FOURTH EDITION

# Focus on
# Grammar 1

**Irene E. Schoenberg**
**Jay Maurer**

**Focus on Grammar 1: An Integrated Skills Approach, Fourth Edition**

Pearson Education, 221 River Street, Hoboken, NJ 07030

**Staff credits:** The people who made up the *Focus on Grammar 1, Fourth Edition* team, representing content creation, design, manufacturing, marketing, multimedia, project management, publishing, rights management, and testing, are Pietro Alongi, Rhea Banker, Elizabeth Barker, Stephanie Bullard, Jennifer Castro, Tracey Cataldo, Aerin Csigay, Mindy DePalma, Dave Dickey, Warren Fischbach, Pam Fishman, Nancy Flaggman, Lester Holmes, Gosia Jaros-White, Leslie Johnson, Barry Katzen, Amy McCormick, Julie Molnar, Brian Panker, Stuart Radcliffe, Jennifer Raspiller, Lindsay Richman, Robert Ruvo, Alexandra Suarez, Paula Van Ells, and Joseph Vella.

**Text design and layout:** Don Williams
**Composition:** Page Designs International
**Project supervision:** Bernard Seal
**Contributing editors:** Julie Schmidt and Bernard Seal

**Cover image:** Andy Roberts / Getty Images

**Library of Congress Cataloging-in-Publication Data**

A catalog record for the print edition is available from the Library of Congress.

Printed in the United States of America
ISBN 10: 0-13-458327-2
ISBN 13: 978-0-13-458327-3

3   17

# Contents

# Contents (continued)

# WELCOME TO
# FOCUS ON GRAMMAR
## NEW EDITION

BUILDING ON THE SUCCESS of previous editions, *Focus on Grammar* continues to provide an integrated-skills approach to engage students and help them understand, practice, and use English grammar. Centered on thematic instruction, *Focus on Grammar* combines comprehensive grammar coverage with abundant practice, critical thinking skills, and ongoing assessment, helping students accomplish their goals of communicating confidently, accurately, and fluently in everyday situations.

## New in This Edition

### New and Updated Content

*Focus on Grammar* continues to offer engaging and motivating content that appeals to learners from various cultural backgrounds. Many readings and activities have been replaced or updated to include topics that are of high interest to today's learners.

### Updated Charts and Redesigned Notes

Clear, corpus-informed grammar presentations reflect real and natural language usage and allow students to grasp the most important aspects of the grammar. Clear signposting draws attention to common usage, the difference between written and spoken registers, and common errors.

### Additional Communicative Activities

The new edition of *Focus on Grammar* has been expanded with additional communicative activities that encourage collaboration and the application of the target grammar in a variety of settings.

### Expanded Writing Practice

Each unit in *Focus on Grammar* now ends with a structured "From Grammar to Writing" section. Supported by pre-writing and editing tasks, students engage in activities that allow them to apply the target grammar in writing.

### New Assessment Program

The new edition of *Focus on Grammar* features a variety of new assessment tools, including course diagnostic tests, formative and summative assessments, and a flexible gradebook. The assessments are closely aligned with unit learning outcomes to inform instruction and measure student progress.

### Revised MyEnglishLab

The updated MyEnglishLab offers students engaging practice and video grammar presentations anywhere, anytime. Immediate feedback and remediation tasks offer additional opportunities for successful mastery of content and help promote accuracy. Instructors receive instant access to digital content and diagnostic tools that allow them to customize the learning environment to meet the needs of their students.

# The *Focus on Grammar* Approach

At the heart of the *Focus on Grammar* series is its unique and successful four-step approach that lets learners move from comprehension to communication within a clear and consistent structure. The books provide an abundance of scaffolded exercises to bridge the gap between identifying grammatical structures and using them with confidence and accuracy. The integration of the four skills allows students to learn grammar holistically, which in turn prepares them to understand and use English more effectively.

**STEP 1: Grammar in Context** integrates grammar and vocabulary in natural contexts such as dialogues and short readings. Students engage with the unit reading and theme and get exposure to grammar as it is used in real life.

**STEP 2: Grammar Presentation** presents the structures in clear and accessible grammar charts and notes with multiple examples of form and meaning. Corpus-informed explanations and examples reflect natural usage of the target forms, differentiate between written and conversational registers whenever appropriate, and highlight common errors to help students avoid typical pitfalls in both speaking and writing.

**STEP 3: Focused Practice** provides numerous and varied contextualized exercises for both the form and meaning of the new structures. Controlled practice ensures students' understanding of the target grammar and leads to mastery of form, meaning, and use.

**STEP 4: Communication Practice** provides practice with the structures in listening exercises as well as in communicative, open-ended speaking activities. These engaging activities provide ample opportunities for personalization and build students' confidence in using English. Students also develop their critical thinking skills through problem-solving activities and discussions.

Each unit now culminates with the **From Grammar to Writing** section. Engaging and motivating writing activities encourage students to apply grammar in writing through structured tasks from pre-writing that contain writing models to editing.

## Recycling

Underpinning the scope and sequence of the *Focus on Grammar* series is practice that allows students to use target structures and vocabulary many times, in different contexts. New grammar and vocabulary are recycled throughout the book. Students have maximum exposure, leading them to become confident in using the language in speech and in writing.

## Assessment

Extensive testing informs instruction and allows teachers and students to measure progress.

- **Unit Reviews** at the end of every unit assess students' understanding of the grammar and allow students to monitor their own progress.

- **Diagnostic Tests** provide teachers with a valid and reliable means to determine how well students know the material they are going to study and to target instruction based on students' needs.

- **Unit Review Tests, Mid- and End-of-Term Review Tests, and Final Exams** measure students' ability to demonstrate mastery of skills taught in the course.

- The **Placement Test** is designed to help teachers place students into one of the five levels of the *Focus on Grammar* course.

## The Importance of Context

A key element of *Focus on Grammar* is presenting important grammatical structures in context. The contexts selected are most relevant to the grammatical forms being introduced. Contextualized grammar practice also plays a key role in improving fluent use of grammar in communicative contexts. It helps learners to develop consistent and correct usage of target structures during all productive practice.

## The Role of Corpus

The most important goal of *Focus on Grammar* has always been to present grammar structures using natural language. To that end, *Focus on Grammar* has incorporated the findings of corpus linguistics,* while never losing sight of what is pedagogically sound and useful. By taking this approach, *Focus on Grammar* ensures that:

- the language presented reflects real, natural usage
- themes and topics provide a good fit with the grammar point and elicit the target grammar naturally
- findings of the corpus research are reflected in the syllabus, readings, charts, grammar notes, and practice activities
- examples illustrate differences between spoken and written registers, and formal and informal language
- students are exposed to common errors in usage and learn how to recognize and avoid errors in their own speech and writing

## *Focus on Grammar* Efficacy

The new edition of *Focus on Grammar* reflects an important efficacy initiative for Pearson courses—to be able to demonstrate that all teaching materials have a positive impact on student learning. To support this, *Focus on Grammar* has been updated and aligned to the **Global Scale of English** and the **Common European Framework** (CEFR) to provide granular insight into the objectives of the course, the progression of learning, and the expected outcomes a learner will be able to demonstrate upon successful completion.

To learn more about the Global Scale of English, visit www.English.com.

# Components

**Student Books with Essential Online Resources** include access codes to the course audio, video, and self-assessment.

**Student Books with MyEnglishLab** offer a blended approach with integration of print and online content.

**Workbooks** contain additional contextualized practice in print format.

**Digital Teacher's Resources** include printable teaching notes, GSE mapping documents, answer keys, audio scripts, and downloadable tests. Access to the digital copy of the student books allows teachers to project the pages for whole-class instruction.

***FOG Go* app** allows users to access the student book audio on their mobile devices.

---

* A principal resource has been Douglas Biber et al, *Longman Grammar of Spoken and Written English*, Harlow: Pearson Education Ltd., 1999.

# The *Focus on Grammar* Unit

*Focus on Grammar* introduces grammar structures in the context of unified themes. All units follow a four-step approach, taking learners from grammar in context to communicative practice. Thematic units add a layer to learning so that by the end of the unit students will be able to discuss the content using the grammar points they have just studied.

## STEP 1   GRAMMAR IN CONTEXT

**Before You Read** activities prepare students for the theme and **essential vocabulary** of the unit. Using a **photo-dictionary approach**, students discover the meanings of the target words before undertaking meaningful practice.

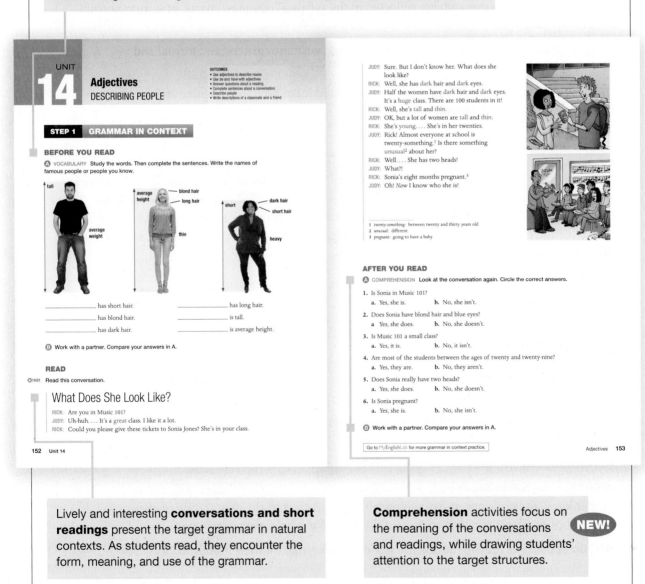

Lively and interesting **conversations and short readings** present the target grammar in natural contexts. As students read, they encounter the form, meaning, and use of the grammar.

**Comprehension** activities focus on the meaning of the conversations and readings, while drawing students' attention to the target structures.

**NEW!**

**Grammar Charts** present the structures in a clear, easy-to-read format.

**NEW!**

The newly designed **Grammar Notes** highlight the main point of each note, making navigation and review easier. Simple corpus-informed **explanations** and **examples** ensure students' understanding.

---

### STEP 2   GRAMMAR PRESENTATION

#### PAST OF *BE*: AFFIRMATIVE STATEMENTS

**Affirmative Statements**

| Was | Were |
|---|---|
| I **was** at a movie last night. | We **were** at a birthday party yesterday. |
| He **was** at home. | You **were** great in the play. |
| She **was** at the gym. | You and Ryan **were** both wonderful. |
| It **was** hot. | They **were** at the soccer game. |

#### PAST OF *BE*: NEGATIVE STATEMENTS

**Negative Statements**

| Was not | Were not |
|---|---|
| I **was not** at home last night. | We **were not** at home last night. |
| He **wasn't** at a movie. | You **weren't** in class yesterday. |
| She **wasn't** at the library. | They **weren't** at the library yesterday. |
| It **wasn't** cold yesterday. | |

#### YES/NO QUESTIONS

**Yes/No Questions**

| Was/Were | | Short Answers | |
|---|---|---|---|
| | | Affirmative | Negative |
| **Was** I right? | | Yes, you **were**. | No, you **weren't**. |
| **Was** he at home? | | Yes, he **was**. | No, he **wasn't**. |
| **Was** she at the game? | | Yes, she **was**. | No, she **wasn't**. |
| **Was** it cold yesterday? | | Yes, it **was**. | No, it **wasn't**. |
| **Were** we right? | | Yes, you **were**. | No, you **weren't**. |
| **Were** you at home? | | Yes, I **was**. | No, I **wasn't**. |
| **Were** they at the game? | | Yes, they **were**. | No, they **weren't**. |

#### GRAMMAR NOTES

**1 Was and Were**

| The past of *be* has two forms: *was* and *were*. Use *was* with *I, he, she,* and *it*. Use *were* with *you, we,* and *they*. | I **was** at a movie last night.<br>The girls **were** at the library yesterday.<br>They **were** at the library yesterday. |
|---|---|

#### GRAMMAR NOTES

**1 There + Be: Affirmative Sentences**

Use *there* + a form of *be* to **state facts** about people or things.

| Use *there is* and *there are* to state facts about people or things in the **present**. Use *there is* with singular nouns. Use *there are* with plural nouns. | **There is** a new **guide** on our tour.<br>**There are** over 6,000 national **parks** in the world. |
|---|---|
| Use *there was* and *there were* to state facts about people or things in the **past**. Use *there was* with singular nouns. Use *there were* with plural nouns. | **There was** an **accident** on the highway.<br>**There were** a lot of **people** on the safari. |
| **USAGE NOTE** We often use *there's* in speaking and informal writing. (*There's = There is*) | **There's** a **park** ten kilometres from here. |
| **BE CAREFUL!** Don't use a plural noun after *there's*. | **There are** a lot of **animals** in the zoo.<br>NOT ~~There's~~ a lot of animals in the zoo. |

**2 There + Be: Negative Sentences**

| Use *there is not* or *there isn't* to state negative facts in the **present** with singular nouns. | **There isn't** a national **park** in our state. |
|---|---|
| Use *there was not* or *there wasn't* to state negative facts in the past with singular nouns. | **There wasn't** a **park** here fifty years ago. |
| Use *there are not* or *there aren't* to state negative facts in the present with plural nouns. | **There aren't** any **elephants** in the national park. |
| Use *there were not* or *there weren't* to state negative facts in the past with plural nouns. | **There weren't** any **cars** on the road. |
| Use *a* or *an* with singular nouns and *any* with plural nouns. | **There isn't a** hotel around here.<br>**There aren't any** volcanoes in my country. |

**3 Yes/No Questions with There**

| To make **yes/no questions** with *there*, put *is, are, was,* or *were* before *there*. | **Are there** (any) volcanoes in your country?<br>**Was there** more rain forest land in the past? |
|---|---|
| Use *there* both in questions and **short answers**. | A: **Is there** a good hotel near the park?<br>B: Yes, **there is.** or No, **there isn't.** or No, **there's not.**<br><br>A: **Were there** many people on the safari?<br>B: Yes, **there were** twenty-five. |

**NEW!**

**Clear signposting** provides corpus-informed notes about common usage, differences between spoken and written registers, and common errors.

---

#### PRONUNCIATION NOTE

🔊 22:02   **A and An Before Singular Count Nouns**

We use *a* before a **consonant sound** and *an* before a **vowel sound**. But sometimes consonants have vowel sounds, and vowels have consonant sounds. We sometimes use *a* before singular count nouns that start with vowels, and *an* before singular count nouns that start with consonants.

Singular count nouns that start with **h**:

| • When the *h* sounds like /h/, we use *a*. | I need **a** hat. |
|---|---|
| • When the *h* is silent, we use *an*. | The trip takes **an** hour. |

Singular count nouns that start with **u**:

| • When the *u* sounds like /yu/, we use *a*. | We have **a** university in our town. |
|---|---|
| • When the *u* sounds like /ə/, we use *an*. | He needs **an** umbrella. |

**Pronunciation Notes** are now included with the grammar presentation to highlight relevant pronunciation aspects of the target structures and to help students understand authentic spoken English.

**NEW!**

# STEP 3   FOCUSED PRACTICE

**Discover the Grammar** activities develop students' recognition and understanding of the target structures before they are asked to produce them.

**Controlled practice activities** lead students to master form, meaning, and use of the target grammar.

---

## STEP 3   FOCUSED PRACTICE

### EXERCISE 1   DISCOVER THE GRAMMAR

Ⓐ GRAMMAR NOTES 1–4   Read the paragraph. Underline the sixteen nouns that are food and drinks. Circle the quantifiers.

My favorite meal is lunch—my big meal of the day. I start with a bowl of soup, and I usually have crackers with it. Next, I have some meat. I also have vegetables: maybe carrots, peas, or beans. I almost always have rice. For dessert, I sometimes have a cookie, and I usually have some fruit—an orange, or an apple, or a banana. Sometimes I have a bowl of ice cream. I usually drink a cup of coffee, but once in a while I have tea. I'm never hungry after lunch.

Ⓑ Look at the paragraph in A again. Write the underlined nouns in the correct columns in the chart.

| Count Nouns | Non-Count Nouns |
|---|---|
| crackers | soup |

### EXERCISE 2   QUANTIFIERS

Ⓐ GRAMMAR NOTES 3–4   Complete the conversation. Circle the correct answers (Ø = no article or quantifier).

SERVER: All right, folks. What do you want to order?

MARY: I want a bag of / some chicken and rice and a / some mixed vegetables. And please
                     1.                           2.
bring me a cup of / a bowl of hot tea to drink.
                  3.

SERVER: Of course. And for you, young man?

---

### EXERCISE 2   *WH-* QUESTION WORDS

GRAMMAR NOTES 1–2   Read the questions and answers. Complete the questions with *what, where, when,* and *who*.

1. A: ___What___ time did the accident occur?    B: At nine o'clock in the morning.
2. A: _____ did it happen?    B: On the corner of Maple and Elm Street.
3. A: _____ did the police arrive?    B: They came at 9:10.
4. A: _____ did the police do?    B: They asked the drivers a lot of questions.
5. A: _____ did the drivers say?    B: The sun was in their eyes.
6. A: _____ called the police?    B: An old woman.

### EXERCISE 3   *WH-* QUESTIONS

GRAMMAR NOTES 1–2   Complete the questions. Use the correct forms of the verbs in parentheses.

1. What time ___did___ they ___leave___ home?
                          (leave)
2. Why _____ they _____ downtown?
                        (go)
3. Where _____ the accident _____?
                              (happen)
4. Who _____ the ambulance?
      (call)
5. How long _____ it _____ the ambulance to get to the accident?
                        (take)
6. What _____ they _____ in the hospital?
                    (do)

### EXERCISE 4   QUESTIONS WITH *WH-* WORD + NOUN

GRAMMAR NOTE 1   Read the questions and answers. Complete the questions with the words from the box.

| what day | what month | ~~what time~~ | what year |
|---|---|---|---|

1. A: ___What time___ did you get up?
   B: 7:00 a.m.
2. A: _____ did the accident happen?
   B: Monday.
3. A: _____ did you take a road trip?
   B: July.
4. A: _____ did you go to Canada?
   B: 2015.

A **variety of exercise types** engage students and guide them from recognition and understanding to accurate production of the grammar structures.

---

**Editing** exercises allow students to identify and correct typical mistakes.

### EXERCISE 5   EDITING

GRAMMAR NOTES 1–4   There are six mistakes in the email. The first mistake is corrected. Find and correct five more.

| TO kathy344@yoohoo.com  |  FROM amanda70@gomail.com  |  **SUBJECT** Party |
|---|

Hi Kathy,

Josh and I going to have a little party last Sunday. We're going watch the Super
        *are*

Bowl, and we're going to has pizza and dessert. I think the game are going to start

at 3:00, and we be going to eat at about 5:00. Please come.

Amanda

Go to MyEnglishLab for more focused practice.

**Listenings** in a variety of genres allow students to hear the grammar in natural contexts.

STEP 4    COMMUNICATION PRACTICE

**EXERCISE 7  LISTENING**

⊙28:06 **A** Listen to a talk by a national park ranger. What are the people visiting?

_____

_____

_____

⊙28:06 **B** Listen again. Complete the sentences. Circle the correct answers.

1. Victoria Falls is _____ high.
   **a.** 108 meters     **b.** 138 meters     **c.** 208 meters

2. David Livingstone discovered Victoria Falls in _____ century.
   **a.** the seventeenth     **b.** the eighteenth     **c.** the nineteenth

3. Livingstone named Victoria Falls after _____.
   **a.** a French Queen     **b.** a British Queen     **c.** a South African Queen

4. There are many animals in Victoria Falls National Park, but there aren't any _____.
   **a.** elephants     **b.** giraffes     **c.** tigers

5. There are _____ tourists at Victoria Falls every year.
   **a.** a few     **b.** some     **c.** a lot of

6. People don't want to hear _____.
   **a.** airplane noise     **b.** waterfall noise     **c.** noise from animals

7. The pollution problem is _____.
   **a.** noise pollution     **b.** air pollution     **c.** water pollution

8. There is a rain forest _____ the falls.
   **a.** in     **b.** next to     **c.** far away from

**C** Work with a partner. Ask and answer questions with *there* about the place in the listening.

EXAMPLE:  A:  Is there a waterfall in the national park?
              B:  Yes, there is. . . . Are there elephants in the park?
              B:  Yes, there are.

There is, There are, There was, and There were    **331**

In the **listening activities**, students practice a range of listening skills. A **new step** has been added in which partners complete an activity that relates to the listening and uses the target grammar.

**NEW!**

Engaging **communicative activities** (conversations, discussions, presentations, surveys, and games) help students synthesize the grammar, develop fluency, and build their problem-solving skills.

**EXERCISE 8  INTRODUCE YOURSELF AND A CLASSMATE**

**A** CONVERSATION  Work with a partner. Practice the conversation with your names. Take turns.

A:  I'm _____.
B:  Nice to meet you, _____. I'm _____.
A:  Nice to meet you, too.

**B** Walk around the classroom. Introduce yourself to four classmates.

**C** Introduce one classmate to the class.

EXAMPLE:  A:  This is Eun Young.
              B:  Nice to meet you, Eun Young. I'm . . .

**EXERCISE 9  TALK ABOUT PHOTOS**

CONVERSATION  Bring photos of your family or friends to class. Then work in a group. Talk about the photos.

EXAMPLE:  A:  Is this your mother?
              B:  Yes. She's in Poland right now.
              C:  This is my boyfriend. He's in Mumbai.
              D:  These are my friends. Asha is on the right, and Nancy is on the left.

14    Unit 1

Go to MyEnglishLab for more communication practice.

## FROM GRAMMAR TO WRITING

A **From Grammar to Writing** section, now in every unit, helps students to confidently apply the unit's grammar to their own writing. **NEW!**

---

### FROM GRAMMAR TO WRITING

**A** BEFORE YOU WRITE  Read about Ali, a man of many abilities. Then work with a partner. Tell your partner about a person you know with different abilities.

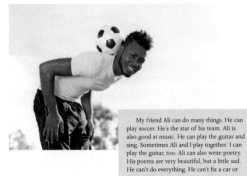

My friend Ali can do many things. He can play soccer. He's the star of his team. Ali is also good at music. He can play the guitar and sing. Sometimes Ali and I play together. I can play the guitar, too. Ali can also write poetry. His poems are very beautiful, but a little sad. He can't do everything. He can't fix a car or a computer.

**B** WRITE  Write a paragraph about the abilities of a person you know. Use *can* and *can't*. Use the paragraph in A and your ideas to help you.

**C** CHECK YOUR WORK  Read your paragraph. Underline all examples of *can* or *can't*. Then use the Editing Checklist to check your work.

**Editing Check List**

Did you...?
- [ ] use *can* to mean ability or possibility
- [ ] use *can* or *can't* + the base form of the verb
- [ ] check your spelling

**D** REVISE YOUR WORK  Read your paragraph again. Can you improve your writing? Make changes if necessary.

220   Unit 19        Go to MyEnglishLab for more writing practice.

---

The **Before You Write** task helps students generate ideas for their writing assignment. They typically contain writing models for students to analyze and emulate.

In the **Write** task, students are given a writing assignment and guided to use the target grammar.

**Check Your Work** includes an Editing Checklist that allows students to proofread and edit their compositions.

In **Revise Your Work**, students are given a final opportunity to improve their writing.

---

## UNIT **REVIEW**

**Unit Reviews** give students the opportunity to check their understanding of the target structures. Students can check their answers against the Answer Key at the end of the book. They can also complete the Review on MyEnglishLab.

### UNIT 5 **REVIEW**

Test yourself on the grammar of the unit.

**A** Match the questions and answers.

_____ 1. Are you actors?              **a.** No, they aren't.
_____ 2. Am I late?                   **b.** No, she isn't.
_____ 3. Is John married?             **c.** Yes, you are.
_____ 4. Are your parents teachers?   **d.** Yes, we are.
_____ 5. Is your sister a dentist?    **e.** No, he isn't.

**B** Complete the conversation with *who* or *what*.

A: That's a great photo. _____'s that woman on the right?
                              1.
B: That's my cousin.

A: Oh, really? _____'s her name?
                    2.
B: Amalia.

A: And _____'s that man on her left?
              3.
B: That's her husband, Carlos.

A: I see. _____ does he do?
                 4.
B: He's a police officer.

A: And _____'s that in the middle? Is that their son?
              5.
B: No, that's their daughter!

**C** Correct the conversations. There are five mistakes.

---

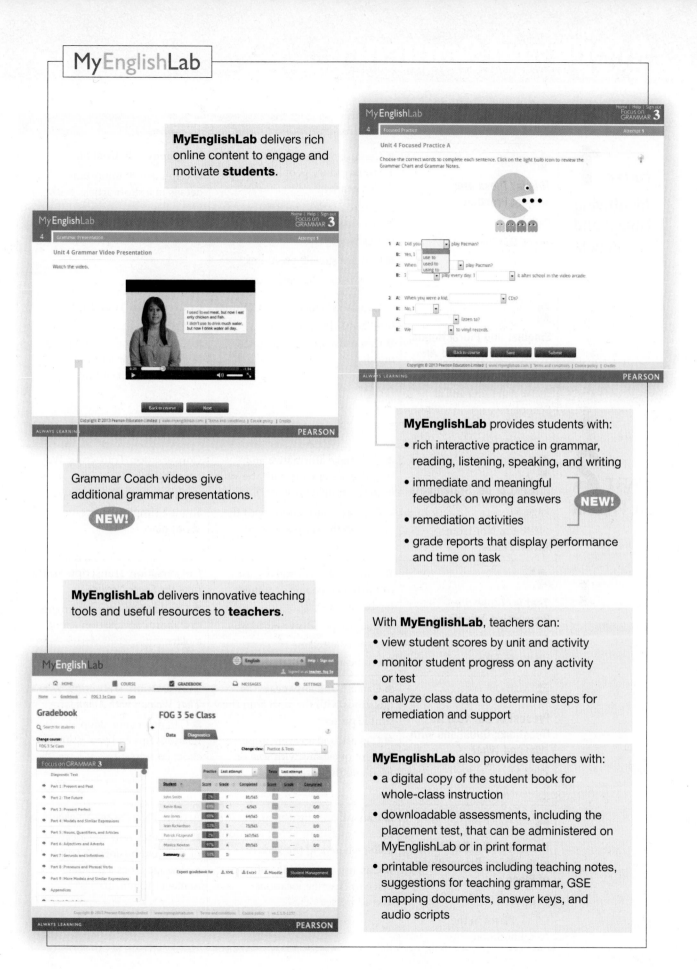

**MyEnglishLab** delivers rich online content to engage and motivate **students**.

Grammar Coach videos give additional grammar presentations.

**NEW!**

**MyEnglishLab** delivers innovative teaching tools and useful resources to **teachers**.

**MyEnglishLab** provides students with:

- rich interactive practice in grammar, reading, listening, speaking, and writing
- immediate and meaningful feedback on wrong answers
- remediation activities

**NEW!**

- grade reports that display performance and time on task

With **MyEnglishLab**, teachers can:

- view student scores by unit and activity
- monitor student progress on any activity or test
- analyze class data to determine steps for remediation and support

**MyEnglishLab** also provides teachers with:

- a digital copy of the student book for whole-class instruction
- downloadable assessments, including the placement test, that can be administered on MyEnglishLab or in print format
- printable resources including teaching notes, suggestions for teaching grammar, GSE mapping documents, answer keys, and audio scripts

# Scope and Sequence

| LISTENING | SPEAKING | WRITING | VOCABULARY |
|---|---|---|---|
| **A conversation about a class**<br>■ Can follow a slow, carefully articulated conversation about everyday topics | ■ Can introduce people using a few basic fixed expressions<br>■ Can ask and answer basic questions about family and friends in a limited way | ■ Can write a simple paragraph about a friend, using a model for support | brother    mother<br>children    parents<br>daughter    sister<br>family    son<br>father    wife<br>husband |
| **A conversation between friends**<br>■ Can follow a slow, carefully articulated conversation about everyday items | ■ Can ask and answer basic questions with *What's this/that?*<br>■ Can identify basic objects and present them to others | ■ Can create vocabulary flash cards and write simple sentences about classroom objects | fork<br>glass<br>knife<br>oven<br>spoon |
| **A conversation between a chef and a student**<br>■ Can identify main points and key details in a slow-paced conversation | ■ Can make basic statements about oneself and classmates, and query statements made by others<br>■ Can express opinions about places | ■ Can write a simple paragraph about a city, using a model for support | boring<br>clean (adj)<br>dirty<br>far<br>fun<br>near |
| **A conversation about family**<br>■ Can identify key details in a slow-paced conversation about family members in a photo | ■ Can ask and answer questions about people's belongings<br>■ Can ask and answer basic questions to confirm locations on a map | ■ Can write a simple paragraph about a place in a photo, using a model for support | museum<br>sports stadium<br>university<br>zoo |
| **A conversation about people**<br>■ Can identify basic information about people in a slow-paced, short conversation | ■ Can have a basic conversation about one's profession<br>■ Can ask and answer *yes/no* questions to determine the identity of a famous person | ■ Can write questions and answers for a short interview | bus driver<br>doctor<br>nurse<br>server<br>writer |
| **A conversation about directions**<br>■ Can identify the locations of people and places in a short conversation, using a map for guidance | ■ Can ask and answer simple questions about the locations of people, objects, and places | ■ Can write a simple paragraph about the addresses and locations of three places | bank (n)<br>drugstore<br>gas station<br>gym<br>hospital<br>supermarket |

| LISTENING | SPEAKING | WRITING | VOCABULARY |
|---|---|---|---|
| **A phone message**<br>■ Can identify true and false statements about where people were and what they were doing from information in a phone message | ■ Can ask and answer questions about past activities<br>■ Can give a brief, basic presentation about a past activity | ■ Can write a simple paragraph about a movie, using a model for support | alone<br>asleep<br>at home<br>at the movies<br>awake |
| **A telephone conversation about weekend activities**<br>■ Can identify the main points in a short conversation about what people did last weekend | ■ Can ask and answer questions about past weather conditions<br>■ Can role-play a conversation about past activities | ■ Can write a short email to a friend about a past vacation | at the beach<br>cold (weather)<br>hot (weather)<br>in the mountains |

| LISTENING | SPEAKING | WRITING | VOCABULARY |
|---|---|---|---|
| **A conversation between students**<br>■ Can complete a paragraph about directions given in a simple conversation | ■ Can make basic, polite requests of others<br>■ Can give directions to someone else, relying on a map for support | ■ Can write a short invitation, providing step-by-step directions to a location | drive (v)<br>park (v)<br>take the bus<br>turn left<br>turn right<br>walk (v) |
| **A conversation between travelers**<br>■ Can identify key details about people and their countries from a slow-paced conversation | ■ Can correct false statements about different people and places<br>■ Can discuss people's likes and dislikes | ■ Can write a short paragraph about a classmate's life and personal preferences, using a model for support | live (v)<br>need (v)<br>speak<br>want |
| **A conversation about preferences**<br>■ Can identify people's preferences in a short, slow-paced conversation | ■ Can ask and answer questions about a person's hobbies and activities<br>■ Can discuss similarities between oneself and classmates | ■ Can write a short conversation about a potential new roommate's preferences and habits | go shopping<br>have a party<br>stay home<br>work out |
| **A conversation about a holiday party**<br>■ Can answer questions regarding a short conversation about a holiday party | ■ Can ask and answer questions about favorite holiday celebrations<br>■ Can ask and answer questions to define new vocabulary | ■ Can write a short conversation about a celebration or well-known event, using a model for support | eat a huge meal<br>play board games<br>see fireworks<br>send cards<br>watch a parade |

| UNIT | GRAMMAR | READING |
|---|---|---|
| ▼ PART **4** CONTINUED | | |
| **13** **Simple Present with Adverbs of Frequency** Page 139 THEME Habits | ■ Can use adverbs of frequency to say how often something happens ■ Can use *ever* with *yes/no* questions and questions with *how often* to ask about frequency | Conversation Transcript: *I Have One Good Habit* ■ Can identify the frequency of different habits described in a short conversation |
| PART **5** **Adjectives** | | |
| **14** **Adjectives** Page 152 THEME Describing People | ■ Can use adjectives to describe nouns ■ Can use nouns to modify or describe other nouns ■ Can use the verbs *be* and *have* in the simple present with adjectives | Conversation Transcript: *What Does She Look Like?* ■ Can identify key details in a simple conversation describing a person in a class |
| **15** **Comparative Adjectives** Page 164 THEME Entertainment | ■ Can form comparatives with short and long regular adjectives ■ Can form comparatives with irregular adjectives like *good, bad,* and *fun* ■ Can use *which* to ask about a comparison of things or places, and *who* to ask about a comparison of people | Conversation Transcript: *That's More Fun* ■ Can complete sentences that compare different people and things, based on information in a simple conversation about a party |
| PART **6** **Present Progressive and *Can*** | | |
| **16** **Present Progressive: Statements** Page 178 THEME Friends from Long Ago | ■ Can use the present progressive to refer to events that are happening now ■ Can make affirmative and negative statements in the present progressive | Email: *A Friend From Long Ago* ■ Can identify key information in an informal email |
| **17** **Present Progressive: *Yes/No* Questions** Page 189 THEME Are You Babysitting? | ■ Can ask and answer *yes/no* questions in the present progressive | Conversation Transcript: *A Night Out* ■ Can answer questions regarding a simple conversation about people's activities on the night of a couple's anniversary |

PART **6** CONTINUES ▼

| LISTENING | SPEAKING | WRITING | VOCABULARY |
|---|---|---|---|
| **A conversation with a relative**<br>■ Can identify important details about the frequency of people's habits in a slow-paced conversation | ■ Can ask and answer questions about personal habits<br>■ Can describe how often people participate in common activities and routines | ■ Can write a short email about everyday activities, using a model for support | eat fast food<br>get up early<br>go to bed<br>sleep late<br>stay up late<br>take a shower |
| **A conversation at a party**<br>■ Can describe a person's physical characteristics and habits after listening to a short, slow-paced conversation | ■ Can describe family members or friends<br>■ Can describe the physical characteristics of a person in a drawing or photo | ■ Can write short descriptions of a classmate and a friend, using a model for support | average height<br>average weight<br>blond hair<br>dark hair<br>heavy<br>long hair<br>short hair<br>tall<br>thin |
| **A conversation about a college student's activities**<br>■ Can identify key details in a simple conversation about a college student's activities and preferences | ■ Can ask and answer questions that compare people, places, or things<br>■ Can participate in a discussion to plan a party, comparing different options | ■ Can write a short paragraph about a favorite form of entertainment, using a model for support | barbecue (n)<br>rap music<br>video games |
| **A conversation about a photo**<br>■ Can identify main ideas in a slow-paced conversation about people in a photo | ■ Can exchange simple information about everyday activities, using visual prompts | ■ Can write a simple conversation describing what people in photos are doing, using a model for support | look at<br>look for<br>lose<br>wait for<br>win |
| **A phone conversation between a brother and a sister**<br>■ Can follow a slow-paced conversation about what people are doing | ■ Can ask and answer simple questions about what people are doing in the classroom and in pictures | ■ Can write a simple conversation that includes questions about what people are doing, using a model for support | babysit<br>clean<br>do laundry<br>get a haircut |

| UNIT | GRAMMAR | READING |
|------|---------|---------|

▼ PART 6 CONTINUED

PART 7 CONTINUES ▼

| LISTENING | SPEAKING | WRITING | VOCABULARY |
|---|---|---|---|
| **A phone conversation between two brothers**<br><br>■ Can answer questions about key details in a slow-paced conversation about what people are doing | ■ Can ask and answer questions about a trip<br><br>■ Can participate in a discussion about people in photos from around the world and what they are doing | ■ Can write a simple conversation between two people meeting at an airport, using a model for support | fly<br>ride a bike<br>take the subway<br>take the metro<br>take a train |
| **A conversation about academic abilities**<br><br>■ Can identify people's abilities after listening to a short, slow-paced conversation | ■ Can express ability or lack of ability with regard to basic activities using *can* or *can't*<br><br>■ Can ask and answer questions with *can* about abilities | ■ Can write a short paragraph about the abilities of someone one knows, using a model for support | dance<br>give a presentation<br>play an instrument<br>play the guitar<br>play the piano<br>sing |

| LISTENING | SPEAKING | WRITING | VOCABULARY | |
|---|---|---|---|---|
| **A conversation about a dinner**<br><br>■ Can identify main ideas and key details in a short, slow-paced conversation about a dinner | ■ Can describe what others are wearing, using a limited range of expressions<br><br>■ Can identify owners of various items, using possessive nouns | ■ Can write short descriptions of people and their clothes, using a model for support | dress (n)<br>earrings<br>handbag<br>high heels<br>jeans<br>ring<br>shoes | sneakers<br>sports jacket<br>suit (n)<br>sweatshirt<br>tie (n)<br>T-shirt |
| **A conversation in a restaurant**<br><br>■ Can correct false statements regarding a short conversation between a restaurant server and two customers | ■ Can ask and answer basic questions about foods people like and dislike<br><br>■ Can role-play a conversation about ordering food in a restaurant | ■ Can write a short paragraph about one's favorite meal, using a model for support | breakfast<br>cereal<br>coffee<br>dinner<br>eggs<br>fruit<br>juice<br>lunch<br>milk<br>pasta | rice<br>salad<br>sandwich<br>soup<br>steak<br>tea<br>toast<br>vegetables<br>yogurt |
| **A conversation about shopping**<br><br>■ Can identify key details in a short, slow-paced conversation about shopping | ■ Can describe shopping habits and preferences, using simple expressions<br><br>■ Can describe people, places, or things with the aid of visual prompts | ■ Can write a short conversation about buying something, using a model for support | order online<br>pay for<br>return<br>try on | |

| UNIT | GRAMMAR | READING |
|---|---|---|

| LISTENING | SPEAKING | WRITING | VOCABULARY |
|---|---|---|---|
| **A conversation about gifts**<br>■ Can identify the recipients of certain gifts based on the information in a short conversation | ■ Can discuss gifts and gift-giving<br>■ Can role-play a conversation asking for a favor | ■ Can write a short paragraph about a good gift for a friend or family member, using a model for support | box of chocolates<br>flowers<br>gift card<br>tickets |
| **A report about a successful business**<br>■ Can identify true and false statements regarding a short report about a shoe business | ■ Can discuss events from one's past<br>■ Can give a short presentation about the life of a successful person | ■ Can write a short paragraph about achievements of a successful businessperson, using a timeline and a model for support | graduate<br>hire<br>move |
| **An interview with an exchange student**<br>■ Can identify key details from a short interview with an exchange student from Japan | ■ Can discuss and conduct Internet research on past events in the lives of famous people<br>■ Can conduct a simple survey about past activities and present the findings | ■ Can write a short paragraph about a famous person, using a model for support | act<br>protect<br>take care of |
| **A telephone conversation**<br>■ Can answer questions about details in a simple conversation about an accident | ■ Can participate in a conversation about accidents<br>■ Can ask and answer questions to fill in missing information in an article about an accident | ■ Can write a short conversation about recent past events, using a model for support | broken headlight<br>bumper<br>car accident<br>dent (n)<br>headlight<br>scratch (n)<br>tire |
| **A news broadcast**<br>■ Can identify true and false statements regarding a short news broadcast about a travel writer | ■ Can participate in a conversation about traveling and everyday activities<br>■ Can discuss answers to a quiz about a travel destination | ■ Can write a short conversation about a past trip, using a model for support | animal<br>flight<br>island<br>plant |
| **A conversation with a national park ranger**<br>■ Can identify specific details in a short conversation between a park ranger and tourists | ■ Can discuss answers to a quiz about places in nature<br>■ Can prepare and deliver a short presentation about one's favorite place in nature | ■ Can write a short descriptive paragraph about a place in nature, using a model for support | desert<br>rain forest<br>volcano<br>waterfall |

| LISTENING | SPEAKING | WRITING | VOCABULARY |
|---|---|---|---|
| A conversation at a soccer game<br><br>■ Can identify true and false statements about a soccer game based on a short conversation between two people at the game | ■ Can conduct a survey about sports and their popularity<br>■ Can participate in a discussion about sports and the future of sports | ■ Can write a short paragraph about an event one is going to attend or watch in the future, using a model for support | baseball<br>basketball<br>football<br>soccer |
| Phone conversations about good news<br><br>■ Can answer questions regarding short conversations about good news at work and at home | ■ Can participate in a conversation about future plans<br>■ Can speculate about what people are going to do with the aid of visual prompts | ■ Can write a short email asking questions about future plans, using a model for support | a business trip<br>a promotion<br>the news |

# About the Authors

**Irene E. Schoenberg** has taught ESL for more than two decades at Hunter College's International English Language Institute and at Columbia University's American Language Program. Ms. Schoenberg holds a master's degree in TESOL from Columbia University. She has trained ESL and EFL teachers at Columbia University's Teachers College and at the New School University. She has given workshops and academic presentations at conferences, English language schools, and universities in Brazil, Chile, Dubai, El Salvador, Guatemala, Japan, Mexico, Nicaragua, Peru, Taiwan, Thailand, Vietnam, and throughout the United States. She is the author of *Talk about Trivia*; *Talk about Values*; *Speaking of Values 1: Conversation and Listening*; *Topics from A to Z*, Books 1 and 2; and *Focus on Grammar 2* (editions 1–5). She is the co-author with Jay Maurer of the *True Colors* series and *Focus on Grammar 1* (editions 1–4). She is one of the authors of *Future 1: English for Results* and *Future 3: English for Results*.

**Jay Maurer** has taught English in binational centers, colleges, and universities in Spain, Portugal, Mexico, the Somali Republic, and the United States; and intensive English at Columbia University's American Language Program. In addition, he has been a teacher of college composition, technical writing, literature, and speech at Santa Fe Community College and Northern New Mexico Community College. Since 1997, he has conducted his own business as an individual English-language coach. He is the author of *Focus on Grammar 5* (editions 1–5). He is the co-author with Penny LaPorte of the three-level *Structure Practice in Context* series. He is the co-author with Irene Schoenberg of the five-level *True Colors* series; the *True Voices* video series; and *Focus on Grammar 1* (editions 1–4). Mr. Maurer holds an M.A. and an M.Ed. in applied linguistics and a Ph.D. in the teaching of English, all from Columbia University. Currently he lives and writes in Arizona and Washington State.

# Acknowledgments

This basic level grammar book was written for teachers who used *Focus on Grammar 2* and asked for a similarly contextualized grammar book for students at a more basic level. Working at a basic level may seem easy, but it is tricky. We could not have done the book without the help of others.

Our greatest thanks for this edition go to our talented developmental editor, **Julie Schmidt**. She worked hard, making certain we kept the material instructive and still on level. Her knowledge and her creativity added a lot to the book.

We wish to thank **Don Williams** for his effort at making the book look very beautiful. We think he succeeded.

We thank **Bernard Seal** for carefully overseeing every part of the book and **Gosia Jaros-White** for all her work in managing the series.

**Marjorie Fuchs**, the author of *Focus on Grammar Levels 3 and 4*, has always been willing to answer FOG-related questions and offer wonderful suggestions.

We cannot complete our acknowledgments without a note thanking **Joanne Dresner**, who had the original idea for this project.

Irene would like to thank **Cristian Gallardo**, director of the International English Language Institute at Hunter College, for allowing her to teach beginning-level classes during the time she was working on this fourth edition.

We would like to thank our families for their love and support. Irene would like to thank **Harris, Dan, Dahlia, Jonathan, Laura, Olivia, Ella**, and **Drew**. Jay would like to thank his wife **Priscilla** for her love and support.

# Reviewers

We are grateful to the following reviewers for their many helpful comments.

**Susanna Aramyan**, Glendale Community College, Glendale, CA; **Homeretta Ayala**, Baltimore Co. Schools, Baltimore, MD; **Barbara Barrett**, University of Miami, Miami, FL; **Rebecca Beck**, Irvine Valley College, Irvine, CA; **Crystal Bock Thiessen**, University of Nebraska-PIESL, Lincoln, NE; **Janna Brink**, Mt. San Antonio College, Walnut, CA; **Erin Butler**, University of California, Riverside, CA; **Joice Cain**, Fullerton College, Fullerton, CA; **Shannonine M. Caruana**, Hudson County Community College, Jersey City, NJ; **Tonya Cobb**, Cypress College, Cypress, CA; **David Cooke**, Mt. San Antonio College, Walnut, CA; **Lindsay Donigan**, Fullerton College, Fullerton, CA; **Mila Dragushanskya**, ASA College, New York, NY; **Jill Fox**, University of Nebraska, Lincoln, NE; **Katalin Gyurindak**, Mt. San Antonio College, Walnut, CA; **Karen Hamilton**, Glendale Community College, Glendale, CA; **Electra Jablons**, International English Language Institute, Hunter College, New York, NY; **Eva Kozlenko**, Hudson County Community College, Jersey City, NJ; **Esther Lee**, American Language Program, California State University, Fullerton, CA; **Yenlan Li**, American Language Program, California State University, Fullerton, CA; **Shirley Lundblade**, Mt. San Antonio College, Walnut, CA; **Thi Thi Ma**, Los Angeles City College, Los Angeles, CA; **Marilyn Martin**, Mt. San Antonio College, Walnut, CA; **Eve Mazereeuw**, University of Guelph English Language Programs, Guelph, Ontario, Canada; **Robert Mott**, Glendale Community College, Glendale, CA; **Wanda Murtha**, Glendale Community College, Glendale, CA; **Susan Niemeyer**, Los Angeles City College, Los Angeles, CA; **Wayne Pate**, Tarrant County College, Fort Worth, TX; **Genevieve Patthey-Chavez**, Los Angeles City College, Los Angeles, CA; **Robin Persiani**, Sierra College, Rocklin, CA; **Denise Phillips**, Hudson County Community College, Jersey City, NJ; **Anna Powell**, American Language Program, California State University, Fullerton, CA; **JoAnna Prado**, Sacramento City Community College, Sacramento, CA; **Mark Rau**, American River College, Sacramento, CA; **Madeleine Schamehorn**, University of California, Riverside, CA; **Richard Skinner**, Hudson County Community College, Jersey City, NJ; **Heather Snavely**, American Language Program, California State University, Fullerton, CA; **Gordana Sokic**, Douglas College, Westminster, British Columbia, Canada; **Lee Spencer**, International English Language Institute, Hunter College, New York, NY; **Heather Stern**, Irvine Valley College, Irvine, CA; **Susan Stern**, Irvine Valley College, Irvine, CA; **Andrea Sunnaa**, Mt. San Antonio College, Walnut, CA; **Margaret Teske**, Mt. San Antonio College, Walnut, CA; **Johanna Van Gendt**, Hudson County Community College, Jersey City, NJ; **Daniela C. Wagner-Loera**, University of Maryland, College Park, MD; **Tamara Williams**, University of Guelph, English Language Programs, Guelph, Ontario, Canada; **Saliha Yagoubi**, Hudson County Community College, Jersey City, NJ; **Pat Zayas**, Glendale Community College, Glendale, CA

# Credits

*Continued on the next page*

Getty Images; **334:** J Hindman/Fotolia; **336–337:** Dima Sidelnikov/
Shutterstock; **338:** (bottom left) Eugene Onischenko/Shutterstock, (bottom
right) Eugene Onischenko/Shutterstock, (top left) Andrey Yurlov/Shutterstock,
(top right) Dotshock/Shutterstock; **339:** Brocreative/Fotolia; **345:** 103tnn/
Fotolia; **347:** Morenovel/Fotolia; **349:** Kzenon/Shutterstock, (bottom) Ake1150/
Fotolia, (top left) Dechevm/Fotolia; **355:** Ross Stevenson/Shutterstock;
**356:** Nikolai Sorokin/Fotolia; **358:** Frantic01010/Fotolia; **359:** (bottom left)
Prasit Rodphan/Shutterstock, (bottom right) Solis Images/Shutterstock, (top
left) DragonImages/Fotolia, (top right) Vasin Lee/Shutterstock; **388:** Flyinglife/
Fotolia; **389:** (background) Isonphoto/Fotolia, (left) WavebreakMediaMicro/Fotolia

## ILLUSTRATION CREDITS

Steve Attoe – pages 1, 3, 6, 7, 8, 10, 11, 18, (top) 31, 42, 45, 46, 52, 75, 78, 84,
  (top) 97, 111, 112, 129, 132, 140, 144, 146, 153, 165, 170, 179, 186, 190, 200,
  211, 225, 228, 236, 241, 252, 260, 265, 277, 291, 297, (top) 311, 342, 350
ElectraGraphics, Inc. – pages 22, (bottom) 31, 114, (bottom) 311
Jock MacRae – pages 69, 159
Tom Newsom – pages 57, 232, 256
Dusan Petricic – pages 58, 81, 90, 100, 218, 343
Tom Sperling – page 237
Gary Torrisi – pages 21, 26, 47, 48, 63, 65, 67, (bottom) 97, 103, 310, 389

# Getting Started

## EXERCISE 1 IN CLASS

GS|01   **A**   Listen and read. Listen again and repeat.

**Look** at page 1.

**Listen** to Exercise 1.

**Read** the sentence.

**Write** the word *English*.

**Circle** the word *English*.

**Underline** the word *English*.

**Ask** a question.

**Answer** the question.

**B**   Work with a partner. Student A, read a sentence from Exercise 1. Student B, point to the sentence. Take turns.

# EXERCISE 2 LEARN THE ALPHABET

GS|02 **A** Listen and read. Listen again and repeat.

| | | | | | | | | |
|---|---|---|---|---|---|---|---|---|
| A a | B b | C c | D d | E e | F f | G g | H h | I i |
| J j | K k | L l | M m | N n | O o | P p | Q q | R r |
| S s | T t | U u | V v | W w | X x | Y y | Z z | |

GS|03 **B** Listen and repeat the vowels.

| | | | | |
|---|---|---|---|---|
| a | e | i | o | u |

GS|04 **C** Listen and repeat the consonants.

| | | | | | | | | |
|---|---|---|---|---|---|---|---|---|
| b | c | d | f | g | h | j | k | l |
| m | n | p | q | r | s | t | v | w |
| x | y | z | | | | | | |

**D** Work with a partner. Spell your first name and your last name.

EXAMPLE: My first name is Maria. M-A-R-I-A. My last name is Alvarado. A-L-V-A-R-A-D-O.

# EXERCISE 3 LEARN THE NUMBERS

GS|05 **A** Listen and read. Listen again and repeat.

| | | | | | | | | | |
|---|---|---|---|---|---|---|---|---|---|
| 1 | 2 | 3 | 4 | 5 | 6 | 7 | 8 | 9 | 10 |
| 11 | 12 | 13 | 14 | 15 | 16 | 17 | 18 | 19 | 20 |

**B** Work with a partner. Look at the alphabet and the numbers again. Then tell your partner these things.

1. the number of people in your family

   EXAMPLE: six people in my family

2. the number of vowels in your first name

3. the number of consonants in your first name

# CAST OF CHARACTERS

These are the people in this book.

**Tim Olson**  **Jessica Olson**  **Jeremy Olson**  **Annie Olson**  **Ben Olson**

**Steve Beck**  **Mary Beck**  **Charles Beck**

**Mark Mason**  **Kathy White**

**Judy Johnson**  **Ken Johnson**

**Josh Wang**  **Amanda Wang**

**Yoshio Tanaka**

# Identifying Things and People

# PART 1

## OUTCOMES

- Use *this is / these are* and *is this / are these* to talk about people and things near you
- Use subject pronouns
- Identify true and false sentences about a reading
- Complete sentences about a conversation
- Introduce yourself and other people
- Write a paragraph about people in a photo

## OUTCOMES

- Use singular, plural, and proper nouns
- Complete sentences about a reading
- Complete sentences about a conversation
- Ask and answer questions about things
- Talk about people and things in the classroom
- Make vocabulary cards for new words

# *This is / These are*; Subject Pronouns

## FAMILY

**OUTCOMES**
- Use *this is / these are* and *is this / are these* to talk about people and things near you
- Use subject pronouns
- Identify true and false sentences about a reading
- Complete sentences about a conversation
- Introduce yourself and other people
- Write a paragraph about people in a photo

---

### STEP 1   GRAMMAR IN CONTEXT

## BEFORE YOU READ

**A**   VOCABULARY   **Study the words. Then check (✓) the things that are true for you.**

**A Family**

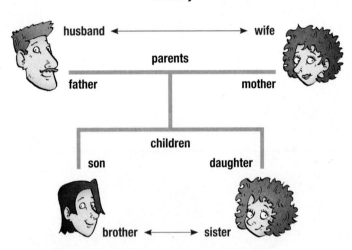

husband ⟷ wife

parents

father       mother

children

son       daughter

brother ⟷ sister

   ☑ **1.** My family is small.

   ☑ **2.** I'm a parent.

   ☐ **3.** I'm a son.

   ☐ **4.** I'm a daughter.

   ☐ **5.** I'm a brother.

   ☐ **6.** I'm a sister.

**B**   **Work with a partner. Compare your answers.**

## READ

▶ 01|01   **Read about Steve Beck and his family.**

## All About Steve

1 *comfortable:* makes us feel good

Hi. I'm Steve Beck. This is my apartment in Seattle. It's small but comfortable.[1]

This is my music. It's great. This is my guitar.

These are my pets. Kip is on the left, and Pam is on the right. They're smart. Kip is two years old. Pam is eight years old, and she talks.

We like our apartment. We're happy here.

My family is wonderful. These are my parents on the left. This is my sister Jessica in the middle, with her husband and children.

## AFTER YOU READ

**A** COMPREHENSION Look at the reading again. For each statement, check (✓) *True* or *False*.

|  | | True | False |
|---|---|:---:|:---:|
| 1. | Steve Beck's apartment is big. | ☐ | ☑ |
| 2. | Steve's apartment is comfortable. | ☑ | ☐ |
| 3. | Steve likes music. | ☑ | ☐ |
| 4. | Pam is eighteen years old, and Kip is five. | ☐ | ☑ |
| 5. | Pam and Kip are children. | ☐ | ☑ |
| 6. | Steve is happy. | ☑ | ☐ |

**B** Work with a partner. Compare your answers in A.

## *THIS IS / THESE ARE*

| Singular | | Plural | |
|---|---|---|---|
| **This is** my friend Pedro. |  | **These are** my friends Maria and Pedro. |  |
| **This is** my seat. |  | **These are** our seats. |  |
| **Is this** your seat? | | **Are these** your seats? | |

## SUBJECT PRONOUNS

| Subject Pronouns | Example Sentences |
|---|---|
| I | **I**'m Steve Beck. |
| you | Hi, Maria. How are **you**? |
| he | **He**'s a teacher. |
| she | **She**'s a reporter. |
| it | This is my apartment. **It**'s in Seattle. |
| we | The apartment is small, but **we**'re happy here. |
| you | Hi, Mom and Dad. How are **you**? |
| they | **They**'re wonderful. |

## GRAMMAR NOTES

| **1** *This is* | |
|---|---|
| Use ***this is*** to introduce or talk about **one** person or thing **near** you. | **This is** my friend Pedro.<br>**This is** my seat. |

| **2** *These are* | |
|---|---|
| Use ***these are*** to introduce or talk about **two or more** people or things **near** you. | **These are** my friends Maria and Pedro. |

## 3 Is this and Are these

| | |
|---|---|
| Use **Is this** and **Are these** to ask questions. | A: **Is this** your cat? <br> B: Yes, it is. <br> A: **Are these** your books? <br> B: No, they aren't. |

## 4 Subject Pronouns and Contractions

| | | |
|---|---|---|
| **I**, **you**, **he**, **she**, **it**, **we**, **you**, and **they** are **subject pronouns**. They replace a **subject noun**. | **SUBJECT NOUN** <br><br> **Pam and Kip** are my pets. <br><br> **Kip** is my cat. | **SUBJECT PRONOUN** <br><br> **They**'re wonderful. <br><br> **He**'s smart. |
| Use **contractions** (short forms) with pronouns and the verb *be* in speaking and informal writing. | I am = **I'm** <br> you are = **you're** <br> he is = **he's** <br> she is = **she's** <br> it is = **it's** <br> we are = **we're** <br> they are = **they're** | |
| **USAGE NOTE** Use *it* or *he* or *she* to talk about an animal. | **It**'s a big cat. **or He**'s a big cat. **or She**'s a big cat. | |

## PRONUNCIATION NOTE

▶ 01|02   *This* and *These*

| | |
|---|---|
| There are two differences in the pronunciation of *this* and *these*. | |
| *This* has a short /ɪ/ vowel. We pronounce the "s" in *this* as /s/. | **This** is my friend Pedro. <br> Is **this** your friend Pedro? |
| *These* has a long /i/ vowel. We pronounce the "s" in *these* as /z/. | **These** are my friends Pedro and Maria. <br> Are **these** your friends Pedro and Maria? |

## REFERENCE NOTE

For **definitions of grammar terms**, see the Glossary on page 375.

## EXERCISE 1   DISCOVER THE GRAMMAR

**A** GRAMMAR NOTES 1–3   **Read the conversations. Underline** *this is*, *is this*, **and** *are these*.

1. A: Is this Mark Mason?
   B: No, this is Steve Beck.

2. A: Are these people Mr. and Mrs. Beck?
   B: No, they're Mr. and Mrs. Olson.

3. A: Is this Judy Johnson?
   B: No, this is Annie Olson.

4. A: Is this Jeremy Olson?
   B: No, this is Ben Olson.

5. A: Is this Josh Wang?
   B: No, this is Ken Johnson.

6. A: Are these people Jeremy and Annie Olson?
   B: No, they're Judy and Ken Johnson.

**B** GRAMMAR NOTE 4   **Read the paragraph. Underline the subject pronouns.**

Jessica is Steve Beck's sister. She is married to Tim Olson. They live in Redmond. They have a very nice house. It's big. Tim and Jessica have three children. Jeremy is 17. He is a basketball player. Annie is 12. She is a soccer player. Ben is 8. He says, "I'm good at sports." Tim and Jessica say, "We are a happy family!"

## EXERCISE 2 *THIS* AND *THESE*

GRAMMAR NOTES 1–3  Complete the sentences. Circle the correct answers.

1. This / (These) are my photos.

2. This / These is my mother.

3. This / These are my sisters.

4. This / These is my father.

5. This / These is my apartment.

6. This / These are my friends.

7. Is this / these your cat?

8. Are this / these your keys?

## EXERCISE 3  SUBJECT PRONOUNS

Ⓐ GRAMMAR NOTE 4  Complete the paragraph about Judy with *She, It,* and *They*.

This is Judy Johnson. ___She___'s a
                         1.

student at the University of Washington.

Elena is her roommate. ___She___'s
                          2.

from Brazil. ___They___'re good friends.
                3.

They like their apartment. ___It___'s
                             4.

small but nice.

Ⓑ Complete Judy's telephone conversation with her mother with *I, you, he, we,*
and *they*.

MOM:  Are ___you___ OK, Judy?
            1.

JUDY:  Yes, ___I___ am. ___I___'m happy here in Seattle.
             2.        3.

MOM:  Good. How are your classes?

JUDY:  ___They___'re good. Elena and I are in the same journalism class. Steve Beck is
          4.

our teacher. Elena and I think ___he___'s a very good teacher. Are ___you___
                                  5.                                    6.

and Dad OK?

MOM:  Yes, ___we___ are. Thanks. ___We___'re very happy.
             7.                      8.

▶ 01|03  Ⓒ LISTEN AND CHECK  Listen to the conversation and check your answers in B.

## EXERCISE 4  *THIS* AND *THESE*

01|04  **A** PRONUNCIATION NOTE  Listen to each sentence. Which word do you hear? Check (✓) *This* or *These*.

|     | **This** | **These** |     | **This** | **These** |     | **This** | **These** |
|-----|----------|-----------|-----|----------|-----------|-----|----------|-----------|
| 1.  | ✓        | ☐         | 3.  | ☐        | ☐         | 5.  | ☐        | ☐         |
| 2.  | ☐        | ☐         | 4.  | ☐        | ☐         |     |          |           |

**B** Work with a partner. For each item, say a sentence, *a* or *b*. Your partner points to the correct sentence.

1. **a.** This is my friend.        **b.** These are my friends.

2. **a.** These are my photos.      **b.** This is my photo.

3. **a.** These are our tickets.    **b.** This is our ticket.

4. **a.** This is my sister.        **b.** These are my sisters.

5. **a.** Is this your key?         **b.** Are these your keys?


## EXERCISE 5  CONTRACTIONS

GRAMMAR NOTE 4  Complete the sentences with subject pronouns and their contractions. Use *I'm*, *it's*, *he's*, *she's*, and *we're*. Use capital letters if necessary.

1. Steve Beck is a teacher. _____He's_____ a teacher at the University of Washington.

2. Jessica Olson is his sister. _____She's_____ a reporter on TV.

3. Jessica says, "I think _____ good at my job."

4. She says, "My job is fun. _____ a great job."

5. Jessica has three children. _____ good at sports.

6. Jessica's children say, "We live in Redmond. _____ happy here."


## EXERCISE 6  EDITING

GRAMMAR NOTES 1–4  There are five mistakes in the conversations. The first mistake is corrected. Correct four more.

1. **A:** ~~These~~ *This* is Pedro.

   **B:** Hi, Pedro.

2. **A:** This are my brothers.

   **B:** Hello.

3. **A:** This Ahmed. He my brother.

   **B:** Hi, Ahmed.

4. **A:** Is this your sister Annie?

   **B:** Yes. He's 12 years old.

## EXERCISE 7  LISTENING

01|05  **A** Listen to the conversation. Write the names *Mr. Singer*, *Hai*, and *Yuan* under the correct people in the picture.

1. _____  2. _____  3. _____

01|05  **B** Listen again. Complete the sentences. Circle the correct answers.

1. This is a photo of _____.
   **a.** a family        **(b.)** an English class

2. Mr. Singer is a _____.
   **a.** teacher         **b.** student

3. Mr. Singer is from _____.
   **a.** the United States   **b.** Canada

4. Hai and Yuan are _____.
   **a.** friends         **b.** brothers

5. Hai and Yuan are from _____.
   **a.** Canada          **b.** China

**C** Work with a partner. Compare your answers in A and B.

## EXERCISE 8  INTRODUCE YOURSELF AND A CLASSMATE

**A** CONVERSATION  Work with a partner. Practice the conversation with your names. Take turns.

A:  I'm _____ .
B:  Nice to meet you, _____ . I'm _____ .
A:  Nice to meet you, too.

**B** Walk around the classroom. Introduce yourself to four classmates.

**C** Introduce one classmate to the class.

EXAMPLE:  A:  This is Eun Young.
            B:  Nice to meet you, Eun Young. I'm . . .

## EXERCISE 9  TALK ABOUT PHOTOS

CONVERSATION  Bring photos of your family or friends to class. Then work in a group. Talk about the photos.

EXAMPLE:  A:  Is this your mother?
            B:  Yes. She's in Poland right now.
            C:  This is my boyfriend. He's in Mumbai.
            D:  These are my friends. Asha is on the right, and Nancy is on the left.

## FROM GRAMMAR TO WRITING

**A** **BEFORE YOU WRITE** Look at the photo. Read the paragraph and the chart. Find a photo of a friend with other people. Complete the chart about the people in your photo. Then work with a partner. Tell your partner about the people in your photo.

This is my friend Miryam on the left. She's from Istanbul, Turkey. She's 21 years old. She's a student at Istanbul University. These are Miryam's parents. This is her mother. She's Sara. She's in the middle. This is her father on the right. He's Erdal. They're in the United States right now.

| Friend's name | Miryam | |
|---|---|---|
| City and country | Istanbul, Turkey | |
| Age | 21 years old | |
| Occupation | student | |
| Other people in the photo | Miryam's parents, Sara and Erdal | |

**B** **WRITE** Write a paragraph about a photo of a friend with other people. Use *this is*, *these are*, and subject pronouns. Use the paragraph in A and your chart to help you.

**C** **CHECK YOUR WORK** Read your paragraph. Underline *this is* and *these are*, and circle subject pronouns. Use the Editing Checklist to check your work.

### Editing Checklist

**Did you . . . ?**

- [ ] use *this* with *is* and *these* with *are*
- [ ] use subject pronouns: *I, he, she, it, we*, and *they*
- [ ] use contractions
- [ ] check your spelling
- [ ] use a capital letter at the beginning of each sentence

**D** **REVISE YOUR WORK** Read your paragraph again. Can you improve your writing? Make changes if necessary.

# UNIT 1 REVIEW

**Test yourself on the grammar of the unit.**

**Ⓐ** Complete the sentences with *This is* or *These are*.

1. _____ my daughter.

2. _____ my sons.

3. _____ my classmate.

4. _____ my apartment.

5. _____ good photos.

**Ⓑ** Complete the sentences with *He*, *She*, *It*, *We*, or *They*.

1. My daughter is a student. _____'s smart.

2. My son is in Seattle. _____'s a reporter.

3. My apartment is small. _____'s near the university.

4. My photos are in my book. _____'re family photos.

5. My father and I are in Seattle. _____'re happy.

**Ⓒ** Correct the sentences. There are five mistakes.

1. This are my parents.

2. This your cat?

3. This is Pete. Is my brother.

4. Is these your photos?

5. I'm happy in this class.

**Now check your answers on page 379.**

# Singular and Plural Nouns; Proper Nouns; *A* and *An*

## AT HOME AND AT SCHOOL

**OUTCOMES**
- Use singular, plural, and proper nouns
- Complete sentences about a reading
- Complete sentences about a conversation
- Ask and answer questions about things
- Talk about people and things in the classroom
- Make vocabulary cards for new words

## STEP 1   GRAMMAR IN CONTEXT

### BEFORE YOU READ

**A** VOCABULARY   Study the words. Then work with a partner. Practice the conversation.

an oven

glasses

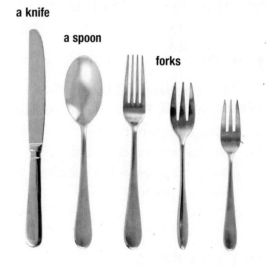

a knife

a spoon

forks

**Conversation**

A: What's this called in English?

B: It's an oven.

A: What are these called?

B: They're glasses.

**B** Now talk about the other words in A.

A: What's this called in English?

B: It's _____.

A: What are these called?

B: They're _____.

## READ

Read this conversation.

# New Words

Judy and Elena are in college. They're roommates. Elena is an English language student. She is from Brazil. They're in the kitchen.

ELENA: Judy, what's this called in English?

JUDY: It's a toaster.

ELENA: A toaster? T-O-A-S-T-E-R?

JUDY: That's right.

ELENA: And this?

JUDY: It's an oven. O-V-E-N.

ELENA: And what's this called?

JUDY: It's a spoon. S-P-O-O-N.

ELENA: Spoon.

ELENA: Is this a knife?

JUDY: Yes. These are knives, and these are forks.

ELENA: Knives? How do you spell "knives"?

JUDY: K-N-I-V-E-S.

ELENA: K?

JUDY: That's right. K-N-I-V-E-S.

ELENA: And forks?

JUDY: F-O-R-K-S.

ELENA: What are these?

JUDY: They're glasses. G-L-A-S-S-E-S.

ELENA: Thank you. You're a good teacher. Now let's go out.

JUDY: Not so fast. Say the words in Portuguese. Now I'm a student, and you're a teacher!

## AFTER YOU READ

**A** COMPREHENSION  Look at the conversation again. Complete the sentences. Circle the correct answers.

1. Judy and Elena are ____.
   a. roommates          b. sisters

2. Elena is from ____.
   a. the United States     b. Brazil

**3.** Elena asks, "What are these?" Judy says, "_____."

    **a.** It's a glass          **b.** They're glasses

**4.** Elena asks, "What's this?" Judy says, "_____."

    **a.** It's an oven         **b.** They're ovens

**5.** Elena wants to learn _____.

    **a.** Portuguese        **b.** English

**B** Work with a partner. Compare your answers in A.

## STEP 2  GRAMMAR PRESENTATION

## NOUNS AND ARTICLES

| Singular and Plural Nouns | |
| --- | --- |
| **Singular Noun** | **Plural Noun** |
| This is a **toaster**. | These are **toasters**. |
| This is a **glass**. | These are **glasses**. |

| Articles: *A* and *An* | |
| --- | --- |
| *a* | *an* |
| This is **a** fork. | This is **an** egg. |

## PROPER NOUNS

| Proper Noun |
| --- |
| **Elena Gomes** is a student. |
| **Elena** is from **Brazil**. |

## GRAMMAR NOTES

| **1** Nouns | |
| --- | --- |
| A **noun** is the word for **a person**, **animal**, **place**, or **thing**. | **Elena** is from Brazil. *(a person)* <br> This is a **dog**. *(an animal)* <br> **Elena** is from **Brazil**. *(a place)* <br> This is a **spoon**. *(a thing)* |
| Nouns are **singular** or **plural**. <br> **Singular** means **one**. <br> **Plural** means **more than one**. | This is a **spoon**. <br> These are **spoons**. |

## 2 Singular Nouns

| | |
|---|---|
| *A* and *an* come before singular nouns. | He's **a teacher**.<br>This is **an apple**. |
| Use *a* before a word that begins with **a consonant sound**. | This is **a f**ork.<br>She's **a s**tudent. |
| Use *an* before a word that begins with **a vowel sound**. | This is **an e**gg.<br>This is **an o**ven. |

## 3 Plural Nouns

| | |
|---|---|
| Add *-s* to most **nouns** to make them **plural**. | This is a **spoon**. *(singular)*<br>These are **spoons**. *(plural)* |
| Add *-es* to nouns that end in *s*, *ss*, *z*, *ch*, *sh*, and *x*. | This is a **glass**. *(singular)*<br>These are **glasses**. *(plural)* |
| **BE CAREFUL!** Do not put *a* or *an* before plural nouns. | These are **glasses**.<br>NOT These are a glasses. |

## 4 Special Plural Forms

| | |
|---|---|
| Some nouns have special plural forms.<br><br>**SINGULAR**  **PLURAL**<br>child  children<br>knife  knives<br>man  men<br>person  people | I have a **child**. She has two **children**.<br>This is a **knife**. These are **knives**.<br>This **man** is American. These **men** are Canadian.<br>I am a **person**. We are **people**. |

## 5 Proper Nouns

| | |
|---|---|
| **Proper nouns** are the **names** of people and places on the map. They start with a **capital letter**. | My roommate **Elena** is from **São Paulo, Brazil**. |
| **BE CAREFUL!** Do not put *a* or *an* before proper nouns. | **Judy** is from **Seattle**.<br>NOT A Judy is from a Seattle. |

# REFERENCE NOTE

For **definitions of grammar terms**, see the Glossary on page 375.

For lists of **spelling and pronunciation rules for plural nouns**, see Appendices 8 and 9 on page 368.

For a list of **irregular plural nouns**, see Appendix 10 on page 368.

## EXERCISE 1 DISCOVER THE GRAMMAR

**Ⓐ** GRAMMAR NOTES 1–5 Circle the singular nouns.

(apple)    forks    knife    kitchens    man

**Ⓑ** Circle the plural nouns.

(men)    spoon    spoons    teacher    teachers    woman

**Ⓒ** Circle the words that begin with a vowel sound.

(apple)    egg    knife    oven    spoon    toaster

**Ⓓ** Circle the proper nouns.

(Brazil)    country    Elena    Judy    São Paulo    student    the United States

## EXERCISE 2 *A*, *AN*, AND PLURAL NOUNS

GRAMMAR NOTES 1–3 Look at the picture. Complete the conversation. Add *a*, *an*, or *-s* to the words in parentheses.

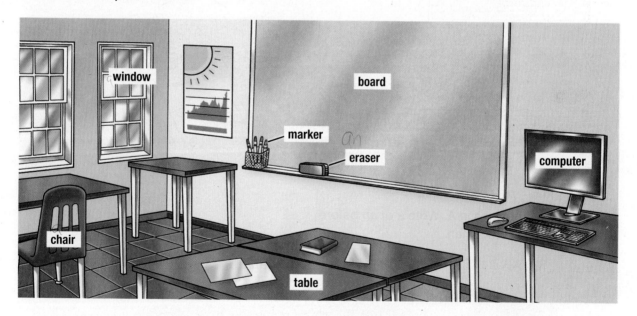

SERGEI: This is our classroom. It's nice. It has _____ a computer _____, _____ a board _____,
(1. computer)          (2. board)

five _____, and two _____ a window _____.
(3. table)          (4. window)

CARLOS: It has four _____ and _____, too.
(5. marker)          (6. eraser)

SERGEI: We just need fifteen _____, and _____!
(7. chair)          (8. teacher)

# EXERCISE 3 A, AN, AND NOUNS

**A** GRAMMAR NOTES 1–4  Look at the things in Steve's kitchen. Complete the sentences. Circle the correct answers.

1. I have (a kitchen) / kitchens.

2. It has a / an refrigerator.

3. (An apple / Apple) is in the refrigerator.

4. My kitchen has a stove / stove.

5. My kitchen has a counter / counter.

6. My kitchen is good for one person / people.

7. When a friend / friends is in my kitchen and we are hungry, we go to a restaurant.

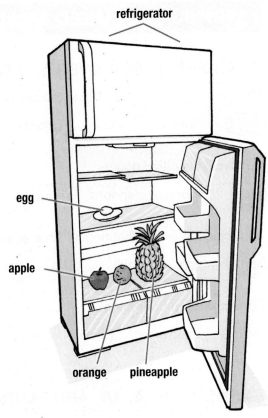

refrigerator

egg

apple

orange    pineapple

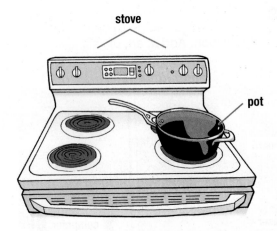

stove

pot

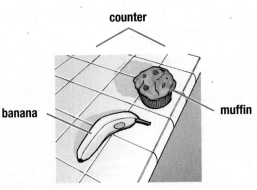

counter

banana    muffin

**B** Look at the pictures in A. Write *a* or *an* before the things in Steve's kitchen.

1. __a__ banana

2. _____ stove

3. __an__ orange

4. _____ egg

5. _____ pineapple

6. _____ counter

7. __an__ apple

8. __a__ muffin

## EXERCISE 4  A, AN, AND PLURAL NOUNS

GRAMMAR NOTES 1–3  Look at Elena's shopping list.
Complete the sentences. Add a, an, or plurals.

TO BUY

| | | |
|---|---|---|
| 1 eraser | 1 dictionary | 1 orange |
| 2 pens | 3 apples | 1 banana |
| 3 notebooks | | |

Elena needs ___an eraser___, ___a pens___, ___a notebook___,
                      1.              2.                    3.

___a dictionary___, _____, _____, and _____.
        4.                       5.                  6.                       7.

## EXERCISE 5  PROPER NOUNS

GRAMMAR NOTE 5  Read the sentences. Cross out the proper nouns. Rewrite them. Start
with a capital letter.

                     Maria
1. My friend is ~~maria~~.

2. mona is from egypt.

3. This is al. He's a teacher. He's from london.

4. She's from são paulo, brazil.

5. seattle is a city. It's in the united states.

## EXERCISE 6  EDITING

GRAMMAR NOTES 1–5  There are six mistakes in the sentences. One mistake is
corrected. Find and correct five more.

1. These are a̶ apples.

4. These banana are good.

2. He's from canada.

5. This is toaster.

3. This is a orange.

6. Two person are not in class.

## EXERCISE 7   LISTENING

⏵02|02   **A**   Listen to the conversation between Elena and Judy. Check (✓) the words Elena asks about.

☑ an apple      ☑ a chair      ☐ eggs      ☑ a kitchen

☐ a banana      ☐ a counter      ☐ forks      ☐ oranges

⏵02|02   **B**   Listen again and complete the sentence.

An _____, a _____, and two _____ are on the counter.
            1.               2.              3.

**C**   Work with a partner. Draw a picture of a word in A. Ask your partner about the picture.

EXAMPLE:   **A:** What's this?
                 **B:** It's an orange.
                 **A:** That's right.

## EXERCISE 8
## WHAT'S THIS CALLED IN ENGLISH?

CONVERSATION   Work with a partner. Touch a thing or things in the class. Ask and answer questions about the things.

EXAMPLE:   **A:** What's this called in English?
                 **B:** It's a computer.
                 **A:** How do you spell "computer"?
                 **B:** C-O-M-P-U-T-E-R. . . . What are these called in English?
                 **A:** They're pens.
                 **B:** How do you spell "pens"?
                 **A:** P . . .

## EXERCISE 9  A TO Z

**GAME**  Work in a group. Name things in your home and in your school. Try to name one thing for each letter of the alphabet. Say *a* or *an* for each thing, or use plural nouns. The group with the most correct words wins.

EXAMPLE:  **A:** an apple
           **B:** bananas

## EXERCISE 10  TREASURE HUNT

**Ⓐ GAME**  Work in a group. Look around your classroom. Find the people and things. Write sentences about them. The first group to find all the people and things in the classroom and write a sentence about them wins.

1. a teacher     _Mr. Brown is a teacher._
2. a sister      _____
3. a brother     _____
4. a father      _____
5. a mother      _____
6. a roommate    _____
7. an apple      _____
8. an eraser     _____
9. a watch       _____
10. phones       _____
11. keys         _____
12. notebooks    _____
13. markers      _____

**Ⓑ** Present the people and things to the class.

EXAMPLE:  **A:** This is Mr. Brown. He's a teacher.
           **B:** This is Marisa. She's a sister.

**A** BEFORE YOU WRITE Look at the things in your classroom. Do you know the words for them in English? Look up five words for things that are new for you. Write each word on a card. Draw a picture of it on the other side of the card. Then work with a partner. Say a sentence for each new word.

EXAMPLE: This is a ruler.

**B** WRITE Write one sentence for each of your new words in A. Use *a*, *an*, and singular and plural nouns. Use the sentences in A to help you.

**C** CHECK YOUR WORK Read your sentences. Underline all nouns and *a* or *an*. Use the Editing Checklist to check your work.

### Editing Checklist

**Did you . . . ?**

- ☐ use *a* or *an* before singular nouns
- ☐ use *a* before nouns that start with a consonant sound
- ☐ use *an* before nouns that start with a vowel sound
- ☐ add -*s* or -*es* for most plural nouns
- ☐ start proper nouns with a capital letter
- ☐ check your spelling

**D** REVISE YOUR WORK Read your sentences again. Can you improve your sentences? Make changes if necessary.

# UNIT 2 REVIEW

**Test yourself on the grammar of the unit.**

**A** Write the plurals.

1. spoon    _spoons_
2. class    _classes_
3. man    _men_
4. teacher    _teacher's_
5. orange    _oranges_   (oranges)

**B** Look at Judy's shopping list. Complete the sentence. Use *a*, *an*, or plurals for the things on the list.

Judy needs _a pineapple_ ,

<u>_bananas_</u> **2.** , <u>_apples_</u> **3.** ,

<u>_an eraser_</u> **4.** , and <u>_a notebook_</u> **5.** .

> **Shopping List**
>
> 1 pineapple
> 5 bananas
> 10 apples
> 1 eraser
> 1 notebook

**C** Correct the sentences. There are five mistakes.

1. This is apple.   This is an apple. /This is an apple/
2. These are fork.   These are forks.
3. It's a oven.   It's an oven. /It's an oven/
4. Three person are in school.   Three person are at school
5. These are knife.   knives is a knife

**Now check your answers on page 379.**

# Be: Present

# PART 2

**OUTCOMES**

- Make simple present statements with the verb *be*
- Correct false sentences about a reading
- Identify true and false sentences about a conversation
- Talk about yourself and a classmate
- Talk and write about cities

**OUTCOMES**

- Use *that is/those are* and *is that/are those* to talk about people and things away from you
- Use possessive adjectives
- Identify true and false sentences about a reading
- Complete sentences about a conversation
- Talk about possessions
- Talk and write about places

**OUTCOMES**

- Ask and answer simple present *yes/no* questions with the verb *be*
- Ask and answer simple present questions with *who* and *what* and the verb *be*
- Complete sentences about a reading
- Answer questions about a conversation
- Talk about people and their jobs
- Write interview questions for a classmate

**OUTCOMES**

- Ask and answer simple present questions with *where* and the verb *be*
- Use prepositions of place
- Complete sentences about a reading
- Answer questions about a conversation
- Ask and answer questions about the locations of people, places, and things
- Write a paragraph about three places in your area

# Present of *Be*: Statements

## I'M NOT FROM AROUND HERE

**OUTCOMES**
- Make simple present statements with the verb *be*
- Correct false sentences about a reading
- Identify true and false sentences about a conversation
- Talk about yourself and a classmate
- Talk and write about cities

---

**STEP 1** **GRAMMAR IN CONTEXT**

## BEFORE YOU READ

**A VOCABULARY** Study the words. Then work with a partner. Practice the conversation.

|  |  |  |  |
|---|---|---|---|
| dirty | clean | far | near |

This is **boring**.

This is **fun**!

### Conversation

A: Are you from around here?
B: No, I'm not. I'm from Sydney, Australia.
A: That's far from here! How's Sydney?
B: It's great. It's fun.

**B** Now talk about the city you are from. Use the words under the pictures in A or other words.

A: Are you from around here?
B: No, I'm not. I'm from _____.
A: That's _____ here! How's _____?
B: It's _____. It's _____.

## READ

▶03|01 Read this conversation.

# We Love Seattle!

**MARK:** Hi, Steve.

**STEVE:** Hi, Mark. Uh, Mark... this is my cousin Amy, and this is her friend Jenny.

**MARK:** Hi. Nice to meet you.

**AMY:** Nice to meet you, too.

**MARK:** So, you're not from around here.

**AMY:** No, we're from Sydney.

**MARK:** Sydney, Australia? That's really far from Seattle.

**AMY:** Yes, it is. How about you? Are you from Seattle?

**MARK:** Yes, I am.

**AMY:** Jenny and I love Seattle. It's a beautiful and clean city. It's fun, and the people are friendly.

**MARK:** How's Sydney?

**AMY:** It's a great city, too—and not just because I live there!

AUSTRALIA

Sydney •
Canberra ★

## AFTER YOU READ

**A** COMPREHENSION  Look at the conversation again. Correct the underlined words.

Jenny and Amy are in Sydney. Steve is Amy's uncle. Steve introduces Jenny and Amy
              1.                            2.

to Mark. Amy talks about her family. Amy says Seattle is not a beautiful city. It's dirty.
                              3.                      4.                          5.

It's boring, and the people are unfriendly.
    6.                              7.

**B**  Work with a partner. Compare your answers in A.

## PRESENT OF THE VERB *BE*

### Affirmative Statements

| Subject | Am | | Subject | Is | | Subject | Are |
|---------|-----|--|---------|-----|--|---------|-----|
| I | **am** from Seattle. | | He She | **is** from Seattle. | | We Jenny and I You Jenny and Amy They | **are** from Sydney. |
| | | | It Seattle | **is** clean. | | | |

### Contractions

| | | |
|--|--|--|
| I am = I**'m** | he is = he**'s** she is = she**'s** it is = it**'s** | we are = we**'re** you are = you**'re** they are = they**'re** |

### Negative Statements

| Subject | Am not | | Subject | Is not | | Subject | Are not |
|---------|--------|--|---------|--------|--|---------|---------|
| I | **am not** from here. | | He She | **is not** from here. | | We You They | **are not** from here. |
| | | | It | **is not** dirty. | | | |

### Contractions

| | | |
|--|--|--|
| I am not = I**'m not** | he is not = he**'s not**    or he **isn't** she is not = she**'s not**    or she **isn't** it is not = it**'s not**    or it **isn't** | we are not = we**'re not**    or we **aren't** you are not = you**'re not**    or you **aren't** they are not = they**'re not**    or they **aren't** |

## GRAMMAR NOTES

### 1 Present of *Be*

| | |
|--|--|
| The **present of the verb** *be* has three forms: *am*, *is*, and *are*. | |
| Use *am*, *is*, or *are* to make an **affirmative statement**. | I **am** from Seattle. It **is** clean. They **are** friendly. |
| Use *am*, *is*, or *are* + *not* to make a **negative statement**. | I **am not** from Sydney. It **is not** dirty. We **are not** cold. |

| | |
|---|---|
| We often use **contractions** (short forms) in speaking and writing. | **I'm** from Seattle. He **isn't** from Seattle. Sydney **isn't** cold. **It's** not cold. |
| **USAGE NOTE** There are **two negative contractions** for *is not* and *are not*. We often use *isn't* or *aren't* after **subject nouns**. We often use *'s not* or *'re not* after **subject pronouns**. | SUBJECT NOUN **Jenny and Amy** aren't cousins. SUBJECT PRONOUN **They're** not cousins. |

## REFERENCE NOTE

For **definitions of grammar terms**, see the Glossary on page 375.

## STEP 3  FOCUSED PRACTICE

## EXERCISE 1  DISCOVER THE GRAMMAR

**A** GRAMMAR NOTES 1–2  Read the sentences. Check (✓) *Affirmative* or *Negative*.

| | Affirmative | Negative |
|---|:---:|:---:|
| 1. She is not from around here. | ☐ | ✓ |
| 2. She is here with a friend. | ☐ | ☐ |
| 3. They're not from Sydney. | ✓ | ☐ |
| 4. We're students. | ☐ | ☐ |
| 5. I'm not from Seattle. | ✓ | ☐ |
| 6. It's a clean city. | ✓ | ☐ |
| 7. Brazil isn't far from Colombia. | ☐ | ☐ |
| 8. The women aren't from New York. | ☐ | ☐ |

**B**  Find six sentences in A with contractions. Write them with the full forms.

1. *They are not from Sydney.*
2. I'm from seattle.
3. The are students students
4. She's from Brazil
5. New York is a bic City
6. He is not from London

## EXERCISE 2 AFFIRMATIVE STATEMENTS

GRAMMAR NOTE 1 Complete the sentences with *I am, She is, He is, It is, We are, You are,* or *They are*.

1. Amy is a student. _____*She is*_____ from Australia.

2. Amy and Jenny are students. _____ from Sydney.

3. Sydney is a great city. _____ in Australia.

4. My friends and I are in school. _____ in Room 2.

5. Mark is a writer. _____ in Seattle.

6. My sister and I are students. _____ at the university.

7. My friend Amy is in class. _____ with her friend Jenny.

8. My name is Elena. _____ an English language student from Brazil.

9. This is your seat. _____ near the teacher.


## EXERCISE 3 CONTRACTIONS

GRAMMAR NOTE 2 Read the sentences. Change the full forms to contractions.

 cold

 hot

*It's*
1. ~~It is~~ cold here.

*isn't*
2. It ~~is not~~ hot in my city.

3. They are not from around here.

4. She is in California.

5. They are not on a bus.

6. We are friends.

7. It is cold in Alaska.

8. My city is not near here.

9. He is not in school.

10. I am not a new student.


## EXERCISE 4 NEGATIVE STATEMENTS

GRAMMAR NOTES 1–2 For each statement, write a negative statement. Add *not*. Then rewrite each sentence with contractions.

1. I am hot.    *I am not hot.*    *I'm not hot.*

2. She is from Peru. _____ _____

3. They are students. _____ _____

4. We are at a restaurant. _____ We are not at a restaurant. _____ We're not at a restaurant.

5. I am a teacher. _____ I'm not a teacher. _____ I'm not a teacher.

6. It is boring. _____ It is not boring. _____ It's not boring.

7. These are good chairs. _____ These aren't good chairs. _____ These're not good chairs.

8. Jenny is my sister. _____ Jenny is not my sister. _____ She's not.

## EXERCISE 5 *BE*: AFFIRMATIVE AND NEGATIVE

Look at the information in the chart about the students in English 1A. Then read incorrect sentences about the students. Write two new sentences. The first sentence is negative. The second sentence is the correct information.

| NAME | SEX | COUNTRY | AGE |
|------|-----|---------|-----|
| Antonio | Male | Mexico | 19 |
| Berat | Male | Turkey | 23 |
| Junko | Female | Japan | 22 |
| Leonardo | Male | Brazil | 33 |
| Min | Female | China | 28 |
| Pinar | Female | Turkey | 18 |
| Saleh | Male | Saudi Arabia | 33 |
| Yumiko | Female | Japan | 18 |

1. Leonardo is from Turkey. _No, he isn't. He's from Brazil._

2. Min is 26. _No, she isn't. She's 28._

3. Saleh is from Mexico. _____ He's from Saudi Arabia.

4. Yumiko and Junko are from China. _____ they are from Japan.

5. Leonardo and Saleh are 29. _____ 33 years old.

6. Pinar is from Japan. _No, she isn't. She's from Turkey._

7. Antonio is from Brazil. _No, he isn't._ _____

8. Yumiko and Pinar are 19. _No, they aren't. They are 18 years old._

9. Berat and Pinar are from Saudi Arabia. _____ They're from Turkey.

## EXERCISE 6 PRESENT OF *BE*

GRAMMAR NOTES 1–2 Complete the email. Circle the correct answers.

Dear Mom and Dad,

Maya and I am / (are) in Seattle, but
1.
we not / we're not at the Western Hotel any
2.
longer. The Western Hotel isn't / aren't good.
3.
It's / It expensive. The people isn't / aren't
4.                                      5.
friendly, and the rooms isn't / aren't clean.
6.
It's / It also far from everything.
7.

Now are / we're at the Pacific Hotel on Second Avenue. It's / Is clean, and it's / it not
8.                                                    9.                   10.
expensive. The people here is / are great. We love Seattle. It is / are a beautiful city, and
11.                                            12.
the food is / are good. It's / Is cool at night, and our umbrella am / is always with us.
13.              14.                                              15.
But are / we're happy to be here.
16.

Love, Julie

## EXERCISE 7 EDITING

GRAMMAR NOTES 1–2 There are six mistakes in the conversations. The first mistake is corrected. Correct five more.

1. A: The food *is* good.

   B: You're right.

2. A: My cousin from Tokyo. She's a student.

   B: I'm from Tokyo. I no am a student.

3. A: Seattle is a big city in California.

   B: No, it's isn't. Seattle is in Washington.

4. A: The people is friendly here.

   B: I know. They're great.

5. A: Sydney is a great city.

   B: Yes. Is beautiful.

## EXERCISE 8  LISTENING

▶03|02  **A**  Listen to the conversation. Which sentence is true? Circle the correct answer.

**a.** The woman is a student, and the man is a chef.

**b.** The woman and the man are chefs.

**c.** The woman is a chef, and the man is a student.

▶03|02  **B**  Listen again. For each statement, check (✓) *True* or *False*.

| | True | False |
|---|---|---|
| 1. The man is from Italy. | ✓ | ☐ |
| 2. The woman is from Australia. | ☐ | ☐ |
| 3. The woman's parents are from Australia. | ☐ | ☐ |
| 4. The woman says Italian food is good. | ☐ | ☐ |
| 5. Italian food is not popular in Australia. | ☐ | ☐ |

a chef

**C**  Work with a partner. Say something true and something false about the woman and the man. Your partner changes the false sentence.

EXAMPLE:  A:  Matteo is from Australia.

B:  Matteo isn't from Australia. He's from . . .

## EXERCISE 9  I'M NOT A TEACHER

**A**  CONVERSATION  Prepare for a conversation. First, write true sentences. Use the words in parentheses.

1. (I / a teacher)  _I am a teacher_

2. (I / from Italy)  _I am from Italy_

3. (I / happy)  _I am happy_

4. (I / from a big city)  _I am from a big city_

5. (I / from a big family)  _I am have a big family_

6. (My parents / from Seattle)  _My parents are from Seattle_

7. (My parents / in Australia)  _My parents are live in Australia_

8. (My city / clean)  _My city is clean_

9. (People in my city / friendly)  _People in my city are friendly_

10. (My city / fun)  _My city is fun._

**B** Work with a partner. Talk about yourself. Use your sentences in A.

EXAMPLE: A: I'm not a teacher. I'm not from Italy. What about you?

B: I'm not a teacher. I am from Italy!

**C** Tell the class three things about you and your partner.

EXAMPLE: A: Oscar and I aren't teachers. Our parents aren't from Seattle. His parents are from Venezuela, and my parents are from China. We're both from big families.

B: Maria and I aren't from a big city. Her city is fun. My city isn't fun. It's boring!

## EXERCISE 10 THAT'S NOT TRUE!

**A** GAME Work in a group. Make up one true statement and one false statement about each student. Use the information in Exercise 9 or your own information.

**B** Work with another group. Say your statements from A. The other group guesses if they are true or false.

EXAMPLE: GROUP A: Ali is from a big family. He's from a big city.

GROUP B: Ali is from a big family. That's true. But he's not from a big city! That's false!

## EXERCISE 11 THE PEOPLE ARE FRIENDLY HERE!

CONVERSATION Work with a partner. Talk about the city you are in and the people in it. Use *I agree* or *I disagree* in your conversation. Use the words in the box.

| boring | cheap | dirty | friendly | great |
|--------|-------|-------|----------|-------|
| beautiful | clean | expensive | fun | unfriendly |

EXAMPLE: A: The people are friendly here.

B: I agree. And the city is clean.

A: Well, some places are dirty. The West Side isn't clean.

B: I disagree. The West Side isn't dirty. It's clean!

**A** BEFORE YOU WRITE  Read about a city. Underline the verb *be*. Then complete the chart about a city you know. Work with a partner. Tell your partner about the city.

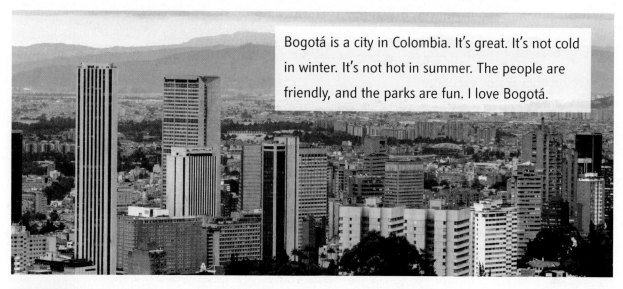

Bogotá is a city in Colombia. It's great. It's not cold in winter. It's not hot in summer. The people are friendly, and the parks are fun. I love Bogotá.

| City | Bogotá | |
| --- | --- | --- |
| Country | Colombia | |
| Weather | good | |
| People | friendly | |
| Parks | fun | |

**B** WRITE  Write a paragraph about a city. Use the present of *be*. Use the paragraph in A and your chart to help you.

**C** CHECK YOUR WORK  Read your paragraph in B. Underline the present of *be*. Then use the Editing Checklist to check your work.

### Editing Checklist

**Did you . . . ?**

- [ ] use *I + am*; *he, she,* and *it + is*; and *we, you, they + are*
- [ ] use *not* after the verb *be* for the negative
- [ ] use a subject and a verb in every sentence
- [ ] check your spelling

**D** REVISE YOUR WORK  Read your paragraph again. Can you improve your writing? Make changes if necessary.

# UNIT 3 REVIEW

**Test yourself on the grammar of the unit.**

**A** Complete the sentences with *She is*, *He is*, *It is*, *We are*, or *They are*.

1. This park isn't clean. _____It is_____ dirty.

2. My brother is not a student. _____He is_____ a teacher.

3. Amy is from Australia. _____She is_____ in Seattle now.

4. Michelle and Lisa are not sisters. _____They are_____ cousins.

5. My friends and I aren't from Japan. _____We are_____ from China.

**B** Rewrite the sentences. Use contractions.

1. It is boring. _____It's boring._____

2. They are not from Brazil. _____They aren't from Brazil. / They're not_____

3. I am not a chef. _____I'm not a chef._____

4. He is not in Australia. _____He isn't in Australia_____

5. We are in class. _____We're in class_____

**C** Correct the conversation. There are five mistakes.

**A:** Ali from Canada. He a student.

**B:** No. Ali no is a student. He's a chef.

**A:** Oh. I a student. I'm a teacher, too. I be an English language student. I'm a

Portuguese language teacher.

**Now check your answers on page 379.**

# 4

## *That is / Those are*; Possessive Adjectives

### FUN PLACES

**OUTCOMES**
- Use *that is / those are* and *is that / are those* to talk about people and things away from you
- Use possessive adjectives
- Identify true and false sentences about a reading
- Complete sentences about a conversation
- Talk about possessions
- Talk and write about places

## STEP 1 · GRAMMAR IN CONTEXT

### BEFORE YOU READ

**A VOCABULARY** Study the words. Then work with a partner. Practice the conversation.

**a university**

**a sports stadium**

**a museum**

**a zoo**

### Conversation

**A:** Is that a museum?
**B:** Yes, it is.
**A:** Is there a museum in your city?
**B:** Yes. It's the Museum of Art. It's big, and it's famous.

**B** Look at the words and photos in A again. Talk about three places in your city.

**A:** Is that _____?
**B:** Yes, it is.
**A:** Is there _____ in your city?
**B:** Yes. It's _____. It's _____.

▶ 04|01   Read this conversation.

# Seattle From the Space Needle

**STEVE:** Well, here we are. That's the Space Needle. How about a photo?

**AMY:** Sure. I have my camera.

**STEVE:** Come on. Let's go up.

*(Amy and Steve go to the top of the Space Needle.)*

CenturyLink Field and Safeco Field

University of Washington

Experience Music Project

**AMY:** Wow! Look at the two buildings over there.

**STEVE:** They're stadiums.

**AMY:** They're big! Are those people next to them? They look so small.

**STEVE:** Yes. Now look over there. That's the University of Washington.

**AMY:** That's your university, right?

**STEVE:** Yes, it is.

**AMY:** Is that the zoo near it?

**STEVE:** Hmm . . . I don't know. . . . OK, now look down. Look at that building with the colors.

**AMY:** The colors are beautiful. Its shape[1] is really interesting.

**STEVE:** That's the EMP.[2] It's a music museum. It belongs to Paul Allen.[3] It's his museum.

**AMY:** Let's go see it.

**STEVE:** That's a great idea.

---

1 *shape:* the form of something—round, square, etc.
2 *EMP:* The Experience Music Project, a music museum in Seattle
3 *Paul Allen:* a businessman, musician, and co-founder of Microsoft

# AFTER YOU READ

**A** COMPREHENSION  Look at the conversation again. For each statement, check (✓) *True* or *False*.

|  | True | False |
|---|:---:|:---:|
| 1. Amy and Steve are in Seattle. | ☐ | ☐ |
| 2. The camera is Amy's camera. | ☐ | ☐ |
| 3. The stadiums are small. | ☐ | ☐ |
| 4. The University of Washington is Amy's university. | ☐ | ☐ |
| 5. The building with many colors is in the zoo. | ☐ | ☑ |
| 6. The EMP is a museum for music. | ☐ | ☐ |

**B** Work with a partner. Read the text. Complete the last sentence. Check your answer on page 385.

> ### Who Am I?
> I am famous in Seattle and in the world. I am very tall—about 600 feet, or 200 meters. My top floor is a good restaurant. The first letters of my name are *S* and *N*. My name is the
>
> S _____.

---

## STEP 2    GRAMMAR PRESENTATION

### THAT IS / THOSE ARE

| Singular |
|---|
| **That is** the stadium. |
| **That's** his car. |
| **Is that** your key? |

| Plural |
|---|
| **Those are** the stadiums. |
| **Those are** his cars. |
| **Are those** your keys? |

### POSSESSIVE ADJECTIVES

| Subject Pronouns | Possessive Adjectives | Example Sentences |
|---|---|---|
| I | my | **I** am Amy. **My** name is Amy. |
| you | your | **You** are Judy. **Your** name is Judy. |
| he | his | **He** is Steve. **His** name is Steve. |
| she | her | **She** is Jenny. **Her** name is Jenny. |
| it | its | **It** is the EMP. **Its** shape is unusual. |
| we | our | **We** have one daughter. **Our** daughter is Judy. |
| you | your | **You** are Steve and Mark, right? **Your** city is very beautiful. |
| they | their | **They** are our children. **Their** names are Judy and Ken. |

# GRAMMAR NOTES

## 1 That is

| | |
|---|---|
| Use **that is** to talk about one person or thing **away from** you. | **That is** the University of Washington. |
| We often contract **that is** to **that's** in speaking and informal writing. | **That's** the Space Needle. |
| **USAGE NOTE** We use **that** when we point at things or people. We also use **that's** with *a good idea* or *a great idea*. | A: How about a picture?<br>B: **That's** a great idea. |

## 2 Those are

| | |
|---|---|
| Use **those are** to talk about two or more people or things **away from** you. | **Those are** our stadiums.<br>**Those are** my pets. |

## 3 Is that and Are those

| | |
|---|---|
| Use **Is that** and **Are those** to ask questions. The answers usually have a **subject pronoun**. | A: **Is that** your dictionary?<br>B: Yes, **it is**.<br>A: **Are those** your keys?<br>B: No, **they aren't**. |

## 4 Possessive Adjectives

| | |
|---|---|
| The possessive adjectives are **my, your, his, her, its, our,** and **their**. They tell who someone or something belongs to. | That's **my** daughter.<br>Those are **her** friends.<br>The car belongs to Steve. It's **his** car. |

# PRONUNCIATION NOTE

04|02  **Same Pronunciation, Different Meaning**

| | |
|---|---|
| Some words sound the same, but they are different in meaning and spelling. | |
| **your** = possessive adjective<br>**you're** = you are | **Your** name is Maria.<br>**You're** a student. |
| **its** = possessive adjective<br>**it's** = it is | **Its** name is the Space Needle.<br>**It's** 600 feet high. |
| **their** = possessive adjective<br>**they're** = they are | **Their** children are happy.<br>**They're** happy. |

# REFERENCE NOTES

For more information about **this, that, these,** and **those,** see Unit 1 on page 8 and Unit 18 on page 201.

For **definitions of grammar terms**, see the Glossary on page 375.

## EXERCISE 1 DISCOVER THE GRAMMAR

GRAMMAR NOTES 1–4 Read the questions and answers. Underline the possessive adjectives. Then match the questions and answers.

_d_ **1.** Are those your books?

_____ **2.** Is that his camera?

_____ **3.** Are those your children?

_____ **4.** Is that the EMP?

_____ **5.** Is that your university?

_____ **6.** Are those stadiums?

_b_ **7.** Is that your sister?

**a.** Yes. They're for sports.

**b.** No. She's my friend.

**c.** Yes. Its shape is interesting, right?

~~**d.**~~ No, they're her books.

**e.** No, it's my camera.

**f.** No, I'm at Columbia University.

**g.** Yes. Their names are Judy and Ken.

## EXERCISE 2 *THAT* AND *THOSE*

GRAMMAR NOTES 1–3 Complete the sentences with *that* or *those*.

**1.** _____That_____'s a big movie theater.

**2.** _____That_____'s a good museum.

**3.** Are _____those_____ your children?

**4.** Is _____that_____ your university?

**5.** _____Those_____ are my friends.

**6.** Is _____that_____ the zoo?

movie theater

## EXERCISE 3 POSSESSIVE ADJECTIVES

GRAMMAR NOTE 4 Look at the pictures. Complete the sentences. Circle the correct answers.

 **1.** Kip and Pam are (my) / our pets.

**2.** Jeremy, Annie, and Ben are my / our children.

 **3.** Annie has her / their books.

**4.** Ben loves her / his school.

 **5.** Ken's car has its / her problems, but he likes it.

**6.** Judy and Ken Johnson like their / your universities very much.

# EXERCISE 4  MORE POSSESSIVE ADJECTIVES

GRAMMAR NOTE 4  Judy is showing photos of her family. Complete the passage with *my*, *his*, *her*, *our*, or *their*.

That's me and ____my____ brother, Ken, with
1.

_____ parents in front of _____ house.
2.                                  3.

We love _____ house. It's close to the sports
4.

stadium. _____ father loves sports. The stadium
5.

is _____ favorite place! _____ mother
6.                            7.

doesn't like sports, so the stadium isn't _____
8.

favorite place! Oh, and Ken is a student. _____us_____
9.

university is near the house, too.

# EXERCISE 5  SAME PRONUNCIATION, DIFFERENT MEANING

04|03 PRONUNCIATION NOTE  Listen to each sentence. Which word do you hear? Circle the correct answer.

1. **a.** Their      (**b.**) They're        4. **a.** your      **b.** you're

2. **a.** Their      **b.** They're         5. **a.** Its       **b.** It's

3. **a.** your       **b.** you're          6. **a.** its       **b.** it's

# EXERCISE 6  EDITING

GRAMMAR NOTES 1–4  There are six mistakes in the conversations. The first mistake is corrected. Correct five more.

       *those*
1. A: Are ~~that~~ your keys?        B: No, they her keys.

2. A: Those is my university.        B: It's really big, right?

3. A: Are that your building?        B: No, it's not.

4. A: Those theater is beautiful.    B: Yes. It name is the Star Theater.

## EXERCISE 7  LISTENING

○04|04  **A**  Listen to Judy and Jessica's conversation. Complete the sentence. Check (✓) the correct answer.

The people in the photo are _____.

☐ Jessica's family          ☐ Judy's family          ☐ Jessica's friends

○04|04  **B**  Now listen again. Complete the sentences. Circle the correct answers.

**1.** Jessica and her husband have _____ children.
  **a.** two          **(b.)** three

**2.** Ben is her _____.
  **a.** dog          **b.** son

**3.** Annie is Jessica's _____.
  **a.** son          **b.** daughter

**4.** In the photo, they are at the _____ stadium.
  **a.** football          **b.** baseball

**5.** The other kids are from _____.
  **a.** their school          **b.** their university

**6.** All the kids love _____.
  **a.** baseball          **b.** football and baseball

**C**  Work with a partner. Compare your answers in B.

## EXERCISE 8  WHO DOES IT BELONG TO?

**A**  GAME  Work with the class. Choose something that belongs to you. Put it on the teacher's table.

**B**  Ask and answer questions about the things on the table.

EXAMPLE:  *(Student A points to a backpack.)*
  A:  Who does it belong to?
  B:  *(B points to Student C.)*
      That's her backpack.
  C:  Right. It's my backpack.
      **or**  *(C points to Student D.)*
      No, that's his backpack.

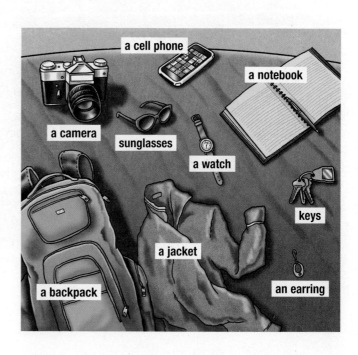

*That is / Those are*; Possessive Adjectives  **47**

# EXERCISE 9  IS THAT A UNIVERSITY?

INFORMATION GAP  Work with a partner. Student A, follow the instructions below. Student B, follow the instructions on page 387.

**STUDENT A**

- Look at the map. Student B has the same map with different information. Ask Student B questions about buildings 2, 4, 6, and 8. Complete the map.

  EXAMPLE:  A: Look at building 2. Is that a university?
  B: No, it isn't. It's . . .

- Answer Student B's questions about buildings 1, 3, 5, and 7 on your map.

  EXAMPLE:  B: Look at building 1. Is that a university?
  A: No, it isn't. It's . . .

- Compare your maps. Are they the same?

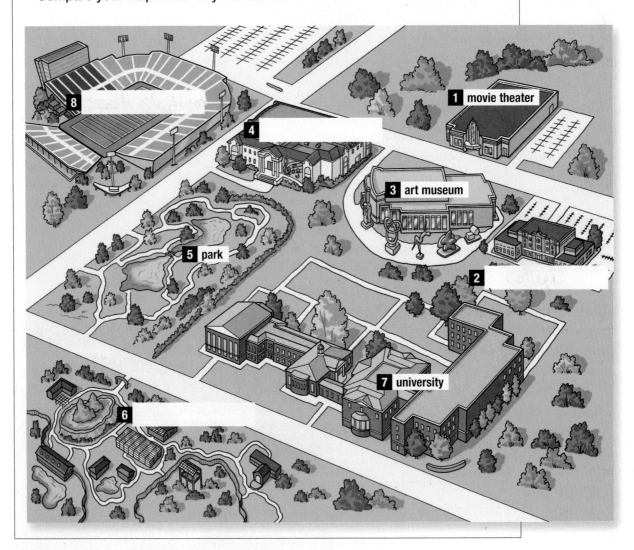

## FROM GRAMMAR TO WRITING

**A** BEFORE YOU WRITE  Read the paragraph and chart, and look at the photo. Underline examples of *that*, *those*, and possessive adjectives. Then find a photo of a place in your town or city. Complete the chart about it. Work with a partner. Tell your partner about the place in the photo.

That's a photo of Safeco Field. That's a sports stadium in my city, Seattle. It's our baseball stadium. Those are baseball players from our team. They are the Seattle Mariners.

| Name of town or city | Seattle | |
|---|---|---|
| Name of place | Safeco Field | |
| Type of place | baseball stadium | |
| People in the place | baseball players | |

**B** WRITE  Write a paragraph about the place in your photo. Use *that*, *those*, and possessive adjectives. Use the paragraph in A and your chart to help you.

**C** CHECK YOUR WORK  Read your paragraph. Underline examples of *that*, *those*, and possessive adjectives. Use the Editing Checklist to check your work.

### Editing Checklist

**Did you...?**

☐ use *that* for one person or thing away from you

☐ use *those* for two or more people or things away from you

☐ use *my*, *your*, *his*, *her*, *our*, or *their* before nouns to show who something belongs to

☐ check your spelling

**D** REVISE YOUR WORK  Read your paragraph again. Can you improve your writing? Make changes if necessary.

# UNIT 4 REVIEW

**Test yourself on the grammar of the unit.**

**A** Complete the sentences with *that* or *those*.

1. ___That___'s an expensive car.

2. Are ___those___ his friends?

3. Is ___That___ your brother?

4. ___That___'s her camera.

5. ___Those___ aren't my keys!

**B** Complete the sentences. Circle the correct answers.

1. He / His is my friend.

2. That's my sister. She / Her name is Lynn.

3. What are you / your names?

4. Those are good cameras. Their / They're very popular.

5. I really like the Barksdale Movie Theater. It's / Its my favorite place.

**C** Correct the conversation. There are five mistakes.

A: Is those your family in the photo?

B: Yes. That's me brother, and that's my sister.

A: What are they're names?

B: He's name is Robert, and her name is Tammy.

A: That your dog?

B: Yes. Its name is Spot.

**Now check your answers on page 379.**

UNIT

**5**

**Present of *Be*: Yes/No Questions; Questions with *Who* and *What***

JOBS

OUTCOMES
- Ask and answer simple present *yes/no* questions with the verb *be*
- Ask and answer simple present questions with *who* and *what* and the verb *be*
- Complete sentences about a reading
- Answer questions about a conversation
- Talk about people and their jobs
- Write interview questions for a classmate

STEP 1    GRAMMAR IN CONTEXT

## BEFORE YOU READ

Study the vocabulary. Then work with a partner. Tell your partner about the jobs of people you know.

EXAMPLE:   A: My father is a bus driver. And my sister is a nurse.
           B: Really? My father is a teacher. My cousin Barbara is a server.

a bus driver

a server

a writer

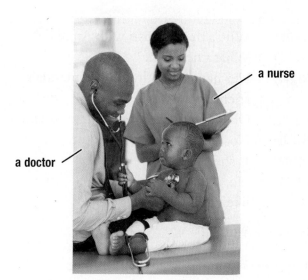

a nurse

a doctor

05|01   Read these conversations at Amanda and Josh's wedding.

# Who's That Woman with Amanda?

STEVE:   Mark?

MARK:    Steve! Are you here for the wedding?

STEVE:   Yes, I am. Amanda is my cousin.
         What about you?

MARK:    Josh and I are friends from school.
         This is a great wedding!

STEVE:   Yes, it is.

KATHY:   Wow, there are a lot of guests
         here. . . . Who's that man with Steve?

AMANDA:  His name is Mark. He and Josh
         are friends.

KATHY:   Hmm. Is he single?

AMANDA:  Yes, he is.

KATHY:   What does he do?[1] Is he a teacher,
         like Steve?

AMANDA:  No, he isn't. He's a writer.

KATHY:   What kind of writer?

AMANDA:  He writes novels.

MARK:    Who's that woman with Amanda?
         What's her name?

STEVE:   Her name is Kathy. She's Amanda's
         friend from work.

MARK:    Oh, yeah? Is she a nurse, like Amanda?

STEVE:   No, she's not. She's a doctor.

MARK:    Is she married?

STEVE:   No, she isn't. She's single . . . just
         like you!

---

1 *What does he do?:*  What is his job?

# AFTER YOU READ

**A** COMPREHENSION  **Look at the conversations again. Complete the sentences. Circle the correct answers.**

1. Steve and Amanda are _____.
   a. brother and sister      **b.** cousins

2. Mark and Josh are _____.
   a. brothers      **b.** friends

3. _____ is single.
   **a.** Kathy      b. Amanda

4. _____ is a writer.
   a. Kathy      **b.** Mark

5. _____ is a doctor.
   **a.** Amanda      b. Kathy

**B** Work with a partner. Compare your answers in A.

## STEP 2 GRAMMAR PRESENTATION

## PRESENT OF *BE*: *YES / NO* QUESTIONS

| Yes/No Questions | | Short Answers | | |
|---|---|---|---|---|
| **Singular** | | **Affirmative** | **Negative** | |
| **Am I** right? | | Yes, **you are.** | No, **you're not.** or No, **you aren't.** | |
| **Are you** a writer? | | Yes, **I am.** | No, **I'm not.** | |
| **Is he** a bus driver? | | Yes, **he is.** | No, **he's not.** or No, **he isn't.** | |
| **Is she** single? | | Yes, **she is.** | No, **she's not.** or No, **she isn't.** | |
| **Is your** car new? | | Yes, **it is.** | No, **it's not.** or No, **it isn't.** | |
| **Plural** | | **Affirmative** | **Negative** | |
| **Are we** late? | | Yes, **we are.** | No, **we're not.** or No, **we aren't.** | |
| **Are you** happy? | | Yes, **you are.** | No, **you're not.** or No, **you aren't.** | |
| **Are they** brothers? | | Yes, **they are.** | No, **they're not.** or No, **they aren't.** | |

## PRESENT OF *BE*: QUESTIONS WITH *WHO* AND *WHAT*

| Questions with *Who/What* | Short Answers | Long Answers |
|---|---|---|
| **Who is** that woman? | Kathy. | That's Kathy. |
| **What's** her name? | Kathy. | It's Kathy. |

# GRAMMAR NOTES

## 1 Yes/No Questions with *Be*

| | |
|---|---|
| In a *yes/no* question with *be*, put **am**, **is**, or **are** before the subject. | SUBJECT<br>**He** is at a wedding. *(statement)*<br><br>SUBJECT<br>Is **he** at a wedding? *(question)* |

## 2 Short Answers

| | |
|---|---|
| **Negative short answers** have two forms. We often use contractions in negative short answers. | A: Is she married?<br>B: No, she**'s not**. **or** No, she **isn't**.<br><br>A: Are they brothers?<br>B: No, they**'re not**. **or** No, they **aren't**. |
| **Affirmative short answers** have only one form. | A: Am I right?<br>B: Yes, **you are**.<br><br>A: Is she single?<br>B: Yes, **she is**. |
| **BE CAREFUL!** Don't use contractions in **affirmative short answers**. | A: Is she a server?<br>B: **Yes, she is.**<br>NOT Yes, ~~she's~~. |

## 3 Questions with *Be*: *Who* and *What*

| | |
|---|---|
| We use *who* and *what* to ask about the **subject** of a sentence. | |
| Use *who* to ask about **people**.<br>Use *what* to ask about **things** or **ideas**. | **Who** is that woman with Amanda?<br>**What** is her name? |
| We often use the contractions *who's* and *what's* in speaking and informal writing. | **Who's** that woman?<br>**What's** her name? |
| **Answers** to these questions can be long or short. | A: Who's that man?<br>B: **That's Mark.** **or** **Mark.** |

# REFERENCE NOTE

For **definitions of grammar terms**, see the Glossary on page 375.

## EXERCISE 1   DISCOVER THE GRAMMAR

GRAMMAR NOTES 1–3   Underline the *yes/no* questions. Circle the *wh-* questions. Then match the questions and answers.

| | | | |
|---|---|---|---|
| _c_ | 1. Is Jenny your sister? | **a.** | No, he isn't. |
| _d_ | 2. Are Jaime and Helen students? | **b.** | Ted is. |
| ____ | 3. Am I right? | **c.** | No, she isn't. She's my cousin. |
| _f_ | 4. What's her name? | **d.** | No, they aren't. They're teachers. |
| ____ | 5. Who's a bus driver? | **e.** | Yes, you are. |
| ____ | 6. Are you and Ed from Chicago? | **f.** | Her name is Kate. |
| ____ | 7. What does Anna do? | **g.** | No, we're from New York. |
| ____ | 8. Is Mark married? | **h.** | She's a doctor. |

## EXERCISE 2   *WHO* AND *WHAT*

GRAMMAR NOTE 3   Complete the conversations with *who* or *what*.

1. A: _____Who_____'s that woman with Mark?
   B: That's my mother.

2. A: _____What_____'s her name?
   B: Mary.

3. A: _____'s his job?
   B: He's a bus driver.

4. A: _____Who_____'s that man with Judy?
   B: That's Mark.

5. A: _____'s the teacher for this class?
   B: Professor Beck. Steve Beck.

6. A: _____What_____'s a nurse?
   B: Amanda is.

## EXERCISE 3   QUESTIONS AND ANSWERS

GRAMMAR NOTES 1–3   Complete the conversation between Ben and Annie and their uncle Steve. Use the correct forms of the words in parentheses. Use contractions.

BEN:   Uncle Steve, _____*who's*_____ a doctor, Kathy or Amanda?
          **1.** (who / be)

STEVE:   Kathy _____ a doctor.
           **2.** (be)

ANNIE:   What about Amanda? _____ her job?
                  **3.** (what / be)

STEVE: _____ *She's* _____ a nurse.
           4. (she / be)

BEN: What about Mark? _____ *He is* _____ a teacher like you?
                            5. (he / be)

STEVE: No, Ben, _____ *he isn't* _____ a teacher. _____ *he is* _____ a writer.
                  6. (he / not / be)                7. (he / be)

ANNIE: _____ *that is* _____ interesting.
           8. (that / be)

## EXERCISE 4  MORE QUESTIONS AND ANSWERS

GRAMMAR NOTES 1–3  **Put the words in the correct order. Make conversations.**

1. A: (Steve / Portland? / Is / from)    A: *Is Steve from Portland?*

   B: (not. / No, / he's)    B: *No, he's not.*

2. A: (a server? / she / Is)    A: *Is she a server?*

   B: (Yes, / is. / she)    B: *Yes, she is.*

3. A: (nurses? / Are / they)    A: *Are they nurses?*

   B: (they're / No, / doctors.)    B: *No, they're doctors.*

4. A: (man? / that / Who / is)    A: *Who is that man*

   B: (my / teacher. / He's)    B: *He's my teacher.*

5. A: (Mark and Kathy / married? / Are)    A: *Are Mark and Kathy married?*

   B: (aren't. / No, / they)    B: *No, they aren't.*

## EXERCISE 5  EDITING

GRAMMAR NOTES 1–3  **There are six mistakes in the conversations. The first mistake is corrected. Correct five more.**

1. A: *Are* ~~Is~~ you a doctor?

   B: Yes, I'm.

2. A: Is she single?

   B: No, she not.

3. A: They chefs?

   B: No, they aren't.

4. A: Is he a bus driver?

   B: No, he's. *n't*

5. A: Is he married?

   B: No, he's not. He single.

## EXERCISE 6 LISTENING

▶05|02 **A** Listen to the conversation. Then listen again. Answer each question with a short answer.

1. Is Mai a chef?                    _No, she's not._ **or** _No, she isn't._

2. Is she married?                   _Yes, she is._

3. Are Jaime and Carlos brothers?    _No, they are not or No, they aren't_

4. Is Alicia single?                 _Yes, she is_

▶05|02 **B** Listen again. Answer the questions. Circle the correct answers.

1. Who is Diego's friend?
   a. Alicia            (b.) Mai

2. What does Mai do?
   a. She's a chef.     b. She's a server.

3. What do Diego's cousins do?
   (a.) They're both chefs.   b. They're both servers.

4. What's the name of Diego's wife?
   a. Mai               b. Alicia

**C** Work with a partner. Compare your answers in A and B.

## EXERCISE 7 WHAT DO YOU DO?

**A** CONVERSATION Work with a partner. Practice the conversation with the jobs in the pictures.

**a dentist**     **a clerk**     **a police officer**     **a mechanic**     **a cashier**

A: What do you do?
B: I'm a _____. What about you?
A: I'm a _____.

**B** Walk around the room. Practice the conversation with different classmates. Use other jobs from this unit or your real job.

**C** Work with your partner again. Ask your partner about other people in the class.

EXAMPLE: A: Who's the man near Mei-ling?

B: That's Hussein.

A: What does he do?

B: He's a bus driver.

## EXERCISE 8  WHO AM I?

GAME  Work in a group. Write the name of a famous living person on a piece of paper. Choose a classmate and put the piece of paper on his or her back. Your classmate asks *yes/no* questions to guess the name of the person.

EXAMPLE: A: Is it a man?

B: No, it isn't.

A: Is she beautiful?

C: Yes, she is.

A: Is she an actor?

D: Yes, she is.

A: Is she Angelina Jolie?

E: Yes, she is!

**A** BEFORE YOU WRITE Read the interview. Underline *who*, *what*, and *yes/no* questions. Then work with a partner. Interview him or her and complete the chart. Ask the questions in Rosa's interview or your own questions. Take turns.

ANNA: What's your name?

ROSA: My name is Rosa Gutierrez.

ANNA: Are you from the United States?

ROSA: No, I'm not. I'm from Tegucigalpa, Honduras.

ANNA: What do you do?

ROSA: I'm a clerk, and I'm a student.

ANNA: Are you married?

ROSA: No, I'm not.

ANNA: Are you happy?

ROSA: Yes, I am. I'm very happy.

| Your Questions | Your Partner's Answers |
|---|---|
|  |  |
|  |  |
|  |  |
|  |  |
|  |  |
|  |  |

**B** WRITE Write your interview questions and your partner's answers. Use *yes/no*, *who*, and *what* questions. Use the interview in A and your chart to help you.

**C** CHECK YOUR WORK Read your interview. Underline *yes/no*, *who*, and *what* questions. Use the Editing Checklist to check your work.

**Editing Checklist**

**Did you...?**

☐ use *am*, *is*, and *are* in *yes/no* questions

☐ use *who* with people and *what* with things

☐ check your spelling

**D** REVISE YOUR WORK Read your paragraph again. Can you improve your writing? Make changes if necessary.

# UNIT 5 REVIEW

**Test yourself on the grammar of the unit.**

**(A)** Match the questions and answers.

_____ 1. Are you actors?

_____ 2. Am I late?

_____ 3. Is John married?

_____ 4. Are your parents teachers?

_____ 5. Is your sister a dentist?

    a. No, they aren't.

    b. No, she isn't.

    c. Yes, you are.

    d. Yes, we are.

    e. No, he isn't.

**(B)** Complete the conversation with *who* or *what*.

A: That's a great photo. _____'s that woman on the right?
    **1.**

B: That's my cousin.

A: Oh, really? _____'s her name?
    **2.**

B: Amalia.

A: And _____'s that man on her left?
    **3.**

B: That's her husband, Carlos.

A: I see. _____ does he do?
    **4.**

B: He's a police officer.

A: And _____'s that in the middle? Is that their son?
    **5.**

B: No, that's their daughter!

**(C)** Correct the conversations. There are five mistakes.

1. A: What his job? Is he a dentist?

    B: No, he's not. He's a doctor.

2. A: Is your sister single?

    B: No, she not.

3. A: Is your mother a nurse?

    B: No, she isn't. She a cashier.

4. A: Is you from Kenya?

    B: Yes, I'm. *am*

**Now check your answers on page 379.**

UNIT

# 6

## Present of *Be*: Questions with *Where*; Prepositions of Place

### PLACES IN THE NEIGHBORHOOD

**OUTCOMES**
- Ask and answer simple present questions with *where* and the verb *be*
- Use prepositions of place
- Complete sentences about a reading
- Answer questions about a conversation
- Ask and answer questions about the locations of people, places, and things
- Write a paragraph about three places in your area

## STEP 1    GRAMMAR IN CONTEXT

### BEFORE YOU READ

**A** VOCABULARY  Study the words. Then work with a partner. Practice the conversation.

a supermarket

a gym

a bank

a drugstore

a hospital

a gas station

**Conversation**

A: Where is the closest supermarket?
B: It's on West Street.
A: And where's the closest bank?
B: It's on Second Avenue.

**B** Talk about places in your neighborhood. Use the words in A and streets in your area.

A: Where is the closest _____?
B: It's on _____.

## READMENT

06|01 Read this article about places in a small town.

# Places in the Neighborhood

**Welcome to Preston Apartments.** Do you know the area? Where is the closest supermarket? Where's the post office? Here is some useful information.

Goodfood Supermarket is on Main Street between First and Second Streets. It's open 24 hours a day. The food is fresh,[1] and the prices are good. Preston Post Office is on Main Street between First and Second Streets, too. It's next to the supermarket. The post office is open Monday to Friday from 9 a.m. to 5 p.m. and Saturday until 12 p.m.

Ella's Gym is on Main Street between Second and Third Streets. It's at 45 Main Street. It's next to Drew's Drugstore. The gym is open every day from 7 a.m. to 10 p.m., and the drugstore is open Monday to Saturday from 9 to 7.

DSL Bank is between Second and Maple Streets. It's open Monday to Friday from 9 a.m. to 4 p.m., and Saturdays from 9 to 12.

Preston Hospital is on the corner of Washington Street and Second Avenue. It's across from a gas station.

Enjoy your new home!

*Olivia Rodriguez, Manager, Preston Apartments*
mr35@qmail.com • 988-656-4346

1 *fresh:* good because it's not old

## AFTER YOU READ

**A** COMPREHENSION  **Look at the reading again. Match the beginnings with the endings of the sentences.**

_____ 1. The supermarket is          **a.** the manager of Preston Apartments.

_____ 2. The post office is           **b.** next to the gym.

_____ 3. The gym is                   **c.** on Main Street between Second and Third Streets.

_____ 4. The drugstore is             **d.** next to the post office.

_____ 5. Olivia Rodriguez is          **e.** open on Saturday until noon.

**B** Work with a partner. Compare your answers in A. Then say something about a supermarket, a gym, or a hospital near you.

## PRESENT OF *BE*: QUESTIONS WITH *WHERE*

| Questions with *Where* | Short Answers | Long Answers |
|---|---|---|
| **Where** is the supermarket? | On First Avenue. | It's on First Avenue. |
| **Where** are your friends? | In Florida. | They're in Florida. |

## PREPOSITIONS OF PLACE

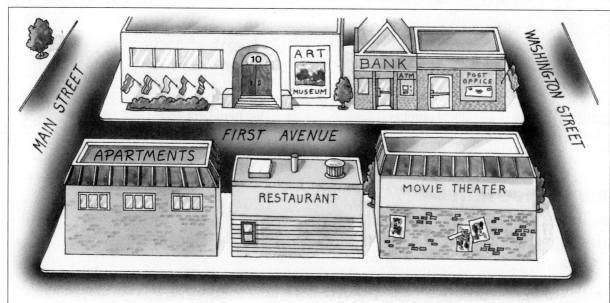

The art museum is **on** First Avenue. It's **across from** an apartment building and a restaurant. It's **at** 10 First Avenue. It's **on the corner of** First Avenue and Main Street.

The bank is **between** the art museum and the post office. The restaurant is **next to** the movie theater.

## GRAMMAR NOTES

### 1 Questions with *Where*

| | |
|---|---|
| Use *where* to ask questions about **location**. | A: **Where** is the restaurant?<br>B: It's on First Avenue. |
| *Where's* is the **short form** for *where is*. | A: **Where's** the bank?<br>B: It's next to the museum. |

### 2 Prepositions of Place

| | |
|---|---|
| *In*, *on*, *at*, *next to*, *between*, and *across from* are prepositions of place. They tell the **location of people, places, and things**. | My school is **in** Seattle.<br>The book is **on** the table.<br>I'm **next to** the door. |

| We use prepositions in **addresses**. | |
|---|---|
| • *in* + **country, state, province, country, or continent** | It is **in** Seattle. |
| • *on* + **street name and floors** | It is **on** Main Street. It's **on** the second (2nd) floor. |
| • *on the corner of* + **streets** | My school is **on the corner of** Main and Third (3rd). |
| • *at* + **street address** | My school is **at** 15 Main Street. |
| **USAGE NOTE** We don't always say *street* or *avenue* in informal speaking or writing. | A: Where's your school?<br>B: It's on **Main.** or It's on **Main Street.** |
| **BE CAREFUL!** Use **ordinal numbers** (*first, second, third,* etc.) for streets and floors. | We live on **Eighth (8th)** Street.<br>NOT We live on ~~Eight~~ Street.<br><br>We're on the **first (1st)** floor.<br>NOT We're on the ~~one~~ floor. |
| **BE CAREFUL!** Use *the* + an ordinal number before floors. | It's on **the third (3rd) floor.**<br>NOT It's ~~on third~~ floor. |

## REFERENCE NOTES

For a list of **ordinal numbers**, see Appendix 4 on page 366.
For **definitions of grammar terms**, see the Glossary on page 375.

**STEP 3    FOCUSED PRACTICE**

## EXERCISE 1  DISCOVER THE GRAMMAR

Ⓐ GRAMMAR NOTES 2–3 Underline the prepositions of place in the sentences.

1. It's <u>on</u> First Avenue between Washington and Main. It's between a movie theater and

   an apartment building.

2. It's on the corner of First Avenue and Washington Street. It's next to a bank.

3. It's next to a restaurant and across from a bank.

Ⓑ Look at the map on page 61. Write the place that each sentence in A is about.

1. *The restaurant* _____

2. _____

3. _____

# EXERCISE 2 PREPOSITIONS IN ADDRESSES

**A** GRAMMAR NOTES 1–3 **Complete the sentences. Circle the correct answers.**

Hi Judy,

Yoko's apartment is in / (on) First Avenue between / in Jackson and Main. I think
         **1.**                      **2.**

it's at / on 10 First Avenue, but I'm not sure. It's across from / in a library and
    **3.**                                        **4.**

next / next to a gym. It's in / on the second floor, Apartment 2A.
    **5.**               **6.**

Take the number 4 bus. It stops on the corner of / next to First and Jackson.
                             **7.**

See you at Yoko's on Sunday afternoon!

Mark

**B** Look at the map. Put an *X* on Yoko's apartment building.

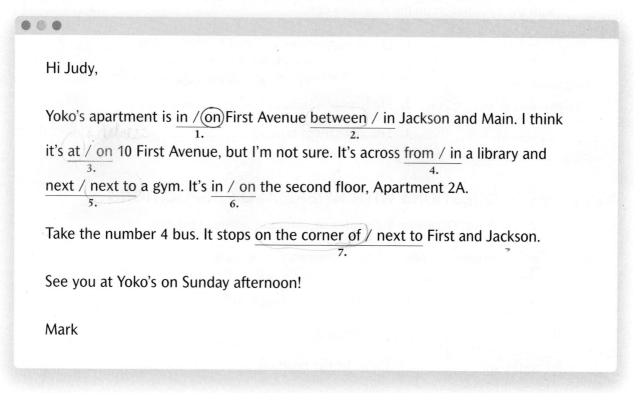

**C** Look at the map again. Write a question with *where* for each answer.

1. **A:** _Where's the gym_____? **B:** It's on the corner of Jackson and First.

2. **A:** _____? **B:** It's on the corner of Main and First.

3. **A:** _____? **B:** It's on First Avenue next to the supermarket.

# EXERCISE 3 PREPOSITIONS OF PLACE IN ADDRESSES

GRAMMAR NOTES 2–3 **Look at the business card. Complete the sentences with the information on the business card.**

DF

Doug Foster

30 16th Avenue, Apt. 3A
Seattle, Washington 98122

1. Doug Foster lives in *Seattle, Washington* _____ .

2. He lives on _____ Avenue.

3. He lives at _____ .

4. His apartment is on the _____ floor.

# EXERCISE 4 QUESTIONS WITH *WHERE* AND PREPOSITIONS

Ⓐ GRAMMAR NOTES 1–3 **Complete the sentences with the words in the box.**

| across | at | between | next | on | where's | ~~where is~~ |
|---|---|---|---|---|---|---|

MAN: Excuse me, _____*where is*_____ the closest drugstore?
1.

WOMAN: It's _____*on*_____ Sixth Avenue. It's _____*between*_____ Foster and
2. 3.

Jefferson. It's _____*next*_____ to the hospital.
4.

MAN: And _____*where's*_____ the closest gas station?
5.

WOMAN: It's _____*at*_____ 50 Sixth Avenue. It's _____*across*_____ from the
6. 7.

movie theater.

MAN: Thanks.

⏵06|02 Ⓑ LISTEN AND CHECK **Listen to the conversation and check your answers in A.**

# EXERCISE 5 EDITING

GRAMMAR NOTES 1–3 **There are six mistakes in the conversations. The first mistake is corrected. Find and correct five more.**

**Conversation 1**

A: Excuse me, ~~where~~ *where's* MidWest Bank?

B: It's in Washington Street. It's next

a supermarket.

A: Is it across a gym?

B: Yes, it is.

**Conversation 2**

A: Where's the party?

B: It's in 359 West Street.

A: That's Bill and Pete's apartment.

B: Are they in the second floor?

A: No, the third floor.

## EXERCISE 6   LISTENING

**A** Look at the map. The letters *N*, *S*, *E*, and *W* stand for *north*, *south*, *east*, and *west*. Match the questions and answers. Then work with a partner. Compare your answers.

<u> *b* </u>   **1.** Where's the art museum?    **a.** It's across from the hospital.

\_\_\_\_\_   **2.** Where's the hospital?    ~~**b.**~~ It's next to the bank.

\_\_\_\_\_   **3.** Where's the bank?    **c.** It's between the art museum and the post office.

\_\_\_\_\_   **4.** Where's the park?    **d.** It's on the northeast corner of Second and Washington.

▶06|03   **B** Listen to the conversation. Look at the map in A. Where are the people? Check (✓) the answer.

☐ Main Street     ☐ Washington Street     ☐ First Avenue

▶06|03   **C** Look at the map and listen again. Write *supermarket* and *flower shop* on the correct buildings on the map.

# EXERCISE 7 FIND THE CLASSROOM

INFORMATION GAP  Work with a partner. Student A follows the instructions below. Student B follows the instructions on page 388.

---

**STUDENT A**

- The directory at Ace Language School is not complete. Ask your partner questions with *where* to complete your list.

  EXAMPLE:  A: Where's English 1?
  B: It's on the first floor in Room 108.

- Answer your partner's questions about his or her directory.

  EXAMPLE:  B: Where's the main office?
  A: It's on the first floor in Room 101.

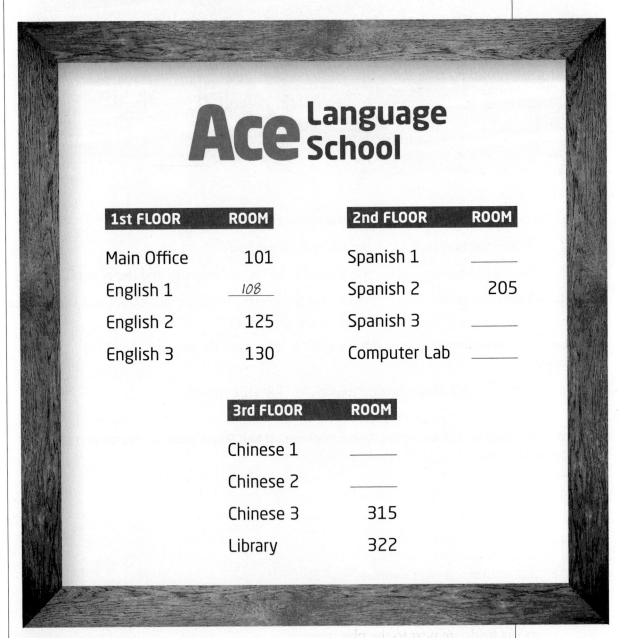

## Ace Language School

| 1st FLOOR | ROOM |
|-----------|------|
| Main Office | 101 |
| English 1 | *108* |
| English 2 | 125 |
| English 3 | 130 |

| 2nd FLOOR | ROOM |
|-----------|------|
| Spanish 1 | ___ |
| Spanish 2 | 205 |
| Spanish 3 | ___ |
| Computer Lab | ___ |

| 3rd FLOOR | ROOM |
|-----------|------|
| Chinese 1 | ___ |
| Chinese 2 | ___ |
| Chinese 3 | 315 |
| Library | 322 |

## EXERCISE 8 GUESS WHERE IT IS

**A** GAME Work in a group. Take turns. Choose four classroom objects. One student places them on the table. The other students don't look.

**B** Students B, C, and D ask Student A *yes/no* questions to find out where the objects are. From Student A's answers, each student draws a picture of the objects on the table.

EXAMPLE: **A:** OK, I'm ready.

    **B:** Is the cell phone next to the book?

    **A:** No, it's not.

    **C:** Is it on the book?

    **A:** Yes, it is.

**C** Look at the objects on the table. Are your drawings correct?

## EXERCISE 9 WHERE'S THE CLOSEST PARK?

ROLE PLAY Work with a partner. Take turns. Ask for the location of places in your area. Ask about the places in the box below or other places. Use *in*, *on*, *at*, *next to*, *between*, *on the corner of*, and *across from* in your answers.

| | | | |
|---|---|---|---|
| a bank | a gas station | a hospital | a park |
| a drugstore | a gym | an Italian restaurant | a post office |

EXAMPLE: **A:** Where's the closest park?

    **B:** It's on Elm Street. It's across from Sinai Hospital.

    **A:** Is it a good park?

    **B:** Yes. It's great. There's a lake. The picnic area is across from the lake. The sports fields are next to the playground.

## FROM GRAMMAR TO WRITING

**A** BEFORE YOU WRITE  Read about Pierre's Café. Then complete the chart for three places in your area. Work with a partner. Tell your partner about the places.

Pierre's Café is at 40 River Street. It's next to West Park. It's across from the library. It's open seven days a week. The food is great.

| Place | Address | What do you think about it? |
|---|---|---|
| Pierre's Café | 40 River Street<br>next to West Park<br>across from the library | great food |
| | | |
| | | |
| | | |

**B** WRITE  Write a paragraph about three places in your area. Use prepositions of place. Use the paragraph about Pierre's Cafe in A and your chart to help you.

**C** CHECK YOUR WORK  Read your paragraph again. Underline the prepositions of place. Use the Editing Checklist to check your work.

### Editing Checklist

**Did you . . . ?**

☐ use *in* before cities and countries, *on* before streets, and *at* before complete addresses

☐ use *across from*, *next to*, and *on the corner of*

☐ use ordinal numbers for streets and avenues

☐ check your spelling

**D** REVISE YOUR WORK  Read your paragraph again. Can you improve your writing? Make changes if necessary.

# UNIT 6 REVIEW

**Test yourself on the grammar of the unit.**

**Ⓐ Complete the paragraph. Circle the correct answers.**

I live in / at Denver. Denver is a big city in / on Colorado. My apartment is in / at
    **1.**                      **2.**                      **3.**

143 Oak Street. It's across from / between 141 Oak Street and 149 Oak Street. I live
                  **4.**

on / on the fourth floor.
  **5.**

**Ⓑ Complete the sentences. Use the words in the box.**

| across | at | in | next to | on |
|---|---|---|---|---|

My school is _____ at _____ 695 Park Avenue. My class is _____ in _____ Room
           **1.**                           **2.**

1502. It's _____ on _____ the 15th floor. My school is _____ across _____ from a small park.
       **3.**                         **4.**

It's _____ next to _____ a supermarket.
   **5.**

**Ⓒ Correct the conversations. There are five mistakes.**

**1. A:** Is your apartment in the second floor?

   **B:** No, it's on the three floor.

**2. A:** Where's the bank?

   **B:** It's First Avenue. It's between from 8th and 9th Streets.

   **A:** Is it next the post office?

   **B:** Yes, it is.

**Now check your answers on pages 379–380.**

# *Be*: Past

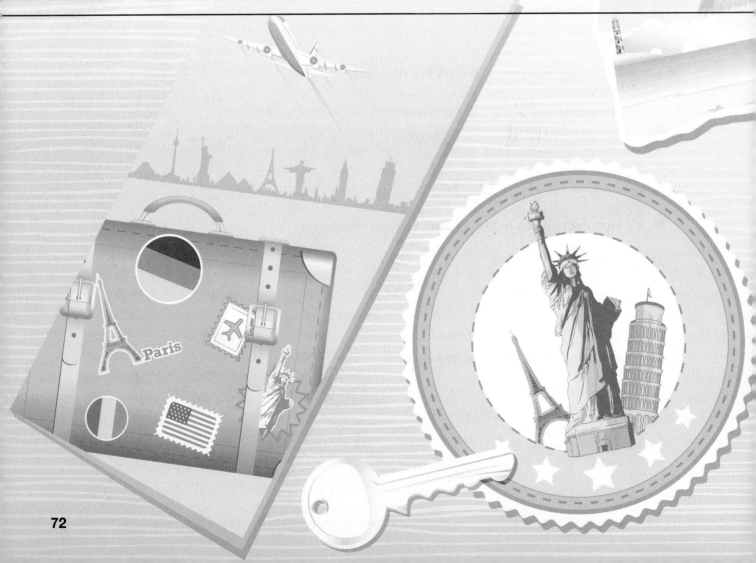

PART **3**

**OUTCOMES**

- Make simple past statements with the verb *be*
- Ask and answer simple past *yes/no* questions with the verb *be*
- Identify true and false sentences about a reading
- Identify true and false sentences about phone messages
- Ask and answer questions about past activities
- Write a paragraph about a movie

**OUTCOMES**

- Ask and answer simple past *wh-* questions with the verb *be*
- Identify true and false sentences about a reading
- Answer questions about a conversation
- Talk about the weather
- Ask and answer questions about past activities
- Write an email with questions about a vacation

The Eiffel Tower

The Taj Mahal

# Past of *Be*: Statements and *Yes/No* Questions

## OUT AND ABOUT

**OUTCOMES**
- Make simple past statements with the verb *be*
- Ask and answer simple past *yes/no* questions with the verb *be*
- Identify true and false sentences about a reading
- Identify true and false sentences about phone messages
- Ask and answer questions about past activities
- Write a paragraph about a movie

## STEP 1   GRAMMAR IN CONTEXT

### BEFORE YOU READ

**A** VOCABULARY   Study the words. Then check (✓) the sentences that are true for you.

alone

asleep

at home

at the movies

awake

☐ **1.** I was asleep at 2 a.m.

☐ **2.** I was awake at 6 a.m. this morning.

☐ **3.** I was alone all day Saturday.

☐ **4.** I was at the movies last night.

☐ **5.** I was at home all day yesterday.

**B** Work with a partner. Compare your answers in A.

## READ

07|01  Read this telephone conversation.

# Out at the Movies

KATHY: Hello?

AMANDA: Hi, Kathy. This is Amanda.

KATHY: Hi, Amanda. How's it going?

AMANDA: Fine. Hey, Josh and I were at your house last night at about 9:00, but you weren't there. Were you at home? Were you asleep?

KATHY: No, I was awake. Actually, I wasn't at home last night. I was at the movies.

AMANDA: Were you with Olivia?

KATHY: No, I wasn't.

AMANDA: With Sally?

KATHY: No.

AMANDA: Were you alone?

KATHY: Uh, no. I was with . . . someone. The movie was great. It was really exciting and funny, too.

AMANDA: Really! What movie was it?

KATHY: *Frankenstein's Uncle.*

## AFTER YOU READ

**A** COMPREHENSION  Look at the conversation again. Check (✓) *True* or *False*.

|  | True | False |
|---|---|---|
| 1. Kathy is at home tonight. | ☐ | ☐ |
| 2. Kathy was asleep last night at 9:00. | ☐ | ☑ |
| 3. Amanda and Josh were at Kathy's house last night. | ☐ | ☐ |
| 4. Kathy wasn't alone at the movies last night. | ☐ | ☐ |
| 5. Kathy was with Sally last night. | ☐ | ☑ |
| 6. The movie was *Young Frankenstein*. | ☐ | ☑ |

**B**  Work with a partner. Compare your answers in A.

## PAST OF *BE*: AFFIRMATIVE STATEMENTS

| Affirmative Statements | |
|---|---|
| Was | Were |
| I **was** at a movie last night.<br>He **was** at home.<br>She **was** at the gym.<br>It **was** hot. | We **were** at a birthday party yesterday.<br>You **were** great in the play.<br>You and Ryan **were** both wonderful.<br>They **were** at the soccer game. |

## PAST OF *BE*: NEGATIVE STATEMENTS

| Negative Statements | |
|---|---|
| Was not | Were not |
| I **was not** at home last night.<br>He **wasn't** at a movie.<br>She **wasn't** at the library.<br>It **wasn't** cold yesterday. | We **were not** at home last night.<br>You **weren't** in class yesterday.<br>They **weren't** at the library yesterday. |

## *YES / NO* QUESTIONS

| Yes/No Questions | Short Answers | |
|---|---|---|
| Was / Were | Affirmative | Negative |
| **Was** I right? | Yes, you **were**. | No, you **weren't**. |
| **Was** he at home? | Yes, he **was**. | No, he **wasn't**. |
| **Was** she at the game? | Yes, she **was**. | No, she **wasn't**. |
| **Was** it cold yesterday? | Yes, it **was**. | No, it **wasn't**. |
| **Were** we right? | Yes, you **were**. | No, you **weren't**. |
| **Were** you at home? | Yes, I **was**. | No, I **wasn't**. |
| **Were** they at the game? | Yes, they **were**. | No, they **weren't**. |

## GRAMMAR NOTES

### 1 *Was* and *Were*

| The past of *be* has two forms: *was* and *were*. Use *was* with *I*, *he*, *she*, and *it*. Use *were* with *you*, *we*, and *they*. | I **was** at a movie last night.<br>The girls **were** at the library yesterday.<br>They **were** at the library yesterday. |
|---|---|

## 2 Negative Statements

| | |
|---|---|
| Use **was** or **were** + **not** to make negative statements. | I **was not** alone.<br>You **were not** at home. |
| We often use the contractions **wasn't** and **weren't** in speaking and informal writing. | I **wasn't** asleep.<br>You **weren't** awake. |

## 3 Yes/No Questions

| | |
|---|---|
| To ask a *yes/no* question, put **was** or **were** before the subject. | **Was** SUBJECT the movie interesting?<br>**Were** SUBJECT you alone at the movie? |

## 4 Short Answers

| | |
|---|---|
| You can use a pronoun and **was**, **wasn't**, **were**, or **weren't** in short answers. | A: Was Mary at the library yesterday?<br>B: Yes, **she was**. |
| You can also just answer *yes* or *no*, and then give more information. | A: Were your friends at home last night?<br>B: No, **they were at a concert**. |

## REFERENCE NOTES

For **definitions of grammar terms**, see the Glossary on page 375.

For information on **simple present questions**, see Unit 11 on page 120 and Unit 12 on page 130.

For more information on **simple past statements and questions**, see Unit 24 on page 274, Unit 25 on page 286, and Unit 26 on page 298.

---

## STEP 3   FOCUSED PRACTICE

## EXERCISE 1   DISCOVER THE GRAMMAR

GRAMMAR NOTES 1–4   Underline all the past forms of *be*. Then match the questions and answers.

_d_   **1.** Were you at home yesterday?     **a.** No, it wasn't. The music was pretty bad.

_____   **2.** Was he in class yesterday?     **b.** Yes, she was. We were both there.

_____   **3.** Was the concert good?     **c.** Yes, I was. It was a really exciting game.

_____   **4.** Was the movie interesting?     ~~**d.**~~ No, I wasn't. I was at a concert.

_____   **5.** Was Susan at the library yesterday?     **e.** No, he wasn't. He was sick.

_____   **6.** Were you at the ball game last night?     **f.** Yes, it was. Johnny Depp is a great actor.

## EXERCISE 2  *WAS* AND *WERE*

GRAMMAR NOTE 1  Look at the pictures. Where were the people last night? Complete the sentences with *was* or *were* and the words in the box.

**Jeremy**

**Tim and Jessica**

**Steve and his father**

**Judy**

**Mark**

**Mary, Annie, and Ben**

| at a concert | at a party | ~~at a play~~ | at a soccer game | at home | at the movies |

1. Last night, Steve and his father _were at a play_____.

2. Mary, Annie, and Ben _were at home_____.

3. Jeremy _was at a concert_____.

4. Mark _was at a soccer game_____.

5. Tim and Jessica _were at the movies_____.

6. Judy _was at a party_____.

## EXERCISE 3  AFFIRMATIVE AND NEGATIVE QUESTIONS AND ANSWERS

GRAMMAR NOTES 1–4  Complete the conversation with *was*, *wasn't*, *were*, or *weren't*.

MAKIKO:  ____Was____ Joan in class yesterday morning?
         **1.**

KELLY:  Yes, she ___was___.
                    **2.**

MAKIKO:  ___were___ you at home last night?
         **3.**

KELLY:  No, I ___wasn't___. I ___was___ at the movies.
              **4.**          **5.**

MAKIKO:  ___Were___ the kids with you?
         **6.**

KELLY:  No, they ___weren't___. They ___were___ at a concert.
                   **7.**              **8.**

78     Unit 7

# EXERCISE 4 AFFIRMATIVE AND NEGATIVE ANSWERS

GRAMMAR NOTES 1–4 **Answer the questions. Use short answers with *was* or *were*. Then use the words in parentheses to give more information.**

1. **A:** Were you late to class yesterday morning?

   **B:** Yes, _____ I was _____. _____ The bus was late. _____
   (The bus / late)

2. **A:** Were you at a concert yesterday evening?

   **B:** No, _____ I wasn't _____. _____ I was at home. _____
   (I / at home)

3. **A:** Were you and Jessica asleep at 10 p.m. last night?

   **B:** No, _____ we weren't _____. _____ we were awake _____
   (We / awake)

4. **A:** Was Annie with you at the library yesterday afternoon?

   **B:** No, _____ she wasn't _____. _____ She was at a soccer game _____
   (She / at a soccer game)

5. **A:** Were you and Tim at the movies last night?

   **B:** Yes, _____ we were _____, but _____ the movie was boring? _____
   (the movie / boring)

6. **A:** Was Jeremy at school yesterday?

   **B:** Yes, _____ he was _____, but _____ He was there _____ only in the morning.
   (he / there)

# EXERCISE 5 EDITING

GRAMMAR NOTES 1–4 **There are six mistakes in the note. The first mistake is corrected. Find and correct five more.**

Mark,

    Sorry I ~~was~~ wasn't at home last night. I were at a basketball

game. Amanda and Josh was with me. It were great.

    Were you at home on Tuesday afternoon? Susan, ~~and~~

Brent and I are at the soccer game, but you were there.

Too bad. It was really fun.

Kathy

## EXERCISE 6  LISTENING

▶07|02  **A**  Listen to the message for Mark on the answering machine. Who is the message from?

"Hello, this is Mark . . . "

_____

▶07|02  **B**  Listen again to the message. For each statement, check (✓) *True*, *False*, or *No Information*.

|  | True | False | No Information |
|---|---|---|---|
| 1. Mark is at home now. | ☐ | ☑ | ☐ |
| 2. Josh was at the movies last night. | ☐ | ☐ | ☐ |
| 3. Amanda was at home last night. | ☐ | ☐ | ☐ |
| 4. Mark was at a concert last night. | ☐ | ☐ | ☐ |
| 5. Josh was alone at the movies. | ☐ | ☐ | ☐ |
| 6. The movie was *Star Wars*. | ☐ | ☐ | ☐ |
| 7. The movie was exciting. | ☐ | ☐ | ☐ |
| 8. The theater was hot. | ☐ | ☐ | ☐ |

**C**  Work with a partner. Compare your answers in A and B.

## EXERCISE 7  WERE YOU AT HOME?

**A**  Q & A  Work with a partner. Ask and answer questions about your partner's activities. Use the time expressions and the places in the box.

| **Time expressions** | | | |
|---|---|---|---|
| yesterday morning | yesterday afternoon | yesterday evening | last night |

| **Places** | | |
|---|---|---|
| at a concert | at a park | at the movies |
| at a museum | at a soccer game | at the zoo |

EXAMPLE:  A: Were you at home last night?
　　　　　　B: No, I wasn't. I was at the movies.

**B**  Work with a new partner. Tell your new partner about your partner in A.

EXAMPLE:  A: Was Ahmed at home last night?
　　　　　　B: No, he wasn't. He was at a soccer game.

## EXERCISE 8  IT WAS EXCITING

**A** PRESENTATION  Prepare for a presentation. First, work with a partner. Tell your partner about a recent activity. Use the words below or your own words.

**boring**

**exciting**

**funny**

**interesting**

**scary**

EXAMPLE:  **A:** I was at a soccer game last night.
**B:** Was it fun?
**A:** Yes! It was exciting.

**B** Work in a group. Give a presentation about your activity in A.

EXAMPLE:  I was at a soccer game last night. My friend Ahmed was with me. The game was really exciting. The teams were the Blues and the Greens. The Greens were the winners, 4-2. About 100 people were there.

**C** Vote on the most interesting or exciting activity.

**A** BEFORE YOU WRITE Read the paragraph. Underline *was* and *were*. Then imagine you were at a movie last night with a friend. Complete the chart. Work with a partner. Tell your partner about the movie.

I was at a movie last night. My friend Alicia was with me. The movie was *Spy*. It was very funny. It wasn't scary. Melissa McCarthy, Rose Byrne, and Jude Law were the actors in it.

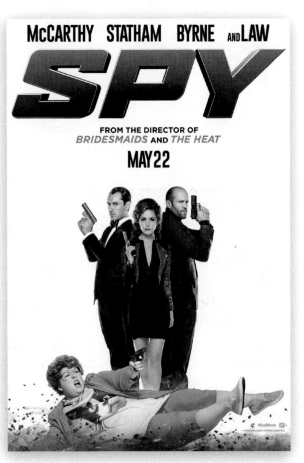

| Name of movie | |
|---|---|
| Friend or friends with me | |
| Opinion about the movie | |
| Actors in the movie | |

**B** WRITE Write a paragraph about a movie. Use *was*, *wasn't*, *were*, and *weren't*. Use the paragraph in A and your chart to help you.

**C** CHECK YOUR WORK Read your paragraph. Underline examples of *was*, *wasn't*, *were*, and *weren't*. Use the Editing Checklist to check your work.

| Editing Checklist |
|---|
| **Did you...?** |
| ☐ use *was* with *I*, *he*, *she*, and *it* |
| ☐ use *were* with *you*, *we*, and *they* |
| ☐ check your spelling |

**D** REVISE YOUR WORK Read your paragraph again. Can you improve your writing? Make changes if necessary.

# UNIT 7 REVIEW

**Test yourself on the grammar of the unit.**

**A** Complete the conversation with *was*, *wasn't*, *were*, or *weren't*.

A: _____ you and your friends at the movies yesterday?
1.

B: No, we _____. We _____ at a baseball game.
2.          3.

A: _____ the game interesting?
4.

B: No, it _____. It _____ boring.
5.          6.

**B** Answer the questions with short and long answers. Use *was*, *wasn't*, *were*, or *weren't* and the words in parentheses.

1. A: Was Tim at home last night?

   B: No, _____. _____
   a. (he)                b. (He / at the library)

2. A: Were your brothers awake at 6 a.m. this morning?

   B: No, _____. _____
   a. (they)              b. (They / asleep)

**C** Find and correct five mistakes in the email.

Kathy,

Sorry I weren't at the basketball game on Tuesday afternoon. I were sick at

home. It be really boring.

Are you at the gym yesterday? Was Amanda and Josh there?

Mark

**Now check your answers on page 380.**

# Past of *Be*:
# *Wh-* Questions
## VACATIONS

## STEP 1   GRAMMAR IN CONTEXT

### BEFORE YOU READ

**Ⓐ VOCABULARY** Study the words. Then work with a partner. Practice the conversation.

hot (weather)

cold (weather)

at the beach

in the mountains

**Conversation**

A: How was your vacation?

B: Great.

A: Where were you?

B: At the beach. It was hot.

**Ⓑ** Now talk about your last vacation.

A: How was your vacation?

B: _____.

A: Where were you?

B: _____.

### READ

⏵08|01   Read this conversation.

## A Vacation in the Sun

JASON: Hi, Mark.

MARK: Hey, Jason.

JASON: Welcome back.[1] How was your vacation?

MARK: Great.

JASON: You look good. Where were you?

MARK: At my cousin's house, in Venice Beach.

---

1 *Welcome back:* something we often say to people when they come back from a trip

| | |
|---|---|
| **JASON:** | Nice! How long were you there? |
| **MARK:** | Ten days. Ten wonderful days. |
| **JASON:** | My parents were on vacation² there last year. It was hot. How was the weather? |
| **MARK:** | It was hot and sunny. I was at the beach every day. |
| **JASON:** | And how was the ocean? |
| **MARK:** | Great. The water was warm. |
| **JASON:** | So . . . were your cousins at the beach with you? |
| **MARK:** | Only on the weekend, but Kathy was there for a week. |
| **JASON:** | Kathy? |
| **MARK:** | She was at Amanda's wedding. The doctor. |
| **JASON:** | Oh, yeah. |
| **MARK:** | Well, she was in Venice Beach, too. |
| **JASON:** | You lucky man! |

---

**2** *on vacation:* away from home and not working

Venice Beach, California

## AFTER YOU READ

Ⓐ COMPREHENSION   Look at the conversation again. For each statement, check (✓)
*True* or *False*. Then change the false sentences to true ones.

|  | True | False |
|---|:---:|:---:|
| **1.** Mark was on vacation for seven days. | ☐ | ☑ |
| **2.** The weather was cold and rainy. | ☐ | ☑ |
| **3.** He was at his cousin's house. | ☑ | ☐ |
| **4.** Jason's parents were in Venice Beach last month. | ☐ | ☑ |
| **5.** Mark's vacation was great. | ☑ | ☐ |
| **6.** Kathy was in Venice Beach, too. | ☐ | ☐ |
| **7.** She was there for ten days. | ☐ | ☐ |

Ⓑ Work with a partner. Compare your answers in A.

## PAST OF *BE*: *WH-* QUESTIONS

| Wh- Questions | Short Answers | Long Answers |
|---|---|---|
| **Where were** you? | (In) California. | I was in California. |
| **Who were** you with? | Friends. | I was there with friends. |
| **How was** the weather? | Hot. | It was hot. |
| **How long were** you there? | Ten days. | I was there for ten days. |

| Questions about the Subject | Short Answers | Long Answers |
|---|---|---|
| **Who was** in California? | Mark (was). | Mark was in California. |

## GRAMMAR NOTES

### 1 *Wh-* Question Words

| | |
|---|---|
| *Wh-* questions start with *where, what, who, when, how,* or *how long*. These words ask for information. | **Where** were you last summer? <br> **Who** was with you? <br> **How long** were you there? |
| We usually use **short answers** in speaking. | A: **How** was your weekend? <br> B: **Great**! |

### 2 *Where, Who, What*

| | |
|---|---|
| Use *where* to ask about a location. | A: **Where** were you? <br> B: At the beach. |
| Use *who* to ask about a person. | A: **Who** was with you at the beach? <br> B: My cousin. |
| Use *what* to ask about a place or a thing. | A: **What** was the name of the beach? <br> B: Venice Beach. |

### 3 *When*

| | |
|---|---|
| Use *when* to ask a time. | A: **When** were you there? <br> B: In June. |

### 4 *How + How long*

| | |
|---|---|
| Use *how* to ask for a description. | A: **How** was your vacation? <br> B: Wonderful! |
| Use *how long* to ask about a length of time. | A: **How long** was your vacation? <br> B: Ten days. |

**5** *It* for the Weather

Use *it* to talk about the weather.

A: **How** was the weather?
B: **It was** hot. **It was** sunny, too.

## REFERENCE NOTES

For **definitions of grammar terms**, see the Glossary on page 375.

For more information on **simple past statements and questions**, see Unit 24 on page 274, Unit 25 on page 286, and Unit 26 on page 298.

## STEP 3   FOCUSED PRACTICE

## EXERCISE 1   DISCOVER THE GRAMMAR

GRAMMAR NOTES 1–5   Read the questions and answers. Circle the question words. Underline the past forms of *be*. Then match the questions and answers.

_b_  **1.** (Where) were you last night?          **a.** It was hot.

_e_  **2.** Who was with you?          ~~**b.**~~ I was at a soccer game.

___  **3.** How was the game?          **c.** Two hours.

___  **4.** How long was the game?          **d.** He was on vacation in Miami.

___  **5.** How was the weather?          **e.** My sister and I were there.

_d_  **6.** Where was your brother?          **f.** Exciting.

## EXERCISE 2   WORD ORDER

GRAMMAR NOTES 1–4   Put the words in the correct order. Make conversations.

**1. A:** _____How was your weekend?_____
(How / your weekend? / was)

**B:** _____It was great._____
(was / It / great.)

**2. A:** _____Where were you?_____
(you? / were / Where)

**B:** _____At a concert._____
(a / concert. / At)

**3. A:** _____When was the concert?_____
(was / When / the concert?)

**B:** _____It was last night._____
(last night. / was / It)

**4. A:** _____Who was in the concert?_____
(in the concert? / Who / was)

**B:** _____Taylor Swift._____
(Taylor Swift.)

**5. A:** _____How long was the concert?_____
(the concert? / long / was / How)

**B:** _____It was two hours._____
(two hours. / It / was)

## EXERCISE 3 *WH-* QUESTION WORDS

GRAMMAR NOTES 1–5  Complete the conversations. Circle the correct answers.

1. A: (How) / When was the weather?

   B: It was cold.

2. A: What / Who was in the mountains ~~mountains~~
   last week?

   B: Mark was.

3. A: Where / When were Pierre and
   Jacques on Monday?

   B: They were in Paris.

4. A: Where / When was the party?

   B: The party was yesterday.

5. A: Who / How was with Kathy?

   B: Mark was with Kathy.

6. A: How / How long was the movie?

   B: The movie was three hours long.

7. A: When / Where were his parents?

   B: His parents were in California.

8. A: How / How long was the game?

   B: It was great.

## EXERCISE 4  PAST *WH-* QUESTIONS

GRAMMAR NOTES 1–5  Complete the conversation. Use *wh-* question words and *was*
or *were*.

BINH:      You weren't in class last week. _____Where were_____ you?
                                                      **1.**

DANUTA:  I was in London for my brother's wedding.

BINH:      _____ the wedding?
                        **2.**

DANUTA:  The wedding was wonderful.

BINH:      _____ the food?
                        **3.**

DANUTA:  It was delicious.

BINH: _____ you in London?
4.

DANUTA: I was in London for four days.

BINH: _____ the weather?
5.

DANUTA: It wasn't good. It was cold and rainy, but the people were great.

## EXERCISE 5 EDITING

GRAMMAR NOTES 1–5  There are five mistakes in the conversations. The first mistake is corrected. Find and correct four more.

OLGA: How ~~were~~ *was* your weekend?

TODD: Saturday evening was great.

OLGA: Where was you?

TODD: At a soccer game.

OLGA: How the game was?

TODD: Exciting and long.

OLGA: How long were it?

TODD: Three hours.

OLGA: Who with you?

TODD: My brother.

OLGA: How was the weather?

TODD: It was hot!

## EXERCISE 6 LISTENING

08|02 **A** Listen to the conversation. Circle the correct answers.

**1.** How was Jason's weekend?

   **a.** Very good.

   **b.** Good.

   **c.** Not so good.

**2.** How was Maria's weekend?

   **a.** Very good.

   **b.** Good.

   **c.** Not so good.

08|02 **B** Listen again. Complete the sentences. Circle the correct answers.

**1.** Jason was _____.

   **a.** at the beach

   **(b.)** in the mountains

   **c.** at home

**2.** The weather was _____.

   **a.** sunny and cool

   **b.** sunny and hot

   **c.** sunny and cold

**3.** Maria was at _____.

   **a.** the beach

   **b.** the movies

   **c.** home

**4.** Maria was busy with _____.

   **a.** work

   **b.** homework

   **c.** friends from high school

**C** Work with a partner. Compare your answers in A and B.

## EXERCISE 7 THE WEATHER LAST WEEK

CONVERSATION Work with a partner. Have a conversation about the weather in your city every day last week. Use the weather words.

EXAMPLE: **A:** How was the weather on Monday?

      **B:** On Monday, it was hot. What about Tuesday? Was it hot on Tuesday?

      **A:** No, it was cloudy. It was warm, but not hot.

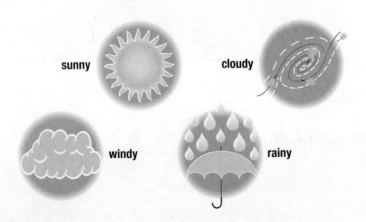

# EXERCISE 8  HOW WAS YOUR WEEKEND?

**A** ROLE PLAY  Work with a partner. Make up a conversation about your weekend. Use the question words in the box or your own ideas.

How / weekend?
Where / you?
When / you / there?
How / the weather?
Were / alone?
Who / with you?

EXAMPLE:  A:  How was your weekend?

B:  It was great.

A:  Where were you?

B:  I was in Hawaii.

A:  Wow!

B:  What about you? How was your weekend?

A:  It was OK.

B:  Where were you?

A:  I was at the library.

**B** Perform your conversation for the class.

# EXERCISE 9  WHO WAS REALLY THERE?

**A** GAME  Work with the class. Three students choose a city, but only one student was really there. All three students say they were there.

**B** The class asks the three students the questions in the box or other questions. Students A, B, and C answer the questions. The class guesses who was really there. Take turns.

I was in Mexico City.

I was in Mexico City.

I was in Mexico City.

When were you there?
How was the weather?
What was your favorite food?
What's a famous place in the city?
What other cities are near the city?
Was the flight expensive?
How long was the flight?
Were the people friendly?

EXAMPLE:  A:  When were you in Mexico City, Adjo?

B:  Last summer.

A:  What about you, Olga? When were you in Mexico City?

C:  I was there last month.

A:  And you, Erik?

D:  I was there three years ago. . . .

# FROM GRAMMAR TO WRITING

**A** BEFORE YOU WRITE  Read the email. Underline all the *wh-* questions.
Then think of a friend who was on vacation. Write questions for your
friend in the chart. Work with a partner. Practice your questions.

Sara,

How was your vacation? I hope it was fun.

I know you were in Florida, but where were you? What city? How
was the weather there? It was cold here.

Florida is far from here. How long was the drive? How was it? Who
was the driver?

Are you free for lunch this week? I want to hear all about your trip.

Alicia

| Where... | |
|---|---|
| When... | |
| Who... | |
| How... | |
| How long... | |

**B** WRITE  Write an email with questions about a friend's vacation. Use *wh-* questions
with *be*. Use the email in A and your chart to help you.

**C** CHECK YOUR WORK  Read your email. Underline examples of *was* and *were*. Circle
*wh-* words. Use the Editing Checklist to check your work.

### Editing Checklist

**Did you...?**

☐ use *wh-* question words with *was* and *were*

☐ start *wh-* questions with a *wh-* question word + *be*

☐ check your spelling

**D** REVISE YOUR WORK  Read your email again. Can you improve your writing? Make
changes if necessary.

# UNIT 8 REVIEW

**Test yourself on the grammar of the unit.**

**A** Complete the conversations with *Who*, *Where*, *When*, *How*, or *How long*.

1. A: _Where_ were you last night?  B: At the supermarket.
2. A: _How_ was the weather?  B: It was freezing.
3. A: _Who_ was with you?  B: My roommate.
4. A: _How long_ was the concert?  B: One hour.
5. A: _When_ were you at the beach?  B: Yesterday.

**B** Put the words in the correct order. Make a conversation.

A: _Where were you last night?_
   1. (were / Where / last night? / you)

B: _I was at the movies_
   2. (at the movies. / was / I)

A: _How was the movie?_
   3. (the movie? / was / How)

B: _It was funny._
   4. (funny. / was / It)

A: _Who was with you?_
   5. (was / with you? / Who)

B: _Drew was with me_
   6. (Drew / with me. / was)

**C** Correct the conversation. There are four mistakes.

A: Hi. What was your vacation?  _How was your vacation?_

B: It was great.

A: Where was you?  _Where were you?_

B: In the mountains.

A: In the mountains? How the weather was?  _How was the weather?_

B: It was rainy.

A: How were you there?  _How long was you there?_

B: A week.

**Now check your answers on page 380.**

# Imperatives and the Simple Present

# PART 4

**OUTCOMES**

- Use the imperative to give directions, instructions, requests, and suggestions
- Draw a route on a map using information from a reading
- Give directions using information from a conversation
- Make requests
- Give directions to places on a map
- Write directions on how to get to a place

**OUTCOMES**

- Make simple present statements
- Identify true and false sentences about a reading
- Complete sentences about a conversation
- Talk about likes and dislikes
- Write a paragraph about a classmate

**OUTCOMES**

- Ask and answer simple present *yes/no* questions
- Answer questions about a questionnaire
- Answer questions about a conversation
- Ask and answer questions about activities, likes, and dislikes
- Write a conversation about a person

**OUTCOMES**

- Ask and answer simple present *wh-* questions
- Identify true and false sentences about a reading
- Answer questions about a conversation
- Ask and answer questions about holidays
- Ask and answer questions about the meaning of words
- Write a conversation about a celebration

**OUTCOMES**

- Use adverbs of frequency to talk about how often something happens
- Complete sentences about a reading
- Complete sentences about a conversation
- Talk about good and bad habits
- Write an email to a friend about what you do every day

# Imperatives
## GIVING DIRECTIONS

---

**STEP 1** **GRAMMAR IN CONTEXT**

## BEFORE YOU READ

Ⓐ Study the words. Then complete the directions to the zoo.

drive

walk

take the bus

park

turn       turn
left       right

### Directions by Car

1. _____ to Exit 10 on Route 4.

2. _____ right on Elm Street.

3. _____ your car at the zoo entrance.

### Directions by Bus

1. _____ the number 4 bus to the zoo. Get off at Elm Street.

2. _____ to the zoo entrance.

Ⓑ Work with a partner. Compare your answers in A.

## READ

09|01 Read this conversation.

## Don't Park Here

MARK: Is the restaurant near here? I'm hungry.

STEVE: Yes, it is.

MARK: Is it good?

STEVE: Don't worry. It's very good. It's Indian food.

MARK: Great! I love Indian food.

STEVE: Now drive to the corner and turn left at Jackson Street.

MARK: At the gas station?

STEVE: Yes. Then go two blocks on Jackson.

MARK: Got it.[1]

STEVE: OK. Turn right at the next corner.

MARK: At Third Avenue?

STEVE: Yes. The restaurant is on the corner on your right.

MARK: Is that it?

STEVE: Yes, it is. Don't park here. It's a bus stop. Park behind the truck.

MARK: OK. Please hand me[2] my jacket. . . . Uh, wait a second. . . . Steve? The restaurant is empty.

STEVE: Really? It's usually packed.[3]

MARK: Is that a sign on the door?

STEVE: Uh-huh. . . . Closed for vacation.

1 *got it:* I understand
2 *hand me:* give me
3 *packed:* full of people

## AFTER YOU READ

Ⓐ COMPREHENSION  Look at the conversation again. Then look at the map. Draw Mark's route. Draw an *X* at the restaurant.

Ⓑ Work with a partner. Compare your answer in A.

## IMPERATIVES

| Affirmative |
|---|
| **Turn** left. |
| **Park** here. |

| Negative |
|---|
| **Don't turn** right. |
| **Don't park** there. |

## GRAMMAR NOTES

### 1 Imperative

| | |
|---|---|
| Use the imperative for **directions, instructions, requests,** and **suggestions**. | **Turn** left. *(direction)* <br> **Answer** the questions. *(instruction)* <br> Please **hand** me my jacket. *(request)* <br> **Try** this cake. *(suggestion)* |
| Use **the base form** of the verb for the imperative. | **Open** the door. |
| **USAGE NOTE** *Please* makes a request **more polite**. *Please* comes at the beginning or the end of the sentence. | **Please** help me. <br> Help me, **please**. |

### 2 Negative Form of the Imperative

| | |
|---|---|
| Use *do not* + **the base form** for the **negative**. | **Do not park** here. |
| ***Don't*** is the short form (contraction) of *do not*. | **Don't park** here. |

## REFERENCE NOTE

For **definitions of grammar terms**, see the Glossary on page 375.

## EXERCISE 1 DISCOVER THE GRAMMAR

**GRAMMAR NOTES 1–2** Read the sentences. Underline the negative imperatives. Then match the sentences.

_c_ **1.** <u>Don't walk.</u>     **a.** Walk. The restaurant is near here.

____ **2.** Don't park there.     **b.** Turn right.

____ **3.** Don't drive to the restaurant.     ~~c.~~ Take the bus.

____ **4.** Don't turn left at the corner.     **d.** It's a bus stop.

____ **5.** Don't worry.     **e.** It's next to you.

____ **6.** Please hand me the dictionary.     **f.** You're not late.

## EXERCISE 2 AFFIRMATIVE AND NEGATIVE IMPERATIVES

Ⓐ **GRAMMAR NOTES 1–2** Complete the conversations with the correct form of the imperative. Use the words in parentheses. Use contractions.

### Conversation 1

AMANDA: Is the restaurant far?

MARK: Yes, it is. _____Don't walk_____ . _____Take_____ the bus.
　　　　　(**1.** not / walk)　　　　　(**2.** take)

AMANDA: OK. So, where's the closest bus stop?

MARK: _____Walk_____ to the corner. Then _____Turn_____ left. The bus stop is
　　　　(**3.** walk)　　　　　　　(**4.** turn)
　　　　at the corner. But _____Don't take_____ the number 4 bus. _____Take_____ the
　　　　　　　　　　　(**5.** not / take)　　　　　　　　(**6.** take)
　　　　number 7. _____Get_____ off at Oak Street. The number 7 stops right in front
　　　　　　　　(**7.** get)
　　　　of the restaurant. The number 4 bus stops a few blocks away.

AMANDA: OK. Thanks.

### Conversation 2

STEVE: Where's the bookstore?

JESSICA: It's on First Street. _____ to Main Street. Then _____
　　　　　　　　　　　　　　　(**8.** drive)　　　　　　　　　　　(**9.** turn)
　　　　right on First. It's on the right side of the street.

STEVE: It's 6 o'clock. Is the bookstore still open?

JESSICA: _____ . It's open until 9 p.m. today.
　　　　　(**10.** not / worry)

STEVE: Thanks.

🔊 09|02 Ⓑ **LISTEN AND CHECK** Listen to the conversations and check your answers in A.

# EXERCISE 3  IMPERATIVE FOR INSTRUCTIONS, REQUESTS, AND SUGGESTIONS

GRAMMAR NOTES 1–2  Look at the pictures. What are the people saying? Write the correct sentences from the box.

| | | |
|---|---|---|
| Close the window, please. | Don't go in the deep water. | Please don't smoke. |
| ~~Please sit down.~~ | Please turn to page six. | Try this cake. |

1. _Please sit down._

2. _Close the window, please_

3. _Please don't smoke._

4. _Please turn to page 6._

5. _Don't go in the deep water_

6. _Try this cake_

## EXERCISE 4  IMPERATIVE FOR INSTRUCTIONS

**(A)** GRAMMAR NOTES 1–2  **Look at the sentence. Follow the instructions.**

1. Underline the word *turn*.

2. Change the word *corner* to *stop sign*.

3. Change *Do not* to the contraction (short form).

4. Write the new sentence on the line.

Do not <u>turn</u> at the corner.

_Don't turn at the stop sign._

**(B)** **Look at the sentence. Follow the instructions.**

1. Add *please* to the sentence.

2. Change *do not* to the short form.

3. Change *driveway* to *garage*.

4. Write the new sentence on the line.

Do not park in the driveway.

_Please Don't park in the garage please_

## EXERCISE 5  EDITING

GRAMMAR NOTES 1–2  **There are six mistakes in the sentences. The first mistake is corrected. Find and correct five more.**

1. Please ~~not to~~ *don't* open your book.

2. You no sit here. It's not your seat.

3. Turn please to page 3.

4. Completes the sentences.

5. No close the window. Keep it open.

6. Don't to park there. Park at the corner.

## EXERCISE 6  LISTENING

▶09|03  **A** Listen to a conversation between a new student and an old student. Complete the statement. Choose from the words in the box.

| cafeteria | computer lab | hall | library | main office | student lounge |

The new student asks for directions to the _____ and the _____.

▶09|03  **B** Listen again. Complete the sentences with directions to both places.

**The First Place:**

_____Walk_____ down the _____. Then _____ right. It's
    **1.**             **2.**              **3.**

between the _____ and the _____.
         **4.**           **5.**

**The Second Place:**

It's on the _____ floor, too. Again, go down the hall. But _____
       **6.**                              **7.**

turn right. Turn _____. It's across from the _____ lounge.
         **8.**                  **9.**

**C** Work with a partner. Give directions to the first place in the listening. Your partner listens and draws a map. Then your partner gives directions to the second place. You draw a map.

```
+-------------------------------------------------------------+
|              Floor Map of the Student Building              |
|                                                             |
|                                                             |
|                                                             |
|                                                             |
|                                                             |
|                                                             |
|                                                             |
|                                                             |
|                                                             |
|                                                             |
|                                                             |
|                                                             |
+-------------------------------------------------------------+
```

# EXERCISE 7 PLEASE OPEN THE DOOR

GAME  Work in groups of four. Take turns. Student A, make a request. Use a verb from the box. Student B, say the negative and make a new request. Students C and D do the same. Then Student D starts with a new verb.

| | |
|---|---|
| close | open |
| give me | turn |
| hand me | write |

EXAMPLE:  A:  Please open the door.
                 B:  Please don't open the door. Open the window.
                 C:  Please don't open the window. Open the dictionary.
                 D:  Please don't open the dictionary. Open the grammar book. . . . Give me a notebook, please.

# EXERCISE 8 WALK TWO BLOCKS ON . . .

GIVING DIRECTIONS  Work with a partner. Take turns. Look at the map. Give directions to a park in downtown Seattle. Your partner listens and names the park.

EXAMPLE:  A:  You are at Union Street and Third Avenue. Walk two blocks on Third Avenue to Pine Street. Turn right. Then go one block. Where are you?
                 B:  I'm at Westlake Park.
                 A:  Right.

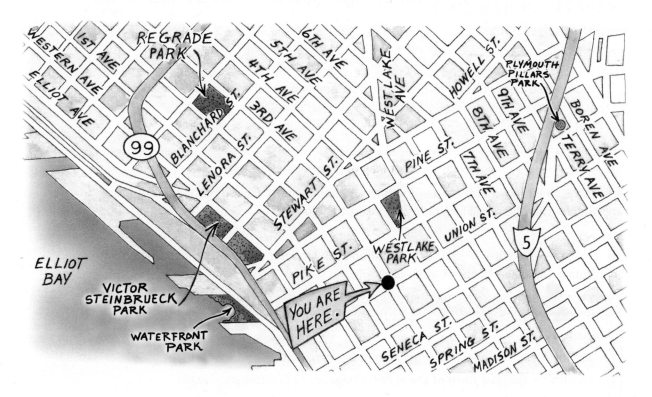

# FROM GRAMMAR TO WRITING

**A** BEFORE YOU WRITE  Read directions to a Thai restaurant from a school. Underline the imperatives. Then think of a place near your school. Complete the chart with directions on how to get there from your school.

Hi Everyone,

I hope you can join me at Thai Gardens tomorrow at 1 p.m.

Take the number 4 train at 14th Street to 4th Street. Get off at 4th Street, and walk east for two blocks. Thai Gardens is on 4th Street between 1st and 2nd Avenues.

The food is delicious at Thai Gardens. Hope to see you there!

| Directions to Thai Gardens | Directions to your place |
|---|---|
| • Take #4 train at 14th Street<br>• Get off at 4th Street<br>• Walk east 2 blocks | |

**B** WRITE  Invite your classmates to meet you somewhere. Give directions. Use the imperative. Use the email in A and your chart to help you.

**C** CHECK YOUR WORK  Read your invitation in B. Underline the imperatives. Then use the Editing Checklist to check your work.

### Editing Checklist

**Did you . . . ?**

- [ ] use the base form of the verb for imperative statements
- [ ] use *don't* + the base form of the verb for negative imperative statements
- [ ] check your spelling

**D** REVISE YOUR WORK  Read your invitation again. Can you improve your writing? Make changes if necessary.

# UNIT 9 **REVIEW**

**Test yourself on the grammar of the unit.**

**A** Complete the sentences. Use the correct forms of the words in the box.

| not / eat | not / open | not / worry | turn | walk |

1. Please ___don't open___ the window. It's cold.
2. ___Don't park right___ to the corner. Then turn left.
3. ___Don't eat___ those cookies. They're terrible.
4. ___Don't worry___. We aren't late.
5. ___Turn___ left at the next corner.

**B** Look at the sentence. Follow the instructions.

1. Add *please* to the sentence.
2. Underline the word *start*.
3. Change *do not* to the short form.
4. Change the number *9* to *10*.
5. Write the new sentence on the line.

Do not <u>start</u> Unit 9.

___Don't start unit 10 please___

**C** Correct the sentences. There are five mistakes.

1. Please to stop at the corner.

2. You not turn left.

3. Turns right, please.

4. Don't please park here.

5. Don't takes the bus.

**Now check your answers on page 380.**

# Simple Present: Statements

## LIKES AND DISLIKES

OUTCOMES
• Make simple present statements
• Identify true and false sentences about a reading
• Complete sentences about a conversation
• Talk about likes and dislikes
• Write a paragraph about a classmate

## STEP 1    GRAMMAR IN CONTEXT

### BEFORE YOU READ

**A** VOCABULARY   Study the words. Then complete the sentences about you.

need

want

live

speak

1. I want _____.

2. I need _____.

3. I live in _____.

4. I speak _____.

**B** Work with a partner. Compare your answers in A.

▶10|01   Read this article.

# Alike or Different?

**Some brothers** are alike,[1] and some are different. John and Larry are good examples. They're both tall, and they look alike. But they like different things.

John is 27 years old. Larry is 25. John lives in New York City. He likes big cities. Larry doesn't like big cities. He lives in Grove City, a small town in Pennsylvania.

Everyone needs friends. John has a lot of[2] friends but not many close friends. Larry doesn't have a lot of friends, but he has a few[3] very good friends. John likes people, and he loves parties. Larry likes people too, but he doesn't like parties very much.

John likes languages. He speaks English, Spanish, and Arabic. Larry just speaks English.

John likes computers. He's a computer programmer. Larry has a computer, but he doesn't use it very much. He loves music, and he's a music teacher.

John isn't married, and he doesn't want children. Larry is married. He and his wife don't have children, but they want them.

John and Larry are very different, but they have fun together.

---

1 *alike:* the same, similar
2 *a lot of:* a large number of
3 *a few:* a small number

## AFTER YOU READ

**Ⓐ COMPREHENSION** **Look at the article again. For each statement, check (✓) True or *False*.**

|  | True | False |
|---|---|---|
| **1.** John and Larry look alike. | ✓ | ☐ |
| **2.** Both John and Larry like big cities. | ☐ | ✓ |
| **3.** Larry speaks a lot of languages. | ☐ | ✓ |
| **4.** Larry is a musician. | ☐ | ☐ |
| **5.** Both John and Larry like people. | ☐ | ☐ |
| **6.** John and Larry are alike. | ☐ | ☐ |

**Ⓑ Work with a partner. Compare your answers in A.**

## THE SIMPLE PRESENT: STATEMENTS

### Affirmative Statements

| Subject | Verb | |
|---|---|---|
| I<br>You*<br>We<br>They | **like** | music. |

### Negative Statements

| Subject | *Do not /<br>Does not* | Base Form<br>of Verb | |
|---|---|---|---|
| I<br>You<br>We<br>They | **do not<br>don't** | **like** | work. |

* *You* is both singular and plural.

### Affirmative Statements

| Subject | Verb | |
|---|---|---|
| He<br>She<br>Maria | **likes** | music. |

### Negative Statements

| Subject | *Does not* | Base Form<br>of Verb | |
|---|---|---|---|
| He<br>She<br>Maria | **does not<br>doesn't** | **like** | big cities. |

### Affirmative Statements

| Subject | Verb | |
|---|---|---|
| It | **rains<br>snows** | a lot here. |

### Negative Statements

| Subject | *Does not* | Base Form<br>of Verb | |
|---|---|---|---|
| It | **does not<br>doesn't** | **rain** | a lot in Los Angeles. |

## GRAMMAR NOTES

### 1 Uses of the Simple Present

| | |
|---|---|
| Use the simple present to talk about **facts** and things that **happen again** and **again**. | I **live** in Redmond. *(a fact)*<br>Everyone **needs** food and water. *(a fact)*<br>He **studies** every evening.<br>    *(a thing that happens again and again)* |

### 2 Affirmative Statements

| | |
|---|---|
| In affirmative statements, use the **base form** of the verb with *I*, *you*, *we*, and *they*. | We **want** a big house.<br>They **like** their home. |
| The verb changes with *he*, *she*, and *it*:<br>• Add -*s* to most verbs. | He **needs** help.<br>It **rains** a lot in New York City. |
| • Add -*ies* to verbs that end in a consonant + *y*. | She **studies** hard. |
| • Add -*es* to verbs that end in -*ch*, -*o*, -*ss*, -*x*, -*s*, or -*z*. | Yukiko **watches** TV every evening.<br>Jomo **goes** to the university every day. |

## 3 Negative Statements

| | |
|---|---|
| In negative statements, use *do not* + the base form of the verb with *I*, *you*, *we*, and *they*. | They **do not live** in the city.<br>You **do not understand**. |
| Use *does not* + the base form of the verb with *he*, *she*, and *it*. | She **does not need** help.<br>It **does not rain** a lot in the desert. |
| We often use the contractions *don't* and *doesn't* in speaking and <u>informal</u> writing. | They **don't live** in the city.<br>She **doesn't need** help. |

## 4 Be and *Have*

| | |
|---|---|
| *Be* and *have* are **irregular verbs**. | I **am** a student. Elena **is** a student, too.<br>Bi-Yun and Sung **are** teachers. |
| | I **have** a lot of friends. Bi-Yun **has** a lot of friends, too.<br>They **have** a beautiful house. |

## PRONUNCIATION NOTE

▶10|02  **Simple Present Verb Endings**

With *he*, *she*, *it*, and words like *everyone*, **simple present verbs** end in *-s* or *-es*. These endings can be pronounced /**s**/, /**z**/, or /**ɪz**/.

| /**s**/ sound:<br>writes<br>likes<br>helps | He **writes** letters.<br>Everyone **likes** music.<br>She **helps** us every night. |
|---|---|
| /**z**/ sound:<br>reads<br>plays<br>needs | She **reads** novels.<br>He **plays** the piano.<br>Mary **needs** help. |
| /**ɪz**/ sound:<br>watches<br>washes<br>misses | She **watches** TV a lot.<br>Bob **washes** the dishes every night.<br>Asha **misses** her children. |

## REFERENCE NOTES

For more information on the verbs *be* and **have**, see Unit 14 on page 154.

For **simple present spelling and pronunciation rules**, see Appendices 13 and 14 on page 370.

For **definitions of grammar terms**, see the Glossary on page 375.

## EXERCISE 1   DISCOVER THE GRAMMAR

GRAMMAR NOTES 1–4   Underline the simple present verbs. Then match the statements.

__e__ 1. John and Larry <u>look</u> alike.

____ 2. Sometimes I <u>like</u> rain.

____ 3. <u>Take</u> some money.

____ 4. Jessica is a musician.

____ 5. John <u>speaks</u> Arabic.

____ 6. Eun-Yung doesn't want coffee.

____ 7. It <u>rains</u> a lot in New York.

____ 8. Asha <u>studies</u> very hard.

a. Yes. She is a very good student.

b. No, thanks. I don't need it.

c. Right. She wants tea.

d. It rains a <u>lot</u> in Seattle, too.

e. Yes. They both have dark hair.

f. Yes. He also speaks Spanish.

g. Yes. I love her music.

h. Really? I don't like rain at all.

## EXERCISE 2   AFFIRMATIVE STATEMENTS

GRAMMAR NOTES 1–2   Write sentences about the people. Use the simple present forms of the verbs *live* and *like*.

1. **Name:** Heng

   **Place:** Beijing, China        _Heng lives in Beijing, China._

   **Favorite music:** rock        _She likes rock._

2. **Name:** Ali

   **Place:** Amman, Jordan        _Ali lives in Amman, Jordan._

   **Favorite sport:** soccer        _He likes soccer._

3. **Names:** Antonio and Rosa

   **Place:** Salvador, Brazil        _Antonio and Rosa live in Salvador, Brazil._

   **Favorite city:** Rio de Janeiro        _They like Rio de Janeiro._

4. **Name:** Carmen

   **Place:** Santiago, Chile        _Carmen lives in Santiago, Chile._

   **Favorite food:** pizza        _She likes pizza._

5. **Names:** Maureen and James

   **Place:** Dublin, Ireland        _Maureen and James live in Dublin, Ireland._

   **Favorite activity:** movies        _They like movies._

# EXERCISE 3 LIKES AND WANTS

**A** GRAMMAR NOTES 1–3 Complete the conversation. Use the simple present forms of the verbs *want* or *like*. Use the affirmative or negative. Use contractions.

WAITER: Can I help you?

TIM: Yes, thanks. The children _____*want*_____ ice cream. My son
               1. (want)
     _____*wants*_____ chocolate.
       2. (want)

BEN: No, Dad. I _____ chocolate. I _____*wants*_____ vanilla.
          3. (not / like)             4. (want)

ANNIE: I _____ chocolate.
      5. (want)

TIM: OK. My son _____*don't wants*_____ chocolate. He ____*wants*____ vanilla.
          6. (not / want)          7. (want)
    My daughter _____*wants*_____ chocolate.
         8. (want)

WAITER: And you, sir?

TIM: I _____ ice cream, so I just _____ a soda.
    9. (not / like)             10. (want)

WAITER: Is that all?

TIM: Yes, thanks.

🔊 10|03 **B** LISTEN AND CHECK Listen to the conversation and check your answers in A.

# EXERCISE 4 AFFIRMATIVE AND NEGATIVE STATEMENTS

GRAMMAR NOTES 1–4 Look at the pictures. Complete the sentences. Use the correct forms of the verbs in parentheses in the affirmative or negative.

**1.** (have)

Jeremy _____*has*_____ an old car.

He ___*doesn't have*___ a new car.

**2.** (like)

Annie _____*likes*_____ pizza.

She ___*doesn't like*___ salad.

**3.** (need)

The man _____ water.

He _____ ice cream.

**4.** (want)

Judy _____ tea.

She _____ coffee.

## EXERCISE 5  SIMPLE PRESENT VERB ENDINGS

▶10|04  **A** PRONUNCIATION NOTE  Listen to the verbs. What is the last sound? Check (✓) the sound you hear.

|  | /s/ | /z/ | /ɪz/ |
|---|---|---|---|
| **1.** has | ☐ | ☑ | ☐ |
| **2.** teaches | ☐ | ☐ | ☐ |
| **3.** writes | ☑ | ☐ | ☐ |
| **4.** drives | ☐ | ☐ | ☐ |
| **5.** watches | ☐ | ☐ | ☑ |
| **6.** understands | ☐ | ☐ | ☐ |
| **7.** works | ☑ | ☐ | ☐ |
| **8.** catches | ☐ | ☐ | ☐ |
| **9.** misses | ☐ | ☐ | ☑ |
| **10.** surprises | ☐ | ☐ | ☐ |

▶10|04  **B** Listen again and repeat the verbs.

# EXERCISE 6 EDITING

**GRAMMAR NOTES 1–4** There are six mistakes in the email. The first mistake is corrected. Find and correct five more.

**To:** Mary Beck
**Fr:** Rose Mendoza
**Re:** Greetings from Mexico

Dear Mary,

Mexico is great. The people are friendly, but they ~~speaks~~ *speak* fast! Jim speak Spanish, but he don't understand everything. He understands a lot. I don't speak Spanish.

It's hot here! We're at my cousin's house. He and his wife lives in a beautiful apartment in Puebla. Juan work in an office downtown. His wife Alicia doesn't works. She stays at home with the children.

See you soon,
Rose

## EXERCISE 7  LISTENING

▶10|05  **A** Listen to the conversation between Tim Olson and a man he meets. Where is the man from?

_____

▶10|05  **B** Listen to the conversation again. Complete the sentences. Circle the correct answers.

ROMANIA

Bucharest ★

*Black Sea*

1. Tim is from _____.
   **a.** Seattle        **b.** Bucharest

2. The man _____ Seattle.
   **a.** likes          **b.** doesn't like

3. The man doesn't live in _____.
   **a.** Portland       **b.** Bucharest

4. A lot of people in the man's country speak _____.
   **a.** three languages   **b.** English

5. The man speaks _____ languages.
   **a.** two            **b.** three

6. People in the man's country _____ English.
   **a.** like           **b.** don't like

7. Tim doesn't speak _____.
   **a.** French         **b.** Spanish

**C** Work with a partner. Compare your answers in A and B. Then talk about languages you speak.

EXAMPLE:  A: I speak Spanish and English.
          B: I speak Korean and English.

## EXERCISE 8 TRUE OR FALSE?

**A** GAME Work with a partner. Use the words to make affirmative sentences in the simple present. <u>Four</u> of the statements are <u>true</u>, and <u>six are false</u>. Correct the false statements. Take turns.

1. Most people / Beijing / speak Spanish

   EXAMPLE: **A:** Most people in Beijing speak Spanish.
   **B:** False. Most people in Beijing speak Chinese.

2. Rihanna / come from / Barbados

3. A lot of people / like / Rihanna's music

4. People / Japan / drive / on the right

5. People / Great Britain / drive / on the left

6. People / live / at the North Pole

7. Penguins / live / in hot places

8. Most people / have / a lot of money

9. It / rain / a lot / the Sahara Desert

10. It / snow / a lot / at the North Pole

**B** Check your answers on page 385. Who got the most answers correct?

## EXERCISE 9 THINGS I REALLY LIKE AND DON'T LIKE

**A** CONVERSATION Work in a group. Say one thing you really like and one thing you don't like for each word in the box. Take turns.

| a city | a food | a movie | an actor | a song |
|--------|--------|---------|----------|--------|

EXAMPLE: I really like steak. I don't like salad.

**B** Tell the class about the people in your group. What do your classmates like? What don't they like?

EXAMPLE: Juan really likes steak. He doesn't like salad.

**A** BEFORE YOU WRITE  Read the paragraph. Underline verbs in the simple present. Then complete the chart about yourself. Work with a partner. Tell your partner about yourself.

**Abla** is from Tanzania. Abla has one brother and one sister. They live in Arusha. Abla speaks Swahili and English. She likes books, and she reads a lot of them. Abla doesn't have a job, but she needs a job. She wants a college degree.

### ABOUT ME

| | |
|---|---|
| From | |
| Family | |
| City | |
| Languages | |
| Likes | |
| Needs | |
| Wants | |

**B** WRITE  Exchange charts with your partner. Write a paragraph about your partner. Use the simple present. Use the paragraph in A and your partner's chart to help you.

**C** CHECK YOUR WORK  Read your paragraph. Underline examples of the simple present. Use the Editing Checklist to check your work.

#### Editing Checklist

**Did you . . . ?**
- ☑ use *does* and *doesn't* with *he*, *she*, and *it*
- ☑ use the base form of the verb with *I*, *you*, *we*, and *they*
- ☑ use *-s* endings with simple present verbs with *he*, *she*, and *it*
- ☑ check your spelling

**D** REVISE YOUR WORK  Read your paragraph again. Can you improve your writing? Make changes if necessary.

# UNIT 10 REVIEW

**Test yourself on the grammar of the unit.**

**Ⓐ** Complete the sentences with the correct forms of the verbs in parentheses. Use contractions when possible.

1.  My roommate _____ likes _____ rap music. He _____ doesn't like _____
    (like)                                          (not / like)

    classical music.

2.  My children _____ doesn't want _____ apples. My son _____ doesn't want _____ ice
    (not / want)                                 (not / want)

    cream. My daughter _____ doesn't want _____ chocolate.
    (not / want)

**Ⓑ** Complete the sentences. Circle the correct answers.

1.  My sister and I (live) / lives in different cities.

2.  She like / (likes) computers, and I (like) / likes books.

3.  She (has) / have blue eyes, and I has / (have) brown eyes.

**Ⓒ** Correct the sentences. There are five mistakes.

1.  This is my brother Nelson. He don't look like me!

2.  Nelson and his wife, Laura, lives in Brazil.

3.  Laura is need a new car.

4.  Nelson work as a mechanic.

5.  They both speaks Portuguese.

**Now check your answers on page 380.**

# Simple Present: Yes/No Questions

## FRIENDS

**OUTCOMES**
- Ask and answer simple present *yes/no* questions
- Answer questions about a questionnaire
- Answer questions about a conversation
- Ask and answer questions about activities, likes, and dislikes
- Write a conversation about a person

| STEP 1 | GRAMMAR IN CONTEXT |

## BEFORE YOU READ

**A** VOCABULARY Study the words. Imagine you don't have school or work. What do you do? Check (✓) the correct answer(s).

go shopping ✓

stay home

have a party

work out

- ☐ go shopping
- ☐ stay home
- ☐ have a party
- ☐ work out
- ☑ something else: _____

**B** Work with a partner. Compare your answers in A.

## READ

▶11|01 **Read Lucy's answers to the questionnaire about her and her friend Nathan.**

# You and Your Friend

Are you and your friend alike? Are you different? Think about your friend. Then answer these questions.

|  | YES | NO |
|---|---|---|
| 1. You have a day off.[1] Do you stay home alone? | ✔ | ☐ |
| Your friend has a day off. Does he or she stay home alone? | ☐ | ✔ |
| 2. You have a day off. Do you see friends? | ☐ | ✔ |
| Your friend has a day off. Does he or she see friends? | ✔ | ☐ |
| 3. It's your birthday. Do you have a party with a lot of people? | ☐ | ✔ |
| It's your friend's birthday. Does he or she have a party with a lot of people? | ✔ | ☐ |
| 4. Do you go shopping for clothes a lot? | ☐ | ✔ |
| Does your friend go shopping for clothes a lot? | ✔ | ☐ |
| 5. Do you work out more than three times a week? | ✔ | ☐ |
| Does your friend work out more than three times a week? | ✔ | ☐ |
| 6. Do you like hot weather? | ☐ | ✔ |
| Does your friend like hot weather? | ✔ | ☐ |
| 7. Do you play sports? | ✔ | ☐ |
| Does your friend play sports? | ✔ | ☐ |
| 8. Do you use your cell phone more than five times a day? | ✔ | ☐ |
| Does your friend use his or her cell phone more than five times a day? | ✔ | ☐ |
| 9. Do you use your computer every day? | ✔ | ☐ |
| Does your friend use his or her computer every day? | ✔ | ☐ |
| 10. Do you like movies? | ✔ | ☐ |
| Does your friend like movies? | ☐ | ✔ |

How many answers are the same for you and for your friend? Count the same answers. Then add the numbers.

7–10 = You are alike.
4–6 = You are a little alike.
1–3 = You are different.

---

[1] *day off:* a day when you do not work

# AFTER YOU READ

Ⓐ COMPREHENSION  Look at the questionnaire again. Answer the questions below. Circle the correct answers.

1. Do both Lucy and Nathan see friends on their day off?

   **a.** Yes, they do.          **b.** No, they don't.

2. Does Lucy go shopping for clothes a lot?

   **a.** Yes, she does.          **b.** No, she doesn't.

3. Do both Lucy and Nathan work out and play sports?

   **a.** Yes, they do.          **b.** No, they don't.

4. Do both Lucy and Nathan use cell phones and computers a lot?

   **a.** Yes, they do.          **b.** No, they don't.

5. Does Nathan like movies?

   **a.** Yes, he does.          **b.** No, he doesn't.

Ⓑ Work with a partner. Compare your answers in A. Then count the same answers for Lucy and Nathan in the questionnaire. Are Lucy and Nathan alike, a little alike, or different?

## STEP 2    GRAMMAR PRESENTATION

## SIMPLE PRESENT: *YES/NO* QUESTIONS

| Yes/No Questions |
| --- |
| **Do** |
| **Do** I **have** your number? |
| **Do** you **like** parties? |
| **Do** we **have** a day off? |
| **Do** they **have** new friends? |

| Short Answers | |
| --- | --- |
| Affirmative | Negative |
| Yes, you **do**. | No, you **don't**. |
| Yes, I **do**. | No, I **don't**. |
| Yes, we **do**. | No, we **don't**. |
| Yes, they **do**. | No, they **don't**. |

| Yes/No Questions |
| --- |
| **Does** |
| **Does** she **wear** red? |
| **Does** he **have** a day off? |
| **Does** that word **mean** "yes"? |

| Short Answers | |
| --- | --- |
| Affirmative | Negative |
| Yes, she **does**. | No, she **doesn't**. |
| Yes, he **does**. | No, he **doesn't**. |
| Yes, it **does**. | No, it **doesn't**. |

# GRAMMAR NOTES

## 1 Yes/No Questions

| | |
|---|---|
| Use *do* or *does* + a subject + the **base form** of the verb to ask *yes/no* **questions** in the simple present. | |
| Use *do* with **I**, *you*, *we*, and *they*. | **Do** you **like** questionnaires?<br>**Do** Laura and Gina **like** questionnaires? |
| Use *does* with *he*, *she*, and *it*. | **Does** she **like** the color red?<br>**Does** Maria **like** the color red? |

## 2 Short Answers

| | |
|---|---|
| We usually use **short answers** in **conversation**. | A: Does he have a day off?<br>B: **Yes.** or **Yes, he does.**<br>A: Do you stay home on Fridays?<br>B: **No.** or **No, we don't.** |
| Sometimes we use **long answers**. | A: Do they stay home on Fridays?<br>B: Yes. **They stay home on Fridays.** |

# REFERENCE NOTES

For **definitions of grammar terms**, see the Glossary on page 375.
For more information on **simple present questions**, see Unit 12 on page 130.

# STEP 3   FOCUSED PRACTICE

## EXERCISE 1   DISCOVER THE GRAMMAR

**GRAMMAR NOTES 1–2** Underline *do* or *does* and the base form of the verb in the questions. Then match the questions and the answers.

_b_ **1.** <u>Does</u> your friend <u>live</u> near you?

_a_ **2.** <u>Do</u> you <u>see</u> your friend every day?

_e_ **3.** Do you <u>text</u> her every day?

_c_ **4.** Do you <u>like</u> the same movies?

_d_ **5.** Do you <u>like</u> the same sports?

_f_ **6.** <u>Does</u> she <u>understand</u> you?

a. Yes, I see her every day.

~~b.~~ Yes, she does. She lives next door.

c. No. I like scary movies, but she doesn't.

d. Yes. We like tennis and basketball.

e. Yes, I do. We text ten times a day.

f. Yes. She always knows what I want.

## EXERCISE 2 YES/NO QUESTIONS

GRAMMAR NOTES 1–2 Complete the yes/no questions. Use the simple present and the words in parentheses.

1. (you / like) ___Do___ ___you___ ___like___ the beach?

2. (Judy / like) ___Does___ ___Judy___ ___like___ the beach?

3. (you / listen to) ___Do___ ___you___ ___listen___ ___to___ music every day?

4. (Jessica and Tim / have) ___Do___ ___Jessica___ ___and___ ___Tim___ ___have___ a lot of parties?

5. (you / have) ___Do___ ___you___ ___have___ a lot of friends?

6. (Steve / have) ___Does___ ___Steve___ ___have___ a few close friends?

7. (you / play) ___Do___ ___you___ ___play___ computer games?

8. (Jeremy / play) ___Does___ ___Jeremy___ ___play___ computer games?

## EXERCISE 3 WORD ORDER OF YES/NO QUESTIONS

GRAMMAR NOTES 1–2 Put the words in the correct order. Write questions.

1. (in a small city / Do / you / live)

   *Do you live in a small city?*

2. (in a big city / live / Does / Elena)

   Does Elena live in a big city?

3. (you / Do / want / a new computer)

   Do you want a new computer?

4. (Does / a day off today / Mark / have)

   Does Mark have a day off today?

5. (your friends / after class / see / you / Do)

   Do you see your friends after class?

6. (stay home / Steve / Does / on Sunday nights)

   Does Steve stay home on Sunday nights?

7. (you / Do / museums / like)

   Do you like museums?

8. (zoos / like / your family / Does)

   Does your family like zoos?

# EXERCISE 4  SHORT ANSWERS

GRAMMAR NOTES 1–2  Write short answers to the questions. Use contractions when possible.

1. A: Do you like the color red?               B: Yes, ___I___ ___do___.

2. A: Does your best friend like the color red?  B: Yes, ___he___ ___does___.

3. A: Do you wear a lot of black?               B: No, ___I___ ___don't___.

4. A: Does your best friend wear a lot of black? B: No, ___she___ ___doesn't___.

5. A: Do they like scary movies?                B: Yes, ___they___ ___do___.

6. A: Does she like funny movies?               B: Yes, ___she___ ___does___.

7. A: Do we need money?                         B: Yes, ___we___ ___do___.

8. A: Do we need love?                          B: Yes, ___we___ ___do___.

# EXERCISE 5  EDITING

GRAMMAR NOTES 1–2  There are five mistakes in the conversation. The first mistake is corrected. Find and correct four more.

JEREMY:  Do you like shopping?

MIA:     Yes, I ~~like~~ do. How about you?

JEREMY:  I no like shopping. Do you likes books?

MIA:     No, I'm not. Do you?

JEREMY:  I love books. You like rock music?

MIA:     No, but I like you.

JEREMY:  I like you, too.

## EXERCISE 6  LISTENING

▶11|02  **A** Listen to the conversation. Circle the things the man and woman talk about.

cities            movies         shopping        weddings

computer games        parties        sports

▶11|02  **B** Listen again. Then check (✓) *Yes*, *No*, or *No Information*.

| | Yes | No | No Information |
|---|---|---|---|
| 1. Does the woman like small parties? | ✓ | ☐ | ☐ |
| 2. Does the man like small parties? | ☐ | ☐ | ☐ |
| 3. Does the woman like big cities? | ☐ | ☐ | ☐ |
| 4. Does the man's brother like big cities? | ☐ | ☐ | ☐ |
| 5. Does the woman like shopping? | ☐ | ☐ | ☐ |

**C** Work with a partner. Ask and answer questions from the listening.

EXAMPLE:  **A:** Do you like big parties?
　　　　　**B:** Not really. I don't like parties.

## EXERCISE 7  MY FRIEND DOESN'T WORK OUT

**A** CONVERSATION  Work with a partner. Ask your partner questions about a close friend. Answer your partner's questions about your friend.

EXAMPLE:  **A:** Are you and your friend alike?
　　　　　**B:** No, we're different.
　　　　　**A:** Does she work out a lot?
　　　　　**B:** No, she doesn't. She doesn't like gyms.
　　　　　**A:** Does she like ...?

**B** Tell the class about your partner's friend.

EXAMPLE:  Dana is Lui's friend.
　　　　　She doesn't work out a lot.

# EXERCISE 8 ARE WE ALIKE?

**A** GAME Find ways that you and your classmates are alike. Ask your classmates *yes/no* questions about the topics in the chart or your own topics. Write their names under *Yes* or *No*. Take turns. You have ten minutes.

| | Question | Yes | No |
|---|---|---|---|
| **Colors** | Do you like black? | Mario, | Lina, |
| **Parties** | | | |
| **Sports** | | | |
| **Music** | | | |
| | | | |
| | | | |

EXAMPLE:  A: Mario, do you like black?
　　　　　B: Yes, I do.
　　　　　A: What about you, Lina? Do you like black?
　　　　　B: No, I don't.

**B** Tell the class about the ways you are like your classmates. The person who finds the most ways wins.

EXAMPLE: I have ten ways that I am like my classmates. Lina and I don't like black. Marta and I don't like big parties. . . .

# FROM GRAMMAR TO WRITING

**A** BEFORE YOU WRITE  Read the conversation between two classmates. Underline *do* and *does* and the base form of the verb. Then work with a partner. What other questions do you want to ask Julio about Adam? Write them in the chart.

JULIO: Do you need a new roommate?

KEN: Yes, I do.

JULIO: What about my friend Adam?

KEN: Does he study English?

JULIO: No, he doesn't. He works.

KEN: Does he stay up late?

JULIO: No, he doesn't.

KEN: Does he like sports?

JULIO: Yes, he does.

| Questions for Julio |
|---|
| 1. |
| 2. |
| 3. |
| 4. |
| 5. |

**B** WRITE  You need a new roommate. Your friend knows someone. You want to know about this person. Write your conversation with your friend. Use *yes/no* questions in the simple present. Use the conversation in A and your questions to help you.

**C** CHECK YOUR WORK  Read your conversation again. Underline *do* or *does* + the base form of the verb. Use the Editing Checklist to check your work.

| Editing Checklist |
|---|
| **Did you . . . ?** |
| ☐ use *do* + the base form of the verb for simple present *yes/no* questions with *I*, *you*, *we*, and *they* |
| ☐ use *does* + the base form of the verb with *he*, *she*, and *it* |
| ☐ use *don't* or *doesn't* with simple present short answers |
| ☐ check your spelling |

**D** REVISE YOUR WORK  Read your questions again. Can you improve your writing? Make changes if necessary.

# UNIT 11 REVIEW

**Test yourself on the grammar of the unit.**

**Ⓐ** Complete the sentences. Use the correct forms of the words in parentheses. Use the simple present.

1. _Do you go shopping_____ every weekend?
   (you / go shopping)
2. _Does your sister stay home_____ on Sunday night?
   (your sister / stay home)
3. _Do your friends like_____ big parties?
   (your friends / like)
4. _Do you see_____ your friends after class?
   (you / see)
5. _Does Carlos speak_____ English after class?
   (Carlos / speak)

**Ⓑ** Ask and answer the questions. Use the simple present forms of the verbs in parentheses.

1. (like)   A: ___Do___ you ___like___ big cities?
            B: No, ___I___, ___don't___.

2. (live)   A: ___Does___ your best friend ___live___ in a big city?
            B: No, ___she___ ___doesn't___.

3. (speak)  A: ___Do___ you and your best friend ___speak___ two languages?
            B: Yes, ___we___ ___do___.

4. (have)   A: ___Do___ you and your classmates ___have___ parties on weekends?
            B: No, ___we___ ___don't___.

5. (work)   A: ___Does___ Maria ___work___ in a big city?
            B: No, ___she___ ___doesn't___.

**Ⓒ** Correct the conversation. There are <u>five</u> mistakes.

A: Do you works out every day?

B: Yes, I am.

A: Do you walk to the gym?

B: No, I not. I drive there.

A: Does Amina works out with you?

B: No, she don't.

**Now check your answers on page 380.**

Simple Present: Yes/No Questions  **127**

# Simple Present:
# *Wh-* Questions

## CELEBRATIONS

**OUTCOMES**
- Ask and answer simple present *wh-* questions
- Identify true and false sentences about a reading
- Answer questions about a conversation
- Ask and answer questions about holidays
- Ask and answer questions about the meaning of words
- Write a conversation about a celebration

## STEP 1    GRAMMAR IN CONTEXT

### BEFORE YOU READ

**A** VOCABULARY **Study the vocabulary. Then complete the sentences. Circle the correct answers.**

**eat a huge meal**

**see fireworks**

**send cards**

**watch a parade**

**play board games**

1. When we eat a huge meal, we eat a lot / a little.

2. We usually see fireworks at noon / at night.

3. Jane is in a July 4th parade every year. She walks / stands still for hours.

4. We usually send cards to people in our house / far away.

5. We usually play board and card games alone / with other people.

**B** Work with a partner. Compare your answers in A.

# What's Your Favorite?

JEREMY:   So how do you like the United States?

YOSHIO:   I like it a lot. But I want to know about celebrations and holidays. What are your favorites?

JEREMY:   Let's see. I think Thanksgiving is my favorite. And New Year's Eve and July 4th are my other favorites.

YOSHIO:   When do you celebrate Thanksgiving?

JEREMY:   On the fourth Thursday in November.

YOSHIO:   What do you do? Who comes? What happens?

JEREMY:   We eat a huge meal. Family members and friends come. We eat and talk and play board games. And we watch football on TV.

YOSHIO:   Why do you call it Thanksgiving?

JEREMY:   Well, on Thanksgiving we say thank you for everything.

YOSHIO:   OK. What about New Year's Eve?

JEREMY:   We stay up until midnight. We have parties. We see fireworks.

YOSHIO:   I love fireworks. They're exciting. What time do you have the fireworks? Before midnight or after?

JEREMY:   The fireworks start before midnight. How do you celebrate New Year's Eve in Japan?

YOSHIO:   We eat special food and get ready for New Year's Day. That's the number one day of the year in Japan. We send special cards to friends and relatives. We play games, too.

JEREMY:   Cards? That's really different. . . . Hey, I have an idea. Come to our Thanksgiving dinner!

YOSHIO:   That sounds great. Thanks.

## AFTER YOU READ

**A** COMPREHENSION  Look at the conversation again. For each statement, check (✓) *True* or *False*.

|  |  | True | False |
|---|---|:---:|:---:|
| 1. | Yoshio likes the United States. | ✓ | ☐ |
| 2. | Americans celebrate Thanksgiving on the fourth Thursday in October. | ☐ | ✓ |
| 3. | Americans watch baseball on TV on Thanksgiving. | ☐ | ☐ |
| 4. | New Year's Day is the number one day of the year in Japan. | ✓ | ☐ |
| 5. | People in Japan get cards on New Year's Day. | ✓ | ☐ |
| 6. | Jeremy invites Yoshio to dinner on New Year's Eve. | ☐ | ✓ |

**B** Work with a partner. Compare your answers in A.

## STEP 2  GRAMMAR PRESENTATION

## SIMPLE PRESENT: *WH-* QUESTIONS

| *Wh-* Questions | Answers |
|---|---|
| **How do** you **like** our country? | I like it a lot. |
| **Why do** you **call** it Thanksgiving? | We say thank you on that day. |
| **When do** you **eat** dinner? | At 6:00 p.m. |
| **Where do** they **live**? | In Seattle. |
| **What does** he **do**? | He's a bus driver. |
| **How long is** the class? | Two hours. |
| **What time does** it **start**? | At seven o'clock. |

| *Wh-* Questions About the Subject | Answers |
|---|---|
| **Who comes** to the dinner?<br>**What happens** on Thanksgiving? | Family and friends.<br>We have a big dinner. |

# GRAMMAR NOTES

## 1 Wh- Questions

| | |
|---|---|
| **Wh- questions** ask for **information**. They often start with **how, when, where, what, why, who,** and **what time**. | **What time do** you **start** class? <br> **How do** I **get** there? <br> **Where does** the parade begin? <br> **How does** she **get** to school? |
| To ask about reasons, use **why** + the verb. | **Why do** you **work** late so much? |
| Use **do** with **I, you, we,** and **they**. Use **does** with **he, she,** and **it**. | What **do they** like? <br> What **does she** mean? |

## 2 Wh- Questions About the Subject

| | |
|---|---|
| To ask a **question about the subject**, use **who** or **what** + the verb. | **Who comes** to the celebrations? <br> **What happens** on the 4th of July? |
| **BE CAREFUL!** Don't use **do** or **does** to ask about the subject. | **Who cooks** your Thanksgiving dinner? <br> **NOT** Who ~~does cook~~ your Thanksgiving dinner? |

## 3 Common Wh- Questions

| | |
|---|---|
| To ask about the meaning of a word, say, **What does . . . mean?** To answer, use **means**. | **A: What does** *little* **mean**? <br> **B:** *Little* **means** *small*. |
| To ask about the spelling of a word, say **How do you spell . . . ?** | **A: How do you spell** *huge*? <br> **B:** H-U-G-E. |
| **BE CAREFUL!** Don't say *what means* or *what does mean* to ask about the meaning of a word. | **What does** *huge* **mean**? <br> **NOT** ~~What means~~ *huge*? <br> **NOT** ~~What does mean~~ *huge*? |

## 4 At and On

| | |
|---|---|
| To answer questions with *when* or *what time*, we can use prepositions of time like *at* and *on*. | |
| Use *at* with exact times or with expressions like *at night*. | **A: What time** do you eat dinner? <br> **B: At** 7 p.m. |
| Use *on* with days of the week and dates. | **A: When** do you see fireworks? <br> **B: On** July 4th. |

# REFERENCE NOTES

For **definitions of grammar terms**, see the Glossary on page 375.

For more information on **simple present questions**, see Unit 11 on page 120.

For more information on **days, months,** and **times**, see Appendices 5 and 7 on page 367.

## EXERCISE 1 DISCOVER THE GRAMMAR

Ⓐ GRAMMAR NOTES 1–4 **Read the conversation. Underline the *wh-* questions in the simple present.**

JOSH: <u>What do you do on Thanksgiving?</u>

MARK: Well, most years, we eat at my sister's house. But she's away on vacation this year.

JOSH: Oh, yeah? Come to dinner at our house! We eat a huge meal. There's food for you, too!

MARK: Great! Thanks a lot. <u>When do you want us there?</u>

JOSH: About three o'clock, I think.

MARK: That sounds good. <u>What do you need for the dinner?</u>

JOSH: Some soda, and maybe some dessert.

MARK: Perfect. So . . . <u>who comes to your Thanksgiving celebrations?</u> Your family? Friends?

JOSH: Friends. . . . Our friend Nicole comes every year. She lives near you, actually.

MARK: Oh, yeah? <u>Where does she live?</u>

JOSH: She lives at 620 15th Avenue.

MARK: That's close to our house. Does she need a ride to dinner?

JOSH: Yes, she does.

MARK: Great. We can give her a ride. <u>What's her phone number?</u>

JOSH: It's 555-268-7029.

MARK: OK. Good. See you on Thursday.

JOSH: See you then.

Ⓑ **Look at the conversation in A again. Answer the questions with complete sentences.**

1. Where does Josh eat Thanksgiving dinner? *He eats it at his house.*

2. What time does the dinner start? _____

3. What does Josh need for the dinner? _____

4. Who lives at 620 15th Avenue? _____

5. What is 555-268-7029? _____

# EXERCISE 2 *WH-* QUESTION WORDS

GRAMMAR NOTES 1–4 Complete the questions with *wh-* question words. Use the question words in the box.

| what | what time | when | where | who | why |
|------|-----------|------|-------|-----|-----|

1. A: _____ *What time* _____ do you get up on New Year's Day?
   B: I get up at noon.

2. A: _____ does the parade begin?
   B: It begins at 34th Street and Broadway.

3. A: _____ *Who* _____ comes to Thanksgiving dinner?
   B: Family members and friends come to Thanksgiving dinner.

4. A: _____ do you celebrate Independence Day?
   B: We celebrate it on July 4th.

5. A: _____ do you send postcards at New Year's?
   B: We send them because we want to send good wishes.

6. A: _____ do you do on Valentine's Day?
   B: We have a party on Valentine's Day.

# EXERCISE 3 *WH-* QUESTIONS

GRAMMAR NOTE 1 Yoshio wants to find out about American holidays. He asks a friend about them. Write his *wh-* questions. Use the simple present and the correct forms of the words in parentheses.

1. *When do you celebrate Valentine's Day?*
   (When / you / celebrate / Valentine's Day)

2. _____
   (How / people / celebrate Valentine's Day)

3. _____
   (Where / the name "Valentine" / come from)

4. _____
   (What day / Americans / celebrate Independence Day)

5. _____
   (Why / people / have fireworks on Independence Day)

6. _____
   (What / the word "independence" / mean)

7. _____
   (When / people / celebrate birthdays)

8. _____
   (How / you / celebrate your birthday)

## EXERCISE 4 *WH-* QUESTIONS

GRAMMAR NOTES 1–3  Read the sentences. Complete *wh-* questions about the underlined words. Use *How, Who, What, Where, Why,* or *What time.*

1. **A:** *What time do you go* _____ to bed on New Year's Eve?
   **B:** I go to bed after midnight on New Year's Eve.

2. **A:** What do you do _____ on New Year's Day?
   **B:** I watch football on New Year's Day.

3. **A:** Why do you send _____ people Valentine cards?
   **B:** We send people Valentine cards because we like them.

4. **A:** What do we have _____ for dinner on Thanksgiving?
   **B:** We have turkey for dinner on Thanksgiving.

5. **A:** What does fascinate _____ mean?
   **B:** "Fascinating" means "very interesting."

6. **A:** How do you spell _____ "valentine"?
   **B:** V-A-L-E-N-T-I-N-E.

7. **A:** Who do you play _____ board games with?
   **B:** I play board games with my parents.

8. **A:** Where do we eat _____ Thanksgiving dinner?
   **B:** We eat it at my mother's house.

## EXERCISE 5  EDITING

GRAMMAR NOTES 1–4  There are five mistakes in the conversation. The first mistake is corrected. Find and correct four more.

JESSICA:  What ~~you do~~ *do you* need for the party? You do need some chips?

MELANIE:  Yes, I do. And some cheese.

JESSICA:  OK. Good. What time does the party start?

MELANIE:  It starts on 9 p.m.

JESSICA:  Where you live?

MELANIE:  At 811 Forster Street.

JESSICA:  OK. How you spell that?

MELANIE:  F-O-R-S-T-E-R.

JESSICA:  Thanks. See you then.

## EXERCISE 6  LISTENING

▷12|02  **A** Listen to the conversation between Trevor and Linda. Check (✓) the true sentence.

☐ Trevor and Linda both drive to work.

☐ Trevor knows a lot of people at work.

☐ Trevor and Linda both live in the same town.

▷12|02  **B** Listen to the conversation again. Answer the questions with complete sentences.

1. Who is new in the company?  *Trevor is new in the company* .

2. How does Trevor like the company?  _____ .

3. What happens at the holiday party?  _____ .

4. What time does the party start?  _____ .

5. When does the last bus leave?  _____ .

6. Where do Linda and Trevor live?  _____ .

**C** Work with a partner. Compare your answers in A and B. Then discuss these questions.

1. What parties do you go to?

2. What do you do at the parties?

## EXERCISE 7  WHAT'S YOUR FAVORITE HOLIDAY?

**CONVERSATION** Work with a partner. Ask your partner questions about his or her favorite holiday. Use *How*, *What*, and *When*. Follow the example.

EXAMPLE:  **A:** What country do you come from?

**B:** I come from Canada.

**A:** What's your favorite celebration or holiday?

**B:** Canada Day is my favorite.

**A:** When do you celebrate it?

**B:** We celebrate it on July 1st.

**A:** How do you celebrate it? . . .

# EXERCISE 8
## WORDS ABOUT CELEBRATIONS

**A** GAME Work with a partner. Ask and answer questions about the meaning of each of the words below. All of the words are in Unit 12. Choose from the definitions in the box. Take turns.

| | |
|---|---|
| 12:00 a.m. | freedom |
| 12:00 p.m. | look at |
| a trip in a car | ~~very big~~ |
| enjoy a special day | very interesting |
| a family member | |

1. huge      *very big* _____

    EXAMPLE: **A:** What does huge mean?
               **B:** Huge means "very big."

2. exciting _____

3. independence _____

4. noon _____

5. midnight _____

6. a ride _____

7. a relative _____

8. watch _____

9. celebrate _____

**B** Now check your answers on page 385. Who has the most correct answers?

## FROM GRAMMAR TO WRITING

**A** BEFORE YOU WRITE  Read the conversation about a celebration in Spain. Underline the *wh-* questions and the simple present verbs. Then interview a partner about a celebration he or she knows about in a different country—not his or her own country. Complete the chart with your partner's answers.

MIGUEL:  What's your favorite celebration in another country?

SASHA:  My favorite is La Tomatina in Spain.

MIGUEL:  What happens in the celebration?

SASHA:  People throw a lot of tomatoes. They watch parades. They have parties on the street, too.

MIGUEL:  Where does it happen?

SASHA:  It happens in Buñol, a town near Valencia.

MIGUEL:  When does it happen?

SASHA:  It happens on the last Wednesday of August.

| Celebration | |
|---|---|
| What / happen | |
| Where / happen | |
| When / happen | |

**B** WRITE  Write a conversation about a celebration. Use *wh-* questions. Use the conversation in A and your chart to help you.

**C** CHECK YOUR WORK  Read your conversation. Underline examples of *wh-* questions. Use the Editing Checklist to check your work.

### Editing Checklist

**Did you...?**

☐ use *do* in *wh-* questions with *I, we, you,* and *they*

☐ use *does* in *wh-* questions with *he, she,* and *it*

☐ check your spelling

**D** REVISE YOUR WORK  Read your paragraph again. Can you improve your writing? Make changes if necessary.

# UNIT 12 REVIEW

**Test yourself on the grammar of the unit.**

**Ⓐ** Complete the conversation with *why, what time, where,* or *when.*

A: _____ does the parade begin?
        1.

B: At 8:00 a.m.

A: At 8:00? That's early! _____ does it start so early?
                    2.

B: It's a very long parade.

A: _____ does it go? And _____ does it end?
    3.                   4.

B: It goes down Fifth Avenue. And it ends about noon.

**Ⓑ** Write *wh-* questions in the simple present. Use the correct forms of the words in parentheses.

1. _____
               (your cousins / Where / live)

2. _____
               (start / the fireworks / When)

3. _____
               (do / What / he)

4. _____
               (like / he / How / his job)

5. _____
               (like / you / Thanksgiving / Why)

6. _____
           (you / get up / on New Year's Day / What time)

**Ⓒ** Correct the conversation. There are five mistakes.

A: How Max celebrates his birthday?

B: He eats a huge meal.

A: What kind of food does he eats? And where he eat it?

B: He eats Italian food at his favorite restaurant, Mangia.

A: How you spell "mangia"? And what means it?

B: M-A-N-G-I-A. It means "eat"!

**Now check your answers on pages 380–381.**

# Simple Present with Adverbs of Frequency

## HABITS

**OUTCOMES**
- Use adverbs of frequency to talk about how often something happens
- Complete sentences about a reading
- Complete sentences about a conversation
- Talk about good and bad habits
- Write an email to a friend about what you do every day

**STEP 1    GRAMMAR IN CONTEXT**

## BEFORE YOU READ

**A** Study the words. Then check (✓) how many times a week you do these things.

go to bed early

stay up late

get up early

sleep late

take a shower

eat fast food

|  | Every day | 3–4 times a week | Once or twice a week |
|---|---|---|---|
| 1. go to bed early | ☐ | ☐ | ☐ |
| 2. stay up late | ☐ | ☐ | ☐ |
| 3. get up early | ☐ | ☐ | ☐ |
| 4. sleep late | ☐ | ☐ | ☐ |
| 5. take a shower | ☐ | ☐ | ☐ |
| 6. eat fast food | ☐ | ☐ | ☐ |

**B** Work with a partner. Compare your answers in A.

🔊 13|01  **Read this conversation.**

# I Have One Good Habit

**JOSH:** How's it going, Steve? You look tired.

**STEVE:** Well, things are OK, but I *am* a little tired. I'm always tired. I only sleep about six hours a night.

**JOSH:** What time do you go to bed?

**STEVE:** I usually stay up late—until 12:30 or 1:00 a.m. And I get up at 6:30 or 7:00 a.m.

**JOSH:** Do you ever sleep late?

**STEVE:** Sometimes—on the weekends.

**JOSH:** Do you always eat lunch?

**STEVE:** Yeah. But I sometimes skip[1] breakfast.

**JOSH:** So you don't eat three meals a day?

**STEVE:** Rarely. I'm usually in a hurry in the morning.

**JOSH:** What do you eat for lunch and dinner?

**STEVE:** I always have a good dinner. But lunch . . . well, I'm always in a hurry then. So I usually go to a fast-food place near the university.

**JOSH:** Hmm. Not enough sleep. No breakfast. Fast food for lunch. Not good, my friend.

**STEVE:** Well, I have one good habit. I work out.

**JOSH:** Great. How often do you work out?

**STEVE:** Two or three times a year.

---

1 *skip:* do not do

## AFTER YOU READ

Ⓐ COMPREHENSION  Look at the conversation again. Circle the correct answers.

1. Steve gets / doesn't get enough sleep.

2. Steve usually goes to bed before / after midnight.

3. Steve always / sometimes skips breakfast.

4. Steve usually / rarely eats three meals a day.

5. Steve always / usually eats fast food for lunch.

6. Steve works out a lot / a little.

Ⓑ Work with a partner. Compare your answers in A.

## ADVERBS OF FREQUENCY

### Adverbs of Frequency with *Be*

|  | *Be* | Adverb |  |
|---|---|---|---|
| I | am | | |
| He<br>She<br>It | is | always<br>usually<br>often | late. |
| We<br>You<br>They | are | rarely<br>never | |

### Adverbs of Frequency with Other Verbs

|  | Adverb | Verb |  |
|---|---|---|---|
| I<br>He<br>They | sometimes<br>never<br>often | skip<br>eats<br>have | lunch.<br>breakfast.<br>parties. |

### Adverbs of Frequency

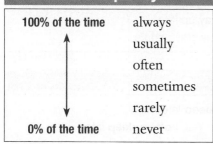

| 100% of the time | always |
|---|---|
| | usually |
| | often |
| | sometimes |
| | rarely |
| 0% of the time | never |

### *Yes/No* Questions

Do you **ever** stay up late?

### Short Answers

| Yes, I | always<br>usually<br>often<br>sometimes | do. |
|---|---|---|
| No, I | rarely<br>never | |

### *Wh-* Questions

| **How often** do you eat fast food? |
| **What time** do you get up? |
| **What** do you do on Saturdays? |

### Answers

| I **usually** eat fast food three times a week. |
| I **always** get up at 7:00 a.m. |
| We **often** go to the movies on Saturdays. |

# GRAMMAR NOTES

## 1 Definition of Adverbs of Frequency

| | |
|---|---|
| **Adverbs of frequency** say **how often** something happens. | I *always* **skip** breakfast.<br>She *sometimes* **skips** lunch.<br>We *never* **work** on Saturdays. |

## 2 Adverbs of Frequency with *Be*

| | |
|---|---|
| Adverbs of frequency come **after** the verb *be*. | I'm *usually* tired in the morning.<br>The food at that restaurant **is** *never* good. |

## 3 Adverbs of Frequency with Other Verbs

| | |
|---|---|
| Adverbs of frequency normally come **before** other verbs. | He *usually* **goes** to a fast-food place.<br>It *always* **rains** on the weekends. |

## 4 *Usually, Sometimes, Rarely,* and *Never*

| | |
|---|---|
| *Usually* and *sometimes* can also come at the **beginning** or the **end** of a sentence with *be* and with other verbs. | **Usually** I get up at 8:00. **or** I get up at 8:00, **usually.**<br>**Sometimes** I'm late for work. **or** I'm late for work, **sometimes.** |
| **BE CAREFUL!** *Rarely* and *never* are negative adverbs. Don't use them in affirmative sentences. | A: Do you ever stay up late?<br>B: No, I **rarely** stay up late.<br>NOT ~~Yes,~~ I rarely stay up late. |

## 5 *Ever* in Yes/No Questions

| | |
|---|---|
| Use *ever* in *yes/no* questions to ask about frequency. *Ever* means "at any time or times." | A: Do you **ever sleep** late?<br>B: Yes, **often. or** Yes, I **often sleep** late. |
| **BE CAREFUL!** Don't use *ever* in affirmative statements. | I **sometimes** sleep late.<br>NOT I ~~ever~~ sleep late. |

## 6 *How Often*

| | |
|---|---|
| Use *how often* questions to ask about frequency. | A: **How often** do you exercise?<br>B: I usually exercise **three times a week.** |

# REFERENCE NOTES

For **definitions of grammar terms**, see the Glossary on page 375.

For more information on **simple present questions**, see Unit 11 on page 120 and Unit 12 on page 130.

## EXERCISE 1 DISCOVER THE GRAMMAR

**A** GRAMMAR NOTES 1–4 Read the paragraph about Josh Wang. Underline the twelve adverbs of frequency. Circle the verbs that go with them. The first adverb is underlined.

Josh Wang has an active life. He gets up at 6 a.m. He <u>usually</u> (runs) two or three miles with his dog. <u>Sometimes</u> he feels tired, but he still runs. When he gets home, he takes a shower. Then he has breakfast with his wife, Amanda. He <u>often</u> has eggs, juice, toast, and coffee, but sometimes he has cereal and fruit. Then Josh goes to work, and he is <u>always</u> on time. He works from 9:00 until 5:00 and <u>rarely</u> stays late. In the evening, Josh and Amanda <u>always</u> have a healthy dinner. They <u>often</u> have fish with rice and vegetables. Josh <u>never</u> has fast food, and he <u>rarely</u> eats sweets. After dinner, both Josh and Amanda read. Josh is also an artist, so <u>sometimes</u> he paints. He and Amanda <u>always</u> go to bed by 10:30.

**B** Look at the paragraph in A again. For each statement, check (✓) *True* or *False*.

|  | True | False |
|---|---|---|
| **1.** Josh Wang often runs with his dog. | ✓ | ☐ |
| **2.** Josh never eats fruit for breakfast. | ☐ | ✓ |
| **3.** Josh always works late. | ☐ | ☐ |
| **4.** Josh always eats healthy food. | ✓ | ☐ |
| **5.** Josh and his wife often go to bed at 11 p.m. | ☐ | ✓ |

## EXERCISE 2 ADVERBS OF FREQUENCY

GRAMMAR NOTES 1–4 Complete the sentences. Circle the correct answers.

**1.** I don't have a car. I (never) / sometimes drive to work.

**2.** Daud loves shopping for clothes. He often / never goes shopping.

**3.** Abla hates to work out. She never / usually goes to the gym.

**4.** Ken likes to get up early. He's often / rarely in bed at 9:00 a.m.

**5.** Pamela takes the bus to work four days a week. She usually / rarely takes the bus.

**6.** Bob eats at a fast-food restaurant two days a week. He usually / sometimes eats fast food.

# EXERCISE 3 ALWAYS, USUALLY, SOMETIMES, NEVER

GRAMMAR NOTES 1–4 Look at the pictures and the chart. Then write two sentences about Jessica Olson for each picture. Use *always, usually, sometimes,* or *never* and the words in parentheses.

|  | Sun | Mon | Tues | Wed | Thurs | Fri | Sat |
|---|---|---|---|---|---|---|---|
| 1. | ✓ | ✓ | ✓ | ✓ | ✓ | ✓ | ✓ |
| 2. |  |  |  |  |  |  |  |
| 3. |  | ✓ | ✓ | ✓ |  | ✓ |  |
| 4. |  | ✓ |  | ✓ |  | ✓ |  |

1. (take a shower)  _She always takes a shower in the morning._

   (skip her shower)  _She never skips her shower._

2. (drive to work)  _She never drives to work._

   (take the bus)  _She always takes the bus_

3. (arrive at work on time)  _She usually arrives at work on time._

   (arrive late)  _She sometimes arrives late_

4. (cook dinner)  _She sometimes cooks dinner._

   (eat in a restaurant)  _She usually eats in a restaurant._

# EXERCISE 4 WORD ORDER

GRAMMAR NOTES 1–6 Put the words in the correct order. Make conversations.

1. A: _Do you ever stay up late?_
   (late? / ever / Do / stay up / you)

   B: _Yes, I do often I do._
   (do. / Yes, / often / I)

2. A: _Are you ever tired in the morning?_
   (you / tired / in the morning? / ever / Are)

   B: _Yes, I'm always tired in the morning._
   (in the morning. / always / I'm / tired / Yes,)

3. A: _How often do you work out?_
   (often / work out? / How / you / do)

   B: _I usually work out five times a week._
   (a week. / five times / usually / work out / I)

4. A: _What do you do usually in the evening?_
   (usually / in the evening? / do / What / do / you)

   B: _I usually play the piano._
   (the piano. / play / I / usually)

# EXERCISE 5 EDITING

GRAMMAR NOTES 1–6 There are five mistakes in the conversation. The first mistake is corrected. Find and correct four more.

JESSICA: Domingo, how ~often~ do you work out?

DOMINGO: I _always_ work out six or seven days a week.

JESSICA: Do ever ~you~ _you_ get tired?

DOMINGO: ~Always I am~ _I am always_ tired. But I enjoy the gym.

JESSICA: OK. How often do you travel?

DOMINGO: Usually I travel three times a month.

JESSICA: Does your wife ever get unhappy because you travel a lot?

DOMINGO: No, she ~ever~ gets unhappy. She travels always with me.

## EXERCISE 6 LISTENING

▶13|02 **A** Listen to the telephone conversation between Ken and his grandmother. Then check (✓) the two true statements.

☐ 1. Ken's grandmother's birthday is today.

☐ 2. Ken is always tired.

☐ 3. Ken has a job.

☐ 4. Ken's grandmother wants him to study more.

▶13|02 **B** Listen again. Complete the statements.

1. Grandma calls Ken because tomorrow is _his birthday_____.

2. Grandma is usually _____.

3. Ken usually starts work at _____.

4. Ken sometimes _____ to study.

5. Ken usually gets _____ of sleep.

6. Grandma says Ken needs _____ of sleep every night.

**C** Work with a partner. Compare your answers in A and B. Then discuss these questions.

1. How often do you see grandparents or other relatives (uncles, aunts, cousins)?

2. What do you usually talk about with them?

## EXERCISE 7 ABOUT YOU

**A** CONVERSATION Work with a partner. Ask and answer *yes/no* questions with *ever*. Use the phrases in the box and an adverb of frequency.

| | | |
|---|---|---|
| be on time to class/work | eat breakfast | go to the movies |
| be tired in the morning | eat fast food | wear a hat |
| do housework | get enough sleep | |

EXAMPLE: **A:** Are you ever on time to class?
　　　　 **B:** Yes! I'm always on time to class.

**B** Tell your classmates about your partner.

EXAMPLE: **A:** Monica is rarely on time to work.
　　　　 **B:** Ben sometimes eats fast food.

# EXERCISE 8 MY GOOD AND BAD HABITS

**A** DISCUSSION Work in a group. First, complete the chart for yourself. For each habit, check (✓) *Always*, *Often*, *Sometimes*, *Rarely*, or *Never*. Then discuss your answers with your classmates.

| How often do you . . . ? | Always | Often | Sometimes | Rarely | Never |
|---|---|---|---|---|---|
| get up early | | | | | |
| sleep late | | | | | |
| go to bed early | | | | | |
| stay up late | | | | | |
| eat regular meals | | | | | |
| skip meals | | | | | |
| take a shower | | | | | |
| watch TV | | | | | |
| work out | | | | | |
| arrive late to work or class | | | | | |
| call your parents | | | | | |

EXAMPLE: **A:** I always get up early. I always eat regular meals. I often call my parents.
          **B:** Really? I often sleep late. I often skip breakfast. I never call my parents.

**B** Report interesting examples to the class.

EXAMPLE: **A:** Tomiko always stays up late.
          **B:** Jomo never watches TV.
          **C:** Henrietta usually goes to bed at 8 p.m.

**A** BEFORE YOU WRITE  You and a good friend, Alfredo, now live in different cities. Read the email from Alfredo. Underline adverbs of frequency. Then work with a partner. Discuss the things you do every day.

Hi!

My life is really different now. I'm a clerk at a big store. I usually start work at 9 a.m. and finish at 5 p.m. Sometimes I take the bus to work, and sometimes I walk.

In the evenings, I usually watch TV or read. On weekends, I go to the movies. I still play my guitar and sing.

What about you?

—Alfredo

**B** WRITE  Answer your friend's email. Talk about what you do every day. Use adverbs of frequency and the simple present. Use the email in A and your discussion to help you.

**C** CHECK YOUR WORK  Read your paragraph. Underline adverbs of frequency. Use the Editing Checklist to check your work.

| Editing Checklist |
| --- |
| **Did you . . . ?** |
| ☐ use adverbs of frequency after *be* |
| ☐ use adverbs of frequency before other verbs |
| ☐ check your spelling |

**D** REVISE YOUR WORK  Read your paragraph again. Can you improve your writing? Make changes if necessary.

# UNIT 13 REVIEW

**Test yourself on the grammar of the unit.**

**A** Match the sentences with similar meanings.

_____ **1.** They always work out.

_____ **2.** They rarely work out.

_____ **3.** They sometimes work out.

_b_ **4.** They usually work out.

**a.** They work out on weekends.

**b.** They work out five days a week.

**c.** They work out every day.

**d.** They work out once a month.

**B** Put the words in the correct order. Make conversations.

**1. A:** _How often do you skip lunch?_
(often / skip / How / you / do / lunch?)

  **B:** _I sometimes skip lunch._
(lunch. / sometimes / I / skip)

**2. A:** _What do you do usually on the weekends?_
(usually / on the weekends? / you / do / What / do)

  **B:** _I often go to the movies._
(to the movies. / go / often / I)

**3. A:** _Do you ever eat fast food for breakfast?_
(for breakfast? / ever / Do / eat / you / fast food)

  **B:** _No, I never do._
(do. / No, / never / I)

**C** Correct the conversation. There are <u>five</u> mistakes.

**A:** Never I get up early. Do you get up early?

**B:** Yes. I get up early usually four days a week.

**A:** Do you see ever your friends after class?

**B:** Sometimes—but I usually see them on the weekends. We play board games always.

  Do you play board games?

**A:** Yes, I rarely play them. They're a lot of fun.

**Now check your answers on page 381.**

# Adjectives

# PART 5

**OUTCOMES**

- Use adjectives to describe nouns
- Use *be* and *have* with adjectives
- Answer questions about a reading
- Complete sentences about a conversation
- Describe people
- Write descriptions of a classmate and a friend

**OUTCOMES**

- Use comparative adjectives to compare two people or things
- Ask and answer questions with *which* and *who*
- Complete sentences about a reading
- Identify true and false sentences about a conversation
- Compare people, places, or things
- Write a paragraph about a favorite type of entertainment

# Adjectives

## DESCRIBING PEOPLE

**OUTCOMES**
• Use adjectives to describe nouns
• Use *be* and *have* with adjectives
• Answer questions about a reading
• Complete sentences about a conversation
• Describe people
• Write descriptions of a classmate and a friend

---

**STEP 1**   **GRAMMAR IN CONTEXT**

## BEFORE YOU READ

**Ⓐ** VOCABULARY  Study the words. Then complete the sentences. Write the names of famous people or people you know.

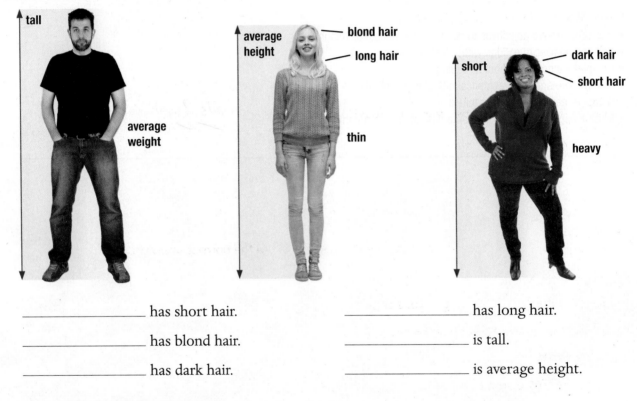

tall

average
height

blond hair

long hair

average
weight

thin

dark hair

short

short hair

heavy

_____ has short hair.

_____ has blond hair.

_____ has dark hair.

_____ has long hair.

_____ is tall.

_____ is average height.

**Ⓑ** Work with a partner. Compare your answers in A.

## READ

▶14|01  Read this conversation.

# What Does She Look Like?

RICK:  Are you in Music 101?

JUDY:  Uh-huh. . . . It's a great class. I like it a lot.

RICK:  Could you please give these tickets to Sonia Jones? She's in your class.

JUDY: Sure. But I don't know her. What does she look like?

RICK: Well, she has dark hair and dark eyes.

JUDY: Half the women have dark hair and dark eyes. It's a huge class. There are 100 students in it!

RICK: Well, she's tall and thin.

JUDY: OK, but a lot of women are tall and thin.

RICK: She's young. . . . She's in her twenties.

JUDY: Rick! Almost everyone at school is twenty-something.[1] Is there something unusual[2] about her?

RICK: Well. . . . She has two heads!

JUDY: What?!

RICK: Sonia's eight months pregnant.[3]

JUDY: Oh! *Now* I know who she is!

---

1 *twenty-something:* between twenty and thirty years old
2 *unusual:* different
3 *pregnant:* going to have a baby

## AFTER YOU READ

**Ⓐ COMPREHENSION** **Look at the conversation again. Circle the correct answers.**

1. Is Sonia in Music 101?
   a. Yes, she is.          b. No, she isn't.

2. Does Sonia have blond hair and blue eyes?
   a Yes, she does.          b. No, she doesn't.

3. Is Music 101 a small class?
   a. Yes, it is.          b. No, it isn't.

4. Are most of the students between the ages of twenty and twenty-nine?
   a. Yes, they are.          b. No, they aren't.

5. Does Sonia really have two heads?
   a. Yes, she does.          b. No, she doesn't.

6. Is Sonia pregnant?
   a. Yes, she is.          b. No, she isn't.

**Ⓑ Work with a partner. Compare your answers in A.**

## ADJECTIVES

### Be + Adjective

| Subject | Be | Adjective |
|---|---|---|
| She | is | tall. |
| They | are | tall. |
| Mary and Joe | are | tall. |

### Adjective + Noun

| | Adjective | Noun |
|---|---|---|
| She is a | **tall** | woman. |
| They are | | women. |
| I have a | **long** | face. |
| We have | | legs. |
| He has an | **old** | computer. |
| They have | | computers. |

### Noun Modifiers

| | Noun Modifier | Noun |
|---|---|---|
| She is a | **music** | teacher. |
| They are | **football** | players. |

## GRAMMAR NOTES

### 1 Adjectives: Form and Meaning

| | |
|---|---|
| Adjectives **describe** nouns. | |
| Adjectives can come **after** the verb *be*. | **SUBJECT NOUN OR PRONOUN** · ***BE*** · **ADJECTIVE**<br>She — is — short.<br>Mary — is — short. |
| Adjectives can come **before a noun**. | **ADJECTIVE** · **NOUN**<br>He is a — tall — man.<br>He has — dark — hair. |
| **BE CAREFUL!** Adjectives **do not follow** nouns. | She is an **old woman**.<br>**NOT** She is a ~~woman old~~. |
| **BE CAREFUL!** Do not add *-s* to adjectives. They have the **same form** before singular and plural nouns. | He is a **thin** man. (*singular*)<br>They are **thin** men. (*plural*)<br>**NOT** They are ~~thins~~ men. |

## 2 *A* or *An* Before an Adjective

When an **adjective** comes before **a singular count noun**, use *a* or *an* before the adjective.

| | |
|---|---|
| Use *a* before the adjective if it begins with a **consonant sound**. | She's **a tall** woman. <br> He has **a long** face. |
| Use *an* before the adjective if it begins with a **vowel sound**. | She has **an old** watch. <br> It's **an unusual** name. |

## 3 Noun Modifiers

**Nouns** can also describe nouns. The modifying nouns have the **same form** before singular and plural nouns.

| | | NOUN | NOUN |
|---|---|---|---|
| He's a | | **baseball** | player. |
| They are | | **baseball** | players. |
| I have an | | **English** | class. |
| They are | | **English** | teachers. |

## 4 *Be* and *Have* + Adjectives

Remember, *be* and *have* are **common irregular verbs**. These verbs are commonly used with **adjectives** or **adjectives + nouns** to describe people and things.

| | | VERB | ADJECTIVE |
|---|---|---|---|
| We can use *be* + an **adjective** alone. | I | **am** | short. |
| | He | **isn't** | tall. |
| | They | **are** | thin. |

| | | VERB | ADJECTIVE | NOUN |
|---|---|---|---|---|
| We use *have* + an **adjective** + a **noun**. | I | **have** | blond | hair. |
| | They | **don't have** | long | hair. |
| | She | **has** | brown | hair. |
| | He | **doesn't have** | brown | hair. |

| | |
|---|---|
| **BE CAREFUL!** We use *be*, not *have*, to talk about **age**. | **A:** How old **are** you? <br> **B:** **I am** twenty-one years old. <br> **NOT** ~~I have twenty-one years~~. |

## REFERENCE NOTE

For **definitions of grammar terms**, see the Glossary on page 375.

## EXERCISE 1  DISCOVER THE GRAMMAR

Ⓐ GRAMMAR NOTES 1–4  Read the conversation. Circle the adjectives.

JUDY: So, Rick, how was the concert?

RICK: It was great, but long.

JUDY: Was Sonia there with her husband?

RICK: Yes, they were both there.

JUDY: What does her husband look like?

RICK: He's tall and heavy. He has brown hair and green eyes.

JUDY: What does he do?

RICK: I think he's a football player.

JUDY: That's an interesting job.

Ⓑ Write the adjectives from A and the nouns they describe.

| Adjective | Noun |
|-----------|------|
| great | concert |
| long | husband |
| tall | hair |
| heavy | football player |
| brown | |
| interesting | job |

Ⓒ Look at the conversation in A. Underline the noun modifier.

## EXERCISE 2  ADJECTIVES WITH A OR AN

GRAMMAR NOTES 1–2, 4  Complete the sentences. Circle the correct words.

1. She has a beautiful / beautiful face.

2. He is a tall / tall.

3. They are a tall / tall men.

4. He is a short / short man.

5. She is a beautiful / beautiful woman.

6. Her eyes are a blue / blue.

7. He has a red / red hair.

8. I need an unusual / a unusual gift.

# EXERCISE 3  WORD ORDER OF ADJECTIVES AND NOUNS

GRAMMAR NOTES 1–4  Write sentences. Put the words in the correct order.

1. My sister has blue eyes and red hair.
   (has / blue / hair / My sister / eyes / and red)

2. I have a sister/funnier.
   (sister / I / funny / a / have)

3. They are heavy men.
   (men / heavy / are / They)

4. He has an exciting job.     *exciting*
   (has / an / job / exciting / He)

5. She has a beautiful smile.
   (smile / has / beautiful / She / a)

6. I'm an English teacher.
   (I'm / teacher / an / English)

7. My parents are tall and thin.
   (tall / are / parents / thin / My / and)

8. I don't have long hair.
   (long / have / don't / hair / I)

9. She is twenty-one years old.
   (She / years old / is / twenty-one)

10. They are average weight.
    (weight / They / average / are)

# EXERCISE 4  ADJECTIVES, *A*, *AN*, *BE*, *HAVE*

GRAMMAR NOTES 1–2, 4  Complete the conversation. Use the words in the box.

| a | an | blue | brown | ~~good~~ | hair | has | is | photo |
|---|----|----|-------|------|------|-----|----|-------|

MARK:  This is my cousin, Francisco.

JUDY:  That's a ___good___ ___photo___ of him.
1.            2.
How old ___is___ he?
3.

MARK:  Twenty-five years old. He lives in São Paulo.

JUDY:  Is he a writer, like you?

MARK:  No. He's ___has___ successful businessman.
4.
He has three businesses.

JUDY:  He looks like you.

MARK:  I know. He has ___brown___ ___hair___
5.            6.
and ___blue___ eyes. He has a beard, too.
7.

JUDY:  He has ___an___ interesting face. Does he have a girlfriend?
8.

MARK:  He's married. He ___has___ a beautiful wife.
9.

beard ——

## EXERCISE 5  *BE* AND *HAVE* + ADJECTIVES

GRAMMAR NOTE 4  Complete the sentences. Use the correct form of *be* or *have*.

1. I _____*have*_____ dark hair. My father _____*has*_____ dark hair, too.

2. I _____*am*_____ short. My mother _____*is*_____ short, too.

3. I __*don't have*__ brown eyes. My mother __*doesn't have*__ brown eyes, either.
    (not)                                    (not)

4. I __*am not*__ twenty. My sister __*isn't*__ twenty, either.
    (not)                          (not)

5. _____ you __*have*__ long hair?

6. __*Is*__ your father old?

7. Who __*has*__ red hair in your family?

8. Who _____ tall and thin?

## EXERCISE 6  EDITING

GRAMMAR NOTES 1–4  There are five mistakes in the paragraph. The first mistake is corrected. Find and correct four more.

THIS IS A PAINTING by the Italian artist Modigliani. The people in Modigliani's paintings usually have ~~longs~~ *long* faces and necks. This woman has a long face and ~~hair brown~~ *brown hair.* Her neck ~~has~~ *is* long, too. Her eyes are ~~blues~~, and her lips are red. It's *an* ~~a~~ interesting painting.

158   Unit 14

## EXERCISE 7  LISTENING

▶14|02  **A** Listen to the conversation. Judy and Mark are at a party. Judy tells Mark about her mom's friend Olivia Lander. What does Olivia do?

**a.** She's a chef.            **b.** She's a writer.            **c.** She's a musician.

▶14|02  **B** Listen again. Complete the sentences. Circle the correct answers.

**1.** Olivia has (red) / blond hair.

**2.** Her hair is short / long.

**3.** She is average height / tall.

**4.** She has a nice smile / nice clothes.

**5.** She likes to wear gray / black clothes.

**6.** She is from Canada / China.

**7.** She's on vacation / on a book tour.

**C** Work with a partner. Look at the pictures. Circle the picture of Olivia. Take turns. Say why the other two women are not Olivia.

EXAMPLE:  The woman in Picture 1 isn't Olivia because she is short.

Picture 1                    Picture 2                    Picture 3

## EXERCISE 8 MY MOTHER IS TALL AND . . .

**A PRESENTATION** Prepare to give a presentation about your family. First, read about people in Melissa's family. Then write the name of the person under his or her picture.

> My cousin Don is eleven. He has wavy blond hair. It's long, too.

> My uncle Joe is average height. He's bald, but he has a mustache and beard.

> My cousin Emma is thin. She has curly blond hair. She has a nice smile.

> My sister Laura has straight brown hair. It's short.

1. _Joe_     2. _____     3. _____     4. _____

**B** Work with a partner. Compare your answers in A. Then discuss the difference between *straight hair*, *curly hair*, *wavy hair*, and *bald*; and the difference between *a beard* and *a moustache*.

**C** Take notes about people in your family. Write short descriptions. Try to use the adjectives in A. Then work in a group and give a presentation about people in your family.

EXAMPLE: My sister Nadia is beautiful. She is thin. She has long brown hair. It's wavy. She . . .

# EXERCISE 9  FACES

**Ⓐ PICTURE DISCUSSION**  Draw three different faces below. Do not show your faces to anyone.

**Ⓑ** Work with a partner. Describe your faces from A to your partner. Do not show the faces. Your partner listens and draws the faces.

EXAMPLE:  **A:** My first face is a man. He has curly brown hair, a curly beard, and a mustache.

**Ⓒ** Compare your drawings in B with your partner's drawings in A. Do they match? Say what is different in the drawings.

EXAMPLE:  The man in your drawing has straight brown hair. The man in my drawing has curly brown hair.

## FROM GRAMMAR TO WRITING

**A** BEFORE YOU WRITE  Read a description of a classmate and of a friend. Underline the adjectives. Then complete the chart about your classmate and your friend. Work with a partner. Tell your partner about your classmate and your friend.

My classmate Maria is short and average weight. She has dark hair and brown eyes. She has a beautiful smile. She's nineteen years old.

My friend Jim has short brown hair and blue eyes. He's average height and weight. He's thirty years old.

|  | Height | Weight | Hair Color | Eye Color | Age |
|---|---|---|---|---|---|
| **Classmate:** |  |  |  |  |  |
| **Friend:** |  |  |  |  |  |

**B** WRITE  Write descriptions of your classmate and your friend. Use adjectives. Use the descriptions in A and your chart to help you.

**C** CHECK YOUR WORK  Read your descriptions. Underline the adjectives. Use the Editing Checklist to check your work.

| **Editing Checklist** |
| --- |
| **Did you . . . ?** |
| ☐ use adjectives before nouns |
| ☐ use adjectives after the verb *be* |
| ☐ use the same form (no -*s*) for adjectives before singular and plural nouns |
| ☐ use the verb *have* with an adjective + noun |
| ☐ check your spelling |

**D** REVISE YOUR WORK  Read your descriptions again. Can you improve your writing? Make changes if necessary.

# UNIT 14 REVIEW

**Test yourself on the grammar of the unit.**

**A** Complete the questions. Circle the correct answers.

1. Who has hair short / short hair?

2. Is Music 101 a / an interesting class?

3. How old has / is she?

4. Are they thin / thins?

5. Is he heavy / a heavy?

**B** Write sentences. Put the words in the correct order.

1. My roommate has a long face.
   (long / My roommate / has / a / face)

2. They are average height.
   (average / are / height / They)

3. He is an unusual person.
   (an / is / person / unusual / He)

4. It is a short book.
   (is / book / It / a / short)

5. He has a nice smile.
   (a / nice / has / He / smile)

**C** Correct the conversation. There are five mistakes.

A: What does your sister look like?

B: She is thin, and she has hair brown and a green eyes.

A: Is she tall or short?

B: She is a short.

A: What about your parents? Are they shorts?

B: No, they're both talls.

**Now check your answers on page 381.**

## UNIT 15

# Comparative Adjectives
## ENTERTAINMENT

---

## STEP 1    GRAMMAR IN CONTEXT

### BEFORE YOU READ

**(A) VOCABULARY**   **Study the words. Then complete the conversations with your opinions.**

rap music

video games

barbecue

### Conversation 1

A: Which is better for dancing, rap music or pop music?

B: I think _____ is better.

### Conversation 2

A: Which are more fun, video games or movies?

B: I think _____ are more fun.

### Conversation 3

A: Which is cheaper, a barbecue at home or dinner at a restaurant?

B: I think _____ is cheaper.

**(B) Work with a partner. Practice the conversations in A.**

15|01 **Read the conversation.**

# That's More Fun

**MARTY:** We need some entertainment for the party. What do you want to do?

**LAURA:** We can listen to music.

**KEN:** Let's dance. That's more fun. I have a lot of great music.

**MARTY:** OK, but don't bring your rap music. Pop music is better than rap for dancing.

**MI YOUNG:** That's not true! Pop music is worse than rap. I love rap!

**LAURA:** Yes, I love rap and hip-hop, too. My older brother has a lot of hip-hop.

**KEN:** Hip-hop is good. And we can have a barbecue. I can buy some steaks.

**MI YOUNG:** Let's get hamburgers. They're easier and quicker than steaks. And they're cheaper.

**LAURA:** OK. What about snacks? How about chips?

**KEN:** I think nuts are tastier than chips.

**MI YOUNG:** Yeah, but chips are more popular than nuts.

**LAURA:** OK, let's have chips *and* nuts. And what about desserts and drinks?

**MI YOUNG:** We have ice cream, and we have soda and juice.

**MARTY:** Do we want to watch movies at the party, too? After we dance?

**LAURA:** Well . . . I'm kind of[1] tired of them. Video games are more fun than movies.

**KEN:** Hey, I know a really great new video game. It's called, "Who's faster?" We can play that.

---

1 *kind of:* a little

# AFTER YOU READ

Ⓐ **COMPREHENSION** Look at the conversation again. Complete the sentences.

1. Ken thinks it's more fun to _____ than listen to music.

2. Marty says ___*Pop music*___ is better than rap for dancing.

3. Mi Young thinks pop music is ___*worse than*___ than rap.

4. _____ are quicker to cook than steak.

5. _____ are more expensive than hamburgers.

6. Laura thinks that, at a party, _____ are more fun than movies.

Ⓑ Work with a partner. Compare your answers in A.

---

| STEP 2 | GRAMMAR PRESENTATION |

## COMPARATIVE ADJECTIVES

### Comparative Adjectives with *-er*

|  |  | Comparative Adjective | *Than* |  |
|---|---|---|---|---|
| The train | is | **quicker** | **than** | the bus. |
| The bus | is | **cheaper**. |  |  |

### Comparative Adjectives with *More*

|  |  | Comparative Adjective | *Than* |  |
|---|---|---|---|---|
| Movies | are | **more interesting** | **than** | television. |
| Cars | are | **more expensive** | **than** | motorcycles. |

| *Which/Who* |  | Comparative Adjective |  |
|---|---|---|---|
| **Which** | are | **more interesting,** | movies or TV shows? |
| **Who** | is | **older,** | Ken or Laura? |

## GRAMMAR NOTES

### 1 Uses of Comparative Adjectives

| Use the **comparative** form of an adjective + *than* to **compare** two people, places, or things. | Ken is **taller than** Laura.<br>Hamburgers are **quicker than** steak. |
|---|---|
| We can omit *than* if the meaning is clear. | They're also **cheaper**. *(cheaper than steak)* |

## 2 Comparatives of Short Adjectives

| To form the comparative of **short (one-syllable)** adjectives, add *-er* to the adjective. | |
|---|---|
| • *young* → *younger* | Laura is **younger than** Ken. |
| If the adjective ends in *-e*, just add *-r*. | |
| • *large* → *larger* | New York is **larger than** Chicago. |

## 3 Comparatives of Two-Syllable Adjectives Ending in *-y*

| To form the comparative of **two-syllable** adjectives that **end in -y**, change the *y* to *i* and add *-er*. | |
|---|---|
| • *easy* → *easier* | For me, algebra is **easier than** geometry. |
| • *tasty* → *tastier* | I think nuts are **tastier than** chips. |

## 4 Comparatives of Long Adjectives

| To form the comparatives of most adjectives of **two or more syllables**, use *more* before the adjective. | |
|---|---|
| • *crowded* → *more crowded* | New York is **more crowded than** Chicago. |
| • *interesting* → *more interesting* | Video games are **more interesting than** movies. |

## 5 Irregular Comparatives

| The adjectives *good*, *bad*, and *fun* have **irregular** comparative forms. | |
|---|---|
| • *good* → *better* | Pop music is **better than** rap for dancing. |
| • *bad* → *worse* | Rap is **worse than** pop music for dancing. |
| • *fun* → *more fun* | For me, volleyball is **more fun than** baseball. |

## 6 *Which* and *Who*

| Use *which* to ask about a comparison of things or places. | A: **Which** is **better**, soda or juice? <br> B: I think juice is **better** (**than** soda). |
|---|---|
| Use *who* to ask about people. | A: **Who**'s **older**, you or your cousin? <br> B: I am. I'm twenty-five, and he's twenty-three. |

## REFERENCE NOTES

For **definitions of grammar terms**, see the Glossary on page 375.

For more information on **adjectives**, see Unit 14 on page 154.

## EXERCISE 1   DISCOVER THE GRAMMAR

**A** GRAMMAR NOTES 1–6   **Read the email. Underline all the comparative adjectives.**

---

**To:** Ian
**Fr:** Laura
**Re:** Party

Hi Ian,

Our party is on Friday, June 10, at 6:00. People are usually <u>busier</u> on Saturday than any other night, and sometimes the traffic is worse on Saturday. So we think Friday is easier than Saturday.

We need food for the barbecue. We want to have hamburgers because steaks are more expensive than hamburgers. But we need something else to barbecue, too. What do you think? Which is better, chicken or hot dogs? I think hot dogs are better than chicken, and they're cheaper and quicker. Also, we have chips and nuts for snacks, but some people don't like chips. Vegetables are healthier. Right?

Please bring some hip-hop music. Bring some video games, too, but don't bring any movies. Video games are more interesting than movies, and they're more fun, too.

See you Friday!

Laura

---

**B**   **Write each adjective from A in the correct category in the chart.**

| Short (One-Syllable) Adjectives | Two-Syllable Adjectives That End in -y | Long Adjectives | Irregular Adjectives |
|---|---|---|---|
|  | *busier* |  |  |
|  |  |  |  |

# EXERCISE 2  COMPARATIVES WITH *THAN*

GRAMMAR NOTE 1  Complete the sentences with phrases from the box and *than*.

| | | | |
|---|---|---|---|
| at the supermarket | classical music | ~~romantic movies~~ | your bike |
| card games | the weather on Tuesday | *Star Trek* | |

1. Scary movies are more exciting *than romantic movies* .

2. I think *Star Wars* is better _____ .

3. Drinks are more expensive at movie theaters _____ .

4. Computer games are more fun _____ .

5. Rock music is better at a party _____ .

6. The weather on Friday was worse _____ .

7. My bike is faster _____ . It's also newer.

# EXERCISE 3  COMPARATIVE FORMS

GRAMMAR NOTES 2–5  Complete the sentences. Circle the correct answers.

1. Hamburgers are more good / (better) than fish for a barbecue.

2. They're cheaper / more cheap, too.

3. Video games are more fun / funner than DVDs.

4. This movie is funnier / more funny than that one.

5. Some people think classical music is interestinger / more interesting than pop music.

6. Gail is friendlier / more friendly than Gertrude.

7. Heavy metal is more bad / worse than rap for dancing.

# EXERCISE 4  COMPARATIVE QUESTIONS

GRAMMAR NOTES 1–6  Put the words in the correct order. Make questions.

1. *Which is worse, cafeteria food or restaurant food* ?
   (worse, / cafeteria food or / is / Which / restaurant food)

2. _____ ?
   (father / you / taller / Are / your / than)

3. _____ ?
   (fun / than DVDs / Are / more / computer games)

4. _____ ?
   (tastier, / is / Which / cake or / ice cream)

5. _____ ?
   (Which / more / baseball games / football games or / are / entertaining,)

6. _____ ?
   (funnier, / Who / Amy Schumer / is / or Chris Rock)

# EXERCISE 5  COMPARATIVE STATEMENTS

**A** GRAMMAR NOTES 1–5  **Look at the picture. Compare the people. Use the words in parentheses.**

1. _Ken is taller than Marty._
   (Marty / Ken / tall)

2. _____
   (Marty / Ken / old)

3. _____
   (Marty's clothes / Ken's clothes / colorful)

4. _____
   (Mi Young / Laura / short)

5. _____
   (Mi Young's hair / Laura's hair / straight)

6. _____ at dancing.
   (Lisa / David / good)

7. _____ at singing.
   (Jason / Maia / bad)

**B**  **Write questions with *Who* about the people in A. Use the words in parentheses. Then answer the questions.**

1. _Who is shorter, Marty or David?_        _Marty._
   (Who / short / Marty / David)

2. _____        _____
   (Who / young / Ken / Marty)

3. _____        _____
   (Who / good at singing / Jason / Maia)

# EXERCISE 6  EDITING

GRAMMAR NOTES 1–6  There are six mistakes in Ben Olson's composition. The first mistake is corrected. Find and correct five more.

Ben Olson

## Which Are Better, Dogs or Cats?

In my opinion, a dog is a ~~gooder~~ *better* pet than a cat. I know

because we have a dog and a cat at home. Our dog is funny

and entertaining, but the cat is boring.

Here are my reasons. First, a dog is friendly than a cat. My

dog is more happy to see me when I come home. Our cat just

doesn't care. Second, a dog is activer. I always take our dog

for a walk. I don't do that with the cat. She only wants to

sleep. Third, a dog is interesting than a cat. Our dog is very

entertaining because he knows a lot of tricks. My cat doesn't

know any tricks at all. Dogs are just more funner than cats.

I think dogs rule.

## EXERCISE 7   LISTENING

▶15|02   Ⓐ   **Listen to Ken's conversation with his grandmother. Check (✓) the subjects Grandma and Ken talk about.**

| | | |
|---|---|---|
| ☐ classes | ☐ Ken's parents | ☐ TV shows |
| ☐ vacations | ☐ food | ☐ sports |

▶15|02   Ⓑ   **Listen again. For each statement, check (✓) True, False, or No Information.**

| | True | False | No Information |
|---|:---:|:---:|:---:|
| 1. Ken's classes are easier than they were last semester. | ☐ | ✓ | ☐ |
| 2. Ken is taking a Spanish class this semester. | ☐ | ☐ | ☐ |
| 3. Ken says his music class is easier than his chemistry class. | ☐ | ☐ | ☐ |
| 4. The chemistry teacher gives higher grades than the music teacher. | ☐ | ☐ | ☐ |
| 5. Ken's friends want him to play the guitar in their band. | ☐ | ☐ | ☐ |
| 6. Ken plays on the school basketball team. | ☐ | ☐ | ☐ |
| 7. Ken thinks basketball is more interesting than music. | ☐ | ☐ | ☐ |
| 8. Ken thinks cheesecake is better than brownies. | ☐ | ☐ | ☐ |

Ⓒ   **Work with a partner. Discuss these questions.**

1. Compare school subjects. Which subjects are harder than other subjects? More interesting?

   EXAMPLE:   Computer science is harder than English, but I think English is
   more interesting...

2. Compare different forms of entertainment. Which activities are more fun than others? Why?

# EXERCISE 8  WHO'S FUNNIER?

**A** SURVEY  Work in a group of four. In the first column in the chart, write a question for each topic. Use *which* and *who* and the comparative form of each adjective. Ask and answer each question. Write students' answers in the chart.

| Topic / Adjective | Student 1 | Student 2 | Student 3 | Student 4 |
|---|---|---|---|---|
| School subject / hard | | | | |
| Actor / funny | | | | |
| Music / good for dancing | | | | |
| Entertainment activities / interesting | | | | |

EXAMPLE:  A:  Which is harder, algebra or psychology?
              B:  I think algebra is harder.
              C:  Who is funnier, . . . or . . . ?

**B** Discuss the results of your survey. Then report your answers to the class.

EXAMPLE:  Three people in our group think algebra is harder than psychology, but one person thinks psychology is harder.

# EXERCISE 9  A REALLY GOOD PARTY

**A** DISCUSSION  Make plans for a party. Think about the topics in the list below. Write down several ideas for a party. Then work in a small group. Discuss your ideas. Decide on the things everyone likes.

EXAMPLE:  A:  For the party food, I think hamburgers are good.
              B:  I think pizza is better than hamburgers. It's easier and it's quicker.

- Food
- Location
- Drinks
- Number of people
- Entertainment

**B** Tell the class about your group's plans for the party. The class votes on the best party plan.

**A** BEFORE YOU WRITE  Read the paragraph. Underline the comparative adjectives. Complete the chart about your favorite kind of entertainment. Compare it to other kinds of entertainment. Then work with a partner. Tell your partner about your favorite kind of entertainment.

Board games are my favorite kind of entertainment. I have two main reasons. First, board games are more fun because they are more interesting than other games. Second, board games are harder than other games. In board games, the winner is usually smarter than the other players.

| My Favorite Entertainment | Reason 1 | Reason 2 |
|---|---|---|
|  |  |  |

**B** WRITE  Write a paragraph about your favorite type of entertainment. Use comparative adjectives. Use the paragraph in A and your chart to help you.

**C** CHECK YOUR WORK  Read your paragraph. Underline the comparative adjectives. Use the Editing Checklist to check your work.

**Editing Checklist**

Did you use . . . ?

- [ ] -er endings for comparative forms of one-syllable adjectives
- [ ] -ier endings for two-syllable adjectives ending in -y
- [ ] more + adjective for long comparative adjectives
- [ ] correct comparative forms for good, bad, and fun

**D** REVISE YOUR WORK  Read your paragraph again. Can you improve your writing? Make changes if necessary.

# UNIT 15 REVIEW

**Test yourself on the grammar of the unit.**

**A** Complete the sentences. Use the comparative forms of the words in parentheses.

1. Board games are _____ than card games.
   (fun)

2. Plays are sometimes _____ than movies.
   (exciting)

3. Video games are _____ than card games.
   (hard)

4. The book was _____ than the movie.
   (good)

5. The weather is _____ this week than it was last week.
   (bad)

6. Chips are _____ than nuts.
   (tasty)

**B** Put the words in the correct order. Make questions.

1. _____ ?
   (entertaining, / is / Which / New York / or / Los Angeles / more)

2. _____ ?
   (than / Are amusement parks / interesting / more / museums)

3. _____ ?
   (sister / older, / your / you or / Who / is)

**C** Correct the description. There are six mistakes.

   I have two interesting pen pals—Jomo and Abla. They are brother and sister, and

they live in Tanzania. Jomo is more older than Abla, and he is also more large. He's

more tall and he's heavyer. Abla is a gooder student, but she's more bad than Jomo at

sports. They go to the same school. It's more crowded than my school.

**Now check your answers on page 381.**

# Present Progressive and *Can*

# PART 6

**OUTCOMES**

- Use the present progressive to talk about events that are happening now
- Complete sentences about an email
- Identify true and false sentences about a conversation
- Describe pictures and talk about what is happening in them
- Write a conversation about what is happening in photos

**OUTCOMES**

- Ask and answer *yes/no* questions in the present progressive
- Answer questions about a reading and a conversation
- Ask and answer questions about events that are happening now
- Write a conversation about what family members are doing

**OUTCOMES**

- Ask and answer *wh-* questions in the present progressive
- Answer questions about a reading and a conversation
- Ask and answer questions about where people are going
- Ask and answer questions about what is happening in photos
- Write a conversation between people meeting at an airport

**OUTCOMES**

- Use *can/can't* to talk about abilities
- Answer questions about a reading
- Complete sentences about a conversation
- Talk about your classmates' abilities
- Write a paragraph about the abilities of a person you know

# Present Progressive: Statements

## FRIENDS FROM LONG AGO

**OUTCOMES**
- Use the present progressive to talk about events that are happening now
- Complete sentences about an email
- Identify true and false sentences about a conversation
- Describe pictures and talk about what is happening in them
- Write a conversation about what is happening in photos

## STEP 1 GRAMMAR IN CONTEXT

### BEFORE YOU READ

**Ⓐ VOCABULARY** Study the words. Then complete the sentences. Write the picture numbers.

**look for**

**look at**

**wait for**

lose

win

1. In picture __4__, she is winning the race.
2. In picture _____, she is looking for her keys.
3. In picture _____, he is waiting for a friend.
4. In picture _____, they are looking at a photo.
5. In picture _____, he is losing the race.

**Ⓑ** Work with a partner. Compare your answers in A.

## READE

**Read this email from Jessica to her friend Lauren.**

# A Friend from Long Ago

Dear Lauren,

I was so happy to hear from you. Of course I remember you. You were one of my best friends in high school!

I'm living in Redmond now with my husband and children. Here are some photos of us.

Tim is my husband. He's in the first photo. He has brown hair, and he's wearing a gray sweatshirt. He's sitting next to my brother, Steve. They're watching a baseball game. They're not smiling because their team is losing. I'm sure you remember Steve. Believe it or not, he's a professor now.

I'm in the second photo between my mom and dad. We're not smiling because we're hungry. We're waiting for the game to end.

In the last photo, my son Jeremy is in the chair. He's fifteen. He's looking at his phone, and he's texting friends. He loves that phone! Annie and Ben are playing cards. Annie is ten, and Ben is seven. They keep us busy.

Call when you're in Seattle. I can't wait to see you. Maybe we can see our old friend Sylvia, too. I know she lives in Seattle. I don't have her phone number, but I can look for it.

Your friend from long ago,
Jessica

## AFTER YOU READ

**A** COMPREHENSION **Look at Jessica's email again. Complete the sentences. Circle the correct answers.**

1. Tim is wearing a gray sweatshirt / gray pants.

2. Steve and Tim are watching soccer / baseball.

3. Steve and Tim are not smiling because their team isn't winning / they're hungry.

4. Jessica is standing between her mom and dad / her son and daughter.

5. Jeremy is texting friends / classmates.

6. Annie and Ben are playing ball / cards.

**B** **Work with a partner. Compare your answers in A.**

## PRESENT PROGRESSIVE: STATEMENTS

### Affirmative Statements

| Am | Is | Are |
|---|---|---|
| I **am listening**. | He **is standing**.<br>She **is sitting**.<br>It **is raining**. | We **are sitting**.<br>You **are standing**.<br>They **are smiling**. |

### Contractions

| | | |
|---|---|---|
| **I'm** listening. | **He's** standing.<br>**She's** sitting.<br>**It's** raining. | **We're** sitting.<br>**You're** standing.<br>**They're** smiling. |

### Negative Statements

| Am not | Is not | Are not |
|---|---|---|
| I **am not talking**. | He **is not standing**.<br>She **is not reading**.<br>It **is not snowing**. | We **are not working**.<br>You **are not listening**.<br>They **are not working**. |

### Contractions

| | | |
|---|---|---|
| **I'm not** talking. | **He's not** standing.<br>Jeremy **isn't** listening.<br>**She's not** talking.<br>Annie **isn't** talking.<br>**It's not** snowing. | **We're not** talking.<br>Tim and I **aren't** talking.<br>**You're not** talking.<br>You and Annie **aren't** talking.<br>**They're not** talking.<br>Tim and Jeremy **aren't** talking. |

## GRAMMAR NOTES

### 1 Present Progressive: Uses

Use the **present progressive** to talk about an action or event that is **happening now**.

I **am sitting** next to Maria.
Jon **is texting**.
We **are talking**.

## 2 Affirmative Statements

| | |
|---|---|
| Use a form of *be* + the **verb** + *-ing* to form the present progressive. <br><br> • *listen* <br> • *talk* <br> • *stand* | I **am listening**. <br> She **is talking**. <br> We **are standing**. |
| We often use **contractions** in speaking and informal writing. | I**'m listening**. <br> She**'s talking**. <br> We**'re standing**. |
| If the **base form** of the verb **ends in** *-e*, drop the *-e* and add *-ing*. <br><br> • *write* | He is writ**ing**. |
| If the base form of the verb is **one syllable** and it ends in **consonant + vowel + consonant**, **double the last consonant**. Then add *-ing*. <br><br> • *run* <br> • *sit* <br> • *shop* | She is run**ning**. <br> They are sit**ting**. <br> We are shop**ping**. |
| **BE CAREFUL!** Do not double the last consonant if the verb ends in *-w*, *-x*, or *-y*. <br><br> • *grow* <br> • *fix* <br> • *play* | We are grow**ing** tomatoes. <br> He is fix**ing** his computer. <br> She is play**ing** ball. |
| **BE CAREFUL!** When one subject refers to two verbs, do not repeat a form of *be*. | He's eating and watching TV. <br> **NOT** He's eating and ~~is~~ watching TV. |

## 3 Negative Statements

| | |
|---|---|
| Use a form of *be* + *not* + the **verb** + *-ing* for **negative statements**. | I **am not wearing** a hat. <br> He **is not talking**. <br> They **are not reading**. |
| We usually use **contractions** in speaking and informal writing. | I**'m not wearing** a hat. <br> She**'s not smiling**. |
| There are **two contractions** for *is not* and *are not*. | Jeremy **isn't talking**. **or** He**'s not talking**. <br> Annie and Ben **aren't reading**. **or** They**'re not reading**. |

## REFERENCE NOTES

For **definitions of grammar terms**, see the Glossary on page 375.

For information on **present progressive questions**, see Unit 17 on page 191 and Unit 18 on page 201.

For information on **present progressive spelling rules**, see Appendix 16 on page 371.

## EXERCISE 1  DISCOVER THE GRAMMAR

**A** **GRAMMAR NOTES 1–3**  Read the email to Jessica from Lauren. Underline all examples of the present progressive.

Hi Jessica,

I'm at the airport in New York, and I'm sitting and waiting for my plane. It's snowing here and my flight is late. My new arrival time is 2:30.

I'm looking at your photos, and I'm smiling. Tim looks like your first boyfriend, Adam. But Tim isn't wearing torn jeans, and he has short hair and a mustache. Your daughter Annie looks just like you. In the photo, she's wearing a purple T-shirt. Purple was your favorite color in high school. Is it still your favorite color? Is it her favorite color, too?

You don't have a photo of me. But I look the same as in high school. I look eighteen! (I'm just kidding!¹) Oh, and I have blond hair now.

See you soon!

Lauren

---

1 *just kidding:* I'm not serious. I'm joking.

**B** Look at the email in A again. For each statement, check (✓) *True*, *False*, or *No Information*.

| | True | False | No Information |
|---|:---:|:---:|:---:|
| 1. Lauren often waits for planes. | ☐ | ☐ | ☑ |
| 2. Lauren is waiting for a plane now. | ☐ | ☐ | ☐ |
| 3. It snows a lot in New York. | ☐ | ☐ | ☐ |
| 4. It's snowing in New York now. | ☑ | ☐ | ☐ |
| 5. Tim is wearing torn jeans. | ☐ | ☐ | ☐ |
| 6. Tim often wears torn jeans. | ☐ | ☐ | ☐ |
| 7. Annie is wearing a purple T-shirt in the photo. | ☑ | ☐ | ☐ |
| 8. Annie wears purple a lot. | ☐ | ☐ | ☐ |

# EXERCISE 2 AFFIRMATIVE STATEMENTS

GRAMMAR NOTES 1–2 Complete the sentences. Use the present progressive forms of the verbs in the box. Do not use contractions.

| carry | cook | fix | listen to | look at | look for | play | rain | wait for | write |
|-------|------|-----|-----------|---------|----------|------|------|----------|-------|

1. Joe ____is____ ____waiting____ ____for____ his brother.

2. Li Heng ____ ____playing____ computer games with a friend in China.

3. Eduarda ____ ____looking____ ____for____ her book bag. Is it under the table?

4. Bea ____ ____cooking____ chicken and rice.

5. Grandpa and Dad ____are____ ____fixing____ the car.

6. Maria ____ ____writing____ an email to her friend.

7. It ____ ____raining____ outside.

8. People ____are____ ____carrying____ umbrellas.

9. Oscar ____is____ ____listening____ ____to____ music. Music helps him relax.

10. My aunt ____ ____looking____ ____at____ pictures from long ago. She's smiling because everyone looks young in the pictures.

# EXERCISE 3 PRESENT PROGRESSIVE

**A** GRAMMAR NOTES 1–3 Complete the conversation. Use the words in parentheses and the present progressive. Use contractions when possible.

JESSICA: This is a picture of me when I was sixteen years old.

TIM: ____You're kidding!____
1. (You / kid)

JESSICA: No. Really. ____I'm wearing____ sunglasses and a funny hat. My hair is long,
2. (I / wear)

and ____I'm not wearing____ makeup.
3. (I / not / wear)

TIM: Oh. Well, what are you doing?

JESSICA: _____ cards.
4. (Lauren and I / play)

TIM: That's Lauren? She looks very unhappy.

JESSICA: She is unhappy. It's hot and _____ in the sun.
5. (she / sit)

_____ the game. Lauren hates hot weather.
6. (She / lose)

_____ a good day. _____ about her
7. (She / not / have)     8. (She / think)

cool apartment.

▶ 16 02 **B** LISTEN AND CHECK Listen to the conversation and check your answers in A.

# EXERCISE 4 AFFIRMATIVE AND NEGATIVE STATEMENTS

GRAMMAR NOTES 1–3 Look at the pictures. Complete the sentences. Use the words in parentheses. Write one affirmative and one negative sentence.

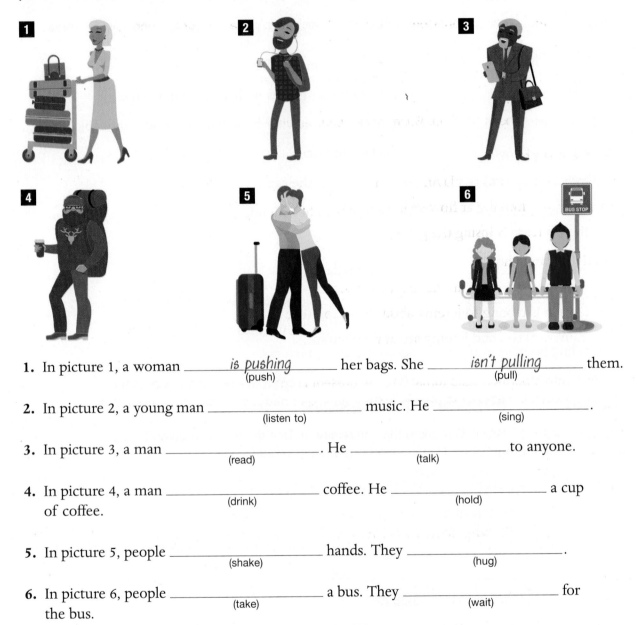

1. In picture 1, a woman _____*is pushing*_____ her bags. She _____*isn't pulling*_____ them.
   (push)                                            (pull)

2. In picture 2, a young man _____ music. He _____.
   (listen to)                                (sing)

3. In picture 3, a man _____. He _____ to anyone.
   (read)                              (talk)

4. In picture 4, a man _____ coffee. He _____ a cup
   (drink)                            (hold)
   of coffee.

5. In picture 5, people _____ hands. They _____.
   (shake)                                (hug)

6. In picture 6, people _____ a bus. They _____ for
   (take)                              (wait)
   the bus.

# EXERCISE 5 EDITING

GRAMMAR NOTES 1–3 There are five mistakes in the sentences. The first mistake is corrected. Find and correct four more.

1. She is ~~wait~~ *waiting* for her friend at the airport. She no is looking for a taxi.

2. They watching a soccer game. Their team is lose.

3. We're playing cards and are listening to music.

## EXERCISE 6 LISTENING

▶16|03 Ⓐ Listen to the conversation. Complete the sentence. Circle the correct answer.

Steve and Jessica are talking and looking at _____.

a. photos of Lauren's visit     b. photos of soccer games

▶16|03 Ⓑ Listen again. Check (✓) *True*, *False*, or *No Information*.

|  |  | True | False | No Information |
|---|---|---|---|---|
| **1.** In the first photo: |  |  |  |  |
|  | a. Steve's students are playing soccer. | ✓ | ☐ | ☐ |
|  | b. Lauren is looking at flowers in the park. | ☐ | ☐ | ☐ |
|  | c. Steve's team is losing the game. | ☐ | ☐ | ☐ |
| **2.** In the second photo: |  |  |  |  |
|  | a. Lauren and Jeremy are talking about soccer. | ☐ | ☐ | ☐ |
|  | b. Lauren is talking to Jeremy about New York University. | ☐ | ☐ | ☐ |
|  | c. Lauren, Steve, and Jeremy are at a restaurant. | ☐ | ☐ | ☐ |

Ⓒ Work with a partner. Take turns. Use the present progressive and the words in the box. Say something about the people in the listening or about you and your classmates.

| look at | play | stand | talk about | watch |
|---|---|---|---|---|

EXAMPLE: A: Eva is looking at Oscar.
B: No. Eva is looking at the board.
C: That's right. I'm not looking at Oscar.
D: In the listening, Steve's students are playing soccer in the park.

## EXERCISE 7 BEA ISN'T SLEEPING!

Ⓐ GAME Work in small groups. Take a photo of your group. Each student does something different in the photo. Use the words in the box for ideas.

Ⓑ Write three true and three false sentences about the photo. Use the present progressive.

*Bea is sleeping.*     *Oscar is looking for his phone.*

Ⓒ Give your photo and your sentences to another group. The other group finds the false sentences and changes them to true ones. Take turns.

EXAMPLE: In this photo, Bea isn't sleeping. She's listening to music.

listen to
look at
look for
play
read
sleep
smile
write

# EXERCISE 8 WHAT'S THE DIFFERENCE?

**Ⓐ PICTURE DISCUSSION** Work with a partner. Find five differences between pictures 1 and 2.

EXAMPLE: **A:** In Picture 1, the two young people are looking at a cell phone.

**B:** Right. And in Picture 2, the same people are taking pictures. I think they're students.

Picture 1

Picture 2

**Ⓑ** Work in a group. Pretend to be one of the people in the pictures in A. Your group says what you are doing.

EXAMPLE: *(A pretends to eat and look at his cell phone.)*

**B:** You're eating and looking at your cell phone.

**A:** That's right.

**A** BEFORE YOU WRITE Read a conversation between two friends. They are looking online for friends from their past. Then work with a partner. Look online for photos of friends from your past. Complete the chart about each photo. Use the present progressive. Then tell your partner about the people in your photos.

ANN: Look at this photo of Lydia and her kids. They're sitting on a beach in Virginia.

BILL: That's nice. They're having a lot of fun.

ANN: And here's a photo of her husband. He's running in a race. Here's another photo of the kids. They're singing happy birthday to their dad.

BILL: Hey, look at this photo. This is my friend Sam. He's visiting Boston.

ANN: That's a great photo of him.

| Photo #1 | |
| --- | --- |
| Photo #2 | |
| Photo #3 | |
| Photo #4 | |

**B** WRITE Write a conversation about your photos from A. Use the present progressive. Use the conversation in A and your chart to help you.

**C** CHECK YOUR WORK Read your conversation again. Underline examples of the present progressive. Use the Editing Checklist to check your work.

### Editing Checklist

**Did you . . . ?**

☐ use a form of *be* + the verb + *-ing* for affirmative statements

☐ put *not* after *be* + the verb + *-ing* for negative statements

☐ check your spelling

**D** REVISE YOUR WORK Read your conversation again. Can you improve your writing? Make changes if necessary.

# UNIT 16 **REVIEW**

**Test yourself on the grammar of the unit.**

**Ⓐ Complete the sentences. Circle the correct answers.**

1. Jeremy is listen / listening to music.

2. Ben and Annie is playing / are playing cards.

3. It not raining / isn't raining outside.

4. They're watching / watching a ball game.

5. I'm no looking / not looking for my cell phone.

**Ⓑ Complete the conversation. Use the present progressive form of the words in parentheses. Do not use contractions.**

1. Ben _____ baseball in the park.
   (play)

2. Jeremy and his friend _____ a friend in college.
   (visit)

3. Jessica and Tim _____ a friend's dog.
   (walk)

4. Annie _____.
   (sleep)

5. Steve _____ and _____ in the living room.
   (sit)                                    (read)

**Ⓒ Correct the sentences. There are four mistakes. Use contractions.**

1. He not standing. He's sitting.

2. Bob and Maya are wait for us.

3. They're listen to a CD.

4. We not playing cards.

**Now check your answers on page 381.**

# Present Progressive: *Yes/No* Questions

## ARE YOU BABYSITTING?

OUTCOMES
• Ask and answer *yes/no* questions in the present progressive
• Answer questions about a reading and a conversation
• Ask and answer questions about events that are happening now
• Write a conversation about what family members are doing

---

## STEP 1 | GRAMMAR IN CONTEXT

### BEFORE YOU READ

**A** VOCABULARY  Study the words. Then match the beginnings of the sentences with the endings.

babysit

get a haircut

clean

do laundry

_____ **1.** The woman with long hair

_____ **2.** The woman in a blue shirt

_____ **3.** The father, the son, and the daughter

_____ **4.** The man in a white t-shirt

a. is doing laundry.

b. are cleaning.

c. is babysitting.

d. is getting a haircut.

**B** Work with a partner. Compare your answers in A.

# A Night Out

**TIM:**  Hi, hon. Happy anniversary![1]

**JESSICA:** Thanks!

**TIM:**  Is everyone OK at home? Is Jeremy watching Ben and Annie?

**JESSICA:** No. Jeremy's at a basketball game with Steve.

**TIM:**  Oh. So, are your parents watching them?

**JESSICA:** No. Their party is tomorrow. So they're cooking and doing laundry.

**TIM:**  Oh, right. Is Mrs. Brown babysitting?

**JESSICA:** No. She's busy, too. Her granddaughter Kelly is watching the kids.

*(Later. Jessica calls Kelly.)*

**KELLY:** Hello?

**JESSICA:** Hi, Kelly. This is Mrs. Olson. How's everything? Are the children listening to you?

**KELLY:** Sure. Everything's fine.

**JESSICA:** Are you helping Ben with his math? Is he doing all his homework?

**KELLY:** No, not now. He's cooking something. It's for you.

**JESSICA:** Oh? Is he cleaning up, too? I hope so. What about Annie? Is she studying for her science test?

**KELLY:** I think so. Her friend Gail is here. They're in Annie's room and it's quiet. They're probably studying.

**JESSICA:** Kelly, please go to her room and check.

**KELLY:** OK, Mrs. Olson. Look. Don't worry. Everything's cool.[2] Enjoy your anniversary dinner.

**JESSICA:** Thanks, Kelly. See you at around 10:00.

**KELLY:** See you then. Bye.

1 *anniversary:* the month and day that two people got married
2 *cool:* OK

## AFTER YOU READ

**A** COMPREHENSION **Look at the conversations again. Circle the correct answers.**

**1.** Are Tim and Jessica celebrating their anniversary?

   **a.** Yes, they are.        **b.** No, they aren't.

**2.** Is Mrs. Brown babysitting?

   **a.** Yes, she is.          **b.** No, she isn't.

**3.** Who is Kelly?

   **a.** Jessica's daughter     **b.** Mrs. Brown's granddaughter

**4.** Is Kelly helping Ben with his math?

   **a.** No, she isn't.        **b.** Yes, she is.

**5.** Are Annie and Gail studying?

   **a.** Yes, they are.        **b.** No, they aren't.

**6.** Is Gail getting a haircut?

   **a.** Yes, she is.          **b.** No, she isn't.

**B** **Work with a partner. Compare your answers in A.**

## STEP 2    GRAMMAR PRESENTATION

## PRESENT PROGRESSIVE: *YES/NO* QUESTIONS

| *Yes/No* Questions | Short Answers | | |
|---|---|---|---|
| **Am** I **making** a mess? | Yes, you **are**. | No, you**'re not**.   or | No, you **aren't**. |
| **Is** he **studying**? | Yes, he **is**. | No, he**'s not**.   or | No, he **isn't**. |
| **Are** they **playing**? | Yes, they **are**. | No, they**'re not**.   or | No, they **aren't**. |

## GRAMMAR NOTES

**1** **Present Progressive: *Yes/No* Questions**

| | |
|---|---|
| In a *yes/no* **question** in the present progressive, put *am*, *is*, or *are* before the subject. | SUBJECT<br>You  **are working**. *(statement)*<br><br>SUBJECT<br>**Are**  you  **working**? *(question)* |

## 2 Short Answers

| | |
|---|---|
| We often use **short answers** in speaking and informal writing. | A: Are you doing your homework?<br>B: **Yes, I am.** or **Yes.**<br>C: **No, I'm not.** or **No.** |
| **BE CAREFUL!** **Don't use contractions** in affirmative short answers. | A: Is he reading?<br>B: Yes, **he is.**<br>NOT Yes, ~~he's.~~ |

## STEP 3 FOCUSED PRACTICE

## EXERCISE 1 DISCOVER THE GRAMMAR

**A** GRAMMAR NOTES 1–2 Underline the questions in the present progressive. Then look at the cartoon. Match the questions and answers.

_d_ 1. Are the parents going out?

____ 2. Are the parents coming home?

____ 3. Is the babysitter asleep?

____ 4. Is the babysitter reading?

____ 5. Is the little boy eating a sandwich?

____ 6. Is the little boy asleep?

~~a.~~ No, they aren't.

**b.** Yes, he is.

**c.** No, he isn't.

**d.** Yes, they are.

**e.** No, she isn't.

**f.** Yes, she is.

**B** Look at the cartoon again. Why does the little boy say, "Now you need to pay me. Right?" Check (✓) the correct answer.

☑ The babysitter is not babysitting.

☐ The little boy is not sleeping.

**DENNIS THE MENACE**

"The sitter is sleeping. Now you
need to pay me. Right?"

# EXERCISE 2 YES/NO QUESTIONS

GRAMMAR NOTE 1  Complete the questions with the present progressive of the verbs in parentheses.

1. (get)    A: _____ *Is* _____ Victor _____ *getting* _____ a haircut?
            B: Yes, he is. His hair was really long.

2. (do)     A: _____ *Are* _____ the kids _____ *doing* _____ homework?
            B: No. They're playing outside.

3. (clean)  A: _____ *Is* _____ your brother _____ *cleanning* _____?
            B: No. He's watching TV. He never cleans. I always do.

4. (help)   A: _____ *Are* _____ you _____ *helping* _____ Grandpa in the garden?
            B: Yes, we are, Mom.

5. (sleep)  A: _____ *Is* _____ Jay _____ *sleeping* _____ at our house today?
            B: I don't know. Ask Bill.

6. (rain)   A: _____ *Is* _____ it _____ *raining* _____ in California now?
            B: Yes, it is.

# EXERCISE 3 YES/NO QUESTIONS AND ANSWERS

**A** GRAMMAR NOTES 1–2  Complete the conversation. Write yes/no questions and answers. Use the present progressive and the correct forms of the words in parentheses.

MIA:    What's that noise? _____ *Are you playing a game* _____ on your phone?
        **1.** (you / play / a game)

KELLY:  No, I'm not. _____ *I'm texting* _____
        **2.** (I / text.)

MIA:    Oh. _____ *Are you texting your mom?* _____
        **3.** (you / text / your mom?)

KELLY:  Well... No, I'm not. _____ *I'm texting Jeremy!* _____
        **4.** (I / text / Jeremy!)

MIA:    Jeremy?? _____ *Are you talking about Jeremy Olson?* _____
        **5.** (you / talk / about Jeremy Olson?)

KELLY:  Yes, I am!

MIA:    Wow!... Why? _____ *Are you asking him* _____ about homework?
        **6.** (you / ask / him)

KELLY:  No. _____ *I'm not answering a texting* _____ from him! He wants to take me to
        **7.** (I / answer / a text)
        the Bruno Mars concert!

MIA:    What?? _____ *Are you kidding?* _____
        **8.** (you / kid?)

KELLY:  Yes. _____ *I'm kidding* _____. _____ *He isn't texting me* _____
        **9.** (I / kid.)                      **10.** (He / not / text / me.)
        _____ *My mom texting me* _____. She wants me to come home.
        **11.** (My mom / text / me.)

🔊 17|02  **B** LISTEN AND CHECK  Listen to the conversation and check your answers in A.

# EXERCISE 4  *YES/NO* QUESTIONS AND SHORT ANSWERS

GRAMMAR NOTES 1–2  Write *yes/no* questions and short answers. Use the present progressive and the correct forms of the words in parentheses. Use contractions when possible.

1. (Dad / watch / the game?)

   A: *Is Dad watching the game?*

   B: No, *he isn't* .

2. (the kids / eat chips?)

   A: *Are the kids eating chips?*

   B: No, *they aren't* .

3. (it / rain?)

   A: *Is it raining?*

   B: Yes, *it is* .

4. (Dan / get / a haircut?)

   A: *Is Dan getting a haircut?*

   B: No, *he isn't* .

5. (Dahlia and Jonathan / celebrate / their anniversary?)

   A: *Are Dahlia and Jonathan celebrating their anniversary?*

   B: Yes, *they are* .

# EXERCISE 5  EDITING

GRAMMAR NOTES 1–2  There are five mistakes in the conversation. The first mistake is corrected. Find and correct four more.

LISA: Is Dad ~~help~~ *helping* you with your homework?

ROB: No, he don't. Grandma is. Dad is do the laundry.

LISA: Is the baby OK? Is Grandpa watches him?

ROB: Yes.

LISA: Are Aunt Janet and Uncle Dan cook?

ROB: Yes, they are. They're making chicken and pasta.

## EXERCISE 6   LISTENING

▶17|03   **A**   Listen to the telephone conversation between Steve and his sister Jessica. Circle the two things Steve is doing now.

**a.** He's cleaning.     **c.** He's doing laundry.     **e.** He's playing basketball.

**b.** He's cooking.     **d.** He's playing a computer game.     **f.** He's writing.

▶17|03   **B**   Listen again. Answer the questions. Use short answers.

**1.** Is Steve writing an article for *The Daily Times* website?    *Yes, he is.* _____

**2.** Is Ben playing with Steve's gift?    _____

**3.** Is Annie cleaning her room?    _____

**4.** Is Annie playing basketball?    _____

**5.** Is Annie writing for *The Daily Times*?    _____

**6.** Is Annie writing for her school paper?    _____

**C**   Work with a partner. Take turns. Ask and answer *yes/no* questions in the present progressive. Give a time and ask about your partner and his friends and family. Use the words in the box or your own words.

| cook | do laundry | write an article for a website |
|------|------------|-------------------------------|
| clean | play computer games | write a paper for school |

EXAMPLE:   **A:** It's 7:00 p.m. Is your mother cooking dinner?
         **B:** No, she isn't. My father is cooking dinner. . . . It's Saturday afternoon. Are you cleaning?
         **A:** No, I'm not. I'm . . .

## EXERCISE 7   IS DOV LOOKING AT HIS BOOK?

CONVERSATION   Work with a partner. Look at your classmates. What are they doing? Ask *yes/no* questions with the present progressive.

EXAMPLE:   **A:** Is Dov looking at his book?
         **B:** Yes, he is. . . . Is Maria helping Carmen?
         **A:** No, she isn't. She's helping Keiko. . . . Are Ali and Hye Won writing?
         **B:** Yes, they are.

## EXERCISE 8 ARE YOU TALKING ON THE PHONE?

**A** CHARADES  Write two sentences in the present progressive on two pieces of paper. Use *you* and verbs from the box or your own verbs. Then you and your classmates put your sentences in a bag.

| | | | |
|---|---|---|---|
| babysit | do laundry | get a haircut | talk on the phone |
| clean | drink | help | worry |
| cook | eat | look for | write |

**B**  Pick a sentence from the bag and then act it out. You can work with a partner. The class asks *yes/no* questions to guess the action. Take turns.

> *You're talking on the phone.*

EXAMPLE:  **A:** Are you talking on the phone?
  **B:** Yes, I am.

## EXERCISE 9  IS THE FATHER READING?

**A**  GAME  Work in groups of three. Student A looks at the picture below for one minute. Then he or she closes his or her book. Students B and C ask *yes/no* questions about the photo.

EXAMPLE:  *(A closes his book.)*
  **B:** Is the father reading?
  **A:** No, he isn't. He's watching TV.
  **C:** Is the boy near the TV wearing a red shirt?
  **A:** Yes, he is.
  **C:** No, he isn't. He's wearing a blue shirt.

**B**  Find two more pictures in this book. Student B looks at one of the pictures, and then closes his or her book. Students A and C ask *yes/no* questions about the photo. Then Student C looks at the other picture and Students A and B ask *yes/no* questions about it. Who remembers the most about their picture?

# FROM GRAMMAR TO WRITING

**A** BEFORE YOU WRITE  Read a phone conversation between two sisters. Then imagine a phone conversation with someone in your family. Ask about other family members. In the chart, write the names of your family members and present progressive *yes/no* questions about them.

ALIA:  Hi, Stefa.

STEFA:  Hi, Alia. How are you?

ALIA:  Great. And you?

STEFA:  Good. So, how's Mom? Is she working now?

ALIA:  No. She's isn't working. She's watching Borys.

STEFA:  Is Dad helping her?

ALINA:  No, he isn't. He's helping Uncle Marek at the bakery.

STEFA:  Oh. That's good. What about Pavel? Is he studying?

ALINA:  Yes, he is.

| Family Member | Yes/No Questions |
|---|---|
|  |  |
|  |  |
|  |  |
|  |  |
|  |  |

**B** WRITE  Write a conversation between you and a family member. Ask about other family members. Use *yes/no* questions in the present progressive. Use the conversation in A and your chart to help you.

**C** CHECK YOUR WORK  Read your conversation again. Underline *yes/no* questions in the present progressive. Use the Editing Checklist to check your work.

### Editing Checklist

**Did you...?**

☐ begin *yes/no* questions with the verb *be* (*am, is, are*)

☐ follow *be* with the subject + the verb + *-ing*

☐ use the present progressive for something happening now

☐ check your spelling

**D** REVISE YOUR WORK  Read your questions again. Can you improve them? Make changes if necessary.

# UNIT 17 REVIEW

**Test yourself on the grammar of the unit.**

**A** Match the questions and answers.

_____ **1.** Is Jon cooking?

_____ **2.** Is your sister babysitting?

_____ **3.** Are you doing your homework?

_____ **4.** Am I helping you?

_____ **5.** Are they studying Spanish?

**a.** Yes, you are. Thank you.

**b.** No, they aren't.

**c.** No, he isn't.

**d.** No, I'm not. I'm reading.

**e.** Yes, she is. She's watching Bobby.

**B** Write questions and complete the answers. Use the present progressive and the words in parentheses. Use contractions whenever possible.

**1.** (Ron / get a haircut)

A: _Is Ron getting a haircut?_____

B: Yes, _He is_____.

**2.** (Dan and Janet / celebrate their anniversary)

A: _Are Dan and Janet celebrating their anniversary?_____

B: No, _they aren't_____. They're celebrating Janet's birthday.

**3.** (it / rain)

A: _Is it raining_____?_____

B: Yes, _it is_____. Take your umbrella.

**C** Correct the conversations. There are four mistakes.

**1.** A: Is Annie clean her room?

B: No, she not. She's writing a story.

**2.** A: Is Ben and Jeremy doing homework?

B: No, they isn't. But it's OK. Tomorrow is a school holiday.

**Now check your answers on pages 381–382.**

# Present Progressive: *Wh-* Questions

## GETTING AROUND

**OUTCOMES**
- Ask and answer *wh-* questions in the present progressive
- Answer questions about a reading and a conversation
- Ask and answer questions about where people are going
- Ask and answer questions about what is happening in photos
- Write a conversation between people meeting at an airport

---

## STEP 1    GRAMMAR IN CONTEXT

### BEFORE YOU READ

VOCABULARY   Study the words. Then work with a partner. Ask and answer *yes/no* questions about the people in each picture. Take turns.

EXAMPLE:   *(Student A points to Picture 1.)*
> A: Is he taking a train?
> B: No, he's not. He's riding a bike.

ride a bike

take the subway / take the metro

take a train

fly

🔘 18|01   Read this conversation.

# Nick's Travels

MARK:  Hello?

NICK:   Hey, little brother . . . what's happening?

MARK:  Nick? Is it really you?

NICK:   Yes. This is your big brother.

MARK:  I don't believe this. Why are you calling me? You hate phones.

NICK:   I know. . . . But you don't answer your emails.

MARK:  What are you doing? Are you still in Kenya?

NICK:   No, I'm back in the United States. I'm going to a job interview[1] in San Francisco.

MARK:  In California? Wow! Do you want to leave Kenya?

NICK:   I'm not sure. Maybe.

MARK:  How are you getting to San Francisco? I think I hear a car engine. Are you taking a bus?

NICK:   No, I'm riding a bike.

MARK:  Come on!

NICK:   OK, I'm taking the subway.

MARK:  Get serious, Nick!

NICK:   OK. You still have good ears. Right now we're driving through Utah.

MARK:  It's a long way from Utah to San Francisco. People usually fly. Why are you driving?

NICK:   I'm spending time with an old friend. Do you remember Jerry Gomez? He's driving me to San Francisco.

MARK:  Sure, I remember him. How's Jerry these days?

NICK:   He's fine. Hey, here's an idea. Come and visit us in San Francisco.

MARK:  Good idea, but I don't want to fly. It's too expensive.

NICK:   Take a train. It's not so expensive.

MARK:  I'll think about it.

---

1  *interview:* a meeting to find a job

## AFTER YOU READ

**A** COMPREHENSION Look at the conversation again. Circle the correct answers.

**1.** Who is Nick calling?
   **a.** His friend.                          **b.** His brother.

**2.** Why is Nick calling?
   **a.** Mark doesn't answer his emails.       **b.** Nick loves phones.

**3.** Where is Nick?
   **a.** In Kenya.                             **b.** In the United States.

**4.** How is Nick getting to San Francisco?
   **a.** He's driving.                         **b.** He's taking the train.

**5.** Who is Nick traveling with?
   **a.** His brother.                          **b.** His friend.

**6.** Does Mark want to go to San Francisco?
   **a.** Yes, he does.                         **b.** No, he doesn't.

**B** Work with a partner. Compare your answers in A.

## STEP 2   GRAMMAR PRESENTATION

## PRESENT PROGRESSIVE: *WH-* QUESTIONS

| Wh- Questions | | | | | Short Answers |
| --- | --- | --- | --- | --- | --- |
| **Wh- Word** | *Be* | Subject | Verb + *-ing* | | |
| What | are | you | **making**? | | Coffee. |
| Where | are | you | **going**? | | To an interview. |
| Why | are | you | **smiling**? | | I'm happy. |
| Who | are | you | **talking** to? | | Nick. |
| How | are | you | **doing**? | | Fine. |

| Wh- Questions About the Subject | | | | Short Answers |
| --- | --- | --- | --- | --- |
| **Wh- Word** | *Be* | Verb + *-ing* | | |
| Who | is | **calling**? | | Nick. **or** Nick is. |
| What | is | **happening**? | | Nothing. |

# GRAMMAR NOTES

## 1 Wh- Questions: Form

| | |
|---|---|
| Most **wh- questions** in the present progressive begin with a question word such as *what*, *where*, *why*, *who*, or *how*. We use a **wh- question word** + *am*, *is*, or *are* + **subject** + **the -ing form of the verb**. | WH- WORD + *BE* + SUBJECT + *-ING* FORM<br>**What** are you **doing**?<br>**Who** are you **talking** to? |

## 2 Wh- Questions About the Subject

| | |
|---|---|
| To ask present progressive **wh-** questions about the **subject** of a sentence, use a **wh- question word** + *am*, *is*, or *are* + **the -ing form of the verb**. Remember that we can use **who** or **what** to ask questions about the subject. (See Unit 12, page 131.) | WH- WORD + *BE* + *-ING* FORM<br>**Who** is **driving**?<br>**What** is **happening**? |

## 3 Short Answers

| | |
|---|---|
| We usually use **short answers** in conversation and informal writing. | A: Where is Nick going?<br>B: **To San Francisco.**<br>A: Who is driving?<br>B: **His friend.** |
| **BE CAREFUL!** Remember not to use contractions in affirmative short answers. | A: Who's driving?<br>B: **Jerry.** or **Jerry is.**<br>NOT ~~Jerry's~~. |

# REFERENCE NOTES

For **definitions of grammar terms**, see the Glossary on page 375.

For more information on **present progressive statements**, see Unit 16 on page 180.

For more information on **present progressive *yes/no* questions**, see Unit 17 on page 191.

For information on **present progressive spelling rules**, see Appendix 16 on page 371.

## EXERCISE 1　DISCOVER THE GRAMMAR

GRAMMAR NOTES 1–3　Circle the *wh-* question words. Then match the questions and the answers.

_d_ 1. (Where) are you going?　　　　　a. They're playing a board game.

____ 2. How are you getting there?　　　b. Planes are very expensive.

____ 3. Why is she driving to Chicago?　c. I'm taking the subway.

____ 4. How's the trip going?　　　　　d. To the office.

____ 5. Who is he talking to?　　　　　e. It's going great! She loves road trips.

____ 6. What are they doing right now?　f. His friend Rashid Jama.

## EXERCISE 2　*WH-* QUESTION WORDS

GRAMMAR NOTES 1–3　Complete the sentences. Circle the correct answers.

1. A: Why / (Where) are you going?

   B: To the university.

2. A: How / Why are you traveling?

   B: I'm taking the bus.

3. A: How / Why are you taking the bus?

   B: My car isn't working.

4. A: Who / What are you doing with your phone?

   B: I'm texting.

5. A: What / Who are you texting?

   B: My friend James.

6. A: Who / What are you and James texting about?

   B: My birthday party!

*who → quién*

# EXERCISE 3 PRESENT PROGRESSIVE QUESTIONS

GRAMMAR NOTES 1–3 Write questions in the present progressive. Use the correct forms of the words in parentheses. Then match the questions and answers.

__d__ 1. _Why are you wearing a suit?_
(Why / you / wear / a suit)

__ 2. _How are your parents travelling to New York_
(How / your parents / travel / to New York)

__ 3. _Who are you driving to work today_
(Who / drive / you / to work today)

__ 4. _Where are_
(Where / your brother / go)

__ 5. _Who is Eun Young talking to_
(Who / Eun Young / talk to)

a. My dad is driving me.

b. He's going to a concert.

c. She's talking to her friend.

~~d.~~ I have a job interview.

e. They're taking the train.

# EXERCISE 4 *WH-* QUESTIONS AND ANSWERS

GRAMMAR NOTES 1–3 Look at the photos. Write questions. Use the *wh-* words in the box and the present progressive forms of the verbs in parentheses. Use some words in the box two times.

| how | what | where | who | why |
|-----|------|-------|-----|-----|

1. A: _Where are you going right now_ ?
(you / go / right now)

   B: To the store.

2. A: _Why are you riding a bike_ ?
(you / ride a bike)

   B: I need some exercise.

**3.** **A:** _What are you doing_ ?
(you / do)

**B:** I'm taking a trip to New York.

**4.** **A:** _How are you getting there_ ?
(you / get there)

**B:** I'm flying.

**5.** **A:** _Who are you flying with_ ?
(you / fly with)

**B:** My wife and the kids.

**6.** **A:** _Where are you going_ ?
(you / go)

**B:** To work.

**7.** **A:** _Why are you taking the bus_ ?
(you / take the bus)

**B:** My car isn't working.

## EXERCISE 5 EDITING

GRAMMAR NOTES 1–3 There are six mistakes in the conversations. The first mistake is corrected. Find and correct five more.

**1.** **A:** Why ~~John is~~ _is John_ sleeping?

**B:** He's not feeling well.

**2.** **A:** Who's driving you to school?

**B:** My mom's.

**3.** **A:** Why _are you_ you are walking, Asha?

**B:** My bike isn't working.

**4.** **A:** Why _are_ you wearing a dress today?

**B:** I have an important appointment.

**5.** **A:** Who are you talk _ing_ to right now?

**B:** My sister.

**6.** **A:** Where _are_ you going?

**B:** To school.

## EXERCISE 6  LISTENING

▶18|02  **A**  Listen to the conversation. Check (✓) the true sentence.

☐  **1.** Mark is alone.

☐  **2.** Mark is listening to music.

☐  **3.** The job interview was really good.

☐  **4.** Mark wants to visit Nick in San Francisco.

▶18|02  **B**  Listen again. Answer the questions. Use long answers.

**1.** Who is calling Mark? _Nick is calling Mark._ _____

**2.** What is Mark doing now? _____

**3.** What is he watching? _____

**4.** Who is he watching it with? _____

**5.** What is Nick doing right now? _____

**6.** Why is Jerry taking the subway? _____

**7.** What is Nick buying? _____

**C**  Work with a partner. Compare your answers in A and B. Then ask and answer these questions.

**1.** What are you doing right now?

**2.** Who are you doing it with?

## EXERCISE 7  WHERE ARE YOU GOING?

DISCUSSION  Work in a group. Imagine you are traveling right now. Your classmates ask you *wh-* questions in the present progressive about your trip.

EXAMPLE:  A:  Where are you going?
           B:  I'm going to Sunset Beach.
           C:  How are you getting there?
           B:  I'm driving there.
           D:  Who are you traveling with?
           B:  I'm traveling with . . .

# EXERCISE 8 THEY'RE RIDING CAMELS

Ⓐ PICTURE DISCUSSION Work in a group. Study the photos. What countries are the people in? What languages are they speaking? Choose from the countries and languages in the box.

| | | |
|---|---|---|
| Brazil / Portuguese | Kenya / Swahili | Russia / Russian |
| Egypt / Arabic | China / Chinese | United States / English |

EXAMPLE: In Picture 1, the people are in Egypt. They are speaking Arabic.

**ride camels / the Pyramids**

**walk / Mount Kilimanjaro**

**drink coconut juice / Sugarloaf mountain**

**stand and talk / Red Square**

**visit / Washington, D.C.**

**ride bikes / Shanghai**

Ⓑ Ask and answer present progressive *wh-* questions about the people in each picture in A. Take turns.

EXAMPLE: A: What are the people in Picture 1 doing?
B: They're riding camels. . . . What are they looking at?
C: They're looking at the Pyramids. . . .

## FROM GRAMMAR TO WRITING

**A** BEFORE YOU WRITE  Read Sally and Diego's phone conversation. Underline *wh-* questions in the present progressive. Then imagine that your own relative is coming to visit and you are looking for that person at the airport. You call your relative. Write questions for your relative in the chart. Work with a partner. Practice your questions.

SALLY:  Diego? I'm here at the airport. What are you doing? Are you looking for me?

DIEGO:  Yes, I am. I'm at the airport, too.

SALLY:  Where are you standing?

DIEGO:  I'm standing in McBurgers, the fast-food restaurant.

SALLY:  Why are you standing in McBurgers?

DIEGO:  Because I'm hungry!

SALLY:  OK. . . . I'm walking to McBurgers. What are you wearing?

DIEGO:  I'm wearing a green shirt and a red baseball cap.

SALLY:  OK. . . . Ah, now I see you!

| | |
|---|---|
| What | |
| Why | |
| Who | |
| Where | |
| | |

**B** WRITE  Write your conversation with your relative at the airport in A. Use *wh-* questions in the present progressive. Use the conversation in A and your chart to help you.

**C** CHECK YOUR WORK  Read your paragraph. Underline *wh-* questions in the present progressive. Use the Editing Checklist to check your work.

### Editing Checklist

**Did you . . . ?**

- [ ] use *wh-* question + *be* + subject + verb + *-ing* for most questions
- [ ] use *wh-* question + *be* + verb + *-ing* for questions about the subject
- [ ] check your spelling

**D** REVISE YOUR WORK  Read your paragraph again. Can you improve your writing? Make changes if necessary.

# UNIT 18 REVIEW

**Test yourself on the grammar of the unit.**

**Ⓐ Match the questions and answers.**

_____ **1.** Where are you going?

_____ **2.** How are you getting to work?

_____ **3.** Who are you driving to work with?

_____ **4.** What is she doing?

_____ **5.** Why are you driving to work?

**a.** The bus is very slow.

**b.** I'm driving.

**c.** She's reading.

**d.** To my office.

**e.** My friend Maria.

**Ⓑ Put the words in the correct order. Make questions.**

**1.** _____
(watching / on TV / What / Steve / is)

**2.** _____
(are / me now / calling / you / Why)

**3.** _____
(in the class / What / studying / you / are)

**4.** _____
(you / is / Who / to work / taking)

**5.** _____
(taking / you / the train / are / Why)

**Ⓒ Correct the conversations. There are five mistakes. Use contractions if possible.**

**1.** **A:** Who teaching the class?

   **B:** Mark's.

**2.** **A:** Why you are smiling?

   **B:** I'm watch a funny movie.

**3.** **A:** What's your sister wear?

   **B:** A blue shirt and jeans.

**Now check your answers on page 382.**

# *Can* and *Can't*

## ABILITIES

**OUTCOMES**
• Use *can/can't* to talk about abilities
• Answer questions about a reading
• Complete sentences about a conversation
• Talk about your classmates' abilities
• Write a paragraph about the abilities of a person you know

| STEP 1 | GRAMMAR IN CONTEXT |
| --- | --- |

## BEFORE YOU READ

**A** VOCABULARY Study the words. Then work with a partner. Read the statements. Check (✓) *True* or *False*.

**give a presentation**

**play the piano**

**play the guitar**

**play an instrument**

**sing**

**dance**

|  | True | False |
| --- | --- | --- |
| 1. I can give a presentation to many people. | ☐ | ☐ |
| 2. I can play the piano. | ✓ | ☐ |
| 3. I can play the guitar. | ☐ | ☐ |
| 4. I can't play an instrument. | ☐ | ✓ |
| 5. I can sing a song in English. | ✓ | ☐ |
| 6. I can't dance. | ☐ | ✓ |

**B** Work with a partner. Compare your answers in A.

🔘 19|01 **Read this conversation.**

# Help with Spanish

**JESSICA:** What's the matter, Jeremy? You look really down.[1]

**JEREMY:** I can't understand my Spanish teacher, and he can't understand me. My pronunciation[2] isn't good. I need to give a presentation on Friday. I can't do it.

**JESSICA:** But last year you were so good in Spanish.

**JEREMY:** It wasn't a conversation class. I can read. I just can't speak.

**JESSICA:** Can someone in the class help?

**JEREMY:** Hmm. . . . Well, Rose is good at Spanish. Actually, Rose is good at everything. She can give a presentation in Spanish. She can understand sign language.[3] She can play the piano, and she can dance.

**JESSICA:** Wow.

**JEREMY:** But there's a problem. She's taking a Chinese class at the college after school, so she's very busy this year. . . . Hmm. Maybe Jorge can help me. He can speak Spanish, and he's a really nice guy. You know, he's not good at math. Maybe I can help him in math. I'm a whiz at[4] math, you know. Then he can help me in Spanish.

**JESSICA:** There you go.

---

1  *look really down:* look sad
2  *pronunciation:* way of speaking
3  *sign language:* language for people who cannot hear or talk
4  *a whiz at:* very good at

# AFTER YOU READ

**A** COMPREHENSION  Look at the conversation again. Circle the correct answers.

1. Why is Jeremy unhappy?
   a. His teacher can't speak Spanish.   b. He can't understand his Spanish teacher.

2. Why was Jeremy good in Spanish last year?
   a. It wasn't a conversation class.   b. It was an easy class.

3. What instrument can Rose play?
   a. She can play the piano.   b. She can play the guitar.

4. Why is Rose busy?
   a. She's teaching Chinese after school.   b. She's learning Chinese after school.

5. How can Jeremy help Jorge?
   a. He can help him with math.   b. He can help him with Spanish.

**B**  Work with a partner. Compare your answers in A.

---

**STEP 2   GRAMMAR PRESENTATION**

## CAN AND CAN'T

### Affirmative and Negative Statements

| Subject | Can/Can't | Base Form of Verb |
|---|---|---|
| I<br>You<br>He<br>She<br>We<br>You<br>They | can<br>can't | speak Russian. |

### Yes/No Questions

| |
|---|
| **Can** you **do** me a favor? |
| **Can** he **understand** French? |

### Short Answers

| |
|---|
| **Yes**, I **can**. |
| **No**, he **can't**. |

### Wh- Questions

| |
|---|
| **What can** I **do**? |
| **Who can help**? |

### Answers

| |
|---|
| You **can carry** the boxes. (**Carry** the boxes.) |
| Pierre **can help**. (Pierre **can**.) |

212    Unit 19

# GRAMMAR NOTES

## 1 Can

| | |
|---|---|
| *Can* has different meanings. We use *can* to talk about **ability** and **possibility**. | I **can understand** Korean. *(ability)*<br>I **can meet** you at 4:00. *(possibility)* |
| *Can* comes before the verb. The verb is always in the **base form**. | He **can dance**. |
| **BE CAREFUL!** Do not use *to* after *can*. Do not add *-s* or *-ing* to verbs that follow *can*. | He **can speak** English.<br>NOT He can ~~to speak~~ English.<br>NOT He can ~~speaks~~ English.<br>NOT He can ~~speaking~~ English. |

## 2 Can't

| | |
|---|---|
| The negative of *can* is *can't*. | I **can't** understand you. |
| **USAGE NOTE** *Cannot* is a form of the negative. It is not very common in speaking. | I **cannot** understand you. |

## 3 Can: Yes/No Questions and Answers

| | |
|---|---|
| For *yes/no* questions, put *can* before the subject. We use short answers in speaking. | Q: **Can** they speak Russian?<br>A: Yes, they **can**. or Yes.<br><br>Q: **Can** she write well?<br>A: No, she **can't**. or No. |

## 4 Can: Wh- Questions and Answers

| | |
|---|---|
| For **most *wh*- questions**, use a *wh*- question word + *can* + the subject + the base form of the verb. | Q: **When can** you work?<br>A: I **can** work in the morning. or In the morning. |
| For questions about the **subject**, use a *wh*- question word + *can* + the base form of the verb. | Q: **Who can** sing?<br>A: Rosa **can** sing. or Rosa **can**. |

# PRONUNCIATION NOTE

▶19|02 **Stress on *Can* and *Can't***

| | |
|---|---|
| When *can* comes before a base form of the verb, we usually pronounce it /kən/ or /kn/ and stress the verb. | She can **SING**. |
| When *can't* comes before a base form of the verb, we usually pronounce it /kænt/ and stress both *can't* and the verb. | She **CAN'T SING**. |

## EXERCISE 1  DISCOVER THE GRAMMAR

**GRAMMAR NOTES 1–4** Read the questions and answers. Underline *can* and *can't*. Circle the verbs that go with *can* or *can't*. Then match the questions and answers.

___c___ 1. Can Luisa (dance?)

_____ 2. I can't (understand) this French phrase.

_____ 3. Can you (pronounce) this word?

_____ 4. Can you (play) the guitar?

_____ 5. Where can we (meet?)

_____ 6. Can Bob (play) soccer?

    **a.** No, I can't. It's hard to say it.

    **b.** At the library. OK?

    **c.** No, but her sister can dance.

    **d.** Yes. I can play the guitar and the piano.

    **e.** *Au revoir* means good-bye.

    **f.** Oh, yes. He loves the game.

## EXERCISE 2  *CAN* AND *CAN'T*

**GRAMMAR NOTES 1–2** Complete the sentences. Use *can* or *can't* and the verbs in parentheses.

1. I ____can't pronounce____ your name. Can you repeat it?
      (not / pronounce)

2. I don't want to be in the school chorus because I _____.
                                         (not / sing)

3. Ali _____ 100 laps. He's a great swimmer.
    (swim)

4. Maria and Pedro _____ for hours. They love to dance.
          (dance)

5. She _____ tennis, but she's a good soccer player.
    (not / play)

6. Ella _____ a presentation to the class. She's a good speaker.
    (give)

7. Oscar and Joe _____ the guitar. They're giving a concert in the park right now.
      (play)

# EXERCISE 3 CAN AND CAN'T: STATEMENTS AND QUESTIONS

GRAMMAR NOTES 1–3 Complete the conversations. Use *can* or *can't* and the words in parentheses.

1. **JEREMY:** Jorge, I have to give a talk about computers in Spanish. _____Can_____ you

   _____help_____ me?
   (help)

   **JORGE:** Well, I don't know about computers, but I _____can help_____ you with your
   (help)

   pronunciation in Spanish.

2. **JEREMY:** There are so many words in Spanish. I _____can't remember_____ all of them.
   (not / remember)

   **JORGE:** Well, you _____can keep_____ a notebook of new words. Then we
   (keep)

   _____can review_____ the new words each week.
   (review)

   **JEREMY:** That's a good idea.

3. **OLIVER:** Mom, I _____can't understand_____ these math problems. _____Can_____ you
   (not / understand)

   _____help_____ me?
   (help)

   **MOM:** What? I _____can't hear_____ you.
   (not / hear)

   **OLIVER:** I _____can't do_____ these math problems. _____Can_____ you _____explain_____
   (not / do)                                      (explain)

   them to me?

   **MOM:** Oh! OK.

4. **MARY:** It's time for Chinese class.

   **ROSE:** Sorry. I _____can come_____ to class today. I feel sick.
   (come)

   **MARY:** That's too bad. I hope you feel better soon.

5. **ROSE:** That woman is speaking sign language. _____Can_____ you _____understand_____ her?
   (understand)

   **MARY:** No, I _____can't_____. I know a few signs, but not enough to understand her.
   (not)

6. **JEREMY:** OK. Now let's shoot some hoops.[1]

   **JORGE:** Great. We _____can play_____ in East Park.
   (play)

   **JEREMY:** No, we _____can't_____. Some college kids are playing there now. But we
   (not)

   _____can play_____ at the middle school. Those courts are usually empty now.
   (play)

7. **JEREMY:** Hi, Yoshio. This is Jeremy. _____Can you join_____ us? We're playing basketball.
   (you / join)

   **YOSHIO:** Sorry, I _____can't_____. I'm studying for the math test.
   (not)

---

1 *shoot some hoops:* play basketball

# EXERCISE 4  *CAN* AND *CAN'T*: STATEMENTS

GRAMMAR NOTES 1–2  Complete the sentences. Use *can* or *can't* and the correct verbs from the box.

| ~~find~~ | give | open | play | speak | understand |
|---|---|---|---|---|---|

1. I'm looking for my phone. I _____ can't find _____ it anywhere.

2. When John travels in Spain and Italy, he talks to everyone
   because he ___ can speak ___ Spanish and Italian.

3. Our classroom is locked. We ___ can't open ___
   the door.

4. I ___ can't give ___ a presentation about the moon.
   I don't know anything about it.

5. We ___ can't understand ___ you. Please speak slowly.

6. He's a good athlete. He ___ can play ___ baseball
   and soccer well. He's on the baseball and soccer teams.

# EXERCISE 5  STRESS ON *CAN* AND *CAN'T*

▶19|03  Ⓐ  PRONUNCIATION NOTE  Listen and complete the conversations with *can* or *can't*.

1. A: We ___ can't ___ understand you.
   B: Sorry. I'll speak slowly.

2. A: We ___ can ___ understand you.
   B: That's good.

3. A: Lin ___ can ___ sing.
   B: I know. And she ___ can't ___ play the piano.

4. A: I ___ can't ___ sing, and I ___ can ___ play the guitar.
   B: Oh. Are you in a band?

5. A: I ___ can't ___ see the board.
   B: Do you want to change seats?

6. A: I ___ can ___ see the board.
   B: Good. Please read the first sentence.

▶19|03  Ⓑ  Listen again to the conversations in A and repeat.

# EXERCISE 6  EDITING

GRAMMAR NOTES 1–4  There are <u>seven</u> mistakes in the sentences. The first mistake is corrected. Find and correct six more.

1. Erika can ~~to~~ understand English, but she no can speak it well.

2. Mei Liang can't plays the guitar. She plays the piano.

3. Can they to give presentations?

4. Can he plays soccer?

5. She no can understand sign language.

6. How I can get to the library?

## STEP 4    COMMUNICATION PRACTICE

## EXERCISE 7  LISTENING

19|04  **A** Listen to the conversation. Complete the sentence. Circle the correct answer.

Jeremy and his mother are talking about Jeremy's _____ .

  **a.** Spanish and math classes      **b.** homework      **c.** soccer team

19|04  **B** Listen again. Complete the sentences. Circle the correct answers.

1. Jeremy <u>can</u> / <u>(can't)</u> give presentations in Spanish now.

2. Jeremy <u>can</u> / <u>can't</u> understand his teacher's Spanish.

3. Jeremy <u>can</u> / <u>can't</u> pronounce words in Spanish very well.

4. Jorge <u>can</u> / <u>can't</u> do math well now.

5. Jeremy <u>can</u> / <u>can't</u> be a math teacher.

**C** Work with a partner. Ask your partner questions about his or her abilities. Use the phrases in the box.

| | |
|---|---|
| give a presentation in Spanish | teach someone math |
| pronounce your classmates' names in English | understand your teacher |

EXAMPLE:  A:  Can you give a presentation in Spanish?
            B:  Yes, I can. Can you?
            A:  No, I can't.

# EXERCISE 8 FIND SOMEONE WHO . . .

GAME  Look at the pictures. Then walk around the class. Ask and answer questions with *can*. Find someone who can do each activity. Write the name of the student below the picture. When you have three names in any direction, you win.

EXAMPLE:  MARIA:  Can you water ski?

KEIKO:  Yes, I can. Can you?

*(Maria writes Keiko's name in the box with "water ski.")*

| | | |
|---|---|---|
| 嗨，你好吗 | 很好，谢谢，你呢 | |
| 1. *Keiko* | 1. *Can you speak Chinese.* | 1. *Can you change (and tire)* |
| 2. _____ | 2. _____ | 2. *Can you fixes the card?* |
| 3. _____ | 3. _____ | 3. _____ |
| Buona sera | | |
| 1. *Can you play guitar* | 1. *Can you understand* | 1. _____ |
| 2. *guitar* | 2. *Italian* | 2. _____ |
| 3. _____ | 3. _____ | 3. _____ |
| 1. *Can you play golf* | 1. *Can you dance* | 1. _____ |
| 2. _____ | 2. *tango ?* | 2. _____ |
| 3. _____ | 3. _____ | 3. _____ |

## EXERCISE 9
## BORIS CAN WRITE POETRY

**A** GAME Work in groups. Find out interesting abilities of the people in your group. Write them down.

Boris can write poetry.

Samir can speak three languages.

Sara can do gymnastics.

Gustavo can fix cars.

Machiko can train a dog.

Bea can make a wedding cake.

**B** Read the abilities of your group to the class, but do not say the name of the person with the ability. The class guesses who it is.

EXAMPLE: **A:** This person can write poetry.
        **B:** We think Samir can write poetry.
        **A:** No, he can't. Boris can.

## EXERCISE 10  I CAN READ, BUT I CAN'T WRITE

**A** DISCUSSION Work in a group. To be good at a language, you need different abilities. Make a list of the abilities of a good language learner.

can remember a lot of new words
can write
can understand other people

**B** Discuss your language ability in English with your group. Use *can* and *can't* in your discussion.

EXAMPLE: **A:** I can understand English, but I can't speak well.
        **B:** Me, too. I also can't speak, but I can read well.
        **C:** My problem is grammar. I can't . . .

# FROM GRAMMAR TO WRITING

**A** BEFORE YOU WRITE  Read about Ali, a man of many abilities. Then work with a partner. Tell your partner about a person you know with different abilities.

My friend Ali can do many things. He can play soccer. He's the star of his team. Ali is also good at music. He can play the guitar and sing. Sometimes Ali and I play together. I can play the guitar, too. Ali can also write poetry. His poems are very beautiful, but a little sad. He can't do everything. He can't fix a car or a computer.

**B** WRITE  Write a paragraph about the abilities of a person you know. Use *can* and *can't*. Use the paragraph in A and your ideas to help you.

**C** CHECK YOUR WORK  Read your paragraph. Underline all examples of *can* or *can't*. Then use the Editing Checklist to check your work.

| Editing Check List |
| --- |
| **Did you . . . ?** |
| ☐ use *can* to mean ability or possibility |
| ☐ use *can* or *can't* + the base form of the verb |
| ☐ check your spelling |

**D** REVISE YOUR WORK  Read your paragraph again. Can you improve your writing? Make changes if necessary.

# UNIT 19 REVIEW

**Test yourself on the grammar of the unit.**

**A** Complete the conversation. Circle the correct answers.

A: Sorry. I can / (can't) remember your name.
     **1.**

B: It's Elmer.

A: I'm sorry. I can / can't hear you. Can / Cannot you say that again?
                      **2.**                **3.**

B: OK. It's ELMER!

A: Um. . . . Can you spell it?

B: Yes, I can / can't. It's E-L-M-E-R.
          **4.**

**B** Complete the conversations. Use *can* or *can't* and the verbs in parentheses.

1. A: _____Can_____ you ____understand____ this message?
                                  (understand)

   B: No, it's in French, and I ____can't read____ French.
                                    (not / read)

   A: Maybe Marie ____can help____. She knows French.
                          (help)

2. A: We ____can't watch____ TV. The TV isn't working.
              (not / watch)

   B: That's too bad. Do you want to play basketball?

   A: We ____can't play____ basketball. It's raining.
              (not / play)

   B: Well, we ____can do____ the laundry. We have a lot of laundry.
                  (do)

   A: I guess so.

**C** Correct the sentences. There are five mistakes.

A: Pietro can't dances, but he can to play the piano.

B: Can he to sing?

A: Yes, he can. He can also teach music.

B: Then he can helping me. I want a music teacher for my son. Can he teach on weekends?

A: No, he no can teach on weekends. He never works on weekends.

**Now check your answers on page 382.**

# Nouns, Articles, and Pronouns

# PART 7

**OUTCOMES**

- Use possessive nouns to show belonging
- Use *this*, *that*, *these*, and *those* to introduce people and things
- Complete a paragraph about a reading
- Complete sentences about a conversation
- Talk about things that people are wearing or have
- Write a paragraph about two people and the clothes they are wearing

**OUTCOMES**

- Use count and non-count nouns
- Use quantifiers with count and non-count nouns
- Complete sentences about a reading
- Identify true and false sentences about a conversation
- Talk about food you like and dislike
- Role-play ordering food in a restaurant
- Write a paragraph about your favorite meal

**OUTCOMES**

- Use the indefinite articles *an*/*a* and the definite article *the*
- Use *one* to replace a singular noun and *ones* to replace a plural noun
- Identify true and false sentences about a reading
- Complete sentences about a conversation
- Talk about shopping
- Describe a picture
- Write a conversation about things you want to buy

**OUTCOMES**

- Use subject and object pronouns
- Identify true and false sentences about a reading
- Complete a chart with information from a conversation
- Ask and answer questions about gifts
- Role-play asking for a favor in a conversation
- Write a paragraph about a gift for someone you know

# Possessive Nouns; *This*, *That*, *These*, and *Those*

## CLOTHING

## STEP 1    GRAMMAR IN CONTEXT

### BEFORE YOU READ

**A** VOCABULARY  Study the words. Then work with a partner. Practice the conversation.

Sara — a T-shirt — jeans

Joe — a sweatshirt — sneakers

Al — a tie — a suit

Mia — a dress — high heels

Brad — a sports jacket — shoes

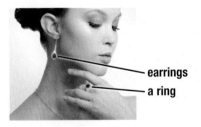

earrings
a ring

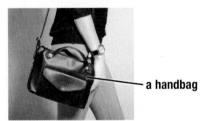

a handbag

**Conversation**

A:  What color is Sara's T-shirt?

B:  Sara's T-shirt is gray.

A:  What color are her jeans?

B:  They're blue.

**B**  What clothes from A do you see in class now? Talk about your classmates' clothes. Complete the conversation.

A:  What color is _____?

B:  _____ is _____.

A:  What color are _____?

B:  _____.

20|01 **Read this conversation.**

# Meet the Parents

**MARK:** Judy, do I look OK?

**JUDY:** Yeah. You look really sharp.[1] What's the occasion?

**MARK:** A special dinner at the Water Grill Restaurant. Kathy and her parents are waiting for me there. It's her parents' anniversary.

**JUDY:** Is that a new jacket?

**MARK:** No. It's my brother's jacket.

**JUDY:** It's a good fit.[2]

**MARK:** Actually, I feel funny in these formal clothes.[3] I like T-shirts, jeans, and sweatshirts. Is the tie OK?

**JUDY:** Sure. It goes well with that sports jacket.

**MARK:** Thanks. Actually, this isn't my tie. It's my roommate's tie. I almost never wear a tie.

**JUDY:** I know. You're wearing all these clothes from other people!

**MARK:** That's true. I'm not wearing my clothes today . . . but how do you like my new goatee?

**JUDY:** It looks good! You know, that goatee makes you look like an artist.

**MARK:** An artist? No kidding. I guess that's good. Now I need to remember—Kathy's mom is Bea Harlow, and her dad is Lee White.

**JUDY:** Relax, Mark. Be yourself.[4] Everyone likes you.

---

1 *sharp:* really good
2 *a good fit:* the right size on you
3 *formal clothes:* special clothes to wear for important events
4 *be yourself:* act as you always do

## AFTER YOU READ

Ⓐ COMPREHENSION  Look at the conversation again. Complete the paragraph. Circle the correct words.

Kathy's sister and brother / mother and father are waiting for Mark at a
    1.
restaurant / hotel. Mark likes / doesn't like formal clothes, but he's / he isn't wearing
    2.                            3.                                    4.
formal clothes now. He's wearing his father's / brother's sports jacket and his
                                              5.
cousin's / roommate's tie. Mark is saying names. Lee is Kathy's dad / mom. Bea is
    6.                                                                7.
Kathy's sister / mom. Mark is a little nervous, so Judy says, "Relax, Mark. Be yourself.
               8.
Everyone likes / listens to you."
             9.

Ⓑ  Work with a partner. Compare your answers in A.

## STEP 2    GRAMMAR PRESENTATION

### POSSESSIVE NOUNS

| Possessive Nouns | |
| --- | --- |
| Singular | Plural |
| My **sister's** car is red. | My **parents'** car is blue. |
| The **actress's** first name is Rosa. | Her **daughters'** names are Tina and Marie. |

### THIS, THAT, THESE, AND THOSE

| This, That, These, Those | |
| --- | --- |
| Pronouns | Adjectives |
| **This** is my cell phone. | **This** cell phone is great. |
| **That** is your jacket. | **That** tie is Steve's. |
| **These** are my keys. | **These** keys don't work. |
| **Those** are your keys. | **Those** keys are Steve's. |

# GRAMMAR NOTES

## 1 Possessive Nouns

| | |
|---|---|
| **Possessive nouns** show **belonging**. | I'm wearing my **roommate's** shoes.<br>*(The shoes belong to my roommate.)*<br>He's wearing **Joe's** sports jacket.<br>*(The sports jacket belongs to Joe.)* |
| Add an **apostrophe** (') + -*s* to a singular noun or an irregular plural noun. | That's my **father's** jacket.<br>Where's the **men's** restroom? |
| Add only an **apostrophe** (') to a plural noun ending in -*s*. | It's her **parents'** anniversary.<br>It's the **Becks'** house. |

## 2 *This, That, These, Those*

| | |
|---|---|
| *This, that, these,* and *those* can be **pronouns** or **adjectives**. When they are adjectives, they come before a **noun**. | PRONOUN<br>**This**     is my hat.<br>ADJECTIVE   NOUN<br>**This**     **hat**     is new.<br><br>PRONOUN<br>**These**     are my sunglasses.<br>ADJECTIVE   NOUN<br>**These**    **sunglasses**    are Robert's. |
| Remember that *this* and *that* are **singular**; *these* and *those* are **plural**. (See Units 2 and 4.) | **This is** my T-shirt.<br>**These are** my T-shirts. |
| Use *this* and *these* for things that are **near**. Use *that* and *those* for things that are **away** from you. | **This** cell phone **in my hand** is new.<br>**That** cell phone **on the table** is old. |
| USAGE NOTE   *That's* is often used in speaking and informal writing. It refers to the idea that was just stated. | A: I really like her parents.<br>B: **That's** great.<br>A: I really don't like her brother.<br>B: **That's** too bad.<br>A: He's in Boston. **That's** why he's not here. |

# PRONUNCIATION NOTE

20|02

### Possessive Noun Endings

| | |
|---|---|
| The *'s* in a **possessive noun** sounds like /**s**/, /**z**/, or /**ɪz**/. | |
| • /s/ | This is my **aunt's** hat. |
| • /z/ | My **uncle's** hat is on the table. |
| • /ɪz/ (This sound adds an' extra syllable.) | His **boss's** name is Mr. Lee. |

# REFERENCE NOTES

For **definitions of grammar terms**, see the Glossary on page 375.

## EXERCISE 1  DISCOVER THE GRAMMAR

GRAMMAR NOTES 1–2  **Read the sentences. Underline** *this*, *that*, *these*, **and** *those*. **Circle the possessive nouns. Then match the sentences.**

_c_ **1.** Do you want to visit (Kathy's) grandmother?

____ **2.** Are those your father's pants?

____ **3.** This is my sister's friend Lulu.

____ **4.** What color are your roommate's shoes?

____ **5.** Bob's son is in the hospital.

**a.** Nice to meet you. I'm Kathy's friend Mark.

**b.** They're black.

**c.** That's a good idea. She loves visitors.

**d.** That's too bad. What's the problem?

**e.** No, they're not. They're my brother's pants.

## EXERCISE 2  *THIS, THAT, THESE,* AND *THOSE*

GRAMMAR NOTE 2  **Complete the conversations with** *this*, *that*, *these*, **or** *those*.

**1. KATHY:** Mom, Dad, _____ *this* _____ is Mark. Mark,

_____ these _____ are my parents, Lee and Bea.

   **MARK:** Nice to meet you.

**2. LEE:** Bea, is _____ at _____ your phone over there?

   **BEA:** No, Lee. I think it's Kathy's.

**3. MARK:** _____ that _____'s a beautiful ring. It's

   very unusual.

   **BEA:** Thanks. _____ ring is about 100 years

   old. It was my great-grandmother's ring.

**4. BEA:** How do you like the food?

   **MARK:** _____ steak is delicious.

   **KATHY:** And _____ vegetables are really good. The Water Grill was a good choice.

**5. LEE:** Bea, do you see _____ man over there? He's wearing a gray suit and a red

   tie. It's Adam Katz.

   **BEA:** You're right. Let's go say hello.

# EXERCISE 3 POSSESSIVE NOUNS

GRAMMAR NOTE 1 Complete the conversations. Use the possessive form of the nouns in parentheses.

1. **A:** Excuse me. Where's the _____women's_____ restroom?
   (women)

   **B:** It's over there, next to the stairs.

2. **A:** Is your _____roommate's_____ jacket on that chair?
   (roommate)

   **B:** No. That's my jacket.

3. **A:** Is that your handbag?

   **B:** No, it's my _____sister's_____ handbag.
   (sister)

4. **A:** Where's _____Dad's_____ hat?
   (Dad)

   **B:** It's on the sofa over there.

5. **A:** Are those your _____mother's_____ earrings? They're beautiful.
   (mother)

   **B:** No, they're my _____aunt's_____ earrings.
   (aunt)

# EXERCISE 4 POSSESSIVES AND NOUNS

GRAMMAR NOTE 1 Complete the paragraphs. Use the correct forms of the words in parentheses and possessive forms when necessary.

Many women in the United States change their family names to their

_____husbands' family names_____ after they marry. For example, before
**1.** (husbands / family names)

_____Steve Beck's mother_____ was Bill Beck's wife, she was Mary Meyers. Now she
**2.** (Steve Beck / mother)

is Mary Beck.

Some women don't change their names. _____Kathy White's mother_____, Bea
**3.** (Kathy White / mother)

Harlow, is married to Lee White. She is still Bea Harlow after thirty-five years of marriage.

Today, some women are keeping their names and adding their

_____husbands' names_____. For example, _____Kathy's sister_____
**4.** (husbands / names)                    **5.** (Kathy / sister)

Jill is married to Joe Smith. Her married name is Jill White-Smith. So a

_____woman's last name_____ doesn't always match her husband's last name.
**6.** (woman / last name)

## EXERCISE 5  *THAT* OR *THAT'S*

GRAMMAR NOTE 2  Complete the conversations with *That* or *That's*.

1. A: _____*That*_____ restaurant is really good. It has four stars.

   B: I know. Everyone likes it.

2. A: My new suit doesn't fit.

   B: ____*that's*____ too bad.

3. A: ____*that*____ shirt is nice.

   B: Thanks. It's new.

4. A: ____*that's*____ sweatshirt has a spot on it.

   B: Oh. Thanks for telling me.

5. A: Do you want to go to Joe's Shoe Store? It's near here, and it has a big sale today.

   B: ____*that's*____ a good idea.

6. A: Joe's Shoe Store is next to the Water Grill Restaurant, right?

   B: ____*that's*____ right.


## EXERCISE 6  POSSESSIVE NOUN ENDINGS

▶ 20|03  PRONUNCIATION NOTE  Read the sentences. Underline the possessive nouns. Then listen and check the final sound of each possessive noun.

| Possessive Noun | /s/ | /z/ | /ɪz/ |
|---|---|---|---|
| 1. That's my mother's ring. | | ✓ | |
| 2. My father's jacket is on the chair. | | ✓ | |
| 3. Those are their children's shoes. | | ✓ | |
| 4. That's my boss's hat. | | | ✓ |
| 5. Are these your roommate's glasses? | ✓ | ✓ | |
| 6. No, they're Liz's glasses. | | | ✓ |

## EXERCISE 7 EDITING

GRAMMAR NOTES 1–2 There are six mistakes in the conversation. The first mistake is corrected. Find and correct five more.

AMY: Are ~~that~~ *those* the children shoes near the door?

TED: No, the children are wearing their shoes.

AMY: Is that your mother's jacket?

TED: No. It's my sister jacket.

AMY: Is these Bill's sweatshirt?

TED: Yes, it is. I want to buy him a new sweatshirt for his next birthday.

AMY: That a good idea.

## STEP 4 COMMUNICATION PRACTICE

## EXERCISE 8 LISTENING

▶ 20|04 **A** Listen to the conversation. What do Mark and Judy talk about? Circle the correct answer.

**a.** food   **b.** Kathy's parents   **c.** Mark's roommate

▶ 20|04 **B** Listen again. Complete the sentences. Circle the correct answers.

1. _____ has a women's clothes store.
   **a.** Kathy's dad   **b.** Mark's dad   **c.** Kathy's mom

2. _____ is worried about her sister.
   **a.** Kathy's mom   **b.** Kathy   **c.** Kathy's aunt

3. _____ doesn't like Mark's goatee.
   **a.** Kathy's mom   **b.** Kathy's dad   **c.** Kathy

4. _____ likes Mark's sports jacket and tie.
   **a.** Kathy   **b.** Mark's roommate   **c.** Mark's friend

**C** Work with a partner. Say things about Kathy, Kathy's mom, and Kathy's dad.

EXAMPLE: Kathy doesn't like Mark's goatee.

## EXERCISE 9  THAT T-SHIRT IS COOL!

CONVERSATION  Work in a group. Talk about things that people in your class are wearing or have.

EXAMPLE:  **A:** That T-shirt is cool, Ben!
**B:** Thanks, Ranxi. I like those shoes, Adriana. Are they new?
**C:** Yes, they are.... Look at Li's backpack. It's a nice color.

## EXERCISE 10  RENEE IS WEARING AMY'S...

**A** PICTURE DISCUSSION  Work with a partner. Compare the people in pictures 1 and 2.

EXAMPLE:  **A:** In Picture 2, Renee is wearing Amy's hat.
**B:** That's right. And in Picture 2, Juan is wearing...

Picture 1

Picture 2

**B** Work in groups. Look at the people in your group. Study what they're wearing and what they have. One student leaves the room. The other students exchange things like glasses, backpacks, watches, or shoes. The student returns and talks about the changes.

EXAMPLE:  **A:** Yusuf is wearing José's hat.
**B:** That's right, Maria.
**A:** And Marco is wearing glasses now. Those aren't his glasses. They're Yusuf's glasses.
**C:** No, they aren't. They're Young Hee's glasses!

# FROM GRAMMAR TO WRITING

**A BEFORE YOU WRITE** Look at the photos of a student's sister and brother, and read about their clothes. Then find photos of two people you know. Complete the chart about their clothes. Work with a partner. Tell your partner about the clothes.

This is my older sister Marta. Marta's favorite outfit is this red dress. She often wears that black hat and those black high heels with the dress. She looks great.

This is a photo of my brother Paolo. Paolo's jeans are blue, and his T-shirt is gray. He wears these jeans every day, but a different T-shirt. His T-shirts are blue, white, and gray. They're boring. All my brother's clothes are boring.

| Person | Clothes |
|---|---|
|  |  |
|  |  |

**B WRITE** Write about the clothes of the people in your photos. Use possessive nouns and *this*, *that*, *these*, or *those*. Use the paragraphs in A and your chart to help you.

**C CHECK YOUR WORK** Read your paragraph. Underline examples of possessive nouns and *this*, *that*, *these*, or *those*. Use the Editing Checklist to check your work.

### Editing Checklist

**Did you use...?**

☐ *'s* + a singular noun to show belonging

☐ an apostrophe (') for a plural noun ending in *-s* to show belonging

☐ *this* and *that* to talk about one person or thing

☐ *these* and *those* to talk about more than one person or thing

☐ *this* and *these* for people or things nearby

☐ *that* and *those* for people or things away from you

**D REVISE YOUR WORK** Read your paragraph again. Can you improve your writing? Make changes if necessary.

# UNIT 20 REVIEW

**Test yourself on the grammar of the unit.**

**A** Complete the conversations. Circle the correct answers.

1. A: Is <u>this</u> / these your jacket?

   B: No, <u>that's</u> / those are my sister's jacket.

2. A: Are that / <u>those</u> your shoes?

   B: No. This / <u>These</u> are my shoes.

3. A: Today is my birthday.

   B: That / <u>That's</u> great. Happy birthday!

**B** Complete the sentences. Use the possessive form of the nouns in parentheses.

1. That's _____ tie.
   (Mark)

2. Where are the _____ running shoes?
   (children)

3. Is _____ hat in the car?
   (Annie)

4. I like your _____ T-shirt.
   (brother)

**C** Correct the conversations. There are <u>six</u> mistakes.

1. A: Is these your new dress?

   B: No. It's not my dress. It's my sister dress.

2. A: Do you like this glasses?

   B: Yes. I really like that glasses. You look smart in them.

3. A: Why are you wearing your dad jacket?

   B: These isn't his jacket. It's my jacket.

**Now check your answers on page 382.**

# Count and Non-Count Nouns; *Some* and *Any*

## FOOD

**OUTCOMES**
- Use count and non-count nouns
- Use quantifiers with count and non-count nouns
- Complete sentences about a reading
- Identify true and false sentences about a conversation
- Talk about food you like and dislike
- Role-play ordering food in a restaurant
- Write a paragraph about your favorite meal

---

## STEP 1    GRAMMAR IN CONTEXT

### BEFORE YOU READ

**Ⓐ** VOCABULARY   Study the words. Then work with a partner. Talk about what you usually have for breakfast, lunch, or dinner.

EXAMPLE:   **A:** I usually have eggs, toast, and coffee for breakfast.
            **B:** I usually have rice and vegetables for dinner.

breakfast
fruit
coffee
juice
toast
eggs
tea
milk
cereal
yogurt

lunch
a sandwich     soup
salad

dinner
steak     rice
pasta     vegetables

**Ⓑ** Work in a group. Compare your answers in A. What foods do your classmates usually eat for breakfast, lunch, and dinner?

21|01  Read these interviews.

# A Healthy Meal?

JESSICA:    Hello, everyone. This morning we're interviewing people about their eating habits. . . . Excuse me, sir, do you eat breakfast?

MAN:    Yes, I do.

JESSICA:    What do you have?

MAN:    I usually have a slice of toast and a cup of tea.

JESSICA:    That's all? Do you have any juice or anything else to drink?

MAN:    Not usually. Once in a while I have coffee instead of tea. I'm always in a hurry. Bye.

JESSICA:    OK. Thanks. Bye. Now, here's our next person. Ma'am, do you eat lunch?

WOMAN 1:    Yes, I do. I usually have a sandwich and some soup and a glass of juice.

JESSICA:    That's a light lunch. Is that all you have?

WOMAN 1:    Yes. I'm on a diet. I'm *always* on a diet.

JESSICA    OK. Thank you. . . . And what about you, ma'am? What do you have for dinner?

WOMAN 2:    Well, I usually have some meat—maybe steak or chicken—and some rice or pasta.

JESSICA:    Do you eat any vegetables?

WOMAN 2:    Oh, yes, I always have vegetables—maybe some peas, or beans, or carrots.

JESSICA:    Hmm. That sounds healthy.

WOMAN 2:    Yes, I always eat a good dinner.

JESSICA:    All right, thanks. Let's see what our next person says . . .

## AFTER YOU READ

Ⓐ COMPREHENSION   Look at the interviews again. Complete the sentences. Circle the correct answers.

**1.** It is _____.

   **a.** morning       **b.** afternoon       **c.** evening

**2.** The man has _____.

   **a.** a big breakfast       **b.** a small breakfast       **c.** no breakfast at all

**3.** He usually drinks _____.

   **a.** water            **b.** coffee          **c.** tea

**4.** The first woman _____ has lunch.

   **a.** never            **b.** always          **c.** sometimes

**5.** The second woman has _____ for dinner.

   **a.** rice or pasta        **b.** french fries        **c.** eggs

**6.** Jessica thinks the _____ has a healthy dinner.

   **a.** man            **b.** first woman       **c.** second woman

**B** Work with a partner. Compare your answers in A.

---

**STEP 2**    **GRAMMAR PRESENTATION**

## COUNT AND NON-COUNT NOUNS; *SOME* AND *ANY*

**Count Nouns**

| Article + Singular Noun | Plural Noun |
|---|---|
| **a**    sandwich | sandwich**es** |
| **an**   orange | orange**s** |

**Non-count Nouns**

|  |
|---|
| bread<br>yogurt<br>water |

**Quantifiers: *Some* and *Any***

| Count Nouns | Non-count Nouns |
|---|---|
| A: Do you have **any** oranges?<br>B: Yes, I have **some**. **or** No, I don't have **any**. | A: Do you have **any** bread?<br>B: Yes, I have **some**. **or** No, I don't have **any**. |

**Other Quantifiers**

a cup of      a slice of      a bowl of      a bottle of      a glass of
(coffee)       (bread)        (cereal)     (mineral water)     (water)

# GRAMMAR NOTES

## 1 Count Nouns

| | |
|---|---|
| **Count nouns** are easy to count. They have a **singular** and a **plural** form. | I have **one** orange, **two** eggs, and **three** bagels. |
| To form the plural of most count nouns, add -*s* or -*es*. | I want an **orange**. Actually, I want two **oranges**. Please bring me **a sandwich**. He wants **two sandwiches**. |
| Remember that we use *a* and *an* before singular count nouns. Use *a* before a word that starts with a **consonant** sound. Use *an* before a word that begins with a **vowel** sound. | Steve wants ***a banana***. *(starts with a consonant sound)* I want ***an orange***. *(starts with a vowel sound)* |

## 2 Non-Count Nouns

| | |
|---|---|
| We cannot count **non-count nouns** in their basic meaning. | Jane wants **tea**. I want **meat**. She wants **water**. |
| We use **singular verbs** with **non-count nouns**. | Rice **is** good for you. **NOT** Rice ~~are~~ good for you. |
| **USAGE NOTE** We use **plural count nouns** or **non-count nouns** to talk about things we **like** or **don't like**. | I like **bananas**. I don't like **yogurt**. I love **bagels**. I hate **soda**. |
| **BE CAREFUL!** Don't use *a*, *an*, or *some* to talk about things you like or don't like. | I like **bananas**. **NOT** I like ~~a banana~~. I don't like **yogurt**. **NOT** I don't like ~~some yogurt~~. |

## 3 Quantifiers

| | |
|---|---|
| We use **quantifiers** to help us count non-count nouns. Some quantifiers are: *a bag of*    *a cup of* *a bowl of*    *a glass of* *a bottle of*    *a slice of* | Please bring me ***a bowl of*** cereal. I want ***a cup of*** coffee. Please bring him ***a slice of*** bread. |

*Some* and *any* are also quantifiers.

| | |
|---|---|
| Use *some* in **affirmative** statements. | I have **some** fruit. |
| Use *any* in **negative** statements. | I don't have **any** fruit. |
| Use both *some* and *any* in questions. | Do you want **some** eggs? |
| | Do you want **any** french fries? |
| We use *some* and *any* with both **count** and **non-count** nouns. | They want **some** *sandwiches*. *(count)* |
| | They want **some** *fruit*. *(non-count)* |
| | They don't want **any** *eggs*. *(count)* |
| | They don't want **any** *cereal*. *(non-count)* |
| Sometimes we don't use a quantifier with **plural count nouns** and **non-count nouns**. | We have (some) **apples** in the refrigerator. *(plural count noun)* |
| | Do you drink (any) **juice** for breakfast? *(non-count noun)* |
| USAGE NOTE  We usually use *some* in questions when we are **offering** something. | Do you want **some** tea? *(an offer)* |

## PRONUNCIATION NOTE

▶ 21|02 **Plural Noun Endings**

Most plural nouns end in *-s* or *-es*. We pronounce these endings /s/, /z/, or /ɪz/.

| | |
|---|---|
| • /s/ | I drink three **cups** of coffee every morning. |
| • /z/ | I love **eggs** for breakfast. |
| • /ɪz/ | We need a bag of **oranges**. |

## REFERENCE NOTES

For **definitions of grammar terms**, see the Glossary on page 375.

For more information on **regular and irregular plural nouns**, see Appendices 8 and 9 on page 368.

For more information on **pronunciation rules for plural nouns**, see Appendix 10 on page 368.

For a list of **non-count nouns** and **quantifiers**, see Appendices 11 and 12 on page 369.

## EXERCISE 1  DISCOVER THE GRAMMAR

Ⓐ GRAMMAR NOTES 1–4  **Read the paragraph. Underline the sixteen nouns that are food and drinks. Circle the quantifiers.**

My favorite meal is lunch—my big meal of the day. I start with(a bowl of)soup,

and I usually have crackers with it. Next, I have some meat. I also have vegetables:

maybe carrots, peas, or beans. I almost always have rice. For dessert, I sometimes have a

cookie, and I usually have some fruit—an orange, or an apple, or a banana. Sometimes

I have a bowl of ice cream. I usually drink a cup of coffee, but once in a while I have tea.

I'm never hungry after lunch.

Ⓑ **Look at the paragraph in A again. Write the underlined nouns in the correct columns in the chart.**

| Count Nouns | Non-Count Nouns |
|---|---|
| crackers | soup |
| Vegetables | rice |
| carrots | fruit |
| peas | ice cream |
| beans | tea |
| an orange | meat |
| an apple | |
| cookie | |

## EXERCISE 2  QUANTIFIERS

Ⓐ GRAMMAR NOTES 3–4  **Complete the conversation. Circle the correct answers (Ø = no article or quantifier).**

SERVER:  All right, folks. What do you want to order?

MARY:  I want a bag of / (some) chicken and rice and a / some mixed vegetables. And please
                 **1.**                                      **2.**
      bring me a cup of / a bowl of hot tea to drink.
                   **3.**

SERVER:  Of course. And for you, young man?

**BEN:** I want a / some tuna sandwich. Is that OK, Grandma?
**4.**

**MARY:** Yes, that's fine. But how about some / any salad to go with it?
**5.**

**BEN:** I don't want some / any salad, Grandma. I don't like a / Ø salad.
**6.** **7.**

**MARY:** All right. But you need something green. Or a / some fruit. Maybe any / some
**8.** **9.**

fruit salad?

**BEN:** OK, Grandma. I like Ø / some fruit salad.
**10.**

**SERVER:** All right. For you, young lady?

**ANNIE:** I want a slice of / a bowl of soup. And
**11.**

any / some salad.
**12.**

**SERVER:** Of course. And to drink?

**MARY:** Can you bring them each a / a glass of
**13.**

milk?

**SERVER:** Certainly.

▶ 21|03 **B** LISTEN AND CHECK   Listen to the conversation and check your answers in A.

## EXERCISE 3 *SOME* OR *ANY*

**A** GRAMMAR NOTE 4   Complete the conversation. Use *some* or *any* and the nouns
in parentheses.

**AMANDA:** Josh, we need _____*some things*_____ for the party tonight. Can you go to
**1. (things)**

the store now?

**JOSH:** Sure. I know we don't have ____*any soda*____ . And we don't have
**2. (soda)**

____*any chips*____ . What else?
**3. (chips)**

**AMANDA:** We need ____*some fruit*____ . And we need ____*some olives*____ .
**4. (fruit)** **5. (olives)**

But let me check.... Oh, yes! Get *some black olives* . Don't get
**6. (black olives)**

____*any green olives*____ .
**7. (green olives)**

**JOSH:** OK. Anything else? Do you want ____*some candy*____ ?
**8. (candy)**

**AMANDA:** Good idea. Get ____*some chocolate candy*____ .
**9. (chocolate candy)**

▶ 21|04 **B** LISTEN AND CHECK   Listen to the conversation and check your answers in A.

# EXERCISE 4 PLURAL NOUN ENDINGS

**A** PRONUNCIATION NOTE  Look at the sentences. Underline the plural nouns.

1. We need some more <u>bagels</u>.

2. How many eggs do you want—one or two?

3. Do we need any oranges?

4. I really like black olives.

5. Mark had three slices of toast for breakfast.

6. I love chips and salsa.

7. Amy made some sandwiches for the picnic.

8. Bananas are very good on cereal.

9. Vegetables are also very healthy for you.

10. Pancakes are my favorite.

21|05  **B** Listen to the sentences in A. How are the plural noun endings pronounced? Write the nouns in the correct columns.

| /s/ | /z/ | /ɪz/ |
|-----|-----|------|
|     | bagels |   |

# EXERCISE 5 EDITING

GRAMMAR NOTES 1–4  There are six mistakes in the conversations. The first mistake is corrected. Find and correct <u>five</u> more.

1. A: Do you like a ~~bagel~~? *bagels*

   B: No, I don't. But I like a sandwich.

2. A: Can I bring you some coffee?

   B: No, thanks. I don't drink a coffee. *any*

3. A: Are we having egg for lunch?

   B: Yes, we are. We're also having a yogurt.

4. A: Do we need milk?

   B: No, we don't need some milk.

242  Unit 21

## EXERCISE 6 LISTENING

▶ 21|06 **A** Listen to Mark and Judy's conversation with a server. Check (✓) the two true statements.

☐ **1.** It's late in the afternoon.

☐ **2.** Mark and Judy want to order lunch.

☐ **3.** Mark and Judy are having dinner.

☐ **4.** The coffee machine is broken.

▶ 21|06 **B** Listen again. Read the statements. Check (✓) *True*, *False*, or *No Information*. Correct the false statements.

|  | True | False | No Information |
|---|---|---|---|
| 1. The restaurant ~~is~~ *isn't* serving lunch now. | ☐ | ✓ | ☐ |
| 2. Judy wants donuts and coffee. | ☐ | ☐ | ☐ |
| 3. The restaurant has iced tea. | ☐ | ☐ | ☐ |
| 4. Mark likes tea. | ☐ | ☐ | ☐ |
| 5. The restaurant doesn't have donuts. | ☐ | ☐ | ☐ |
| 6. The restaurant has mineral water. | ☐ | ☐ | ☐ |
| 7. The soda is expensive. | ☐ | ☐ | ☐ |
| 8. Mark and Judy like the restaurant. | ☐ | ☐ | ☐ |

**C** Work with a partner. Ask and answer questions about Mark and Judy's visit to the restaurant in the listening.

EXAMPLE: A: Who wants some coffee?

B: Judy wants a cup of coffee, but the restaurant doesn't have any coffee. Does Mark want coffee?

A: No . . .

# EXERCISE 7 WHAT FOODS DO YOU LIKE?

**A** SURVEY Complete this survey. Walk around your classroom and ask the other students if they like these foods. For each answer, place a check mark (✓) in the correct column.

EXAMPLE: **A:** Do you like eggs?
          **B:** Yes, I do. Do you like eggs?
          **A:** No. I don't like eggs.

| Food | Like | Don't Like |
|------|------|------------|
| Eggs | | |
| Yogurt | | |
| Toast | | |
| Cereal | | |
| Coffee | | |
| Tea | | |
| Pizza | | |

| Food | Like | Don't Like |
|------|------|------------|
| Steak | | |
| Chicken | | |
| Pasta | | |
| Rice | | |
| Beans | | |
| Carrots | | |
| Peas | | |

**B** Count the number of "likes" and "don't likes" for each food in A. Then work in a small group. In general, what foods do your classmates like? What foods don't they like? Report to the class.

EXAMPLE: In our class, five people like eggs and five people don't like eggs. Nine people like pizza and one person doesn't like pizza. . . .

# EXERCISE 8 WHAT DO YOU WANT TO ORDER?

**A** ROLE PLAY Work with a partner. Practice the conversation.

**A:** What do you want to order?
**B:** I want chicken and rice.
**A:** Sorry. We don't have chicken and rice.
**B:** OK. Please bring me some pasta.
**A:** Sorry, but we don't have any pasta, either.
**B:** Well, what do you have?
**A:** We have pizza.
**B:** I don't like pizza very much, but OK. Please bring me some pizza.

**B** Imagine you are in a restaurant. One of you is a server, and the other is a customer. Work together to write your own conversation. Then perform your conversation for the class.

**A** BEFORE YOU WRITE  Read the composition. Then work with a partner. Guess the answer to the question at the end of the composition. Then decide on your favorite meal. Complete the chart about it. Describe one of the parts of your meal, but don't say what it is. Can your partner guess what it is?

### My Favorite Meal

My favorite meal is dinner. First, I want some steak. I love steak. I also want some french fries. And I love vegetables. My favorite vegetables are peas, beans, and carrots. I want some dessert, of course! My favorite dessert is sweet and has milk in it. It has different flavors: chocolate, vanilla, strawberry, and many others. It's usually in a bowl. Can you guess what the dessert is?

| My favorite meal | |
|---|---|
| Food 1 | |
| Food 2 | |
| Food 3 | |
| Food to guess | |

**B** WRITE  Write a composition about your favorite meal. End your composition with "Can you guess what it is?" Use the composition in A and your chart to help you. Use count nouns, non-count nouns, and quantifiers.

**C** CHECK YOUR WORK  Read your composition. Underline count and non-count nouns, *some*, and *any*. Use the Editing Checklist to check your work.

### Editing Checklist

**Did you use . . . ?**

- [ ] *a* or *an* before singular count nouns
- [ ] no article before plural count nouns and non-count nouns
- [ ] no quantifiers with *like*, *love*, and *hate*
- [ ] *some* in affirmative sentences and *any* in negative sentences
- [ ] correct spelling

**D** REVISE YOUR WORK  Read your paragraph again. Can you improve your writing? Make changes if necessary.

# UNIT 21 **REVIEW**

**Test yourself on the grammar of the unit.**

**A** Complete the phrases. Circle the correct answers.

1. a cup of eggs / chicken / coffee / pizza

2. a bowl of pizza / toast / cereal / steak

3. a slice of yogurt / candy / pizza / chocolate

4. a bottle of fruit / water / rice / chicken

5. a glass of milk / salad / olives / eggs

**B** Complete the conversation. Circle the correct answers.

A: What do you want to order?

B: I want a / an egg salad sandwich.
       **1.**

A: Sorry, we don't have some / any eggs. How about a / an chicken sandwich?
                     **2.**                       **3.**

B: No, I don't like some / Ø chicken. Just bring me a bowl of / cup of coffee.
                         **4.**                         **5.**

**C** Correct the paragraph. There are <u>five</u> mistakes.

    I always drink two cup of coffee for breakfast. Usually I have an cereal

and slice of toast. Sometimes I have fruit, like a bananas. I also like any milk

and yogurt.

**Now check your answers on page 382.**

# A, An, and *The*; *One* and *Ones*

## SHOPPING

**OUTCOMES**
- Use the indefinite articles *an/a* and the definite article *the*
- Use *one* to replace a singular noun and *ones* to replace a plural noun
- Identify true and false sentences about a reading
- Complete sentences about a conversation
- Talk about shopping
- Describe a picture
- Write a conversation about things you want to buy

---

**STEP 1 GRAMMAR IN CONTEXT**

## BEFORE YOU READ

**Ⓐ VOCABULARY** Study the words. Then complete the sentences with the words.

order online

try on

pay for

return

1. _____ that shirt before you buy it. It looks big.

2. I _____ things with my credit card.

3. I don't like this phone. I want to _____ it.

4. You use your computer to _____ .

**Ⓑ Work with a partner. Compare your answers in A.**

# Online or at a Store?

Here's a question: You need a new suit very soon. Do you order the new suit online, or do you go to a store? Both kinds of shopping have their pros and cons.[1]

### Online Shopping: The Pros

- The Internet never closes, so you can order things anytime, day or night.
- There is a good selection[2] online.
- You don't need a car. You don't need money for gas.
- It's easy to send gifts to family members or friends far away.
- It's easy to pay for things with a credit card.

### Online Shopping: The Cons

- Online companies send you the things you buy. That costs money, and it can take a long time.
- Sometimes packages get lost, and you don't receive them.
- Sometimes it's hard to return things online.

### Shopping at a Store: The Pros

- You can see and touch things in a store.
- You can try on many clothes, and you can buy only the good ones. You don't make mistakes and buy the wrong ones.

### Shopping at a Store: The Cons

- You need to go back to the store to return things, and you need a receipt.[3]
- Stores aren't always open. The store hours aren't always good for us.
- Sometimes stores don't have a good selection. For example, they have suits, but they don't always have a good one.

---

Which is better, online shopping or shopping at a store? Actually, they're both good, and bad, in their own ways.

---

1 *pros and cons:* good, positive points and bad, negative points
2 *selection:* many things to choose from
3 *a receipt:* a paper that shows payment

## AFTER YOU READ

**A** COMPREHENSION  Look at the article again. For each statement, check (✓) *True* or *False*.

|  | True | False |
|---|:---:|:---:|
| 1. The Internet sometimes closes. | ☐ | ✓ |
| 2. We can use a credit card to pay for things online. | ✓ | ☐ |
| 3. It is sometimes difficult to return things online. | ✓ | ☐ |
| 4. You need a receipt when you return something to a store. | ☐ | ☐ |
| 5. Stores are always open. | ☐ | ✓ |
| 6. Stores don't always have a lot of things. | ✓ | ☐ |

**B**  Work with a partner. Compare your answers in A.

## STEP 2    GRAMMAR PRESENTATION

## A, AN, AND THE; ONE AND ONES

### Indefinite Articles (A and An)

| Singular Nouns | Plural Nouns |
|---|---|
| I'm looking for **a suit**. | **Suits** are expensive. |
| I have **an interview** tomorrow. | I don't like **interviews**. |

### The Definite Article (The)

| Singular Nouns | Plural Nouns |
|---|---|
| I like **the** blue **suit**. | I don't like **the** black **suits**. |

### One and Ones

| Singular Pronouns | Plural Pronouns |
|---|---|
| I hope my interview is **a** good **one**. | They sell **some** good **ones**. |
| I like **the** blue **one**. | I don't like **the** black **ones**. |

# GRAMMAR NOTES

## 1 A and An

| | |
|---|---|
| *A* and *an* are **indefinite articles**. Use *a* or *an* to talk about a person or thing for the **first time**. You can also use it to talk about people or things in **general**, when it is **not clear** which person or thing you mean. | We have **a** new **car**.<br>Jomo is wearing **an** orange **shirt**. |
| Remember that we use *a* before a **consonant** sound. Use *an* before a **vowel** sound. (See Unit 21.) | A: Do you have **a house**?<br>B: No, we live in **an apartment**. |
| **BE CAREFUL!** Don't put *a* or *an* before a **plural noun** or a **non-count noun**. | He's reading **a** book.<br>**NOT** He's reading ~~a books~~.<br>She's eating meat.<br>**NOT** She's eating ~~a meat~~. |

## 2 The

| | |
|---|---|
| *The* is the **definite article**. Use *the* when you are talking about a **specific** person or thing. It is **clear** which person or thing you mean. | Our car is **the red car**.<br>Abla is in **the kitchen**. |
| You can use *the* before **singular count nouns**, **plural count nouns**, and **non-count nouns**. | **The teacher** is funny.<br>**The students** like her.<br>**The air** is fresh and clean today. |

## 3 One and Ones

| | |
|---|---|
| We use *one* to replace a **singular noun**. | A: Do you have **a car**?<br>B: Yes, I have **one**. |
| We often use *a* or *an* + **an adjective** before *one*. | A: Is this Miryam's phone?<br>B: No, she has **a new one**. |
| We also use *the* + an adjective before *one*. | They have two suits on sale. I like **the blue one**, but I don't like **the brown one**. |
| We use *ones* to replace a **plural noun**. | They sell a lot of chairs here. I like the expensive **ones**, but I also like the cheap **ones**. |

# PRONUNCIATION NOTE

▶ 22|02 **A and *An* Before Singular Count Nouns**

We use *a* before a **consonant sound** and *an* before a **vowel sound**. But sometimes consonants have vowel sounds, and vowels have consonant sounds. We sometimes use *a* before singular count nouns that start with vowels, and *an* before singular count nouns that start with consonants.

| | |
|---|---|
| Singular count nouns that start with *h*: | |
| • When the *h* sounds like /h/, we use *a*. | I need **a h**at. |
| • When the *h* is silent, we use *an*. | The trip takes **an h**our. |
| Singular count nouns that start with *u*: | |
| • When the *u* sounds like /yu/, we use *a*. | We have **a u**niversity in our town. |
| • When the *u* sounds like /ə/, we use *an*. | He needs **an u**mbrella. |

## STEP 3   FOCUSED PRACTICE

## EXERCISE 1   DISCOVER THE GRAMMAR

GRAMMAR NOTES 1–3   Read the conversations and look at the underlined words. Then answer the questions about them. Circle the correct answers.

1. ANNE:   Do you want to buy some clothes online?
   BOB:    Yes, I need a jacket.

   Does Bob know which specific jacket he wants?
   **a.** Yes, he does.
   **b.** No, he doesn't.

2. FRED:   Do you want to buy a car?
   RITA:   Yes, I want to buy a new one.

   Does Rita know which specific car she wants to buy?
   **a.** Yes, she does.
   **b.** No, she doesn't.

3. KATHY:  Which dress are you trying on?
   VICKY:  I'm trying on the green dress.

   Is it clear which dress Vicky is trying on?
   **a.** Yes, it is.
   **b.** No, it isn't.

**4.** ASHA:  I have three new shirts. Do you like them?

JAMA:  Well, I like <u>the red one</u>.

Is "the red one" Asha's shirt?

**a.** Yes, it is.

**b.** No, it isn't.

**5.** JUDY:  Do you like these four books?

ELENA:  I like <u>the one</u> by J. K. Rowling.

What is "the one"?

**a.** A book by J. K. Rowling.

**b.** Judy's four books.

**6.** KATHY:  Are the CDs in this store good?

MARK:  Yes. <u>The classical ones</u> are really good.

What are "the classical ones"?

**a.** All classical CDs.

**b.** The classical CDs in the store.

## EXERCISE 2  ARTICLES

**Ⓐ** GRAMMAR NOTES 1–3  Complete the conversation. Circle the correct answers. (Ø = no article or quantifier.)

KEN:  Laura, let's go to ⓐ/ an / Ø shoe store. I have a / an / Ø interview next week.
<br>　　　　　　　　　　　　　1.　　　　　　　　　　　　　　2.

　　　I need new shoes for it.

LAURA:  OK, we can buy a / an / Ø shoes at
<br>　　　　　　　　　　　　　3.

　　　that store over there.

*(in the store)*

CLERK:  Can I help you?

KEN:  Yes. I need a / the / Ø shoes.
<br>　　　　　　　　　4.

CLERK:  OK. A / An / The men's shoes are over
<br>　　　　　　　　5.

　　　here. What size?

KEN:  Ten medium.

LAURA:  I like a / the / Ø black ones. What do
<br>　　　　　　　　　6.

　　　you think?

KEN: No. I don't like a / the / Ø formal shoes. These are really dark. And I don't like
7.

a / the / Ø style.
8.

CLERK: What about these?

KEN: A / The / Ø tan ones? Very nice! I like them.
9.

CLERK: Do you want to try them on?

KEN: Yes, please.

CLERK: How do they feel?

KEN: Perfect. Laura, what do you think?

LAURA: Well, a / the / Ø shoes look nice. But there's a / the / Ø problem. They're casual.[1] Can
10.                                                    11.

you wear a / the / Ø shoes at your interview?
12.

KEN: Don't worry. They're fine.

_____

1 *casual*: not formal

▶22|03  **B  LISTEN AND CHECK**  Listen to the conversation and check your answers in A.

## EXERCISE 3  *ONE* AND *ONES*

GRAMMAR NOTE 3  Complete the conversations with *one* and *ones*.

1. A: Which jacket do you like best?

   B: I like the blue ____*one*____ best.

2. A: I really like these orange socks.

   B: I don't. I like the gray ____ones____.

3. A: Do you want those expensive notebooks?

   B: Yes. I hate the cheap ____ones____.

4. A: Does this dress fit you?

   B: No, I need a larger ____one____.

5. A: Do you like these black shoes?

   B: No, I like the brown ____ones____ a lot better.

6. A: Is a new car always better?

   B: Not always. Sometimes an older ____one____ is better.

# EXERCISE 4 _A_ AND _AN_ BEFORE SINGULAR COUNT NOUNS

22|04 **A** PRONUNCIATION NOTE Listen to the conversations. Complete the conversations with _a_ or _an_.

**Conversation 1**

A: What do you want for your birthday?

B: I want __an__ umbrella. Can you get me __a__ red one?

**Conversation 2**

A: I need __a__ hat.

B: How about this one?

A: Well. . . . It's __an__ interesting hat, but I don't like the color.

**Conversation 3**

A: I study English for __an__ hour every day.

B: Wow! That's __a__ long time.

**Conversation 4**

A: There's __a__ university in our city.

B: Yes, I know. It's __an__ expensive school.

22|04 **B** Work with a partner. Listen and check your answers in A. Then practice the conversations.

# EXERCISE 5 EDITING

GRAMMAR NOTES 1–3 There are six mistakes in the email. The first mistake is corrected. Find and correct five more.

Dear Kathy,

Josh and I have a great new house! ~~A~~ The house isn't very big, but it's nice. We have the beautiful

living room, but we need to buy the new sofa for it. We have an old sofa, but a sofa isn't nice.

And we really need an new chair. We have one chair, but it's a terrible old ones.

Come visit us soon!

Love,
Amanda

## EXERCISE 6 LISTENING

▶ 22|05 **A** Listen to the conversation. Why are Amanda and Josh shopping?

_____

▶ 22|05 **B** Listen again. Complete the sentences. Circle the correct answers.

**1.** Josh's sister's birthday is today / (tomorrow)

**2.** Amanda suggests a laptop / an iPad for Josh's sister.

**3.** Josh thinks a laptop / an iPad is a better gift.

**4.** Josh's sister already has / doesn't want an iPad.

**5.** Josh's sister has an old / a new computer now.

**6.** The selection online / in the store is good.

**7.** Josh and Amanda buy the expensive / cheaper computer.

**8.** They can / can't get the computer tomorrow.

**C** Work with a partner. Talk about the things in the Listening. Do you want them or not?

EXAMPLE: **A:** Do you want an iPad?
**B:** No, I don't want one. I already have one.

BIG COMPUTER SALE!

This week only! Buy now!

50% Price $230 $460

## EXERCISE 7 WHAT DO YOU THINK?

**A** DISCUSSION Work in a small group. Discuss the questions.

**1.** How do you usually buy things—in a store, online, or do you shop both ways?

**2.** Which do you think is better, shopping in stores or shopping online? Give reasons.

EXAMPLE: **A:** I think stores are better. We have some good ones close to my house. I can try on dresses before I buy them.
**B:** I think shopping online is better. You don't need a car. You can shop on the computer at home. And the selection is better.

**B** Report to the class.

# EXERCISE 8 WHAT'S WRONG WITH THIS PICTURE?

**Ⓐ PICTURE DISCUSSION** Work with a partner. What's wrong with this picture? Find strange or unusual things.

EXAMPLE: **A:** I see a car in the store. It's a pink one. That's strange.
           **B:** The boy is trying on a coat. He needs a smaller one.
           **A:** An old man has a cat in the store. Cats don't go in stores.

**Ⓑ** Work with two other partners. How many wrong or strange things can you find in the picture?

## FROM GRAMMAR TO WRITING

**A** BEFORE YOU WRITE  Read the conversation. Underline the articles *a*, *an*, and *the*.
Circle *one* and *ones*. Then imagine that you want to buy something. Work with a partner.
Ask your partner for advice about the thing you want to buy.

NANCY:  Larry, I want a bike. Where can I buy one?

LARRY:  What kind of bike do you want?

NANCY:  I want a new one. But I don't want an expensive one. Maybe I need an older bike.

LARRY:  Is the bike's color important?

NANCY:  No. I just want a good one.

LARRY:  Bob's Bike-O-Rama is a good store for bikes.

They sell some nice ones. I was there yesterday.

They have an older red bike.

The price is good.

NANCY:  Great! Let's go

to Bob's.

**B** WRITE  Write a conversation about the thing you want to buy. Use the conversation
in A and your discussion with your partner to help you. Use *a*, *an*, *the*, *one*, and *ones*.

**C** CHECK YOUR WORK  Read your composition. Underline the articles *a*, *an*, and *the*.
Circle *one* and *ones*. Use the Editing Checklist to check your work.

| Editing Checklist |
| --- |
| **Did you use...?** |
| ☐ *a* or *an* before singular count nouns when it is not clear which person or thing you mean |
| ☐ *the* before nouns when it is clear which person or thing you mean |
| ☐ *one* and *ones* |
| ☐ correct spelling |

**D** REVISE YOUR WORK  Read your paragraph again. Can you improve your writing?
Make changes if necessary.

# UNIT 22 REVIEW

**Test yourself on the grammar of the unit.**

**Ⓐ Match the questions and answers.**

_____ 1. Which is your jacket?      **a.** The white ones.

_____ 2. Do you like that orange tie?     **b.** No, I need larger ones.

_____ 3. Which are your shoes?     **c.** No, I like the green one.

_____ 4. Do those shoes fit?     **d.** The brown one.

**Ⓑ Complete the sentences with *a*, *an*, *the*, *one*, or *ones*.**

1. It's raining. I need to buy _____ a _____ new umbrella.

2. They sell a lot of chairs here. I don't like the white chairs, but I like the black _____ ones _____.

3. Look at these T-shirts. Do you like _____ the _____ black one?

4. I have a hat, but I need to get a better _____ one _____.

5. I have _____ an _____ old computer.

6. She has a laptop. _____ the _____ laptop is new.

**Ⓒ Correct the sentences. There are <u>five</u> mistakes.**

Bozo's shoes are very strange. Shoes are orange and yellow. An orange shoe is big,

and the yellow ones is small. He's wearing the funny hat, too. He looks like the clown!

**Now check your answers on page 382.**

# 23

## Subject and Object Pronouns

### GIFTS AND FAVORS

**OUTCOMES**
• Use subject and object pronouns
• Identify true and false sentences about a reading
• Complete a chart with information from a conversation
• Ask and answer questions about gifts
• Role-play asking for a favor in a conversation
• Write a paragraph about a gift for someone you know

## STEP 1    GRAMMAR IN CONTEXT

### BEFORE YOU READ

**A** VOCABULARY  Study the words. Then work with a partner. Practice the conversation.

**Conversation**

A: It's your birthday. What gift do you want?

B: I want a gift card. What about you?

A: I want flowers.

B: Flowers are nice.

tickets

flowers

gift card

box of chocolates

**B** Now practice the other words in A.

A: It's your birthday. What gift do you want?

B: I want _____. What about you?

A: I want _____.

B: _____.

23|01    Read this conversation.

# An Appropriate¹ Gift

CARLOS:   Judy, you're an American. What's a good gift?

JUDY:      For what?

CARLOS:   For the party at Bill's house on Saturday. I want to get him a gift.

JUDY:      Right. Let me think.

CARLOS:   How about flowers?

JUDY:      Well, I guess flowers are nice. But you don't usually give flowers to a man.

CARLOS:   He has a wife. Can I give them to her?

JUDY:      Hmm. I'm not sure.

CARLOS:   What about tickets for a concert? I know he likes music. Or maybe a gift card?

JUDY:      No. Not appropriate. You don't give your boss tickets or a gift card.

CARLOS:   Well, what do you suggest?

JUDY:      Why don't you² give him some chocolates? He's always eating them at his desk.

CARLOS:   OK, good idea. A box of chocolates. Now, can you do me a favor?

JUDY:      Sure. What?

CARLOS:   Tomiko and I need a ride to the party. Our car isn't working. Can you take us?

---

1   *appropriate:* the right thing at the right time
2   *Why don't you:* I suggest you

JUDY:    For a price.

CARLOS:  For a price? What do you mean?

JUDY:    Get me a box of chocolates, too.

CARLOS:  I don't believe you. You're kidding!

JUDY:    You're right! I can pick you up[3] at 6:30 on Saturday. OK?

---

**3** *pick you up:* come and get you in my car

## AFTER YOU READ

**Ⓐ COMPREHENSION** Look at the conversation again. For each statement, check (✓) *True* or *False*.

|  | True | False |
|---|---|---|
| **1.** Bill is Carlos's boss. | ☐ | ☐ |
| **2.** Judy says people often give flowers to a man. | ☐ | ☐ |
| **3.** Judy says tickets are a good gift for a boss. | ☐ | ☐ |
| **4.** Carlos's boss likes chocolates. | ☐ | ☐ |
| **5.** Judy has a car. | ☐ | ☐ |
| **6.** Judy doesn't like chocolate. | ☐ | ☐ |

**Ⓑ** Work with a partner. Compare your answers in A.

## STEP 2   GRAMMAR PRESENTATION

### SUBJECT AND OBJECT PRONOUNS

| Subject Pronouns | Example Sentences | Object Pronouns | Example Sentences |
|---|---|---|---|
| I | I like flowers. | Me | Maria usually calls **me**. |
| You | **You** have the tickets. | You | Yusuf likes **you**. |
| He | **He**'s my boss. | Him | Please ask **him**. |
| She | **She** needs help. | Her | Kei knows **her** very well. |
| It | **It**'s for a party. | It | Bring **it** to the party. |
| We | **We** don't know Bill. | Us | Jim is giving **us** a ride. |
| You | **You** seem very happy. | You | I can see **you** this afternoon. |
| They | **They**'re a good gift. | Them | The boss loves **them**. |

# GRAMMAR NOTES

## 1 Subject Pronouns

| | |
|---|---|
| *I*, *you*, *he*, *she*, *it*, *we*, and *they* are **subject pronouns**. They replace a subject noun. | SUBJECT NOUN<br>**The boys** need a ride.    SUBJECT PRONOUN<br>**They** don't have a car. |

## 2 Object Pronouns

| | |
|---|---|
| *Me*, *you*, *him*, *her*, *it*, *us*, and *them* are **object pronouns**. They replace an object noun. | SUBJECT NOUN    OBJECT NOUN<br>**Bill** loves **chocolates**.<br><br>SUBJECT PRONOUN    OBJECT PRONOUN<br>**He** loves **them**. |
| Object pronouns often come after verbs and after prepositions like *to* or *for*. | Give the chocolates *to* **him**.<br>The chocolates are *for* **him**. |

## 3 *You* and *It*

| | |
|---|---|
| *You* and *it* are both subject and object pronouns. | SUBJECT    OBJECT<br>**You**'re kidding. I don't believe **you**.<br><br>SUBJECT    OBJECT<br>**It**'s good music. He likes **it**. |
| The pronoun *you* is the same for singular and plural. | I don't believe **you**. *(you = Judy)*<br>See **you** at 6:30. *(you = you and Tomiko)*<br><br>Are **you** ready for the test? *(you = one student)*<br>Are **you** ready for the test? *(you = the class)* |

## REFERENCE NOTES

For definitions of **grammar terms**, see the Glossary on page 375.

For more information on **subject pronouns**, see Unit 1 on page 8.

## EXERCISE 1   DISCOVER THE GRAMMAR

(A) **GRAMMAR NOTES 1–3**   Read the conversation. Underline the subject pronouns. Circle the object pronouns.

STEVE:    <u>You</u> like parties. Right?

AMANDA:    I love (them) Why?

STEVE:    Well, we're having a party on Sunday at my apartment. You and Josh are

          invited. Are you free at three o'clock?

AMANDA:    I think so. What's the occasion?

STEVE:    It's Jessica's birthday, but I don't know what to get her. What's a good gift?

          Any ideas?

AMANDA:    How about tickets for a concert? Does she like music?

STEVE:    Yes. She listens to it all the time.

AMANDA:    Good. Get her some tickets. You can get them online. Now, tell me again.

          What's your new address?

STEVE:    Fourteen Vine Street, Apartment 202.

AMANDA:    OK. See you then.

(B) **Read the conversation in A again. For each statement, check (✓) *True* or *False*.**

|  | True | False |
|---|:---:|:---:|
| 1. Amanda loves parties. | ✓ | |
| 2. Only Amanda is invited to Jessica's party. | | ✓ |
| 3. Amanda and Josh are free at three o'clock on Sunday. | ✓ | |
| 4. Jessica's birthday is on Saturday. | | |
| 5. Steve knows what to get Jessica for her birthday. | | |
| 6. Jessica likes music. | ✓ | |
| 7. Jessica rarely listens to music. | | |
| 8. Amanda says Steve can get tickets online. | | |

## EXERCISE 2 SUBJECT AND OBJECT PRONOUNS

GRAMMAR NOTES 1–3 Complete the sentences. Circle the correct answers.

1. Jenny needs a ride. Drive she / (her) to the train station.

2. Josh and I love tennis. Can you play with we / (us)?

3. Steve loves books. Why don't you get he / (him) one?

4. Jessica and Tim are at a restaurant. They / Them are celebrating their anniversary.

5. I / Me need to go shopping for Steve's birthday present.

6. We / Us are going to the party. Do you need a ride?

7. How about some bagels? I know you like it / (them).

8. Ana loves shopping at the mall. I can give her / him a gift card from a store there.

## EXERCISE 3 SUBJECT AND OBJECT PRONOUNS

GRAMMAR NOTES 1–3 Complete the conversations. Use subject and object pronouns.

1. A: It's Jessica's birthday on Sunday. What's a good gift for ____her____?

   B: How about a DVD? ____She____ loves movies.

2. A: I need to buy a present for Mark's birthday next week. What's a good present?

   B: Well, ____He____ likes music. Get ____him____ some concert tickets.

3. A: Our car isn't working. Can ____you____ give ____us____ a ride to the party?

   B: Sure. I'll pick ____you____ up at 5:00.

4. A: The Johnsons are having a party on Saturday. What's a good gift for ____them____?

   B: ____They____ love flowers.

5. A: Hello? Steve? Is ____it____ raining there? Do I need my umbrella?

   B: Yes, bring ____it____. It's raining hard.

6. A: My friends are visiting from Portland. ____They____'re a lot of fun.

   B: Well, bring ____them____ on Saturday. We have a lot of food.

# EXERCISE 4 OBJECT PRONOUNS

GRAMMAR NOTE 2  In the pictures, the people are talking about buying presents for
people they know. For each picture, continue the conversation. Use the nouns in
parentheses. For A's question, use *Why don't you get* + noun + *for* + object pronoun. For
B's answer, use a noun + *for* + object pronoun.

1.  A: <u>Why don't you get a travel book for them</u> ?
    (a travel book)

    B: They don't like travel books. I can get <u>a CD for them</u> .
    (a CD)

2.  A: _____ ?
    (a soccer ball)

    B: She has a soccer ball. I can get _____ .
    (this tennis racquet)

3.  A: _____ ?
    (a vest)

    B: He doesn't wear vests. I can get _____ .
    (a jacket)

4.  A: _____ ?
    (a DVD)

    B: You already have a lot of DVDs. I can get _____ .
    (a video game)

## EXERCISE 5
## EDITING

GRAMMAR NOTES 1–3
There are six mistakes
in the invitation.
The first mistake is
corrected. Find and
correct five more.

Dear Sarah,

                    I
Jim and ~~me~~ are having a party on Saturday, June 10,

at 3:00. Is for our son, Bob, and our daughter, Sally.

Them both have birthdays in June. You and Stan are

invited. Please don't bring they any presents. Us have

lots of gifts already. Can you come? Give I a call.

See you soon.
Doris

## STEP 4    COMMUNICATION PRACTICE

## EXERCISE 6  LISTENING

▶ 23|02  **A** Listen to Jessica and Tim's conversation. What is Tim's problem?

_____

▶ 23|02  **B** Listen again. Complete the chart with the words from the box.

| Colors: | blue | green | orange | ~~red~~ | white |

| Gifts: | a DVD | a game | something special | ~~a tennis racquet~~ | concert tickets |

| Color of Package | Who is it for? | Gift |
|---|---|---|
| red | Cousin Martha | a tennis racquet |
| | Mom and Dad | |
| | Jeremy | |
| | Ben and Annie | |
| | Jessica | |

**C** Work with a partner. Look at the chart in B. Ask your partner what Jessica and Tim are giving people. Your partner answers the question. Take turns.

EXAMPLE:  A:  What are Jessica and Tim giving Martha?
          B:  They're giving her a tennis racquet.

## EXERCISE 7  WHAT'S A GOOD GIFT?

**A** DISCUSSION  Work with a partner. Write the names of five people you know. Talk about a good gift for each person.

EXAMPLE:  A:  Theo is my brother. It's his birthday tomorrow. What's a good gift for him?
          B:  Hmm. How old is he?
          A:  Ten.
          B:  Maybe a DVD?
          A:  I don't think so.
          B:  OK, then why don't you get him a soccer ball?
          A:  Good idea.

**B** Report interesting answers to the class.

## EXERCISE 8  CAN YOU DO ME A FAVOR?

**A** ROLE PLAY  Work with a partner. Prepare a role-play conversation. Ask your partner to do you a favor. Choose a favor from the box or use your own favor.

| | | |
|---|---|---|
| buy me some coffee | give me a ride downtown | pick me up at work |
| get me some medicine | lend me $20 | |

EXAMPLE:  A:  Matteo, can you do me a favor?
          B:  Sure. What do you need?
          A:  My car isn't working. Can you pick me up at work?
          B:  Yes. What time do you finish work?
          A:  Five-thirty.
          B:  OK, good. See you at 5:30.

**B** Present your role play to the class.

**A** BEFORE YOU WRITE  Read the paragraph. Underline subject pronouns and circle object pronouns. Then think about a gift for someone you know. Complete the chart. Work with a partner. Tell your partner about the person and the gift.

My sister's seventeenth birthday is this month. What can I buy for her? I have only $30 for a gift. I know! I can get her some books. She loves books, and they aren't very expensive. I can get them at my favorite bookstore. It has a lot of good books.

| Who is the person? | |
| --- | --- |
| What does the person like? | |
| What can I get the person? | |

**B** WRITE  Write a paragraph about a gift for someone you know. Use subject and object pronouns. Use the paragraph in A and your chart to help you.

**C** CHECK YOUR WORK  Read your paragraph. Underline subject pronouns and circle object pronouns. Use the Editing Checklist to check your work.

**Editing Checklist**

**Did you use . . . ?**
- [ ] subject pronouns to replace subject nouns
- [ ] object pronouns to replace object nouns
- [ ] correct spelling

**D** REVISE YOUR WORK  Read your paragraph again. Can you improve your writing? Make changes if necessary.

# UNIT 23 REVIEW

**Test yourself on the grammar of the unit.**

**Ⓐ Complete the conversations. Circle the correct answers.**

1. **A:** It's Steve's birthday on Sunday. What's a good gift for he / him?

   **B:** How about a gift card from a movie theater? He / Him really likes movies.

2. **A:** What's a good gift for the children? Do they / them like games?

   **B:** Yes, buy they / them games. We / Us all love games!

**Ⓑ Look at the nouns in parentheses. Complete the suggestions with the correct object pronouns.**

1. Why don't you get flowers for _____?
   (your wife)

2. Why don't you get a tie for _____?
   (Uncle Toshi)

3. Why don't you take chocolates to _____?
   (your cousins)

4. Why don't we give a gift card to _____?
   (John's sister)

5. Why don't you buy a new TV for _____?
   (Grandma and Grandpa)

**Ⓒ Correct the note. There are five mistakes.**

Dear Doris and Jim,

Thank you for inviting we to the party on June 10. Us can bring some cookies

for dessert. It are really good, and everyone likes they. I don't have your address.

Can you please email them to us?

See you on Saturday!

Sarah and Stan

**Now check your answers on pages 382–383.**

# Simple Past

# PART 8

**OUTCOMES**
- Use regular verbs in simple past statements to talk about the past
- Identify true and false sentences about a reading and a conversation
- Talk about events from your past
- Give a short presentation about the life of a successful businessperson
- Write a paragraph about a successful businessperson

**OUTCOMES**
- Use regular and irregular verbs in the simple past
- Ask and answer *yes/no* questions in the simple past
- Complete sentences about a reading
- Identify true and false statements about a conversation
- Talk about the lives of famous people
- Interview your classmates about what they did last week
- Write a paragraph about a famous person who helped others

**OUTCOMES**
- Ask and answer *wh-* questions in the simple past
- Answer questions about a reading and a conversation
- Ask and answer questions about accidents
- Ask and answer questions about a news report
- Write a conversation about what you saw on your way to school

# Simple Past Statements: Regular Verbs

## SUCCESS STORIES

**OUTCOMES**
• Use regular verbs in simple past statements to talk about the past
• Identify true and false sentences about a reading and a conversation
• Talk about events from your past
• Give a short presentation about the life of a successful businessperson
• Write a paragraph about a successful businessperson

## STEP 1 GRAMMAR IN CONTEXT

### BEFORE YOU READ

**A** VOCABULARY **Study these words. Complete the paragraph with the words from the box.**

move

graduate

Welcome to the company!

Thanks!

hire

| graduated | hired | moved |

   Ten years ago my wife and I _____ graduated _____ from college. We

_____ to Chicago, Illinois. Then we started a shoe business. After a year,
  **2.**

we started to get a lot of customers, and we needed help. So we _____
                                                             **3.**

more workers. Today, thirty people work for us.

**B** Work with a partner. Compare your answers in A.

# BRIAN SCUDAMORE:
# The Business of Junk[1]

**BRIAN SCUDAMORE** was born in San Francisco in 1970. In 1978, his family moved to Vancouver. Brian wasn't a good student. He didn't finish high school, so colleges didn't want him. But Brian wanted to go to college. He talked to professors at a business college. They liked him, and they offered him a place. Brian enrolled at the college.

College was expensive, and Brian needed money. One day he was at a restaurant. An old truck was in the street outside. Brian looked at all the junk in the truck. He realized[2] something important. People didn't want to move their own junk. They wanted someone else to take it away. So, Brian started his own junk removal[3] business. He moved junk from people's homes. He worked hard, and his business expanded.[4]

**Brian Scudamore**

Brian wanted an unusual name for his business. He liked the name 1-800-GOT-JUNK?, but the Department of Transportation of Idaho owned that name. That didn't stop Brian. He talked to the Department, and they agreed to give him the name.

Brian was busy with his business, so he never graduated from college. But that wasn't a problem for him. Today he is a very successful businessman.

What is Brian like? Does he love junk and keep it in his house? He says, "No. I'm very neat, and I don't keep many things."

---

1 *junk:* old things people don't want
2 *realized:* understood
3 *removal:* taking away
4 *expanded:* grew; got bigger

## AFTER YOU READ

**A** COMPREHENSION  Look at the article again. For each statement, check (✓) *True* or *False*.

|  |  | True | False |
|---|---|:---:|:---:|
| 1. | Brian Scudamore lived in San Francisco for eight years. | ✓ | ☐ |
| 2. | Brian Scudamore didn't attend college. | ☐ | ✓ |
| 3. | Brian Scudamore didn't finish college. | ☐ | ✓ |
| 4. | Brian Scudamore's business moved junk from homes. | ✓ | ☐ |
| 5. | Brian Scudamore didn't like the name 1-800-GOT-JUNK?. | ☐ | ✓ |
| 6. | Brian Scudamore has a lot of junk in his house. | ☐ | ☐ |

**B**  Work with a partner. Compare your answers in A.

---

### STEP 2    GRAMMAR PRESENTATION

## SIMPLE PAST: REGULAR VERBS (STATEMENTS)

| Affirmative | | | | Negative | | | |
|---|---|---|---|---|---|---|---|
| Subject | Past Form of Verb | | | Subject | *Did not* | Base Form of Verb | |
| I<br>You<br>He<br>She<br>We<br>You<br>They | **started** | a job last week. | | I<br>You<br>He<br>She<br>We<br>You<br>They | **did not (didn't)** | start | a business. |
| It | | on time. | | It | | | late. |

## PAST TIME EXPRESSIONS

| Past Time Expressions | | |
|---|---|---|
| *Yesterday* | *Ago* | *Last* |
| **yesterday**<br>**yesterday** morning<br>**yesterday** evening | two days **ago**<br>a week **ago**<br>a month **ago**<br>a year **ago** | **last** night<br>**last** week<br>**last** Monday<br>**last** year |

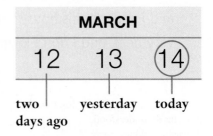

**MARCH**

12    13    (14)

two days ago    yesterday    today

# GRAMMAR NOTES

## 1 Simple Past: Uses

| | |
|---|---|
| Use the **simple past** to talk about an event that **happened in the past**.<br><br>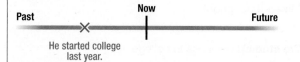 | I **graduated** high school two years ago.<br>He **started** college last year. |

## 2 Simple Past: Affirmative Statements

| | |
|---|---|
| In **simple past affirmative** statements, **regular** verbs end in **-ed**. The ending is the **same** for **all subjects**. | I **start*ed*** a business.<br>She **start*ed*** a business.<br>They **start*ed*** a business. |
| If the base form of the verb ends in **-e**, add only **-d**. | She **graduat*ed*** from college last year. |
| Some verbs end in a **consonant + -y**. Change the -y to **-i** and add **-ed**. | I **stud*ied*** all night. |

## 3 Simple Past: Negative Statements

| | |
|---|---|
| Use **did not** + the **base form** of the verb to make a negative statement in the simple past. | She **did not work** yesterday. |
| **USAGE NOTE** We often use **didn't** for speaking and informal writing. | She **didn't work** yesterday. |
| **BE CAREFUL!** Do not add **-ed** to verbs that follow **didn't**. | She **didn't start** a business.<br>**NOT** She didn't ~~started~~ a business. |

## 4 Past Time Expressions

| | |
|---|---|
| Past time expressions come at the **beginning** or the **end** of a sentence. | **Last night,** I studied Spanish.<br>I studied Spanish test **last night**. |
| | My friend worked **yesterday**.<br>**Yesterday,** my friend worked. |
| | I visited my grandparents **two weeks ago**.<br>**Two weeks ago,** I visited my grandparents. |

## PRONUNCIATION NOTE

24|02 **Simple Past Verb Endings**

> The regular **simple past verb ending** has **three sounds**: /t/, /d/, and /ɪd/. The sound of the past ending depends on the last sound in the base form of the verb.

| | |
|---|---|
| • **/t/ sound:** The simple past of *like* is pronounced /laɪkt/. | I **liked** that school. |
| • **/d/ sound:** The simple past of *study* is pronounced /stʌdid/. | We **studied** business in college. |
| • **/ɪd/ sound:** The simple past of *start* is pronounced /stɑrtɪd/. | I **started** college last year. |

## REFERENCE NOTES

For **definitions of grammar terms**, see the Glossary on page 375.

For more information on the **past of** *be*, see Unit 7 on page 76.

For information on **irregular simple past verbs** and **simple past** *yes/no* **questions**, see Unit 25 on page 286.

For more information on the **simple past spelling and pronunciation rules**, see Appendices 17 and 18 on page 372.

## STEP 3    FOCUSED PRACTICE

## EXERCISE 1  DISCOVER THE GRAMMAR

Ⓐ GRAMMAR NOTES 1–4  Read about Kathy's cousin Ted Geller. Underline the simple past verbs. Circle the negative past tense verbs.

Ten years ago, Ted Geller graduated from college. He finished college in three years.

A year after his graduation, Ted and four friends started an online business. They hired

a lot of people. For three years, everyone worked very hard. They didn't travel. They

didn't relax. Their business expanded. In their fifth year, a company offered them a lot

of money for their business. The five partners agreed to sell it. Ted used half of his

money to help poor children and the other half to start a new business.

Ⓑ Write the base forms of the underlined words in A.

| graduate | start | work | offer | use |
|---|---|---|---|---|
| finish | hire | expand | agree | |

# EXERCISE 2 SIMPLE PAST: AFFIRMATIVE STATEMENTS

GRAMMAR NOTES 1–2 Complete the sentences. Use the past forms of the verbs from the box.

| graduate | help | learn | ~~love~~ | move | open | work |
|---|---|---|---|---|---|---|

As a child, Jane _____**loved**_____ flowers. She always _____ her
      1.                              2.

mother in their garden. Six years ago, Jane _____ from art school. She
                                                        3.

_____ in a flower shop after graduation. She _____ a lot about
  4.                                        5.

flowers and about business. Three years ago, she _____ to a new city and
                                                6.

_____ her own flower shop. Her flower shop is doing very well, and Jane
  7.

wants to open another one.

# EXERCISE 3 AFFIRMATIVE AND NEGATIVE STATEMENTS

GRAMMAR NOTES 1–3 Look at the pictures. Complete the sentences with the past forms of the verbs from the box. Use the affirmative or negative. Use all the verbs twice.

| clean | enjoy | play | rain | stay | watch |
|---|---|---|---|---|---|

On Saturday, it _____**rained**_____ all day long. Judy _____ at home.
               1.                                    2.

She _____ her apartment. Then she _____ TV. She
     3.                                        4.

_____ tennis. Judy wasn't happy. She _____ the day. On
  5.                                            6.

Sunday, it _____. It was a beautiful day. Judy _____ at
          7.                                        8.

home. She _____ TV. She _____ her apartment. She
        9.                                10.

_____ tennis in the park. Judy was happy. She _____ the day.
  11.                                              12.

## EXERCISE 4 PAST TIME EXPRESSIONS

GRAMMAR NOTE 4 Complete the sentences with *last*, *ago*, or *yesterday*.

Five years _____ago_____, I started my career as a server at a restaurant. My boss

was terrible. I changed jobs four years _____ago_____. My new boss was good. He

liked me and I liked him. _____last_____ month, the restaurant moved to a new

location. I moved, too. _____Yesterday_____, we celebrated our first month in the new

location, and I celebrated my new job as head server.

## EXERCISE 5 SIMPLE PAST VERB ENDINGS

24|03 **A** PRONUNCIATION NOTE Read the sentences in the chart. Underline the simple past verbs. Then listen and check (✓) the verb endings you hear.

| Sentence | /t/ | /d/ | /ɪd/ |
|---|---|---|---|
| **1.** He graduated from college last year. | | | ✓ |
| **2.** He and his friends started a business. | | | ✓ |
| **3.** They worked for ten hours every day. | ✓ | | |
| **4.** They hired many people. | | ✓ | |
| **5.** They learned a lot about people. | | ✓ | |
| **6.** They liked their new workers. | ✓ | | |
| **7.** The business expanded a lot. | | | |

24|03 **B** Listen again and repeat the sentences.

## EXERCISE 6 EDITING

GRAMMAR NOTES 1–4 There are six mistakes in the sentences. The first mistake is corrected. Find and correct five more.

**1.** I ~~did~~ hired a new assistant last Thursday.

**2.** We didn't worked yesterday.

**3.** She last month opened a new store.

**4.** I visited them for two days ago.

**5.** We move to the city last year.

**6.** Our business did expanded last month.

## STEP 4 COMMUNICATION PRACTICE

### EXERCISE 7 LISTENING

24|04 **A** Listen to a talk about a successful business. What kind of company is Bucketfeet?

_____

24|04 **B** Listen again. For each statement, check (✓) *True* or *False*.

|  | | True | False |
|---|---|:---:|:---:|
| 1. | Raaji Nemani and Aaron Feinstein were in Austria at the same time. | ☐ | ☑ |
| 2. | Raaji and Aaron helped people in poor areas. | ☐ | ☐ |
| 3. | Aaron painted a backpack for Raaji. | ☐ | ☐ |
| 4. | A lot of people asked about Raaji's sneakers. | ☐ | ☐ |
| 5. | Raaji didn't like his sneakers. | ☐ | ☐ |
| 6. | When Raaji returned from his trip, the two men opened a travel company. | ☐ | ☐ |
| 7. | They hired musicians from around the world. | ☐ | ☐ |
| 8. | Bucketfeet connects people through travel. | ☐ | ☐ |

**C** Work with a partner. Change all the false statements in B to true ones.

EXAMPLE: **A:** They weren't together in Austria.
        **B:** You're right. They were in Argentina at the same time. They helped people in the poor areas.

### EXERCISE 8 GUESS MY SECRET

**A** GAME Write two things your classmates don't know about you. Write one affirmative and one negative sentence on small pieces of paper. Use the simple past and the verbs in the box.

| be | like | move | start | work |
|---|---|---|---|---|
| graduate | live | pass | study | |

*I didn't like school ten years ago.*

*I lived in Paris for two months five years ago.*

**B** Work in a group. Put your sentences in a box. Each student picks a sentence and reads it to the class. The class guesses the person.

EXAMPLE: **A:** This paper says, "When I was six, I moved from a small town to the capital of my country."
        **B:** I think it's Ali. He's from the capital of his country. Is it you, Ali?
        **C:** No, that's not my paper. I didn't move from the country to Cairo. I was born in Cairo.

# EXERCISE 9 HE STARTED ALIBABA

**A PRESENTATION** Prepare for a presentation. Work in a group. First, read about these successful business people from around the world. Match the names and the bios.

__c__ **1.** She is a Filipino-American businesswoman. When she was in college, she needed caregivers[1] for her children, but it was hard to find good ones. So, in 2006, she started the Internet company Care.com. On Care.com, people can find caregivers, and caregivers can find people to help. The website is a huge success.

**a.** Steve Jobs

_____ **2.** He was a poor boy in China. He wanted to learn English, but he didn't have money for school. So, he helped Americans in China, and they helped him learn English. Later he wanted to go to college, but he failed the entrance exam. He looked for jobs, but he didn't find one. But then, in 1998, he started an Internet company called Alibaba. It succeeded, and today Jack Ma is a very rich man.

**b.** Jack Ma

_____ **3.** He was a great boxer. He was a heavyweight champion and an Olympic gold medalist. After 1977, he didn't box anymore. He studied and worked as a minister in a church. Then he was a businessman. He worked with different companies, and one of them produced electric grills. The grills cooked meat in a healthy way, and now, millions of people have them at home.

**c.** Sheila Lirio Marcelo

_____ **4.** This man lived in California. He studied at Reed College in Oregon, but he didn't graduate from college. He traveled to India and studied Eastern religions. He and his partner, Steve Wozniak, started Apple. This computer company makes the iPad and the iPhone.

**d.** George Foreman

**B** Choose one of the people in A. Make a poster about the person. Use the Internet to get more information about the person. Use the verbs in the box for ideas.

| die | start |
| expand | study |
| graduate | succeed |
| live | travel |
| move | |

*When he was a child, Steve Jobs lived near San Francisco, California. He worked on computers in the family garage. Jobs was smart, but he didn't like school. He didn't study...*

**C** Present your poster to the class.

---

1 *caregivers:* people who take care of other people

## FROM GRAMMAR TO WRITING

**A** BEFORE YOU WRITE Look at the timeline about Diego. Then read about him. Underline the past tense verbs. Then make a timeline about a businessperson you know. Work with a partner. Tell your partner about the person.

| born in Lima | started high school | graduated from high school | moved to New York City; enrolled in an English language school | worked in cousin's gym | opened a gym | the gym expanded |
|---|---|---|---|---|---|---|
| 1994 | 2009 | 2013 | 2014 | 2015 | 2016 | 2017 |

I was born in Peru in 1994. I lived with my parents and my two brothers in Lima. When I was a child, I enjoyed sports. I started high school in 2009. In high school, I played soccer. I also studied English. I graduated from high school in 2013. In 2014, I moved to New York City and enrolled in an English language school. The next year, I worked in my cousin's gym. I loved the work. I saved money, and then I opened a small gym in 2016. The gym was popular, and it expanded in 2017.

**B** WRITE Write a paragraph about a businessperson. Use the paragraph in A and your timeline to help you. Use affirmative or negative simple past statements.

**C** CHECK YOUR WORK Read your paragraph in B. Underline the simple past verbs. Then use the Editing Checklist to check your work.

### Editing Checklist

**Did you . . . ?**
- [ ] add *-d* or *-ed* to the base form of regular verbs
- [ ] use *didn't* + the base form to form the negative
- [ ] correct your spelling

**D** REVISE YOUR WORK Read your sentences again. Can you improve your writing? Make changes if necessary.

# UNIT 24 REVIEW

**Test yourself on the grammar of the unit.**

**A** Complete the sentences. Use the <u>simple past form of the words</u> in parentheses.

1. He _____ *moved* _____ from Peru to the United States last year.
   (move)

2. She _____ *didn't graduate* _____ from college. She's still in college.
   (not / graduate)

3. They _____ *didn't start* _____ a business two years ago.
   (not / start)

4. He _____ *hired* _____ an assistant last year.
   (hire)

5. His business _____ *expanded* _____ two months ago.
   (expand)

**B** Complete the sentences. Circle the correct answers.

My cousin <u>attended</u> / did attended Columbia University. He was graduate / <u>graduated</u>
            **1.**                                        **2.**

last year. After graduation, he starts / <u>started</u> a business, but he work not / <u>didn't work</u>
                                   **3.**                        **4.**

hard and he no listen / <u>didn't listen</u> to other people. The business <u>failed</u> / does fail. He
                  **5.**                                                **6.**

started another business. This time he worked very hard, and his business was a success.

**C** Correct the sentences. There are four mistakes.

1. We started last year a business. *We started a business last year.*

2. He no did graduate from high school. *He didn't graduate from high school.*

3. Two weeks ago, I move to a new apartment. *I moved to a new apartment two weeks ago.*

4. She was enjoy her vacation last summer.

**Now check your answers on page 383.**

# Simple Past:
# Irregular Verbs;
# *Yes/No* Questions

## HELPING OTHERS

## STEP 1  GRAMMAR IN CONTEXT

### BEFORE YOU READ

**A** VOCABULARY  **Study the words. Then complete the sentences with the words.**

act

protect

take care of

1. Nurses _____ sick people in hospitals.

2. People _____ when they play characters in movies or plays.

3. Parents _____ their children when they ride in cars.

**B**  Work with a partner. Compare your answers in A.

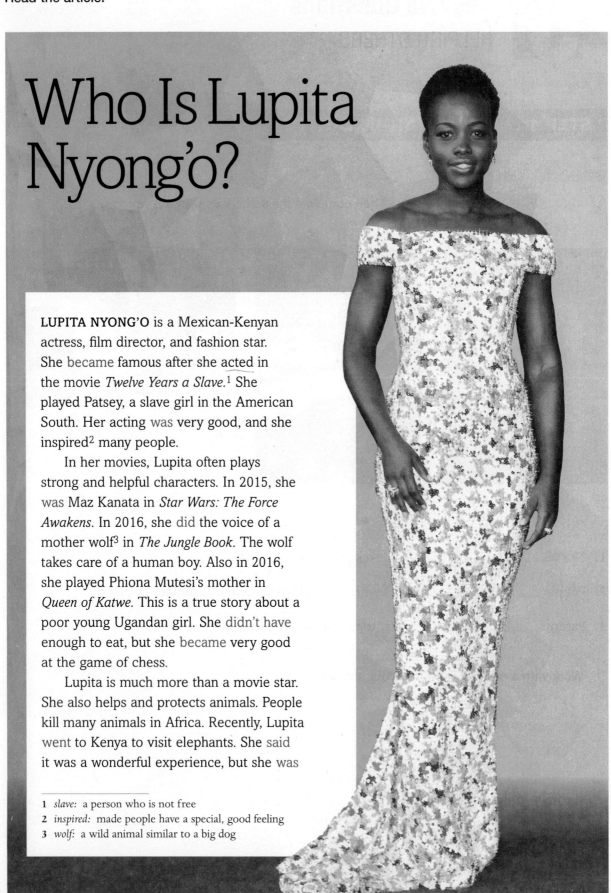

# Who Is Lupita Nyong'o?

**LUPITA NYONG'O** is a Mexican-Kenyan actress, film director, and fashion star. She became famous after she acted in the movie *Twelve Years a Slave*.[1] She played Patsey, a slave girl in the American South. Her acting was very good, and she inspired[2] many people.

In her movies, Lupita often plays strong and helpful characters. In 2015, she was Maz Kanata in *Star Wars: The Force Awakens*. In 2016, she did the voice of a mother wolf[3] in *The Jungle Book*. The wolf takes care of a human boy. Also in 2016, she played Phiona Mutesi's mother in *Queen of Katwe*. This is a true story about a poor young Ugandan girl. She didn't have enough to eat, but she became very good at the game of chess.

Lupita is much more than a movie star. She also helps and protects animals. People kill many animals in Africa. Recently, Lupita went to Kenya to visit elephants. She said it was a wonderful experience, but she was

---

1  *slave:* a person who is not free
2  *inspired:* made people have a special, good feeling
3  *wolf:* a wild animal similar to a big dog

sad when she saw many baby elephants with no mothers. Lupita wants everyone to help her save elephants and other animals.

Lupita also helps girls and women around the world. Recently, Lupita became a member of Mother Health International. This organization helps poor mothers and their children in Africa.

Lupita Nyong'o's film career is important. But she also protects animals and helps girls, women, and babies. That work is even more important.

A scene from *Queen of Katwe*

## AFTER YOU READ

**A** COMPREHENSION Look at the article again. Complete the sentences. Circle the correct answers.

1. Lupita Nyong'o became famous after she was in the movie _____.
   a. *Star Wars: The Force Awakens*   b. *Twelve Years a Slave*

2. The movie *Queen of Katwe* is about _____.
   a. a mother wolf   b. a chess player

3. In Kenya, Lupita visited _____.
   a. elephants   b. girls

4. Elephants are in danger from _____.
   a. other animals   b. people

5. Mother Health International is an organization for _____.
   a. all mothers   b. poor mothers

**B** Work with a partner. Compare your answers in A.

## SIMPLE PAST STATEMENTS (IRREGULAR VERBS)

| Statements | |
|---|---|
| **Affirmative** | **Negative** |
| He **ate** bread. | He **did not eat** regular meals. |
| They **got** married in June. | They **didn't get** married in July. |
| You **had** time to help. | You **didn't have** time to help. |
| She **drank** water. | She **didn't drink** coffee. |
| She **went** to Kenya. | She **didn't go** to Egypt. |

## SIMPLE PAST *YES/NO* QUESTIONS

| *Yes/No* Questions | | | |
|---|---|---|---|
| *Did* | Subject | Base Form | |
| **Did** | I | **wake** | you up? |
| | you | **take care of** | the kids yesterday? |
| | he | **help** | his grandfather? |
| | it | **rain** | last night? |
| | we | **eat** | all the cookies? |
| | they | **cook** | for the hungry people? |

| Short Answers | |
|---|---|
| **Affirmative** | **Negative** |
| Yes, you **did**. | No, you **didn't**. |
| Yes, I **did**. Yes, we **did**. | No, I **didn't**. No, we **didn't**. |
| Yes, he **did**. | No, he **didn't**. |
| Yes, it **did**. | No, it **didn't**. |
| Yes, we **did**. | No, we **didn't**. |
| Yes, they **did**. | No, they **didn't**. |

## GRAMMAR NOTES

### 1 Irregular Verbs

**Irregular verbs have different** forms in the simple past.

Here are several common irregular verbs and their past forms.

| | |
|---|---|
| • *become* → *became* | Jaime **became** a teacher. |
| • *do* → *did* | I **did** a lot of work yesterday. |
| • *grow* → *grew* | She **grew** up in China. |
| • *say* → *said* | He **said** he was hungry. |
| • *see* → *saw* | We **saw** that movie. |
| • *send* → *sent* | They **sent** us a letter. |
| • *sit* → *sat* | Maria **sat** down. |
| • *take* → *took* | We **took** a vacation last summer. |
| • *win* → *won* | Our team **won** the game. |
| • *write* → *wrote* | My grandfather **wrote** many books. |

Remember that the simple past forms of *be* are *was*, *wasn't*, *were*, and *weren't*. (See Unit 7.)

She **was born** in Mexico. She **wasn't born** in Kenya.
We **were born** in Canada. We **weren't born** in Italy.

## 2 Negative Forms of Simple Past Verbs

| | |
|---|---|
| To make **negative sentences** with both regular and irregular verbs in the <u>simple past</u>, use *did not* + the **base form** of the verb. | He **did not eat** much. |
| Use the contraction *didn't* + the **base form** in conversation and informal writing. | He **didn't eat** much. |
| **BE CAREFUL!** Don't use *did* or *didn't* with the past form of the verb. Use the base form. | He **didn't have** breakfast. <br> **NOT** He didn't ~~had~~ breakfast. |

## 3 Yes/No Questions and Short Answers in the Simple Past

| | |
|---|---|
| To make *yes/no* **questions** in the simple past, use *did* + the **subject** + the **base form** of the verb. | **Did** you **stop** for lunch? <br> **Did** she **eat** anything? |
| You can use *did* or *didn't* in the short answer to a question in the simple past. You can also use just the word *yes* or *no*. | A: **Did** it rain? <br> B: Yes, it **did. or Yes.** <br> No, it **didn't. or No.** |

# PRONUNCIATION NOTE

▶ 25|02 **Simple Past Questions with *Did***

| | |
|---|---|
| In *yes/no* questions in the simple past, we often pronounce the last *d* in *did* + a /y/ sound as /ʤ/. When *did* comes before other sounds, we pronounce the last *d* as /d/. | |
| • /d/ + a /y/ sound | **Did you** get up late today? <br> (/diʤu/) <br> **Did your** brother come to visit? <br> (/diʤur/) |
| • /d/ + other sounds | **Did they** call you last night? <br> **Did Ana** finish her homework? |

# REFERENCE NOTES

For **definitions of grammar terms**, see the Glossary on page 375.

For information on **regular verbs in the simple past**, see Unit 24 on page 275.

For information on **simple past *wh-* questions**, see Unit 26 on page 298.

For a list of **irregular verbs and their simple past forms**, see Appendix 19 on page 373.

## EXERCISE 1  DISCOVER THE GRAMMAR

Ⓐ  GRAMMAR NOTES 1–3  Read the conversation. Underline the *yes / no* questions in the simple past. Then circle irregular verbs in simple past statements.

ABLA:  Wow! I'm really hungry. Let's go have lunch. I (didn't) have breakfast.

JOMO:  Why? Did you get up late?

ABLA:  Yeah, I got up at 8:15. I just drank a glass of orange juice.

JOMO:  Did you stay up late last night?

ABLA:  Yes, I did.

JOMO:  Why?

ABLA:  Well, first I babysat for my neighbor. Then I bought some medicine for

my grandmother.

JOMO:  Did you write your paper for drama class?

ABLA:  Yeah. I wrote it on Lupita Nyong'o.

JOMO:  Oh, no! You, too?

Ⓑ  Read the conversation in A again. For each statement, check (✓) *True* or *False*.

|  | True | False |
|---|---|---|
| 1. It is time for breakfast now. | ☐ | ☑ |
| 2. Abla got up early. | ☐ | ☑ |
| 3. Abla had some orange juice after she got up. | ☑ | ☐ |
| 4. Abla went to bed late last night. | ☑ | ☐ |
| 5. Abla babysat for her grandmother. | ☐ | ☐ |
| 6. Abla helped her grandmother last night. | ☐ | ☐ |
| 7. Abla didn't do her paper for drama class. | ☐ | ☑ |
| 8. Jomo wrote his drama paper on Lupita Nyong'o. | ☑ | ☐ |

# EXERCISE 2 REGULAR AND IRREGULAR VERBS

GRAMMAR NOTES 1–2  Complete the paragraph. Use the simple past form of the verbs in parentheses.

Lupita Nyong'o _____was born_____ in Mexico in 1983. Her
                    **1. (be born)**

family _____didn't live_____ in Mexico very long. After three years,
        **2. (not / live)**

they _____went_____ to Kenya, where they were from. Lupita
        **3. (go)**

_____grew_____ up there. When Lupita was sixteen, her
    **4. (grow)**

parents _____sent_____ her back to Mexico to learn Spanish.
        **5. (send)**

Lupita later _____moved_____ to the United States. She _____attended_____ Hampshire
            **6. (move)**                                    **7. (attend)**

College and then Yale University. She _____got_____ a bachelor's degree from
                                        **8. (get)**

Hampshire College and a master's degree from Yale. Then Lupita _____began_____ to
                                                                    **9. (begin)**

act in movies. Many people _____saw_____ Lupita in the movie *Twelve Years a Slave*.
                            **10. (see)**

She _____won_____ an award for that movie. She also _____had_____ roles in the
    **11. (win)**                                        **12. (have)**

movies *Star Wars: The Force Awakens* and *Queen of Katwe*.


# EXERCISE 3 *YES/NO* QUESTIONS

GRAMMAR NOTE 3  Complete the conversations with *yes/no* questions. Use the correct forms of the words in parentheses.

1. A: _____Did you have_____ breakfast this morning, Bi-Yun?
        **(have / you)**

   B: No. I had to drive my mother to work.

2. A: _____Did she write_____ her paper on Lupita Nyong'o?
        **(write / she)**

   B: No, she didn't. She wrote it on Antonio Banderas.

3. A: _____Did it take_____ you a long time to help your grandfather?
        **(take / it)**

   B: Yes, it took me about three hours.

4. A: _____Did you work_____ at the old people's home?
        **(work / you)**

   B: No, I didn't. I worked at the library.

5. A: _____Did you see_____ the movie *Twelve Years a Slave*?
        **(see / you)**

   B: Yes, I did. I saw it in 2014.

6. A: _____Did you help_____ your father in the garden?
        **(help / you)**

   B: Yes, I did. We worked for three hours.

## EXERCISE 4  SIMPLE PAST QUESTIONS WITH *DID*

**A** PRONUNCIATION NOTE  Read and listen to each sentence. How is the last *d* in *did* pronounced? Check (✓) /d/ or /ʤ/.

|  | /d/ | /ʤ/ |
|---|---|---|
| 1. Did you work last night? | ☐ | ☑ |
| 2. Did she go with you? | ☑ | ☐ |
| 3. Did your friends pick the movie? | ☐ | ☑ |
| 4. Did Larry help you with the party? | ☑ | ☐ |
| 5. Did she hurt her back? | ☐ | ☐ |
| 6. Did you cook breakfast this morning? | ☐ | ☐ |
| 7. Did your brother visit New York? | ☐ | ☐ |
| 8. Did they go with you? | ☐ | ☐ |
| 9. Did you visit Uganda, too? | ☐ | ☑ |
| 10. Did Bob finish his work? | ☐ | ☑ |

**B** Listen again and repeat the sentences.


## EXERCISE 5  EDITING

GRAMMAR NOTES 1–3  There are six mistakes in the conversations. The first mistake is corrected. Find and correct five more.

1. A: Yukiko, did you ~~worked~~ *work* at the school yesterday?

   B: Yes, I do. I worked all afternoon.

2. A: Jessica, Jeremy helped you with the garden?

   B: Yes, and he does a good job.

3. A: How many movies you saw last month?

   B: I saw four movies.

4. A: I think Lupita Nyong'o go back to Kenya.

   B: Yes, she only lived in Mexico for three years.

**290**  Unit 25

## EXERCISE 6  LISTENING

▶ 25|04   **A** Listen to the class interview with Yoshio, an exchange student from Japan. Why does he like the Seattle area?

_____

_____

_____

_____

▶ 25|04   **B** Listen again. Check (✓) *True*, *False*, or *No Information*. Correct the false statements.

|   | True | False | No Information |
|---|------|-------|----------------|
| **1.** Yoshio got to the United States four months ago. | ✓ | ☐ | ☐ |
| **2.** Yoshio was born in Hamamatsu. | ☐ | ☐ | ☐ |
| **3.** Yoshio has two sisters and one brother. | ☐ | ☐ | ☐ |
| **4.** Yoshio played soccer in high school. | ☐ | ☐ | ☐ |
| **5.** Yoshio has only a white belt in karate. | ☐ | ☐ | ☐ |
| **6.** Yoshio's family came to the United States. | ☐ | ☐ | ☐ |
| **7.** Yoshio didn't go to Los Angeles. | ☐ | ☐ | ☐ |
| **8.** Yoshio's family went to Seattle when he was ten. | ☐ | ☐ | ☐ |

**C** Work with a partner. Ask and answer simple past *yes/no* questions about Yoshio.

EXAMPLE:  **A:** Did Yoshio play sports in high school?
          **B:** Yes, he did.

## EXERCISE 7  TRUE OR FALSE?

**A** GAME  Work in a small group. First, read the sentences. For each sentence, check (✓) *True* or *False*. Guess the answers.

|  | True | False |
|---|---|---|
| 1. Nelson Mandela became president of South Africa in the 1990s. | ✓ | ☐ |
| 2. The English police sent Nelson Mandela to prison. | ☐ | ☐ |
| 3. Mahatma Gandhi was a famous leader in China. | ☐ | ✓ |
| 4. Mother Teresa went to India to help people. | ✓ | ☐ |
| 5. Albert Schweitzer started a hospital in Africa. | ☐ | ☐ |
| 6. Harriet Tubman helped slaves in Europe. | ☐ | ☐ |
| 7. Martin Luther King Jr. wrote "Letter from New York City Jail." | ☐ | ☐ |
| 8. Martin Luther King Jr. won the Nobel Peace Prize. | ☐ | ☐ |

**B** Do research on the Internet to check your answers in A. Correct the false statements.

EXAMPLE:  **A:** The English police sent Nelson Mandela to prison. That's false.
**B:** Right. The South African police sent Nelson Mandela to prison.

**C** Check your answers on page 385. Then compare with other groups. Which group got the most correct answers?

# EXERCISE 8 LAST WEEK I...

**A** SURVEY  What did your classmates do last week? Write questions for your classmates in the chart. Use the words in the box or your own ideas.

| | |
|---|---|
| call a friend | make breakfast for someone |
| get a gift for someone | pay for someone's meal |
| have an interesting experience | take someone to work |
| help someone | write a message to a relative |

| Questions |
|---|
| *Did you call a friend last week?* |
| |
| |
| |
| |
| |
| |

**B**  Work in a group. Ask a different group member each question in A. Ask them to give long answers.

EXAMPLE:  **A:** Enrique, did you call a friend last week?
   **B:** Yes, I did. I called my friend Armando in Mexico City.
   **A:** Svetlana, did you get a gift for someone last week?
   **C:** Yes, I did. I got a cat for my son.

**C**  Report interesting answers to the class.

EXAMPLE:  Enrique called his friend Armando in Mexico City last week. Svetlana got a cat for her son.

# FROM GRAMMAR TO WRITING

**A** BEFORE YOU WRITE   Read the paragraph. Underline simple past verbs. Guess who the paragraph is about. Then think of a famous person who did something good or helped other people. Complete the chart about your person. Do research on the Internet if necessary.

This person was born on July 18, 1918, in Transkei, South Africa. In South Africa, white people had power. Black Africans were poor and didn't have rights. This person didn't like that. He tried to change the laws in South Africa. The South African government didn't like him. They arrested him in 1956. He was in prison for twenty-seven years. After he got out of prison, he won the Nobel Peace Prize in 1993. In 1994, he became the first black president of South Africa. He was president until 1998. He died on December 5, 2013, in Johannesburg. He was ninety-five years old. Who was this person?

| Person's name | Nelson Mandela |
|---|---|
| Person's date of birth | July 18, 1918 |
| Person's date of death (if not living) | December 5, 2013 |
| Important facts about the person | He first black president of South Africa |
| Person's experiences | |

**B** WRITE   Write a paragraph about a famous person who helped others. Use the paragraph in A and your chart to help you. Use simple past verbs.

**C** CHECK YOUR WORK   Read your composition. Underline simple past verbs. Use the Editing Checklist to check your work.

### Editing Checklist

**Did you use . . . ?**

☐ irregular simple past verbs

☐ *did not* or *didn't* in negative sentences

☐ correct spelling

**D** REVISE YOUR WORK   Read your paragraph again. Can you improve your writing? Make changes if necessary. Then read your paragraph to the class. Your class members try to guess who your paragraph is about.

# UNIT 25 REVIEW

**Test yourself on the grammar of the unit.**

**A** Complete the paragraph. Use the simple past form of the verbs in parentheses.

Yesterday I _____got_____ home about 5:30 p.m. It was my turn, so I
_____made_____ dinner for my wife. We _____ate_____ dinner. Then we
**2.** (make)                 **3.** (eat)
_____saw_____ my mother in the hospital. At home later, I _____wrote_____ an email
**4.** (see)                          **5.** (write)
to our son at the university. Finally, at 11:00 p.m., I _____went_____ to bed.
                                           **6.** (go)

**B** Complete the conversations with simple past *yes/no* questions. Use the correct forms of the words in the box.

| you / get | Alicia / take care of | Jack / babysit | you / take |
|---|---|---|---|

**1. A:** ___Did you get___ Chris to the soccer game on Saturday?

  **B:** Yes, I took him in my car.

**2. A:** ___Did you take___ gifts for your children?

  **B:** Yes, I got them some nice things.

**3. A:** ___Did Alicia take care of___ her grandmother yesterday?

  **B:** Yes, she did. Her grandmother was in an accident.

**4. A:** ___Did Jack babysit___ for your children last night?

  **B:** Yes, he did. He's a great babysitter.

**C** Correct the conversations. There are five mistakes.

**1. A:** You got this book for your friend?

  **B:** No, I don't. She got it for me.

**2. A:** Did you go out last night?

  **B:** No. Katharine makes dinner for me at home. We eated a lot!

**3. A:** Do you pay for your parents' vacation last year?

  **B:** Yes, I did. They went on a trip to Hawaii.

**Now check your answers on page 383.**

# Simple Past:
# *Wh-* Questions

## AN ACCIDENT

**OUTCOMES**
- Ask and answer *wh-* questions in the simple past
- Answer questions about a reading and a conversation
- Ask and answer questions about accidents
- Ask and answer questions about a news report
- Write a conversation about what you saw on your way to school

## STEP 1 GRAMMAR IN CONTEXT

### BEFORE YOU READ

**Ⓐ VOCABULARY** Study the words. Then work with a partner. Practice the conversation.

a car accident

a broken headlight

a dent

a scratch

a headlight

a bumper

a tire

### Conversation

A: I was in a car accident.

B: Oh, no! What happened?

A: I drove into a car. I have a broken headlight.

**Ⓑ** Now talk about other accidents. Use the words in A or other words.

A: I was in _____.

B: Oh, no! What happened?

A: I _____. I have _____.

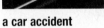

## READ

26|01 **Read Amanda's phone conversation with her brother Rob and her husband Josh.**

# Rob's Accident

AMANDA: Hi, Rob. What's up? . . . Are you OK? . . . Well, that's good. When did it happen? . . . Where did it happen? . . . Are you there now? . . . Why did you drive? . . . Does Dad know?

*(Amanda says goodbye to Rob and talks to Josh.)*

JOSH: What happened?

AMANDA: Rob had a car accident this morning.

JOSH: How is he?

AMANDA: He's fine, but the car isn't.

JOSH: What happened to the car?

AMANDA: There's a big dent in the bumper, and a headlight is broken.

JOSH: How did the accident happen?

AMANDA: I guess the road was slippery.[1] The car hit a sign.

JOSH: That's too bad.

AMANDA: The thing is, Rob took Dad's car because he didn't want to walk to the supermarket in the rain. But he didn't ask Dad first.

JOSH: Uh-oh.

AMANDA: Rob is at Charlie's Auto Repair Shop[2] now. The mechanic replaced[3] the headlight and fixed the dent. He also replaced a tire and fixed some scratches on the car. Now the mechanic wants $1,000.

JOSH: A thousand dollars? Poor Dad.

AMANDA: What do you mean, "Poor Dad?" Poor Rob.

---

1 *slippery:* smooth and easy to fall or have an accident on
2 *auto repair shop:* place that fixes cars
3 *replaced:* got a new thing in place of an old thing

## AFTER YOU READ

**A** COMPREHENSION  Look at the conversations again. Answer the questions.

1. When did the accident happen?
   - **a.** In the morning.
   - **b.** In the afternoon.

2. What happened to Rob in the accident?
   - **a.** He got hurt.
   - **b.** Nothing. He didn't get hurt.

3. Who was the driver?
   - **a.** Rob was.
   - **b.** Dad was.

4. How did the accident happen?
   - **a.** The car hit another car.
   - **b.** The car hit a sign.

5. Where did Rob take the car after the accident?
   - **a.** To his father's office.
   - **b.** To Charlie's Auto Repair Shop.

**B**  Work with a partner. Compare your answers in A.

---

**STEP 2**  **GRAMMAR PRESENTATION**

## SIMPLE PAST: *WH-* QUESTIONS

| Questions | | | | | Answers |
|-----------|---|---|---|---|---------|
| *Wh-* Question Word | *Did* | Subject | Base Form of Verb | | |
| Why | | Rob | **go** | to the store? | He wanted to get some food. |
| How long | | he | **stay** | at the store? | Half an hour. |
| Who | | he | **go** | with? | Nobody. He was alone. |
| Where | did | the accident | **happen?** | | In front of the supermarket. |
| When | | it | **happen?** | | In the morning. |
| What time | | it | **happen?** | | At 10:00 a.m. |
| How | | it | **happen?** | | The car hit a sign. |

| Questions About the Subject | | | Answers | | |
|-----------------------------|---|---|---------|---|---|
| *Wh-* Question Word | Simple Past Verb | | | | |
| What | **happened?** | | Rob | **had** | a car accident. |
| Who | **drove** | the car? | Rob | (did). | |

# GRAMMAR NOTES

## 1 Simple Past *Wh-* Questions: Form

To make most *wh-* questions in the **simple past**, use a *wh-* word + *did* + **the subject** + **the base form of the verb**.

A: **When did** he **call**?
B: In the morning.

A: **Where did** she **go**?
B: To the store.

A: **What did** they **do**?
B: They called an ambulance.

A: **Who did** you **visit**?
B: My mother.

**USAGE NOTE** We often use *wh-* **question words** + **a noun** to get more exact information.

- *What time*

- *What day*

A: **What *time*** did the accident happen?
B: 10:00 a.m.

A: **What *day*** did you go there?
B: Thursday.

## 2 *Wh-* Questions About the Subject

To make *wh-* questions **about the subject**, use a *wh-* word + the **simple past form** of the verb.

A: **Who called?**
B: My brother called.

A: **What happened?**
B: I had a car accident.

**BE CAREFUL!** Do not use *did* with questions about the subject.

Who **drove**?
**NOT** Who ~~did~~ drive?

# REFERENCE NOTES

For **definitions of grammar terms**, see the Glossary on page 375.

For information on **simple past *yes/no* questions**, see Unit 25 on page 286.

For a list of **irregular past tense verbs**, see Appendix 19 on page 373.

## EXERCISE 1   DISCOVER THE GRAMMAR

**Ⓐ** GRAMMAR NOTES 1–2 **Read the conversation. Underline all the *wh-* questions in the past. Circle questions about the subject.**

GINA:   Why are you late? What happened?

CAMERON:   There was an accident on my way here. Traffic was awful.

GINA:   Oh. Where did the accident happen?

CAMERON:   Just before Exit 6 on the highway.

GINA:   What caused[1] the accident?

CAMERON:   A box fell off[2] a truck, and it hit a car. The car stopped, and another car hit it.

GINA:   What time did it happen?

CAMERON:   About 3:30 p.m.

GINA:   Did anyone call the police?

CAMERON:   Yes. The police were there.

GINA:   What did the police do?

CAMERON:   They closed two lanes of the highway.

GINA:   Did anyone get hurt?

CAMERON:   No, but the cars had a lot of damage.

**Ⓑ** **Read the conversation in A again. Circle the correct answers.**

1. Why did Cameron come late?
   a. He was in an accident.    **b.** He saw an accident.

2. When did the accident happen?
   a. in the morning    b. in the afternoon

3. What did the police close?
   a. two lanes of the highway    b. the highway

4. Who got hurt?
   a. one of the drivers    b. nobody

---

1 *caused:* made something happen
2 *fell off:* dropped down to the ground

# EXERCISE 2 *WH-* QUESTION WORDS

GRAMMAR NOTES 1–2 Read the questions and answers. Complete the questions with *what*, *where*, *when*, and *who*.

1. A: ___What___ time did the accident occur?    B: At nine o'clock in the morning.

2. A: ___where___ did it happen?    B: On the corner of Maple and Elm Street.

3. A: _____ did the police arrive?    B: They came at 9:10.

4. A: _____ did the police do?    B: They asked the drivers a lot of questions.

5. A: _____ did the drivers say?    B: The sun was in their eyes.

6. A: ___who___ called the police?    B: An old woman.

# EXERCISE 3 *WH-* QUESTIONS

GRAMMAR NOTES 1–2 Complete the questions. Use the correct forms of the verbs in parentheses.

1. What time ___did___ they ___leave___ home?
                                    (leave)

2. Why ___did___ they ___go___ downtown?
                              (go)

3. Where ___did___ the accident ___happen___?
                                        (happen)

4. Who ___called___ the ambulance?
            (call)

5. How long ___did___ it ___take___ the ambulance to get to the accident?
                                (take)

6. What ___did___ they ___do___ in the hospital?
                            (do)

# EXERCISE 4 QUESTIONS WITH *WH-* WORD + NOUN

GRAMMAR NOTE 1 Read the questions and answers. Complete the questions with the words from the box.

| what day | what month | ~~what time~~ | what year |
|----------|-----------|--------------|-----------|

1. A: ___What time___ did you get up?
   B: 7:00 a.m.

2. A: ___what day___ did the accident happen?
   B: Monday.

3. A: ___what month___ did you take a road trip?
   B: July.

4. A: ___what year___ did you go to Canada?
   B: 2015.

## EXERCISE 5  *WH-* QUESTIONS

**A** GRAMMAR NOTE 1  **Complete the conversation with questions in the simple past. Use the correct forms of the words in the parentheses.**

AL:     Guess what? Yesterday, I saw Jake Arrieta.

DREW:   Really? _____Where did you see him_____?
        1. (Where / you / see him)

AL:     On Pike Street.

DREW:   _____What time did you see him_____?
        2. (What time / you / see him)

AL:     It was about 3:00 in the afternoon.

DREW:   _____What did he look like_____?
        3. (What / he / look like)

AL:     Like Jake Arrieta, of course.

DREW:   Did you talk to him?

AL:     Yes. I asked him for his autograph.

DREW:   _____What did he do_____?
        4. (What / he / do)

AL:     He wrote his name on a piece of paper!

**Jake Arrieta**

▶26|02 **B** LISTEN AND CHECK  **Listen to the conversation and check your answers in A.**

## EXERCISE 6  WORD ORDER OF *WH-* QUESTIONS

**A** GRAMMAR NOTES 1–2  **Put the words in the correct order. Write questions.**

JOSH:       You know, I once drove without a driver's license.

AMANDA:     _____When did you do that?_____
            1. (you / when / do / did / that?)

JOSH:       Oh, about ten years ago. I was fifteen, and I drove to my grandmother's house.

AMANDA:     _____Why did you drive there?_____
            2. (you / why / there / did / drive?)

JOSH:       My grandmother called and said she was sick. My parents were away for the day,

            and there was no bus or train to her house.

AMANDA:     So _____What happened?_____
            3. (happened / what?)

JOSH:       Well, I drove to her house and she was very sick. I took her to the hospital.

AMANDA:     _____How long did the drive take?_____
            4. (the drive / how long / did / take?)

JOSH:       About thirty minutes.

AMANDA:     _____What did your parents say?_____
            5. (your parents / did / say / what?)

JOSH:       They said I did the right thing. I got my license the next month.

▶26|03 **B** LISTEN AND CHECK  **Listen to the conversation and check your answers in A.**

# EXERCISE 7  *WHO* QUESTIONS ABOUT THE SUBJECT

GRAMMAR NOTES 1–2  Complete the conversations with simple past questions with *Who*.
Use the correct forms of the words in parentheses.

1. A: _____Who taught you to drive?_____
     (teach you to drive)
   B: My uncle taught me how to drive.

2. A: _____
     (hit your car)
   B: I don't know. I came out of the restaurant and I
      saw the dent and some scratches.

3. A: _____
     (cause the accident)
   B: The truck driver did. He drove through a red light.

4. A: _____
     (call the police)
   B: A driver of another car.

5. A: _____
     (go to the auto repair shop with you)
   B: My brother went with me.

6. A: _____
     (drive you home)
   B: My brother did.

# EXERCISE 8  EDITING

GRAMMAR NOTES 1–2  There are five mistakes in the conversation. The first mistake is
corrected. Find and correct four more.

ROB:  Hello, this is Rob Peck. I'd like to report an accident.

GAIL:  Thank you, Mr. Peck. What time ~did~ the accident happen?

ROB:  It did happen at 9:30 this morning.

GAIL:  Where did it happened?

ROB:  On Oak Street between First and Second Avenues.

GAIL:  How it did happen?

ROB:  A cat ran into the street and the car in front of me stopped. I hit the car. The

      police came and wrote a report.

GAIL:  Who did called the police?

ROB:  I did. And I took pictures, too.

GAIL:  Thank you for reporting the accident.

## EXERCISE 9   LISTENING

▶ 26|04   **A**   Listen to a telephone conversation between Amanda and Rob. Then answer the question. Where did Amanda go on Saturday? Check (✓) all the places.

☑ her parents' home      ☐ the bank      ☐ the post office

☐ the auto repair shop      ☐ the gym      ☐ the supermarket

▶ 26|04   **B**   Listen again. Then answer the questions. Circle the correct answers.

1. What did Rob promise to do?

   **a.** pay for the car repairs      **b.** fix his father's car

2. What did Amanda lose?

   **a.** her watch      **b.** her credit card

3. Who helped her find it?

   **a.** her father      **b.** her brother Rob

4. Where did she find it?

   **a.** in her bag      **b.** in her car

**C**   Work with a partner. Take turns. Ask and answer *wh-* questions in the past about the conversation between Amanda and Rob.

EXAMPLE:   A: Who lost a credit card?
           B: Amanda did.

## EXERCISE 10   I HAD AN ACCIDENT

DISCUSSION   Work in small groups. Tell your group about an accident you saw or were in. Your group members ask questions with *what time*, *where*, *how*, *what*, *why*, or *how long*.

EXAMPLE:   A: I had a bike accident.
           B: Where did it happen?
           A: In Westlake Park.
           C: When...?

# EXERCISE 11  BOY SAVES MOM

INFORMATION GAP  Work with a partner. Student A, follow the instructions below. Student B, follow the instructions on page 389.

---

**STUDENT A**

- You and your partner have the same story, "Boy Saves Mom." Some information is missing from your story. Ask your partner *wh-* questions in the past to find out the information.

EXAMPLE:  A: When did Ann Green have an accident?
          B: On Wednesday, April 20.

# Boy Saves Mom

On _____*Wednesday, April 20*_____, Ann Green had an accident. The accident happened in Ann's kitchen. She fell off a chair and hit her head. _____ found her. Max is four years old, but he's very smart. He called the police. A policeman answered. He asked Max, "_____?" Max said, "Mommy fell off a chair." The policeman _____ to the Green's home. The ambulance took Ann to a hospital. She is doing well there. Yesterday, she _____. She said, "My son saved my life."

- Your partner's story is also missing some information. The information is in your story. Answer your partner's questions.

EXAMPLE:  B: Where did the accident happen?
          A: In Ann's kitchen.

# FROM GRAMMAR TO WRITING

**A** BEFORE YOU WRITE Read part of a conversation between two students. Think about something you saw on the way to school. Then work with a partner. Tell your partner about the thing you saw. Your partner asks questions about it. Write your partner's questions in the chart below.

A: On my way to school, I saw a beautiful bird.
B: Where did you see it?
A: I saw it in East Park.
B: When did you see it?
A: At 8:30.
B: What did it look like?
A: It had beautiful red feathers and . . .

| Your Partner's Questions |
|---|
| 1. |
| 2. |
| 3. |
| 4. |

**B** WRITE Write a conversation that begins, "On my way to school, I saw . . ." Use the conversation in A and your chart to help you. Use simple past *wh-* questions.

**C** CHECK YOUR WORK Look at your conversation. Underline the *wh-* questions. Use the Editing Checklist to check your work.

### Editing Checklist

**Did you . . . ?**

☐ use a *wh-* word + *did* + a subject + the base form of the verb for most *wh-* questions

☐ use a *wh-* word + the past form for questions about the subject

☐ check your spelling

**D** REVISE YOUR WORK Read your conversation again. Can you improve your writing? Make changes if necessary.

# UNIT 26 REVIEW

**Test yourself on the grammar of the unit.**

### A Match the questions and answers.

_____ **1.** Who got a job yesterday?

_____ **2.** Where did he get a job?

_____ **3.** Why did he get a job?

_____ **4.** When did he start his job?

_____ **5.** Who hired him?

**a.** A couple of days ago. ~~maneaupai di dias~~

**b.** Mr. Stram. He owns the drugstore.

**c.** My brother. He's really happy.

**d.** At a drugstore.

**e.** He needed money for car repairs.

### B Put the words in the correct order. Write simple past *wh-* questions.

1. _____*When did the accident happen?*_____
(the accident / happen / did / When)

2. _____*How did the accident happen*_____
(happen / did / How / the accident)

3. _____*Why did he drive to the supermarket?*_____
(he / Why / to the supermarket / drive / did)

4. _____*Who did he drive with?*_____
(did / Who / with / he / drive)

5. _____*Where did he take the car?*_____
(take / he / Where / the car / did)

### C Correct the conversation. There are five mistakes.

**A:** What time ~~did~~ you get to work this morning?

**B:** At 10:00 a.m. I was late because there was an accident on the bus.

**A:** Oh, no! What happen? ~~did?~~

**B:** The bus hit a car. It was scary. People got hurt.

**A:** Oh, no. Who they got hurt?

**B:** The people in the car. An ambulance came to get them, but it took a long time.

**A:** How long ~~did~~ the ambulance take?

**B:** About twenty minutes.

**A:** Why it did take so long?

**B:** I don't know. But the people were OK.

**Now check your answers on page 383.**

# Asking About and Expressing Quantity

# PART 9

## OUTCOMES

- Use *how many* and *how much* to ask questions about quantities
- Use *a few*, *not many*, *a little*, and *not much* to describe quantities
- Answer questions about a reading
- Identify true and false sentences about a news report
- Ask and answer questions about traveling and everyday activities
- Write a conversation about a place you visited

## OUTCOMES

- Use *there is*, *there are*, *there was*, and *there were* to state facts about people and things
- Identify true and false sentences about a reading
- Complete sentences about a conversation
- Identify true and false statements about places in nature
- Give a presentation about your favorite place in nature
- Write a paragraph about a place in nature that needs protection

## *How many* and *How much*; Quantity Expressions

### A TRIP

**OUTCOMES**
- Use *how many* and *how much* to ask questions about quantities
- Use *a few, not many, a little,* and *not much* to describe quantities
- Answer questions about a reading
- Identify true and false sentences about a news report
- Ask and answer questions about traveling and everyday activities
- Write a conversation about a place you visited

| STEP 1 | GRAMMAR IN CONTEXT |
|---|---|

### BEFORE YOU READ

**A** VOCABULARY  Study the words. Then complete the sentences with the words.

an island

an animal

a plant

a flight

1. We can take a(n) _____ to Ecuador.

2. A place with water all around is a(n) _____.

3. A(n) _____ has leaves and needs water and sun to grow.

4. A dog is a(n) _____.

**B** Work with a partner. Compare your answers in A. Then name an island, a plant, and an animal. Take turns.

EXAMPLE:  A:  Hong Kong is an island.
B:  Madagascar is an island, too.

🔊 27|01   Read this conversation.

# A Great Trip

**STEVE:** So how was Ecuador?

**JESSICA:** Great.

**STEVE:** How many days were you away?

**JESSICA:** Ten. We were in Guayaquil, and we were on the Galápagos Islands, too.

**MARK:** The Galápagos Islands? That sounds exciting. How much time did you spend there?

**TIM:** Not much. Only four days. But it was fantastic. We took hundreds of photos of the plants and animals. We slept and ate on a boat.

**MARK:** Really? How many people were on the boat?

**JESSICA:** Twelve.

**STEVE:** How much did the trip cost?

**JESSICA:** Just a little. Tim won it. We only paid for our food.

**MARK:** Was the flight free, too?

**JESSICA:** Yes, it was.

**MARK:** Lucky you! I love to travel.

**TIM:** I agree. Nothing beats travel.[1]

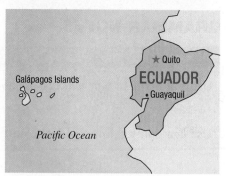

---

**1** *Nothing beats travel:* travel is a lot of fun

## AFTER YOU READ

**Ⓐ COMPREHENSION** Look at the conversation again. Answer the questions. Use the words from the box.

| A little | Hundreds | Two | Ten | Twelve |
|----------|----------|-----|-----|--------|

**1.** How many photos did Steve and Jessica take? _____

**2.** How many days did Steve and Jessica spend in Ecuador? _____

**3.** How much money did Steve and Jessica spend? _____

**4.** How many people were on the boat? _____

**5.** How many places did Steve and Jessica visit? _____

**Ⓑ** Work with a partner. Compare your answers in A.

## *HOW MANY* AND *HOW MUCH*; QUANTITY EXPRESSIONS

| *How many* + Count Nouns | | | Quantity Expressions |
|---|---|---|---|
| How many | photos | did you take? | A lot.<br>Not many.<br>A few.<br>Sixty. |

| *How much* + Non-Count Nouns | | | Quantity Expressions |
|---|---|---|---|
| How much | time | did you spend there? | A lot.<br>Not much.<br>A little. |

## GRAMMAR NOTES

### 1 *How many* and *How much*

Use *how many* or *how much* to ask about the quantity of something.

| | |
|---|---|
| Use *how many* before a **plural count noun**. | PLURAL<br>COUNT NOUN<br>A: **How many days** were you there?<br>B: Fifteen. |
| Use *how much* before a **non-count noun**. | NON-COUNT<br>NOUN<br>A: **How much rain** do they usually get in May?<br>B: Not much. |
| USAGE NOTE Use *how much* to ask about the **cost** of something. When we talk about cost, we often use *how much* **without a noun**. The reader or listener knows we're asking about the cost. | A: **How much** was your flight?<br>B: Three hundred dollars. |

### 2 *A lot of*

To answer questions with *how many* or *how much*, use *a lot* or *a lot of* for **large quantities or amounts**.

| | |
|---|---|
| Use *a lot of* before **plural count nouns** and **non-count nouns**. | A: How many people live in Quito?<br>B: **A lot. or A lot of people** live in Quito. |
| BE CAREFUL! Use *a lot* without *of* for short answers. | A: How much time did you spend on the boat?<br>B: **A lot.**<br>NOT A lot of. |

## 3 A few, Not many, A little, Not much

To answer questions with *how many* or *how much*, use *a few*, *not many*, *a little*, and *a few* for **small amounts**.

| | |
|---|---|
| Use *a few* or *not many* before **plural count nouns**. | **A:** How many people were on the boat? <br> **B:** **A few people** were on the boat. **or A few.** |
| You can also use *a few* and *not many* as short answers without a noun. | **A:** How many days did you go swimming? <br> **B:** **Not many.** *(We didn't swim many days.)* |
| Use *a little* or *not much* before **non-count nouns**. | **A:** How much tea did you drink? <br> **B:** I drank **a little tea.** **or A little.** |
| You can also use *a little* and *not much* as short answers without a noun. | **A:** How much time did you spend in Guayaquil? <br> **B:** **Not much.** |

## REFERENCE NOTES

For **definitions of grammatical terms**, see the Glossary on page 375.

For more information on **count and non-count nouns**, see Unit 21 on page 237.

## STEP 3   FOCUSED PRACTICE

## EXERCISE 1   DISCOVER THE GRAMMAR

**A** GRAMMAR NOTES 1–3   **Read the conversations. Underline** *how many* **and** *how much*, **and circle the nouns they go with.**

1. **A:** How many (flights) go to the Galápagos Islands from Guayaquil?

   **B:** A few each day.

2. **A:** How many seats are available on Flight 1?

   **B:** Not many. You need to make a reservation now.

3. **A:** How much time does it take to get to the airport?

   **B:** Not much. Only about thirty minutes.

4. **A:** How much money does the flight cost?

   **B:** About $550.

5. **A:** How many tourists visit the Galápagos Islands in May?

   **B:** A lot. Most tourists go there in April, May, and November.

6. **A:** Is there a lot of rain in July?

   **B:** No, there isn't. There's just a little light rain called "garúa."

**B** Look at the conversations in A again. Write the quantity or quantity expression that answers each question.

1. _A few_ _____

2. _____

3. _____

4. _____

5. _____

6. _____

## EXERCISE 2  *HOW MANY* AND *HOW MUCH*

GRAMMAR NOTE 1  Read an ad for a trip to Washington, D.C. Match the questions and answers.

COME TO WASHINGTON, D.C.!

See the beautiful cherry blossoms. Visit the White House. See the Capitol.

**Includes:**

• Airfare from Seattle
• Two nights, three days at the Eastern Hotel
• Double rooms
• Lunch and dinner for three days
• Tour of Washington, D.C.
• Free bus from airport to hotel

*All this for only $800!*

_b_ 1. How many days is the trip?

___ 2. How many meals does the trip include?

___ 3. How much does the trip cost?

___ 4. How many people share a room?

___ 5. How much is the bus ride from the airport?

**a.** Two.

~~b.~~ Three.

**c.** Six.

**d.** Nothing.

**e.** $800.

# EXERCISE 3  *A LOT, A FEW, A LITTLE, NOT MANY, NOT MUCH*

GRAMMAR NOTES 2–3  **Read the questions. Complete the answers. Circle the correct words.**

1.  A: How much time do you spend with your parents?

    B: Not many / (Not much) I live in New York, and they live in Mazatlán, Mexico.

2.  A: How much does a flight to Mazatlán cost?

    B: (A lot) / Not many. It costs more than $700.

3.  A: How many trips to Mexico do you take every year?

    B: (A few) / A little. I usually visit Mazatlán three times a year.

4.  A: How much money do you spend when you're in Mexico?

    B: Just (a little) / a few. I always stay with my parents, and we all cook at their house.

5.  A: How many people live in your parents' house?

    B: (Not many) / Not much. Just my parents and my sister.

6.  A: On your last trip, how many days did you go to the beach?

    B: Only (a few) / a little. I don't like the beach. I like shopping more.

7.  A: How many photos did you take?

    B: (Not many) / Not much. My sister usually takes a lot of photos, but I don't.

8.  A: How much sunny weather did you have?

    B: (A lot) / A little. It's usually hot in Mazatlán.

Mazatlán, Mexico

## EXERCISE 4  QUESTIONS WITH *HOW MANY* AND *HOW MUCH*

GRAMMAR NOTE 1  Read the ad for a trip to Boston and the conversation. Complete the conversation. Write questions with *how many* or *how much*.

VISIT **BOSTON** ONLY $1,000!

**Includes:**
- Airfare from Seattle
- Five days and four nights at Motel 9
- Four to a room
- Delicious breakfast every day
- Three-hour sightseeing tour of Boston

**Visit the Freedom Trail, Faneuil Hall, Quincy Market, and Old North Church**

JUDY:  I'm thinking of visiting New York or Boston.

MARK:  Well, here's an ad for a trip to Boston.

JUDY:  <u>How much does it cost? or How much is it?</u>
1.

MARK:  A thousand dollars.

JUDY:  <u>How many days is the trip?</u>
2.

MARK:  Five days.

JUDY:  Do they include meals?

MARK:  Some.

JUDY:  <u>How many meals does the trip include?</u>
3.

MARK:  Five breakfasts.

JUDY:  Do you get your own room?

MARK:  Uh, no.

JUDY:  <u>How many people share a room?</u>
4.

MARK:  Four people share a room.

JUDY:  Oh. That's not for me.

# EXERCISE 5  HOW MANY, HOW MUCH, A LOT, A FEW, A LITTLE

GRAMMAR NOTES 1–3  Complete the questions with *how many* or *how much*. Complete the answers with *a lot*, *a few*, or *a little*.

1. A: _____How many_____ people were on the bus to the airport?

   B: Only _____a few_____. Maybe six. The bus was almost empty.

2. A: ____How many____ cities did you visit?

   B: ____a lot____. We were in ten different cities!

3. A: ____How much____ time did you spend in shops?

   B: Just ____a little____. I didn't want to buy a lot of things.

4. A: ____How many____ children were on the trip?

   B: ____a few____. Only three. They were ten, eleven, and fourteen years old.

5. A: ____How many____ T-shirts did you take?

   B: Just ____a few____. I only took two white and two blue T-shirts.

# EXERCISE 6  EDITING

GRAMMAR NOTES 1–3  There are <u>seven</u> mistakes in the conversations. The first mistake is corrected. Find and correct <u>six</u> more.

1. A: How ~~much~~ many people did you travel with?

   B: Only one other person, but we met a little people on the trip.

2. A: How many days were you away?

   B: Not much, only three days. But we were on a small island.

3. A: How much time did you spend in your hotel room?

   B: Not many. We left early and returned late.

4. A: How much trips do you usually take in a year?

   B: A lot of. I travel for work about five times a year, and I travel with my family three

   times a year.

## EXERCISE 7  LISTENING

▶27|02  **A**  **Listen to the news report. What is it about?**

**a.** a travel writer's new book          **b.** a travel writer's death

▶27|02  **B**  **Listen again. Read the statements about John Levin. For each statement, check (✓)**
*True* or *False*.

|  |  | True | False |
|---|---|:---:|:---:|
| **1.** | He wrote a lot of books. | ✓ | ☐ |
| **2.** | He had four children. | ☐ | ☐ |
| **3.** | He had a few grandchildren. | ☐ | ☐ |
| **4.** | He had a lot of money. | ☐ | ☐ |
| **5.** | He left his money to his first son. | ☐ | ☐ |
| **6.** | He spent a lot of time with his family. | ☐ | ☐ |

**C**  **Work with a partner. Take turns. Ask your partner questions about John Levin from
the listening. Use *how many* or *how much* in each question. Use the words in the box.
Your partner answers the questions.**

| books | children | grandchildren | money | time |
|---|---|---|---|---|

EXAMPLE:  **A:**  How many books did John Levin write?
                 **B:**  A lot.

## EXERCISE 8  ALL ABOUT ME

**A**  Q & A  **Work in a group. Ask questions with *how
many* and *how much*. Your classmates answer with
*a lot*, *a little*, *a few*, *not many*, or *not much*, or give
an exact amount. Use the ideas from the box or
your own ideas.**

trips / take in a year
people / usually travel with
photos / take on trips
gifts / buy on trips
time / like to spend away from home
different animals / see on an average day
plants / have in your home
texts / send and receive in a day
people / help each day

EXAMPLE:  **A:**  How many trips do you take in a year?
                 **B:**  One. But I don't take a trip every year.

**B**  **Report to the class. Tell your class two things
about each person in your group.**

EXAMPLE:  Maria doesn't travel a lot. She helps her
                 grandmother every day.

# EXERCISE 9  GALÁPAGOS QUIZ

**A** GAME  Work in small groups. Guess the answers to the questions below.

1. How much does a male giant tortoise weigh?

   **a.** about 25 kilograms    **b.** about 250 kilograms    **c.** about 2,250 kilograms

2. How many giant tortoises are there on the Galápagos Islands?

   **a.** a lot    **b.** a few    **c.** none

3. How many elephants are there on the Galápagos Islands?

   **a.** a lot    **b.** a few    **c.** none

4. How much time does it take to fly to the Galápagos Islands from Guayaquil?

   **a.** about two hours    **b.** about five hours    **c.** about eight hours

5. How many main islands are there in the Galápagos Islands?

   **a.** 18    **b.** 80    **c.** 180

6. How many people live on the Galápagos Islands all year round?

   **a.** 2,500    **b.** 25,000    **c.** 2,500,000

**B** Work with another group. Compare your answers. Explain why you think your answers are correct. Then check answers on page 385.

EXAMPLE:  **GROUP A:**  We think a male giant tortoise weighs about 2,250 kilograms. How much do you think it weighs?

**GROUP B:**  2,250 kilograms is a lot! We think it weighs about 225 kilograms.

**A** BEFORE YOU WRITE Read this conversation about Washington, D.C. Then think about a place you visited. Work with a partner. Your partner asks *how many* or *how much* questions about that place.

A: I was in Washington, D.C., last August.
B: Oh. How was it?
A: Great. But it rained a lot.
B: Did you visit any museums?
A: Oh, yes. I loved the Smithsonian.
B: How much did it cost?
A: Nothing. It's free.
B: That's good. Was the Metro crowded?
A: Yes, sometimes.
B: How many people live in Washington, D.C.?
A: A lot. About 700,000. Over 20 million people visit it each year.
B: How many?
A: Over 20 million.
B: Wow. That's a lot of tourists.

**B** WRITE Write a conversation about the place you talked about in A. Include three *how many* or *how much* questions and answers. Include quantifiers in your answers.

**C** CHECK YOUR WORK Look at your conversation again. Underline *how many* and *how much* and the nouns that follow them. Circle quantifiers in your answers. Use the Editing Checklist to check your work.

| Editing Checklist |
| --- |
| **Did you use . . . ?** |
| ☐ *How many* before plural count nouns? |
| ☐ *How much* before non-count nouns |
| ☐ *A lot, a few,* and *not many* before plural count nouns |
| ☐ *A lot, a little,* and *not much* before non-count nouns |
| ☐ check your spelling |

**D** REVISE YOUR WORK Read your conversation again. Can you improve your writing? Make changes if necessary.

# UNIT 27 REVIEW

**Test yourself on the grammar of the unit.**

**Ⓐ Complete the conversations with *how many* or *how much*.**

1. **A:** _How much_ time did you spend away from home?  **B:** A lot. Four weeks.

2. **A:** _How many_ countries did you visit last summer?  **B:** Four countries.

3. **A:** _How many_ days were you in Spain?  **B:** Five days.

4. **A:** _How much_ rain was there in Spain?  **B:** Not much.

5. **A:** _How much_ did your trip cost?  **B:** A lot.

**Ⓑ Complete the conversations. Circle the correct answers.**

1. **A:** How much water do you need?  **B:** (A lot) / Much. About ten bottles.

2. **A:** How many miles is the hike?  **B:** (Not many) / Not much. Just five.

3. **A:** How much cheese did you bring?  **B:** Just a little / (a few.)

4. **A:** How many people want to join you?  **B:** (A lot) / Much. Almost thirty.

5. **A:** How much bread do you want?  **B:** (Not much) / Not many.

**Ⓒ Correct the conversations. There are <u>five</u> mistakes.**

1. **A:** How much time did you spend on a boat?

   **B:** Not ~~many~~ *much* time. Only a ~~couple~~ *couple* of days.

2. **A:** How ~~much~~ *many* trips did you take last year?

   **B:** Not many. Only two short ones.

3. **A:** How ~~much~~ *many* email messages do you send each day?

   **B:** Each day? Only one or two. But I send ~~much of~~ *a lot* text messages—maybe twenty or thirty.

4. **A:** How much time do you spend online?

   **B:** A lot of *time*. Maybe six hours a day!

**Now check your answers on page 383.**

# There is, There are, There was, and There were

## NATURE

**OUTCOMES**
• Use *there is, there are, there was,* and *there were* to state facts about people and things
• Identify true and false sentences about a reading
• Complete sentences about a conversation
• Identify true and false statements about places in nature
• Give a presentation about your favorite place in nature
• Write a paragraph about a place in nature that needs protection

---

## STEP 1    GRAMMAR IN CONTEXT

### BEFORE YOU READ

**A** VOCABULARY  Study the words. Then work with a partner. Practice the conversation.

**a rain forest**

**a waterfall**

**a volcano**

**a desert**

### Conversation

A: I'm from Brazil. There is a rain forest in Brazil.

B: Really? I'm from Saudi Arabia. There aren't any rain forests in Saudi Arabia.

**B** Work in a group. Which of the things in A are in your country? Talk about them. Complete the conversation.

A: I'm from _____. There _____ in _____.

B: Really? I'm from _____. There _____ in _____.

28|01  Read this article about national parks.

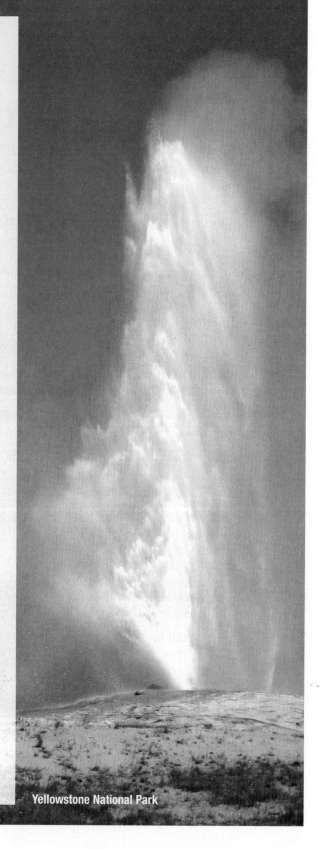

# Can We Protect Nature?

There are many parts of nature. Nature is plants and animals. It is volcanoes, waterfalls, deserts, rain forests, and mountains. We farm nature's plants and hunt its animals. We also pollute[1] nature. So, it needs protection from us. Are there things we can do to protect nature? Yes, there are.

First, we can make more national parks. Before 1872, there weren't any national parks. Before there were national parks, people hunted, farmed, and mined[2] in many beautiful places. But some thought there was a need to protect these places. National parks protect nature. In 1872, Yellowstone became the world's first national park. Today, there are more than 6,000 national parks. They are in about 100 countries.

There's also a need to protect rain forests. In rain forests, there is a lot of rain, and the weather isn't very cold. Number one in the world is the Amazon Rain Forest. There are many plants and animals in it. But there are many farmers near the rain forest. They want more land, so they cut down trees. This hurts the plants and animals in the rain forest.

In the Amazon and all around the world, there are things we can do to protect nature. We can limit[3] farming, hunting, and pollution. We need to save the beautiful world of nature for our children and our children's children.

1 *pollute:* put bad or dangerous things in nature
2 *mined:* took minerals out of the earth
3 *limit:* to keep at or under a certain amount

**Yellowstone National Park**

## AFTER YOU READ

**A** COMPREHENSION  Look at the article again. Check (✓) *True* or *False*. Correct the false statements.

|  | True | False |
|---|---|---|
| **1.** Volcanoes and waterfalls are part of nature. | ☐ | ☐ |
| **2.** There were national parks before 1872. | ☐ | ☐ |
| **3.** Yellowstone was the first national park in the world. | ☐ | ☐ |
| **4.** Today there are more than 10,000 national parks in the world. | ☐ | ☐ |
| **5.** Animals don't need rain forest trees. | ☐ | ☐ |
| **6.** We need to protect the Amazon Rain Forest. | ☐ | ☐ |

**B** Work with a partner. Compare your answers in A.

---

## STEP 2   GRAMMAR PRESENTATION

### *THERE IS*, *THERE ARE*, *THERE WAS*, AND *THERE WERE*

**Statements**

| Singular | Plural |
|---|---|
| **There is a national park** in Hawaii.<br>**There was a need** to protect nature. | **There are** many **volcanoes** in the world.<br>**There were** no **national parks** before 1872. |

**Yes/No Questions and Answers**

| Singular | Plural |
|---|---|
| A: **Is there a waterfall** in the park?<br>B: Yes, **there is.** or  No, **there isn't.** | A: **Are there** any **national parks** in the area?<br>B: Yes, **there are.** or  No, **there aren't.** |
| A: **Was there** a hotel near the park?<br>B: Yes, **there was.** or  No, **there wasn't.** | A: **Were there** any animals in the national park?<br>B: Yes, **there were.** or  No, **there weren't.** |

**There, It, and They**

| *There* | *It* and *They* |
|---|---|
| **There is** a rain forest in my country.<br>**There are** many animals in rain forests. | **It is** very beautiful.<br>**They are** wild animals. |

# GRAMMAR NOTES

## 1 *There + Be*: Affirmative Sentences

Use *there* + a form of *be* to **state facts** about people or things.

| | |
|---|---|
| Use *there is* and *there are* to state facts about people or things in the **present**. Use *there is* with singular nouns. Use *there are* with plural nouns. | **There is** a new **guide** on our tour. <br> **There are** over 6,000 national **parks** in the world. |
| Use *there was* and *there were* to state facts about people or things in the **past**. Use *there was* with singular nouns. Use *there were* with plural nouns. | **There was** an **accident** on the highway. <br> **There were** a lot of **people** on the safari. |
| **USAGE NOTE** We often use *there's* in speaking and informal writing. (*There's* = *There is*) | **There's** a **park** ten kilometres from here. |
| **BE CAREFUL!** Don't use a plural noun after *there's*. | **There are** a lot of **animals** in the zoo. <br> NOT ~~There's~~ a lot of animals in the zoo. |

## 2 *There + Be*: Negative Sentences

| | |
|---|---|
| Use *there is not* or *there isn't* to state negative facts in the **present** with singular nouns. | **There isn't** a national **park** in our state. |
| Use *there was not* or *there wasn't* to state negative facts in the **past** with singular nouns. | **There wasn't** a **park** here fifty years ago. |
| Use *there are not* or *there aren't* to state negative facts in the present with plural nouns. | **There aren't** any **elephants** in the national park. |
| Use *there were not* or *there weren't* to state negative facts in the past with plural nouns. | **There weren't** any **cars** on the road. |
| Use *a* or *an* with singular nouns and *any* with plural nouns. | There isn't **a** hotel around here. <br> There aren't **any** volcanoes in my country. |

## 3 *Yes/No* Questions with *There*

| | |
|---|---|
| To make *yes/no* **questions** with *there*, put *is, are, was,* or *were* before *there*. | **Are there** (any) volcanoes in your country? <br> **Was there** more rain forest land in the past? |
| Use *there* both in questions and **short answers**. | A: **Is there** a good hotel near the park? <br> B: Yes, **there is.** or No, **there isn't.** or No, **there's not.** <br><br> A: **Were there** many people on the safari? <br> B: Yes, **there were** twenty-five. |

## 4 *There* and *It* or *They*

| | |
|---|---|
| Use *there* the **first time** you talk about something. When you talk about the thing again, use *it* if the noun is singular. | **A:** Is **there** a zoo in your city? <br> **B:** Yes, **there is**. **It**'s a very large zoo. |
| Use *they* if the noun is plural. | **A:** Were **there** any guides on your tour? <br> **B:** Yes, **there were**. **They** were very good speakers. |

## PRONUNCIATION NOTE

▶28|02  **There are and They're**

| | |
|---|---|
| It is sometimes difficult to hear the difference between *there are* and the contraction *they're*. | |
| • *There are* has two syllables. | **There are** five national parks in my state. |
| • *They're* has one syllable. | **They're** all beautiful and interesting. |

## STEP 3   FOCUSED PRACTICE

### EXERCISE 1   DISCOVER THE GRAMMAR

**A** GRAMMAR NOTES 1–4   Read the conversation about Josh and Amanda's visit to Yosemite National Park. Underline *there + be*. Draw an arrow between each example of *there* and the noun or nouns it refers to.

MRS. GRANT:   Hello. Are you Josh and Amanda Wang? I'm Amy Grant. Welcome. Can you

please sign the guest book? There's a pen right over there.

JOSH:   Thank you. We're glad there's a room for us.

MRS. GRANT:   Actually, there are two rooms to choose from. We have a room on the second

floor and a room on the third. The one on the third floor has a nice view of

the waterfall, but there isn't an elevator.[1] Sorry about that.

AMANDA:   Oh, that's fine. We want the one with the nice view. Is there a shower[2] in

the room?

MRS. GRANT:   No. There's just one bathroom per floor. But we don't have many guests.

---

1 *elevator:* a machine to take people from one floor to another
2 *shower:* a machine that gives water; people stand under the water to get clean

a moose

deer

**AMANDA:**    Are there any animals around the hotel?

**MRS. GRANT:**    Sometimes, yes. Yesterday there was a moose in the front yard, and on Friday there were two deer across the road.... Anyway, let's see.... Breakfast is from 6:30 until 9:00. There's coffee in your room, and there are also snacks. Your room is up that stairway. See you in the morning.

**JOSH:**    Thanks a lot. See you then.

**B** Look at the conversation in A. Read the statements. Check (✓) *True* or *False*. Correct the false statements.

|  | True | False |
|---|---|---|
| 1. Mrs. Grant's hotel has two available rooms. | ✓ | ☐ |
| 2. There's a waterfall near the hotel. | ☐ | ☐ |
| 3. Josh and Amanda's room has a shower. | ☐ | ☐ |
| 4. There are always animals around the hotel. | ☐ | ☐ |
| 5. A moose visited the hotel area yesterday. | ☐ | ☐ |
| 6. Many deer visited the hotel area on Friday. | ☐ | ☐ |
| 7. Josh and Amanda can drink coffee and eat snacks in their room. | ☐ | ☐ |

## EXERCISE 2  *THERE IS, IT IS, THERE ARE, THEY ARE*

**A** GRAMMAR NOTES 1, 3–4  **Complete the conversation. Circle the correct words.**

MAN:     What are your plans for today? Are you going into the park?

AMANDA:  Yes, we are. (Is there) / There's a bus to the park? We don't want to drive.
         **1.**

MAN:     Yes, there is / it is. The number 10 bus takes you there. And there's / there are
         **2.**                                                      **3.**

         a bus stop just down the street from the hotel.

JOSH:    Great. . . . Hmm. What about lunch? Is there / Are there any places to eat in
         **4.**

         the park?

MAN:     Yes, there's / it's a good park restaurant, and they are / there are a
         **5.**                                **6.**

         couple of coffee shops. There's / It's a shopping area a few miles away.
         **7.**

         There are / They are a lot of restaurants there, and there are / they are pretty
         **8.**                                               **9.**

         good. So, have a great day. See you this evening.

⏵28|03  **B** LISTEN AND CHECK  **Listen to the conversation and check your answers in A.**

## EXERCISE 3  *THERE, IT, AND THEY*

GRAMMAR NOTES 1, 3–4  **Complete the conversations with *there*, *it*, and *they*.**

**Conversation 1**

A: OK, this is the national park. Where do we go first?

B: Well, ____there____'s an information center. ____It____ opens in fifteen minutes.
   **1.**                                        **2.**

A: Are ____there____ any animals in the center?
   **3.**

B: No, ____there____ aren't any animals in the center. ____They____ are all outside in the park.
   **4.**                                               **5.**

**Conversation 2**

A: Is ____there____ anything else to see in this area?
   **6.**

B: Yes. ____there____ are a lot of beautiful waterfalls and mountains.
   **7.**

A: Are ____they____ close?
   **8.**

B: Yes, ____they____ are all pretty close.
   **9.**

# EXERCISE 4
## *THERE* + PAST OF *BE*

**A** GRAMMAR NOTES 1–4 Complete the conversation with *there* + past forms of *be*. Write negative statements or questions if necessary. Use contractions.

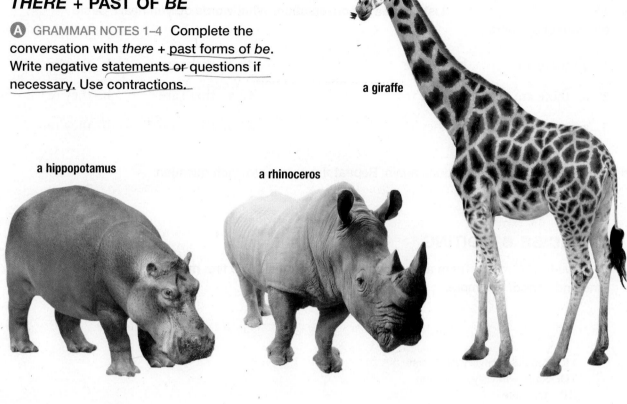

a giraffe

a hippopotamus

a rhinoceros

ALICIA: How was your trip?

MI-YOUNG: It was great. _____*There were*_____ a lot of terrific things to see.
1.

ALICIA: Sounds good. _____*There were*_____ a lot of people in your group?
2.

MI-YOUNG: _____*there were*_____ about twenty-five. Most of them were friendly, but
3.
_____*there was*_____ one unfriendly guy. We didn't like him.
4.

ALICIA: _____*Was there*_____ a guide for your group?
5.

MI-YOUNG: Yes, _____*there was*_____. He was really good.
6.

ALICIA: _____*Were there*_____ many interesting animals to see?
7.

MI-YOUNG: Oh, yeah, _____*there were*_____ a lot of them. _____*there were*_____ elephants
8.                                                   9.
and lions. And _____*there was*_____ one rhinoceros. *rhinoceros*
10.

ALICIA: _____*Was there*_____ a hippopotamus?
11.

MI-YOUNG: No, _____*there wasn't*_____. _____*there weren't*_____ any giraffes, either.
12.                      13.

ALICIA: Wow. I want to take a trip like that.

▶28|04 **B** LISTEN AND CHECK Listen to the conversation and check your answers in A.

## EXERCISE 5  *THERE ARE* AND *THEY'RE*

▶28|05  Ⓐ PRONUNCIATION NOTE  Listen to each conversation. What words do you hear? Circle the correct answers.

1. a. there are       b. they're          4. a. there are       b. they're

2. a. there are       b. they're          5. a. there are       b. they're

3. a. there are       b. they're          6. a. there are       b. they're

▶28|05  Ⓑ Listen to the conversations again. Repeat the answer to each question.

## EXERCISE 6  EDITING

GRAMMAR NOTES 1–4  There are six mistakes in the email. The first mistake is corrected. Find and correct five more.

---

FR: Amandawang@yoohoo.com
TO: Kathywhite@yoohoo.com
RE: Yosemite

Dear Kathy,

Greetings from Yosemite. We're having a wonderful time. ~~It is~~ *There are* so many beautiful places here! There are a lot of great views, and they're a big waterfall. There's a lot of animals in the park, and there really interesting. And then there's the gift shop. You know I love gift shops. They're interesting things to buy in it. We're staying at a really nice hotel called Grants' Inn. Is a nice place, and there are a lot of interesting people from different countries.

Say hi to Mark and everyone else.

Love,
Amanda

---

### EXERCISE 7 LISTENING

28|06 **A** Listen to a talk by a national park ranger. What are the people visiting?

_____

_____

_____

28|06 **B** Listen again. Complete the sentences. Circle the correct answers.

1. Victoria Falls is _____ high.
   **a.** 108 meters       **b.** 138 meters       **c.** 208 meters

2. David Livingstone discovered Victoria Falls in _____ century.
   **a.** the seventeenth       **b.** the eighteenth       **c.** the nineteenth

3. Livingstone named Victoria Falls after _____.
   **a.** a French Queen       **b.** a British Queen       **c.** a South African Queen

4. There are many animals in Victoria Falls National Park, but there aren't any _____.
   **a.** elephants       **b.** giraffes       **c.** tigers

5. There are _____ tourists at Victoria Falls every year.
   **a.** a few       **b.** some       **c.** a lot of

6. People don't want to hear _____.
   **a.** airplane noise       **b.** waterfall noise       **c.** noise from animals

7. The pollution problem is _____.
   **a.** noise pollution       **b.** air pollution       **c.** water pollution

8. There is a rain forest _____ the falls.
   **a.** in       **b.** next to       **c.** far away from

**C** Work with a partner. Ask and answer questions with *there* about the place in the listening.

EXAMPLE: **A:** Is there a waterfall in the national park?
   **B:** Yes, there is. . . . Are there elephants in the park?
   **B:** Yes, there are.

# EXERCISE 8  HOW MUCH DO YOU REMEMBER?

**A** GAME  Divide into two teams: Team A and Team B. Read the questions. All the information to answer the questions is in Unit 28. Find the answers to the questions.

1. Are there ways to protect nature?

2. Were there five national parks in the United States in 1871?

3. Is there a national park called Yellowstone National Park in Canada?

4. Are there 10,000 national parks in the world?

5. Are there many plants and animals in rain forests?

6. Are there any farmers near the Amazon Rain Forest?

7. Are there any moose and deer in Yosemite National Park?

8. Is there a big waterfall in Yosemite National Park?

9. Is there a famous national park in Zimbabwe?

10. Were there a lot of tourists at Victoria Falls in the nineteenth century?

11. Was there a British king named Victor in the nineteenth century?

12. Is there a lot of noise at Victoria Falls?

**B**  Work with the other team. Take turns asking and answering the questions in A. Use your memory. Don't look back at the unit, and try to give more information when you answer. Then check your answers on page 385.

EXAMPLE:  TEAM A:  Are there ways to protect nature?
    TEAM B:  Yes, there are. We can make more national parks, and we can limit farming, hunting, and pollution.

**C**  Close your books. Work with your team. Make up five new nature questions. They can be from the unit or your own questions. Ask the other team your questions, and answer their questions.

EXAMPLE:  TEAM A:  Are there any rain forests in the desert?
    TEAM B:  No, there aren't. There is a lot of rain in rain forests. There isn't much rain in the desert.

# EXERCISE 9  MY FAVORITE PLACE IN NATURE

**A** PRESENTATION  Prepare for a presentation. Think of your favorite place in nature. Work with a partner. Your partner asks you questions with *there* about the place. Take notes on your answers. Take turns.

EXAMPLE:  A: What's your favorite place in nature?

B: My favorite place in nature is Rwenzori Mountains National Park. It's in Uganda.

A: Are there a lot of mountains in the park?

B: Yes, there are. They are high.

A: Are there a lot of animals?

B: Yes, there are a lot of animals. There are elephants, monkeys, and chimpanzees. . . .

**B** Write a presentation about your favorite place. Use your notes in A.

**C** Give your presentation to the class.

EXAMPLE:  My favorite place in nature is Rwenzori Mountains National Park in Uganda. It's very beautiful. There are a lot of mountains in the park. Mount Baker is a very high one. There are also many interesting animals. There are elephants, monkeys, chimpanzees, and many types of birds. . . .

Mount Baker in Rwenzori Mountains National Park

**A** BEFORE YOU WRITE  Read the paragraph. Underline uses of *there is*, *there are*, *there was*, and *there were*. Then think of a beautiful place in nature that needs protection, or choose one of the places in the box. Do some research on the Internet. Then work with a partner. Tell your partner about the place.

The Everglades National Park in Florida is a beautiful place. It needs protection. There are a lot of problems in the Everglades. There is a very big problem with water. In the past, there was more water than there is today. A lot of water in the Everglades comes from Lake Okeechobee. People need water. Cities take water out of the lake. But there are many more people in Florida than there were before. We need to protect the water in the Everglades and the animals.

| | |
|---|---|
| Galápagos Islands (Ecuador) | Serengeti National Park (Tanzania) |
| Grand Canyon National Park (USA) | Torres del Paine (Chile) |
| Kruger National Park (South Africa) | Yellowstone National Park (USA) |
| Sagarmatha National Park (Nepal) | Yosemite National Park (USA) |

**B** WRITE  Write a paragraph about the place in nature you talked about in A. Use the paragraph in A and your information from the Internet to help you. Use *there + be*.

**C** CHECK YOUR WORK  Read your paragraph. Underline uses of *there + be*. Use the Editing Checklist to check your work.

### Editing Checklist

**Did you use . . . ?**

- [ ] *there is* or *was* + a singular noun
- [ ] *there are* or *were* + a plural noun
- [ ] *there* for the first time you talk about something
- [ ] *it* or *they* when your listener knows what you are talking about
- [ ] correct spelling

**D** REVISE YOUR WORK  Read your paragraph again. Can you improve your writing? Make changes if necessary.

# UNIT 28 REVIEW

**Test yourself on the grammar of the unit.**

**A** Complete the conversation. Circle the correct answers.

A: Is there / There's a visitor center in the park?
_____
    1.

B: Yes, there is / it is. It's just half a mile from here.
        _____
          2.

A: And is there / are there any interesting animals there?
              _____
                3.

B: Yes, there are / they are a lot of deer and buffaloes.
        _____
          4.

A: It is / Are they easy to find?
   _____
      5.

B: Yes, they are.


**B** Complete the conversation with *there* or *they*.

A: Good afternoon. Grants Inn, Yosemite.

B: Hi, are ____there____ any rooms for tonight?
              1.

A: Yes, ____they____ are two rooms available. ____there____'re both on the third floor.
           2.                                      3.

B: Do ____they____ have TVs?
        4.

A: Yes. ____there____'s a TV in every room.
          5.


**C** Correct the conversation. There are five mistakes.

A: How was your trip to Hawaii?

B: Wonderful! There was fantastic beaches, and were a lot of friendly people.

A: Is there interesting things to do in Hawaii?

B: Yes. You can swim in the ocean. It's a lot of beautiful fish. And they is a volcano. You

need to go to Hawaii.


**Now check your answers on pages 383–384.**

# Future with *Be going to*

# PART 10

**OUTCOMES**
- Use statements with *be going to* to talk about the future
- Identify true and false sentences about a reading and a conversation
- Talk about sports
- Discuss the future of sports
- Write a paragraph about an event you are going to attend or watch

**OUTCOMES**
- Ask and answer questions with *be going to*
- Identify true and false sentences about a reading
- Answer questions about a conversation
- Discuss pictures and talk about possible events in the future
- Talk about your plans for the future
- Write an email to your friend with questions about the future

# Future with *Be going to*: Statements

## SPORTS

**OUTCOMES**

• Use statements with *be going to* to talk about the future
• Identify true and false sentences about a reading and a conversation
• Talk about sports
• Discuss the future of sports
• Write a paragraph about an event you are going to attend or watch

---

**STEP 1** | **GRAMMAR IN CONTEXT**

### BEFORE YOU READ

**A** VOCABULARY   Study the words. Then rank the four sports in the order you like them. Your favorite is number one.

**soccer**

**basketball**

**football**

**baseball**

**B** Work in a small group. Discuss your rankings in A.

EXAMPLE:   A:  My number one sport is football.

B:  Really? Football is my number three. My number one is basketball.

🔊 29|01  Read this article about sports.

# Future Changes in the Sports World

**SPORTS ARE VERY IMPORTANT for many people around the world.** That is not going to change in the future. But many changes are going to happen in the sports world in the next twenty or thirty years.

Today, soccer ("football" outside North America) is the number one sport in the world. It's safer than many other sports. In the future, soccer is probably going to be even more popular than it is now. More and more people are going to play it.

The game of soccer is probably not going to change much, but American football is. It has a big problem: concussions.[1] They can be very dangerous to players. Officials want to protect players, so they are going to change the game in some ways.

Other sports, like baseball and basketball, are probably going to change, too. Athletes are going to be stronger. Doctors are going to change their bodies. They aren't going to have many injuries. There are also going to be new kinds of athletes. Players of video and computer games are going to become famous athletes. People are going to pay to see them.

Finally, sports fans are going to see a lot of improvements.[2] For example, it's going to be easy to attend games with self-parking cars. At games, fans are going to watch their own videos with their favorite players.

One thing is sure: Sports in the future are going to be different from the sports we watch and play today.

---

1 *concussions:* injuries to the head and brain
2 *improvements:* things that are better than in the past

# AFTER YOU READ

**A** COMPREHENSION  Look at the article again. For each statement, check (✓) *True* or *False*. Correct the false statements.

|  | True | False |
|---|:---:|:---:|
| 1. Sports are not going to change in the future. | ☐ | ☐ |
| 2. Baseball is the most popular sport in the world today. | ☐ | ☐ |
| 3. American football officials are going to make the game safer. | ☐ | ☐ |
| 4. Doctors are not going to change the bodies of athletes. | ☐ | ☐ |
| 5. Athletes aren't going to have many injuries in the future. | ☐ | ☐ |
| 6. It's going to be hard to get to stadiums in the future. | ☐ | ☐ |

**B**  Work with a partner. Compare your answers in A.

## STEP 2   GRAMMAR PRESENTATION

## FUTURE WITH *BE GOING TO*: STATEMENTS

### Affirmative Statements

| Am going to | Is going to | Are going to |
|---|---|---|
| I **am going to play** volleyball this weekend. <br> I **am going to have** a party next weekend. | He **is going to graduate** in June. <br> She **is going to be** an Olympic athlete. <br> It **is going to rain** today. | We **are going to see** a movie tonight. <br> You **are going to enjoy** this party. <br> There **are going to be** improvements in the future. |

### Negative Statements

| Am not going to | Is not going to | Are not going to |
|---|---|---|
| I **am not going to drive** fast. <br> I**'m not going to drive** fast. | He **is not going to graduate** in June. <br> It **is not going to rain** today. <br> It**'s not going to rain** today. <br> It **isn't going to rain** today. | We **are not going to be** late. <br> We**'re not going to be** late. <br> We **aren't going to be** late. |

# GRAMMAR NOTES

## 1 Be going to: Uses

| | |
|---|---|
| You can use **be going to** to talk about the future. | We**'re going to be** late.<br>It**'s going to rain**. |

## 2 Be going to: Affirmative Statements

| | |
|---|---|
| To make **affirmative** future statements with *be going to*, use *am*, *is*, or *are* + *going to* + the **base form** of the verb. | I **am going to play** soccer.<br>We **are going to win**. |
| **USAGE NOTE** We often use **contractions** in conversation and informal writing. | We**'re going to win**.<br>The game**'s going to** start soon. |

## 3 Be going to: Negative Statements

| | |
|---|---|
| To make **negative** future statements with *be going to*, place *not* before *going to*. We often use contractions with negative statements. | They **are not going to lose**.<br>It **is not going to snow**.<br>They **aren't going to lose**.<br>It **isn't going to snow**. |

## 4 Time Expressions with Be going to

To talk about the future, we can use expressions such as *this / next* + period of time, *tonight*, and *tomorrow*. We can also use prepositions of time such as *in*.

| | |
|---|---|
| • *this / next* + period of time | He's going to study **this afternoon**.<br>They're going to play soccer **next weekend**. |
| • *tonight* | We're going to watch TV **tonight**. |
| • *tomorrow* | It's going to rain **tomorrow**. |
| • *in* + period of time | They're going to arrive **in a few minutes**.<br>He is going to graduate **in June**.<br>Spain is going to win the World Cup **in 2018**. |

# PRONUNCIATION NOTE

▶ 29|02 **Going to and Gonna**

| | |
|---|---|
| In conversation, we often pronounce *going to* as *gonna*. Don't use *gonna* in writing. | |
| • *Going to* (standard pronunciation) | We **are going to see** a movie tonight. |
| • *Gonna* | We're **gonna see** a movie tonight. |

# REFERENCE NOTES

For **definitions of grammar terms**, see the Glossary on page 375.

For information on **questions with *be going to***, see Unit 30 on page 351.

## EXERCISE 1  DISCOVER THE GRAMMAR

Ⓐ GRAMMAR NOTES 1–4  Read the conversation. Underline the examples of *be going to* + the base form of the verb.

LAURA: Ken, hurry up! We're going to be late!

KEN:   What's the hurry? It's just a silly little soccer game! I think it's going to be boring.

LAURA: It's not silly, and it's not little. And it's not boring. Sam is on the team! It's a big game. I think they're going to win.

KEN:   I know. That's what you told me. Is your brother a good player?

LAURA: He's really good.

KEN:   Do I need an umbrella?

LAURA: No. It's not going to rain.... Come on.

*(Later)*

LAURA: Can you drive any faster?

KEN:   No. I'm not going to drive faster than the speed limit.

LAURA: Oh, no! A traffic jam! The game is going to start in a few minutes.

KEN:   Laura, relax! We're going to make it on time.

Ⓑ Look at the conversation in A again. Complete the sentences. Circle the correct answers.

1. Ken knows / (doesn't know) a lot about soccer.

2. Laura thinks they are / aren't going to be late to the game.

3. Ken thinks the game is / isn't going to be boring.

4. Laura says it is / isn't going to rain.

5. Ken says he is / isn't going to drive faster than the speed limit.

6. Laura is afraid they are / aren't going to make it to the soccer game on time.

7. Ken says that they are / aren't going to be late.

## EXERCISE 2 *BE GOING TO*: AFFIRMATIVE STATEMENTS

GRAMMAR NOTES 1–2  Complete the sentences. Use the correct forms of *be going to* and the words in parentheses. Use contractions with pronoun subjects.

It's Saturday. Annie Olson is on a soccer team. ___*They're going to play*___
**1.** (They / play)
this afternoon. ___*It's going to be*___ warm. Everybody in the family
**2.** (It / be)
___*are going to attend*___. Ben ___is going to invite___
**3.** (attend)                  **4.** (invite)
four friends, and Jeremy ___is going to take___ his girlfriend. Tim and
**5.** (take)
Jessica ___are going to film___ the game. Mary and Bill Beck
**6.** (film)
___are going to ask___ a few of their friends to go. Everyone thinks
**7.** (ask)
Annie's team ___is going to win___ — everyone but Annie. She says,
**8.** (win)
"I'm not sure ___I'm going to play___ very well."
**9.** (I / play)

## EXERCISE 3 *BE GOING TO*: AFFIRMATIVE AND NEGATIVE STATEMENTS

GRAMMAR NOTES 1–3  Look at the pictures. Complete the sentences. Use the correct forms of *be going to* and the verbs in parentheses. Use the affirmative or negative.

**1.** Skier 34 ___*is going to win*___.
            (win)

**2.** Skier 21 ___isn't going to finish___ second.
            (finish)

**3.** The Porpoises ___aren't going to win___.
            (win)

**4.** The Dolphins ___are going to win___.
            (win)

**5.** Runner 81 ___isn't going to lose___.
            (lose)

**6.** Runner 6 ___isn't going to win___.
            (win)

**7.** Magic Dancer ___is going to win___.
            (win)

**8.** Petunia ___isn't going to finish___ last.
            (finish)

# EXERCISE 4  *GOING TO* AND *GONNA*

▶29|03  Ⓐ PRONUNCIATION NOTE  Read and listen to the conversations. Then listen again and complete the sentences with the correct forms of *be going to*.

**Conversation 1**

A: I don't think ___*I'm going to pass*___ this course.
                                1.

B: Of course ___you are going to pass___ it! Don't worry.
                       2.

**Conversation 2**

A: My team ___is going to win___ the game.
                    3.

B: No, it isn't.

A: Yes, it is. ___We are going to win___ for sure.
                      4.

**Conversation 3**

A: The traffic is terrible. ___I am not going to be___ it on time.
                                   5.

B: Don't worry. ___You are going to make___ it. The game
                        6.

___is going to start___ in twenty minutes.
        7.

Ⓑ Read the conversations in A out loud. Pronounce *going to* as "gonna."


# EXERCISE 5  EDITING

GRAMMAR NOTES 1–4  There are six mistakes in the email. The first mistake is corrected. Find and correct five more.

---

**TO** kathy344@yoohoo.com  |  **FROM** amanda70@gomail.com  |  **SUBJECT** Party

Hi Kathy,

                  are
Josh and I ̭going to have a little party ~~last~~ Sunday. We're going ^to^ watch the Super

Bowl, and we're going to ~~has~~ pizza and dessert. I think the game ~~are~~ going to start

at 3:00, and we ~~be~~ going to eat at about 5:00. Please come.

Amanda

---

## EXERCISE 6   LISTENING

▶ 29|04   **A**   Listen to the conversation. Does Sam's team win or lose their soccer game?

_____

▶ 29|04   **B**   Listen to the conversation again. For each statement, check (✓) *True* or *False*.

| | True | False |
|---|---|---|
| **1.** Ken thinks the game is boring. | ☐ | ☑ |
| **2.** Ken thinks it's going to rain. | ☐ | ☐ |
| **3.** Laura thinks it's going to rain. | ☐ | ☐ |
| **4.** The score is 2–1. | ☐ | ☐ |
| **5.** Ken thinks Sam's team is going to win. | ☐ | ☐ |
| **6.** Laura thinks Sam's team is going to win. | ☐ | ☐ |
| **7.** Sam's penalty kick went in the goal. | ☐ | ☐ |
| **8.** Ken and Laura are going to go to Sam's game in two weeks. | ☐ | ☐ |

**C**   Work with a partner. Discuss these statements. Are they true or false? Explain why.

**1.** Laura is going to attend a lot of soccer games in the future.

**2.** Ken is going to attend a lot of soccer games in the future.

**3.** I am going to attend a lot of soccer games in the future.

EXAMPLE: The first statement is true. Laura is going to attend a lot of soccer games in the future because . . .

# EXERCISE 7 WHAT SPORTS ARE POPULAR IN YOUR COUNTRY?

Ⓐ SURVEY Work in a group of three. Find out what sports are popular in each person's country. Check (✓) if the sport is popular.

| Sport | Country 1: | Country 2: | Country 3: |
|---|---|---|---|
| American football | | | |
| Baseball | | | |
| Basketball | | | |
| Soccer | | | |
| Gymnastics | | | |
| Hockey | | | |
| Track and field (running) | | | |
| Volleyball | | | |

Ⓑ Discuss each sport. In your countries, do you think the sport is going to become more popular or less popular in the next twenty years?

EXAMPLE:  A: In the United States, basketball is very popular. But I think basketball is going to be more popular in twenty years.
B: Basketball is going to be more popular in China, too.

Ⓒ Report your results to the class.

EXAMPLE:  Our group thinks basketball is going to be more popular in the United States and China. We think baseball is going to be less popular.

# EXERCISE 8 PEOPLE ARE STILL GOING TO WATCH FOOTBALL

Ⓐ DISCUSSION Work in a group. Look at these two statements about sports in the future. Choose one of the statements and discuss it. Is this change really going to happen? Is it going to be good or bad? Explain why.

1. People aren't going to watch football and basketball in the future. They're going to watch video games.

   EXAMPLE:  I think people are going to watch football and basketball in the future. They're going to watch these sports because . . .

2. Sports fans are going to watch only their favorite players in games. They aren't going to watch all the players.

Ⓑ Report your ideas to the class.

# FROM GRAMMAR TO WRITING

**A** BEFORE YOU WRITE  Read the paragraph. Underline uses of *be going to*. Then think of a sports event or other event you are going to attend or watch on TV in the future. Complete the chart about your plans for the event. Work with a partner. Tell your partner about the event you're going to see.

The next Summer Olympics are going to be fun. I can't go to the Olympics. I'm going to watch them on TV. I like a lot of different sports, so I'm going to watch a lot of different events. But I love cycling. I ride on a cycling team, so my teammates and I are going to watch all the cycling events. France, Germany, and Great Britain are good at cycling. They're probably going to win a lot of medals.

| Name of event | |
|---|---|
| Your favorite part of the event | |
| Why you like it | |
| People or groups in the event | |

**B** WRITE  Write a paragraph about the event you are going to attend or watch. Use the model and your chart in A to help you. Read your paragraph to the class.

**C** CHECK YOUR WORK  Read your paragraph. Underline statements with *be going to*. Use the Editing Checklist to check your work.

**Editing Checklist**

**Did you use . . . ?**
- [ ] *am going to* with *I*
- [ ] *is going to* with *he* and *she*
- [ ] *are going to* with *we*, *you*, and *they*
- [ ] the base form of the verb after *be going to*
- [ ] correct spelling

**D** REVISE YOUR WORK  Read your paragraph again. Can you improve your writing? Make changes if necessary.

# UNIT 29 REVIEW

**Test yourself on the grammar of the unit.**

**A** Complete the sentences. Use the correct form of *be going to* and the words in parentheses. Use contractions when possible.

1. _I am not going to play baseball_ this weekend.
   (I / not / play baseball)

2. I think _Argentina is going to win_ the World Cup.
   (Argentina / win)

3. _It is not going to rain_ at the game tonight.
   (It / not / rain)

4. _We aren't going to have dinner_ at the game.
   (We / not / have dinner)

5. _You are going to love_ the beautiful stadium.
   (You / love)

**B** Put the words in the correct order. Make sentences.

1. _They are going to win_
   (are / going / to / They / win)

2. _We are going to be late._
   (We / going / to / late / be / are)

3. _The sun is not going to shine_
   (shine / is / not / The sun / going / to)

4. _The game is going to start soon_
   (going / to / soon / game / is / The / start)

5. _We are going to get there on time._
   (get there / We / on time / going / to / are)

**C** Correct the sentences. There are five mistakes.

Jorge and I going to go to a basketball game this Saturday afternoon at 2:00 p.m. But there's one little problem. Our friend's son be going to graduate from high school on Saturday, too. The graduation is going end at 2:00 p.m., so we going to be late for the game. But we not going to miss more than half an hour of the game.

**Now check your answers on page 384.**

UNIT
30

# Future with *Be going to*: Questions

## CAREER PLANS AND GOALS

---

### STEP 1   GRAMMAR IN CONTEXT

## BEFORE YOU READ

**Ⓐ VOCABULARY** Study the words. Match the words and phrases.

the news

You are now a sales manager. Congratulations!

a promotion

a business trip

_____ **1.** information about things happening now

_____ **2.** a higher level job

_____ **3.** travel for work

**a.** a business trip

**b.** a promotion

**c.** the news

**Ⓑ** Work with a partner. Compare your answers in A. Then complete the sentences. Circle the words that are true for you.

**1.** I watch / listen to / read the news.

**2.** My friend / co-worker / brother got a promotion last year.

**3.** I often / sometimes / never take business trips.

🔊 30|01  Read this conversation.

# A Job Offer

**TIM:** How was your day?

**JESSICA:** Actually, I had an interesting call from Dan Evans, the TV producer.[1]

**TIM:** Oh?

**JESSICA:** He's planning a TV news show, and he wants me in it.

**JEREMY:** Cool! What are you going to do in the show?

**JESSICA:** I'm going to present the news.

**JEREMY:** Are you going to accept the job offer?

**JESSICA:** I don't know yet.

**JEREMY:** Is it going to be a big promotion?

**JESSICA:** Uh-huh.

**JEREMY:** What about the salary?[2] Are we going to be rich?

**JESSICA:** We didn't talk about money. But I'm sure it's going to be a raise[3] from my present job.

**TIM:** Are you going to be away a lot? Are you going to have a lot of business trips?

**JESSICA:** I think so.

**ANNIE:** Don't take the job, Mom. I want you to stay home.

**BEN:** Yeah. You always help me with my homework. Who's going to help me with my homework? How are you going to drive me to soccer practice?

**TIM:** Hey, guys, I'm still going to be here. I can do those things.

**JESSICA:** Listen, kids, don't worry. This is all very new. The TV show isn't going to start for a long time.

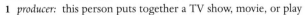

1  *producer:* this person puts together a TV show, movie, or play
2  *salary:* pay you receive every month or week from the place you work
3  *raise:* more money for your work

# AFTER YOU READ

**A COMPREHENSION** Look at the conversation again. For each statement, check (✓) *True* or *False*.

| | True | False |
|---|---|---|
| 1. Dan Evans has an idea for a movie. | ☐ | ☐ |
| 2. Dan wants Jessica to work on a news show. | ☐ | ☐ |
| 3. Jessica's new job is going to start right away. | ☐ | ☐ |
| 4. Jessica is going to get a promotion. | ☐ | ☐ |
| 5. Jeremy is unhappy about Jessica's new job. | ☐ | ☐ |
| 6. Jessica helps Ben with homework. | ☐ | ☐ |
| 7. Tim drives Ben to soccer practice. | ☐ | ☐ |

**B** Work with a partner. Correct the false statements in A.

## STEP 2    GRAMMAR PRESENTATION

## FUTURE WITH *BE GOING TO*: QUESTIONS

### Yes/No Questions

| Be | Subject | Going to + Base Form |
|---|---|---|
| Am | I | **going to get** the job? |
| Is | the program | **going to start** soon? |
| Are | we | **going to move**? |

### Short Answers

| | |
|---|---|
| Yes, **you are.** | No, **you're not.** or No, **you aren't.** |
| Yes, **it is.** | No, **it's not.** or No, **it isn't.** |
| Yes, **we are.** | No, **we're not.** or No, **we aren't.** |

### Wh- Questions

| Wh- Question Word | Be | Subject | Going to + Base Form |
|---|---|---|---|
| **When** | **are** | you | **going to start**? |
| **How** | **are** | they | **going to get** there? |

### Short Answers

| |
|---|
| Next Monday. |
| By bus. |

### Wh- Questions About the Subject

| Wh- Question Word | Be | Going to + Base Form |
|---|---|---|
| **Who** | **is** | **going to help** us? |

### Short Answers

| |
|---|
| I am. |

# GRAMMAR NOTES

## 1 Be going to: Yes/No Questions

| | |
|---|---|
| To make **yes/no questions** with *be going to*, put **am**, **is**, or **are** before the subject. | **Am I going to have** a big part? <br> **Is he going to change** jobs? <br> **Are they going to buy** a house? |
| We usually use **contractions** in negative short answers. | A: Is he going to change jobs? <br> B: No, he**'s not**. or No, he **isn't**. |
| **BE CAREFUL!** Do not use contractions with affirmative short answers. | A: Are they going to play soccer this weekend? <br> B: Yes, they **are**. <br> NOT Yes, ~~they're~~. |

## 2 Be going to: Wh- Questions

| | |
|---|---|
| To form most **wh- questions** with *be going to*, use a **wh- question word** + *be* + **subject** + *going to* + the **base form** of the verb. | A: **When is it going to begin**? <br> B: Next year. |
| To form a **wh- question about the subject**, use **who** or **what** + **is** + **going to** + the **base form** of the verb. | A: **Who is going to be** the producer? <br> B: Dan Evans is. |
| We usually use **short answers** for *wh-* questions with *be going to*. We can also use long answers. | A: What are you going to do this summer? <br> B: **Study Chinese.** <br> or <br> B: **I'm going to study Chinese.** <br><br> A: Who is going to teach the class? <br> B: **Professor Chang.** <br> or <br> B: **Professor Chang is going to teach the class.** |

# REFERENCE NOTES

For **definitions of grammar terms**, see the Glossary on page 375.

For information on **statements with *be going to***, see Unit 29 on page 340.

For information on the **pronunciation of *going to***, see Unit 29 on page 341.

## EXERCISE 1  DISCOVER THE GRAMMAR

**A** GRAMMAR NOTES 1–2  **Read the conversation. Underline the** *yes/no* **questions about the future. Circle the** *wh-* **questions about the future.**

JILL: (When are you going to start college?)

RUSS: Next September.

JILL: <u>Are you going to go to a college near your home?</u>

RUSS: No. I'm going to go to an out-of-town college.

JILL: Where are you going to go?

RUSS: I'm going to go to a college in Alaska.

JILL: That's far. What are you going to major in?

RUSS: Math.

JILL: Are you going to work this summer?

RUSS: Yes, I am. I have an interview at the library this afternoon. I'm going to get a job

to help pay for college.

**B** **Look at the conversation in A again. Answer the questions. Circle the correct answers.**

1. What is Russ going to do in September?
   **a.** get a job          **(b.)** go to college

2. Is Russ going to go to a college near home?
   **a.** Yes, he is.          **b.** No, he isn't.

3. Is Russ going to take a lot of math courses?
   **a.** Yes, he is.          **b.** No, he isn't.

4. What is Russ going to do in the summer?
   **a.** study at the library          **b.** get a summer job

# EXERCISE 2 YES/NO QUESTIONS AND SHORT ANSWERS

GRAMMAR NOTE 1  Complete the conversations. Use the correct forms of the verbs in parentheses.

1. **A:** ____Are____ you ____going to work____ next year?
   (work)

   **B:** No, ____I'm not____. I'm going to study full-time.

2. **A:** ____Is____ she ____going to graduate____ in June?
   (graduate)

   **B:** No, ____she isn't____. She's going to graduate next January.

3. **A:** ____Is____ he ____going to get____ a promotion?
   (get)

   **B:** Yes, ____He is____. He's going to be the head chef.

4. **A:** ____Is____ she ____going to be____ a teacher?
   (be)

   **B:** Yes, ____she is____. She's going to start next September.

5. **A:** ____Are____ you ____going to ask____ for a raise? more money
   (ask)

   **B:** No, ____I'm not____. I just started this job last month.

6. **A:** ____Are____ they ____going to start____ their own business?
   (start)

   **B:** Yes, ____they are____. They're going to start an online hat business.

# EXERCISE 3  YES/NO QUESTIONS

GRAMMAR NOTE 1  Read the sentences. Write yes/no questions with be going to for the future. Use the correct forms of the words in parentheses.

1. John is working today. _Is he going to work tomorrow?_
   (he / work / tomorrow?)

2. Mary was late this morning. _Is she going to be late tomorrow morning?_
   (she / be / late tomorrow morning?)

3. Oscar and Greta left early last Monday. _Are they going to leave early next Monday?_
   (they / leave / early next Monday?)

4. You took a business trip last month. _Are you going to take a business trip next month?_
   (you / take / a business trip next month?)

5. It's raining now. _Is it_
   (it / rain / this afternoon?)

6. Elsa asked for a raise a few months ago. _Is she going to ask for a raise this month?_
   (she / ask / for a raise this month?)

# EXERCISE 4 WH- QUESTIONS

**A** GRAMMAR NOTE 2 Write *wh-* questions with *be going to*. Use the correct forms of the words in parentheses.

OLIVIA: Hey, Drew! What are your summer plans?

DREW: I'm going to take a class.

OLIVIA: Oh, yeah! <u>*What are you going to take?*</u>
   **1.** (What / you / take?)

DREW: A psychology class.

OLIVIA: Not me. I'm not going to take any classes. I have a job.

DREW: Really? <u>What are you going to do?</u>
   **2.** (What / you / do?)

OLIVIA: I'm going to be a dog walker.

DREW: <u>Why are you going to do</u> that?
   **3.** (Why / you / do)

OLIVIA: Because I love dogs. And people need dog walkers in this city.

DREW: <u>Where are you going to walk</u> the dogs?
   **4.** (Where / you / walk)

OLIVIA: In West Park.

DREW: <u>When are you going to start?</u>
   **5.** (When / you / start?)

OLIVIA: Next Monday. I have two customers.

DREW: That's not many. <u>How are you going to get</u> more customers?
   **6.** (How / you / get)

OLIVIA: I have a website, and I'm going to put signs in buildings near the park.

DREW: <u>What hours are you going to work?</u>
   **7.** (What hours / you / work?)

OLIVIA: Eleven to 1:30, Monday to Friday.

DREW: Well, good luck!

**30|02** **B** LISTEN AND CHECK Listen to the conversation and check your answers in A.

# EXERCISE 5  PAST, PRESENT, FUTURE:  REVIEW

GRAMMAR NOTES 1–2  Complete the conversations. Use the simple past, the simple present, the present progressive, or *be going to* for the future. Use the correct forms of the verbs in parentheses. Use contractions when possible.

**1.** (rain)

TIM:  It _____ *rained* _____ yesterday.

It _____ *'s raining* _____ now.

_____ *Is* _____ it

_____ *going to rain* _____ tomorrow?

JESSICA:  I'm afraid so. That's what the

weather channel says.

**2.** (get)

TIM:  Robert _____ a raise last March.

_____ he _____ a raise this March?

MARY:  I think so. He's a great salesman, and they want him to stay at the company. And

you and I _____ raises, too.

TIM:  That's great!

**3.** (graduate)

RON:  I can't see you tonight because my family is going to have a big celebration.

My cousin _____ from college last week.

I _____ from high school next week, and my sister

_____ from middle school tomorrow.

JEREMY:  Nice! Have fun.

**4.** (work)

JESSICA:  You _____ late now. You _____ late

last night. _____ you _____ late

tomorrow night, too?

TIM:  Yes, I am. This is always a busy time at work.

**5.** (have)

JEREMY: I'm tired of tofu. We _____ tofu last night. We

_____ tofu now. _____ we

_____ tofu tomorrow?

TIM: No, we're not. Tomorrow we _____ veggie burgers.

**6.** (play)

JESSICA: You always _____ that video game. You

_____ it every day last week.

You _____ it now. _____ you

_____ it tomorrow?

JEREMY: Probably. It's really fun!

**7.** (watch)

TIM: You _____ that news program yesterday. Why

_____ you _____ it again now?

JESSICA: It's awesome. I _____ it again tonight at 11:00. I can

watch news shows over and over again.

## EXERCISE 6 EDITING

GRAMMAR NOTES 1–2 **There are five mistakes in the phone messages. The first mistake is corrected. Find and correct four more.**

1. Hi, Jessica. This is Dan. Are you going ^*to* be in Seattle on Tuesday? I have a meeting there

   and I want to see you. Call or text me at 990-287-2295.

2. Hi, honey. I forgot my date book. Is Fred and Janet going to meet us at 8:00 or 8:30?

   Please call.

3. This message is for Jessica Olson. This is George Selig. When is the conference going start?

4. Hi, Mom. I want to study with Jorge. Are Grandma and Grandpa going to watching Ben

   and Annie?

5. Hi, Jessica. This is Meg Smith. What time the meeting going to be? Please call me at

   989-555-0007.

## EXERCISE 7   LISTENING

▶ 30|03   Ⓐ   **Listen to Josh's conversation with Mark and Josh's telephone conversation with Amanda. What is Amanda going to have soon?**

**a.** A new job.          **b.** A baby.

▶ 30|03   Ⓑ   **Listen again. Answer the questions.**

1.  What is Josh going to work on?
    (a.) The company's website.
    **b.** The company's newspaper.

2.  What is Josh going to be?
    **a.** An assistant.
    **b.** A manager.

3.  Is Josh going to go rock climbing for his job?
    **a.** Yes, he is.
    **b.** No, he isn't.

4.  Is Amanda going to go rock climbing?
    **a.** Yes, she is.
    **b.** No, she isn't.

Ⓒ   **Work with a partner. Josh and Amanda's lives are going to change in many ways. What are three more questions Amanda is asking herself? What are three more questions Josh is asking himself?**

Amanda's questions:                        Josh's questions:

*Is Josh going to work many hours?*           *Are we going to need a bigger home?*

## EXERCISE 8   IN TEN YEARS, I'M GOING TO . . .

Ⓐ   DISCUSSION   Think about your plans for the future. Complete the sentences below.

Next year, I'm going to ____. In five years, I'm going to ____. In ten years, I'm going to ____.

*Next year, I'm going to move to California.*
*In five years, I'm going to graduate from college.*
*In ten years, I'm going to start my own business.*

**B** Work in small groups. Tell your group about your plans for next year, five years from now, and ten years from now. Your classmates ask *yes/no* and *wh-* questions about your plans for the future.

EXAMPLE: **A:** Next year, I'm going to move to California.

**B:** Why are you going to move there?

**A:** I'm going to move there because I have family there.

**C:** Are you going to live with your family?

**A:** Yes, for the first year. Then I'm going to . . .

## EXERCISE 9 THINK OF THE POSSIBILITIES

**A** PICTURE DISCUSSION  Work in small groups. Look at the pictures. Write as many *yes/no* and *wh-* questions with *be going to* about the pictures as you can.

*In picture 1, are the women going to work together in the future?*
*What are they going to do?*
*Is the woman in the blue shirt going to be the other woman's boss?*

**B** Work with another group. Read all your group's questions to the other group. They answer your questions, using their imaginations. Take turns.

EXAMPLE: **A:** Are the women in Picture 1 going to work together?

**B:** Yes, they are. The woman in the blue shirt is a manager, and the woman in the middle is going to be her assistant.

**A** BEFORE YOU WRITE  A man got a promotion. Read a message from his friend. Underline questions with *be going to*. Then imagine your friend got a job, a promotion, or acceptance at a school or college. Write a list of questions for your friend in the chart below.

○ ○ ●

Hi Gabriel,

Congratulations! I hear that you're going to be a manager at Goodbuys. I'm so happy for you. When are you going to begin? Are you going to work evenings? Are you going to take business trips? Are you going to live in this area?

Please tell me all about you and your new job.

Gustavo

| Questions for Your Friend |
|---|
| 1. |
| 2. |
| 3. |
| 4. |

**B** WRITE  Your friend got a job, a promotion, or acceptance to a school. Write an email to your friend. Ask your friend questions. Use the message in A and your chart to help you. Use *be going to* for the future.

**C** CHECK YOUR WORK  Read your letter again. Underline the questions with *be going to*. Use the Editing Checklist to check your work.

| Editing Checklist |
|---|

**Did you . . . ?**

☐ use *is, am, are* + subject + *going to* + the base form of the verb for *yes/no* questions in the future

☐ use a *wh-* question word + *be* + subject + *going to* + the base form of the verb for most *wh-* questions in the future

☐ use a *wh-* question word + *be* + *going to* + the base form of the verb for *wh-* questions about the subject

☐ check your spelling

**D** REVISE YOUR WORK  Read your letter again. Can you improve your writing? Make changes if necessary.

# UNIT 30 REVIEW

**Test yourself on the grammar of the unit.**

**A** Match the questions and short answers.

___b___ **1.** Is Josh going to be a father?

___d___ **2.** Are Josh and Amanda going to move right away?

___e___ **3.** Is it going to cost a lot to have a child?

___a___ **4.** Is Amanda's mom going to watch the baby?

___c___ **5.** Are you going to help Amanda's mom?

**a.** Yes, she is.

**b.** Yes, he is.

**c.** No, I'm not.

**d.** No, they're not.

**e.** Yes, it is.

**B** Complete the questions about a business meeting. Use the correct forms of *be going to* and the verbs in parentheses.

1. Where ___is___ the meeting ___going to be___ ?
   (be)

2. When ___is___ it ___going to start___ ?
   (start)

3. How ___are___ you ___going to get___ there?
   (get)

4. Who ___are___ you ___going to go___ with?
   (go)

5. What ___are___ they ___going to talk (to)___ about at the meeting?
   (talk)

**C** Correct the conversation. There are five mistakes.

**A:** I got a new job. I'm going to be a producer.

**B:** ~~Is~~ Are you going to work full-time?

**A:** Yes, I'm. I am

**B:** When ~~you are~~ are you going to start?

**A:** Next month.

**B:** Are you going to take a vacation?

**A:** Yes, I'm going to go to Toronto next week.

**B:** Who are you going to stay with?

**A:** My aunt.

**Now check your answers on page 384.**

# Appendices

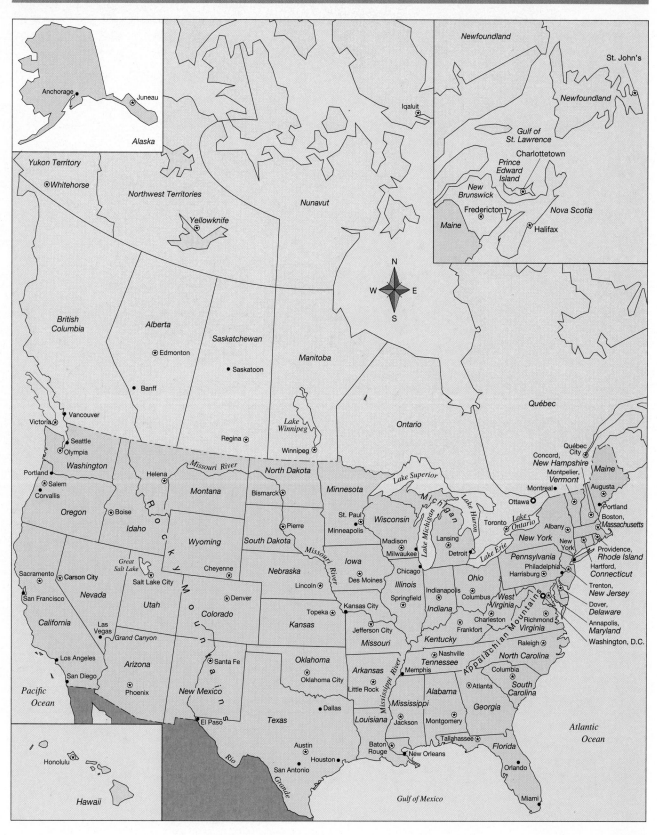

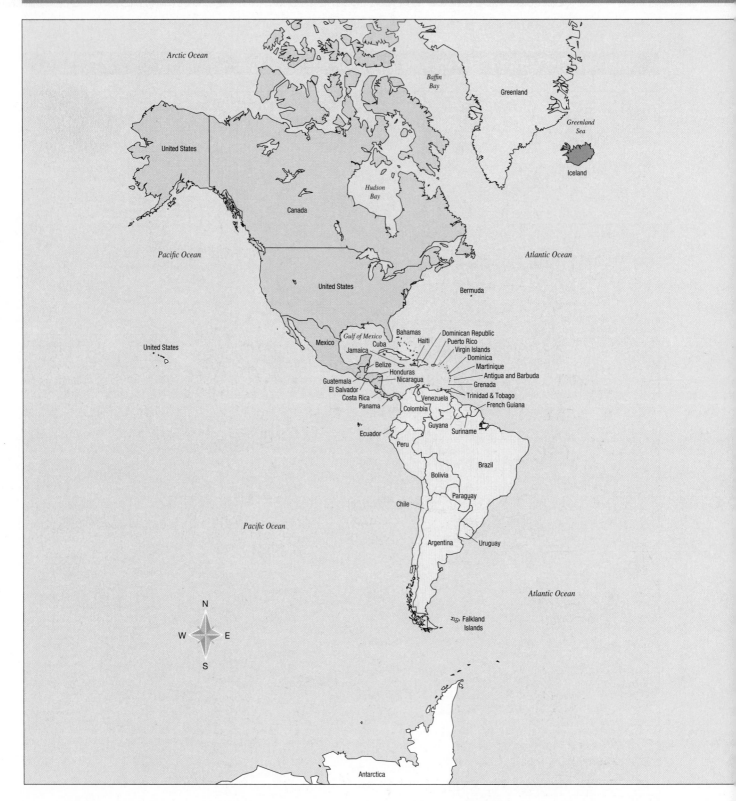

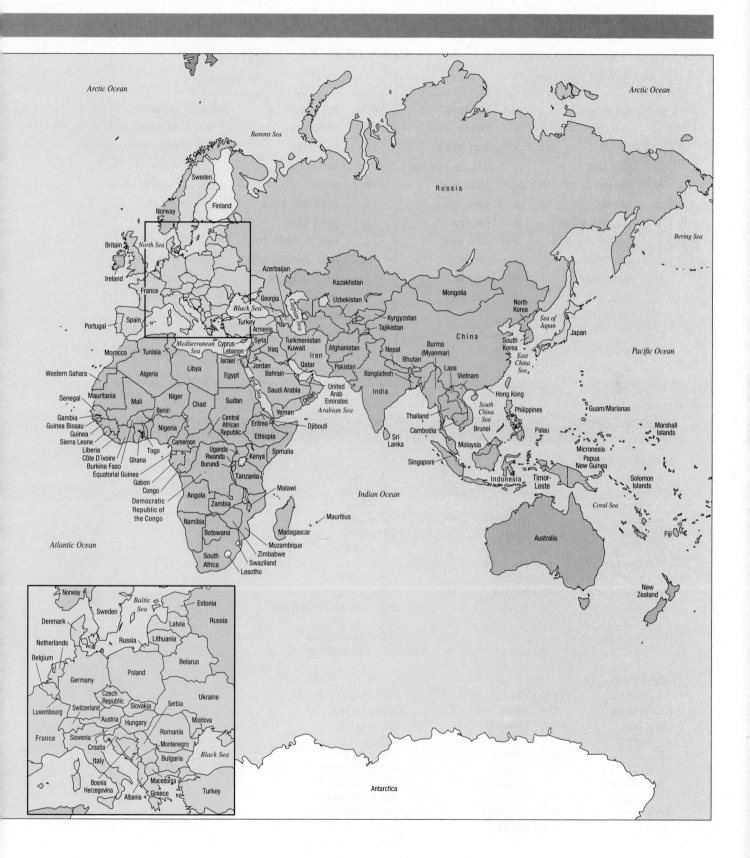

Arctic Ocean

Arctic Ocean

Barents Sea

Bering Sea

Sweden

Finland

Russia

Norway

*Bering Sea*

Britain

*North Sea*

Azerbaijan

Kazakhstan

Mongolia

Ireland

France

Georgia

Uzbekistan

North Korea

*Sea of Japan*

*Black Sea*

*Caspian Sea*

Kyrgyzstan

China

Portugal

Spain

Turkey

Armenia

Turkmenistan

Tajikistan

South Korea

Japan

Pacific Ocean

Syria

Afghanistan

*Mediterranean Sea*

Cyprus

Lebanon

Iraq

Kuwait

Iran

Nepal

Burma (Myanmar)

*East China Sea*

Morocco

Tunisia

Israel

Jordan

Pakistan

Bhutan

Laos

Western Sahara

Algeria

Libya

Egypt

Bahrain

Qatar

Saudi Arabia

Oman

United Arab Emirates

*Red Sea*

India

Bangladesh

Vietnam

Hong Kong

Guam/Marianas

Senegal

Mauritania

Mali

Niger

Chad

Sudan

*Arabian Sea*

Yemen

Eritrea

Djibouti

Thailand

*South China Sea*

Philippines

Palau

Marshall Islands

Gambia

Guinea Bissau

Guinea

Sierra Leone

Liberia

Côte D'ivoire

Benin

Nigeria

Cameroon

Togo

Ghana

Central African Republic

Ethiopia

Somalia

Cambodia

Brunei

Micronesia

Burkina Faso

Equatorial Guinea

Gabon

Congo

Uganda

Rwanda

Burundi

Kenya

Malaysia

Singapore

Papua New Guinea

Solomon Islands

Democratic Republic of the Congo

Angola

Zambia

Tanzania

Malawi

Indonesia

Timor-Leste

Namibia

Botswana

Madagascar

Mauritius

Indian Ocean

Australia

*Coral Sea*

Fiji

Atlantic Ocean

South Africa

Mozambique

Zimbabwe

Swaziland

Lesotho

New Zealand

Norway

*Baltic Sea*

Estonia

Denmark

Sweden

Russia

Latvia

Netherlands

Russia

Lithuania

Belgium

Luxembourg

Germany

Poland

Belarus

France

Switzerland

Czech Republic

Slovakia

Ukraine

Austria

Hungary

Serbia

Moldova

Slovenia

Croatia

Romania

Italy

Montenegro

Bulgaria

*Black Sea*

Bosnia Herzegovina

Macedonia

Albania

Greece

Turkey

Antarctica

## 3 Pronunciation Table

▶ A|01  These are the pronunciation symbols used in this text. Listen to the pronunciation of the key words.

| | VOWELS | | | | CONSONANTS | | |
|---|---|---|---|---|---|---|---|
| SYMBOL | KEY WORD | SYMBOL | KEY WORD | SYMBOL | KEY WORD | SYMBOL | KEY WORD |
| i | beat, see | ə | banana, among | p | pack, happy | z | zip, please, goes |
| ɪ | bit, did | ɚ | shirt, murder | b | back, rubber | ʃ | ship, machine, station, |
| eɪ | date, paid | aɪ | bite, cry, buy, eye | t | tie | | special, discussion |
| ɛ | bet, bed | aʊ | about, how | d | die | ʒ | measure, usually |
| æ | bat, bad | ɔɪ | voice, boy | k | came, key, quick | h | hot, who |
| ɑ | box, odd, father | ɪr | ear, deer | g | game, guest | m | men |
| ɔ | bought, dog, saw | ɛr | care, wear | tʃ | church, nature, watch | n | sun, know |
| oʊ | boat, road | ɑr | car, farm | ʤ | judge, general, major | ŋ | bring, singing |
| ʊ | book, good | ɔr | door, or | f | fan, photograph | w | wet, white |
| u | boot, food, student | ʊr | tour, poor | v | van, save | l | light, long |
| ʌ | but, mud, mother | | | θ | thing, breath | r | right, wrong |
| | | | | ð | then, breathe | y | yes, use, music |
| | | | | s | sip, city, psychology | ṭ | butter, bottle |

## 4 Numbers

### CARDINAL NUMBERS

| | | |
|---|---|---|
| 1 = one | 11 = eleven | 21 = twenty-one |
| 2 = two | 12 = twelve | 30 = thirty |
| 3 = three | 13 = thirteen | 40 = forty |
| 4 = four | 14 = fourteen | 50 = fifty |
| 5 = five | 15 = fifteen | 60 = sixty |
| 6 = six | 16 = sixteen | 70 = seventy |
| 7 = seven | 17 = seventeen | 80 = eighty |
| 8 = eight | 18 = eighteen | 90 = ninety |
| 9 = nine | 19 = nineteen | 100 = one hundred |
| 10 = ten | 20 = twenty | 101 = one hundred and one |
| | | 200 = two hundred |
| | | 1,000 = one thousand |
| | | 1,000,000 = one million |

### ORDINAL NUMBERS

| | | |
|---|---|---|
| 1st = first | 11th = eleventh | 21st = twenty-first |
| 2nd = second | 12th = twelfth | 30th = thirtieth |
| 3rd = third | 13th = thirteenth | 40th = fortieth |
| 4th = fourth | 14th = fourteenth | 50th = fiftieth |
| 5th = fifth | 15th = fifteenth | 60th = sixtieth |
| 6th = sixth | 16th = sixteenth | 70th = seventieth |
| 7th = seventh | 17th = seventeenth | 80th = eightieth |
| 8th = eighth | 18th = eighteenth | 90th = ninetieth |
| 9th = ninth | 19th = nineteenth | 100th = one hundredth |
| 10th = tenth | 20th = twentieth | 101st = one hundred and first |
| | | 200th = two hundredth |
| | | 1,000th = one thousandth |
| | | 1,000,000th = one millionth |

## 5 Days, Months, and Seasons

**DAYS OF THE WEEK**

| Weekdays | Weekend |
|---|---|
| Monday | Saturday |
| Tuesday | Sunday |
| Wednesday | |
| Thursday | |
| Friday | |

**MONTHS OF THE YEAR**

| Month | Abbreviation | Month | Abbreviation |
|---|---|---|---|
| January | Jan. | July | Jul. |
| February | Feb. | August | Aug. |
| March | Mar. | September | Sept. |
| April | Apr. | October | Oct. |
| May | May | November | Nov. |
| June | Jun. | December | Dec. |

**SEASONS**

Spring
Summer
Autumn or Fall
Winter

## 6 Titles

**Mr. (Mister)** /mɪstər/    unmarried or married man
**Ms.** /mɪz/    unmarried or married woman
**Miss** /mɪs/    unmarried woman
**Mrs.** /mɪsɪz/    married woman
**Dr. (Doctor)** /dɑktər/    doctor (medical doctor or Ph.D.)

## 7 Time

It's one o'clock.
(It's 1:00.)

It's five after one.
(It's 1:05.)

It's one-ten.
It's ten after one.
(It's 1:10.)

It's one-fifteen.
It's a quarter after one.
(It's 1:15.)

It's one twenty-five.
It's twenty-five after one.
(It's 1:25.)

It's one-thirty.
It's half past one.
(It's 1:30.)

It's one forty-five.
It's a quarter to two.
(It's 1:45.)

It's one-fifty.
It's ten to two.
(It's 1:50.)

**1** You can ask for and give the time in this way:

A: **What time is it?**
B: It's one **o'clock**.

**2** We often write time with numbers.

It's one o'clock. = It's **1:00**.
It's two-twenty. = It's **2:20**.

**3** We use the abbreviation **a.m.** for times from midnight to noon.
It's 10:00 **a.m.**

We use the abbreviation **p.m.** for times from noon to midnight.
It's 10:00 **p.m.**

**4** When people say 12:00 a.m., they mean midnight. When people say 12:00 p.m., they mean noon.

## 8 Regular Plural Nouns: Spelling Rules

**1** Add *-s* to most nouns.

| | |
|---|---|
| book | book**s** |
| table | table**s** |
| cup | cup**s** |

**2** Add *-es* to nouns that end in *-ch*, *-s*, *-sh*, or *-x*.

| | |
|---|---|
| watch | watch**es** |
| bus | bus**es** |
| dish | dish**es** |
| box | box**es** |

**3** Add *-s* to nouns that end in **vowel + y**.

| | |
|---|---|
| day | day**s** |
| key | key**s** |

**4** Change the **y** to **i** and add *-es* to nouns that end in **consonant + y**.

| | |
|---|---|
| baby | bab**ies** |
| city | cit**ies** |
| strawberry | strawberr**ies** |

**5** Add *-s* to nouns that end in **vowel + o**.

| | |
|---|---|
| radio | radio**s** |
| video | video**s** |
| zoo | zoo**s** |

**6** Add *-es* to nouns that end in **consonant + o**.

| | |
|---|---|
| potato | potato**es** |
| tomato | tomato**es** |

EXCEPTIONS:

| | |
|---|---|
| kilo | kilo**s** |
| photo | photo**s** |
| piano | piano**s** |

## 9 Irregular Plural Nouns

| SINGULAR | PLURAL |
|---|---|
| half | halves |
| knife | knives |
| leaf | leaves |
| life | lives |
| shelf | shelves |
| wife | wives |

| SINGULAR | PLURAL |
|---|---|
| child | children |
| foot | feet |
| man | men |
| mouse | mice |
| person | people |
| tooth | teeth |
| woman | women |

| SINGULAR | PLURAL |
|---|---|
| clothes | clothes |
| deer | deer |
| fish | fish |
| pants | pants |
| scissors | scissors |
| sheep | sheep |

## 10 Plural Nouns: Pronunciation Rules

**1** The **final sounds** for regular plural nouns are /s/, /z/, and /ɪz/.

| | | |
|---|---|---|
| boots | boys | horses |

**2** The plural is pronounced /s/ after the **voiceless sounds** /p/, /t/, /k/, /f/, and /θ/.

| | |
|---|---|
| cups | cuffs |
| hats | myths |
| works | |

**3** The plural is pronounced /z/ after the **voiced sounds** /b/, /d/, /g/, /v/, /m/, /n/, /ŋ/, /l/, /r/, and /ð/.

| | | |
|---|---|---|
| crabs | doves | rings |
| cards | drums | girls |
| rugs | fans | stores |

**4** The plural **s** is pronounced /z/ **after** all **vowel sounds**.

| | |
|---|---|
| day | days |
| toe | toes |

**5** The plural **s** is pronounced /ɪz/ **after the sounds** /s/, /z/, /ʃ/, /tʃ/, and /dʒ/. (This adds another syllable to the word.)

| | |
|---|---|
| races | churches |
| causes | judges |
| dishes | |

Non-count nouns are singular.

| CITY PROBLEMS | FOOD AND DRINKS | | GASES | MATERIALS | SCHOOL SUBJECTS | SPORTS | THINGS TOO SMALL TO COUNT | WEATHER |
|---|---|---|---|---|---|---|---|---|
| crime | bread | juice | oxygen | clay | Arabic | baseball | cereal | fog |
| pollution | broccoli | lettuce | smoke | cotton | art | biking | dust | ice |
| traffic | butter | meat | | glass | English | football | pepper | rain |
| | cake | milk | IDEAS AND FEELINGS | gold | geography | golf | rice | snow |
| | cheese | pasta | | leather | history | hiking | salt | sunshine |
| | chicken | pizza | friendship | paper | mathematics | running | sand | wind |
| | chocolate | salad | happiness | silk | music | soccer | sugar | |
| | coffee | soda | love | silver | photography | swimming | | |
| | corn | soup | | wood | psychology | tennis | | |
| | fish | spinach | | wool | science | | | |
| | flour | tea | | | Spanish | | | |
| | fruit | water | | | | | | |
| | ice cream | yogurt | | | | | | |

### NAMES OF CATEGORIES

| clothing | (BUT: coats, hats, shoes ...) |
|---|---|
| equipment | (BUT: computers, phones ...) |
| food | (BUT: bananas, eggs ...) |
| furniture | (BUT: beds, chairs, lamps ...) |
| homework | (BUT: assignments, problems ...) |
| jewelry | (BUT: earrings, necklaces ...) |
| mail | (BUT: letters, packages ...) |
| money | (BUT: dollars, euros, pounds ...) |
| time | (BUT: minutes, months ...) |
| work | (BUT: jobs, projects ...) |

### OTHER

Some non-count nouns don't fit into any list.
You must memorize these non-count nouns.

advice
air
garbage/trash
help
information
news

## 12 Quantifying Non-Count Nouns

a bottle of (milk, soda, ketchup)
a bowl of (cereal, soup, rice)
a can of (soda, beans, tuna fish)
a cup of (hot chocolate, coffee, tea)
a foot of (snow, water)
a gallon of (juice, gas, paint)

a head of (lettuce)
a loaf of (bread)
an inch of (snow, rain)
a pair of (pants, gloves)
a piece of (paper, cake, pie)
a pint of (ice cream, cream)

a quart of (milk)
a roll of (toilet paper, paper towels)
a slice of (toast, cheese, meat)
a tablespoon of (flour, sugar, baking soda)
a teaspoon of (sugar, salt, pepper)
a tube of (toothpaste, glue)

## 13 The Simple Present: Spelling Rules

**1** Add *-s* for most verbs.

| | |
|---|---|
| work | works |
| buy | buys |
| ride | rides |
| return | returns |

**2** Add *-es* for verbs that end in *-ch*, *-s*, *-sh*, *-x*, or *-z*.

| | |
|---|---|
| watch | watches |
| pass | passes |
| rush | rushes |
| relax | relaxes |
| buzz | buzzes |

**3** Change the *y* to *i* and add *-es* when the base form ends in **consonant + y**.

| | |
|---|---|
| study | studies |
| hurry | hurries |
| dry | dries |

**4** Do not change the *y* when the base form ends in **vowel + y**. Add *-s*.

| | |
|---|---|
| play | plays |
| enjoy | enjoys |

**5** A few verbs have **irregular forms**.

| | |
|---|---|
| be | is |
| do | does |
| go | goes |
| have | has |

## 14 The Simple Present: Pronunciation Rules

**1** The third-person singular in the simple present always ends in the letter *-s*. There are three different pronunciations for the final sound of the third-person singular.

| /s/ | /z/ | /ɪz/ |
|---|---|---|
| talks | loves | dances |

**2** The final sound is pronounced /s/ after the voiceless sounds /p/, /t/, /k/, and /f/.

| | |
|---|---|
| top | tops |
| get | gets |
| take | takes |
| laugh | laughs |

**3** The final sound is pronounced /z/ after the voiced sounds /b/, /d/, /g/, /v/, /m/, /n/, /ŋ/, /l/, /r/, and /ð/.

| | |
|---|---|
| describe | describes |
| spend | spends |
| hug | hugs |
| live | lives |
| seem | seems |
| remain | remains |
| sing | sings |
| tell | tells |
| lower | lowers |
| bathe | bathes |

**4** The final sound is pronounced /z/ after all **vowel sounds**.

| | |
|---|---|
| agree | agrees |
| try | tries |
| stay | stays |
| know | knows |

**5** The final sound is pronounced /ɪz/ after the sounds /s/, /z/, /ʃ/, /ʒ/, /tʃ/, and /dʒ/. /ɪz/ adds a syllable to the verb.

| | |
|---|---|
| miss | misses |
| freeze | freezes |
| rush | rushes |
| massage | massages |
| watch | watches |
| judge | judges |

**6** *Do* and *say* have a change in vowel sound.

| | |
|---|---|
| do /du/ | does /dʌz/ |
| say /seɪ/ | says /sɛz/ |

## 15 Non-Action Verbs

| STATE OF BEING | EMOTIONS | MEASUREMENT | MENTAL STATES | POSSESSION AND RELATIONSHIP | SENSES | WANTS AND PREFERENCES |
|---|---|---|---|---|---|---|
| be | dislike | cost | agree | belong | feel | need |
| | hate | weigh | believe | have | hear | prefer |
| | like | owe | disagree | owe | look | want |
| | love | | guess | own | see | |
| | miss | | know | | smell | |
| | | | remember | | sound | |
| | | | seem | | taste | |
| | | | think | | | |
| | | | understand | | | |

## 16 The Present Progressive: Spelling Rules

**1** Add *-ing* to the base form of the verb.

read      read**ing**
stand     stand**ing**

**2** If the verb ends in a **silent -e**, drop the final *-e* and add *-ing*.

leave     leav**ing**
take      tak**ing**

**3** In **one-syllable** verbs, if the last three letters are consonant-vowel-consonant (CVC), double the last consonant and add *-ing*.

C V C
↓ ↓ ↓
s i t      sit**ting**

C V C
↓ ↓ ↓
p l a n     plan**ning**

EXCEPTION: Do not double the last consonant in verbs that end in *-w*, *-x*, or *-y*.

sew      sew**ing**
fix       fix**ing**
play      play**ing**

**4** In verbs of **two or more syllables** that end in consonant-vowel-consonant, double the last consonant only if the last syllable is stressed.

admít     admit**ting**    *(The last syllable is stressed.)*

whísper   whisper**ing**   *(The last syllable is not stressed, so don't double the -**r**.)*

**5** If the verb ends in *-ie*, change the *ie* to *y* before adding *-ing*.

die      d**ying**
lie       l**ying**

---

**Stress**
´ shows main stress.

## 17 The Simple Past: Spelling Rules

**1** If the verb ends in a **consonant**, add *-ed*.

return     return**ed**
help       help**ed**

**2** If the verb ends in *-e*, add *-d*.

live        live**d**
create    create**d**
die         die**d**

**3** In **one-syllable** verbs, if the last three letters are consonant-vowel-consonant (CVC), double the last consonant and add *-ed*.

C V C
↓ ↓ ↓
h o p      hop**ped**

C V C
↓ ↓ ↓
g r a b     grab**bed**

EXCEPTION: Do not double the last consonant in **one-syllable** verbs that end in *-w*, *-x*, or *-y*.

bow      bow**ed**
mix       mix**ed**
play      play**ed**

**4** In verbs of **two or more syllables** that end in consonant-vowel-consonant, double the last consonant only if the last syllable is stressed.

prefer     prefer**red**    *(The last syllable is stressed.)*

visit       visit**ed**      *(The last syllable is not stressed, so don't double the -t.)*

**5** If the verb ends in **consonant + y**, change the **y** to **i** and add *-ed*.

worry     worr**ied**
carry     carr**ied**

**6** If the verb ends in **vowel + y**, add *-ed*. (Do not change the **y** to **i**.)

play     play**ed**
annoy   annoy**ed**

EXCEPTIONS:
lay     la**id**
pay     pa**id**
say     sa**id**

## 18 The Simple Past: Pronunciation Rules

**1** The regular simple past always ends in the letter *-d*. There are three different pronunciations for the final sound of the regular simple past.

/t/      /d/      /ɪd/
rac**ed**   liv**ed**   attend**ed**

**2** The final sound is pronounced /t/ after the voiceless sounds /p/, /k/, /f/, /s/, /ʃ/, and /tʃ/.

hop        hop**ped**
work      work**ed**
laugh     laugh**ed**
address   address**ed**
publish   publish**ed**
watch     watch**ed**

**3** The final sound is pronounced /d/ after the voiced sounds /b/, /g/, /v/, /z/, /ʒ/, /dʒ/, /m/, /n/, /ŋ/, /l/, /r/, and /ð/.

rub        rub**bed**      rhyme    rhy**med**
hug       hug**ged**      return    return**ed**
live        liv**ed**       bang     bang**ed**
surprise   surpris**ed**   enroll    enroll**ed**
massage   massag**ed**   appear   appear**ed**
change    chang**ed**     bathe    bath**ed**

**4** The final sound is pronounced /d/ after all **vowel sounds**.

agree    agr**eed**
die       di**ed**
play     pl**ayed**
enjoy    enj**oyed**
snow    sn**owed**

**5** The final sound is pronounced /ɪd/ after /t/ and /d/. /ɪd/ adds a syllable to the verb.

start     star**ted**
decide   deci**ded**

## 19 Irregular Past Tense Verbs

| BASE FORM | PAST FORM | BASE FORM | PAST FORM | BASE FORM | PAST FORM | BASE FORM | PAST FORM |
|-----------|-----------|-----------|-----------|-----------|-----------|-----------|-----------|
| be | was, were | eat | ate | hear | heard | see | saw |
| become | became | feel | felt | know | knew | send | sent |
| begin | began | find | found | leave | left | sit | sat |
| break | broke | fly | flew | make | made | sleep | slept |
| buy | bought | forget | forgot | meet | met | speak | spoke |
| come | came | get | got | pay | paid | take | took |
| cost | cost | give | gave | put | put | teach | taught |
| do | did | go | went | read* | read* | tell | told |
| drink | drank | grow | grew | run | ran | win | won |
| drive | drove | have | had | say | said | write | wrote |

*Pronounce the base form /rid/. Pronounce the past form /rɛd/.

## 20 Capitalization and Punctuation Rules

| | USE FOR . . . | EXAMPLES |
|---|---|---|
| capital letter | • the pronoun *I*<br>• proper nouns<br>• the first word of a sentence | My friend and **I** are on vacation.<br>**Ali** is from Turkey.<br>**They** live in Spain. |
| apostrophe (') | • possessive nouns<br>• contractions | Is that **Marta's** coat?<br>**That's** not hers. **It's** mine. |
| comma (,) | • after items in a list<br>• to connect two sentences with *and* or *but*<br>• after the name of a person you are writing to | He bought apples**,** pears**,** oranges**,** and bananas.<br>They watched TV**,** and she played video games.<br>Dear John**,** |
| exclamation point (!) | • at the end of a sentence to show surprise or a strong feeling | You're here**!** That's great**!**<br>Stop**!** A car is coming**!** |
| period (.) | • at the end of a statement<br>• after abbreviations | Today is Wednesday**.**<br>The party is on Nov**.** 3. |
| question mark (?) | • at the end of a question | What day is today**?** |

# Glossary of Grammar Terms

**action verb** A verb that describes an action. It can be used in the progressive.

Sachiko **is planning** a big party.

**adjective** A word that describes (or modifies) a noun or pronoun.

That's a **great** idea.

**adverb** A word that describes (or modifies) an action verb, another adverb, an adjective, or a sentence.

She drives **slowly**.

**adverb of frequency** A word that tells the frequency of something.

We **usually** eat lunch at noon.

**affirmative statement** A sentence that does not use a negative verb form (*not*).

**I have a car.**

**apostrophe** A punctuation mark used to show possession and to write a short form (contraction).

He**'**s in my father**'**s car.

**base form** The form of the verb without any ending such as *-ing*, *-ed*, or *-s*. It is the same as the infinitive without *to*.

Arnold will **come** at 8:00. We should **eat** then.

**be going to future** A verb form used to make predictions, express general facts in the future, or talk about definite plans that were made before now.

Mei-Ling says it**'s going to be** cold, so she**'s going to take** a coat.

**capital letter** The big form of a letter of the alphabet. Sentences start with a capital letter.

**A, B, C**, etc.

**comma** Punctuation used to separate single things in a list or parts of a sentence.

We went to a restaurant**,** and we ate chicken**,** potatoes**,** and broccoli.

**common noun** A noun for a person, an animal, a place, or a thing. It is not capitalized.

The **man** got a **book** at the **library**.

**comparative form** An adjective ending in *-er* or following *more*. It is used in comparing two things.

My sister is **older** and **more intelligent** than my brother.
But he studies **harder** and **more carefully**.

**consonant** The letters *b, c, d, f, g, h, j, k, l, m, n, p, q, r, s, t, v, w, x, y, z*.

**contraction** A short form of two words. An apostrophe (') replaces the missing letter.

**It is** late, and **I am** tired. I **cannot** stay up so late.
**It's** late, and **I'm** tired. I **can't** stay up so late.

**count noun** A noun you can count. It usually has a singular and a plural form.

In the **park**, there was a **man** with two **children** and a **dog**.

**definite article** *The*; makes a noun specific.

We saw a movie. **The** movie starred Sean Penn.

**exclamation point** A punctuation mark (!) used at the end of a statement. It shows strong emotion.

Help! Call the police**!**

**formal language** Language we usually use in business settings, academic settings, and with people we don't know.

**Good morning, ladies** and **gentlemen. May** we begin?

**imperative** A sentence used to give an instruction, a direction, a command, or a suggestion. It uses the base form of the verb. The subject (*you*) is not a part of the sentence.

**Turn** right at the corner. **Drive** to the end of the street. **Stop!**

**indefinite article** *A* and *an*; used before singular, nonspecific non-count nouns.

Jaime brought **a** sandwich and **an** apple for lunch.

**infinitive** *To* + the base form of a verb.

> I want **to see** the world.

**informal language** The language we usually use with family and friends, in email messages, and in other informal settings.

> **Hey, Doug, what's up?**

**irregular verb** A verb that does not form the simple past by adding *-d* or *-ed*.

> They **ate** a fancy meal last night. The boss **came** to dinner.

**modal** A verb that comes before the main verb. Modals can express ability, possibility, obligation, and necessity.

> He **can** play the guitar, but he **can't** play the piano.

**negative statement** A statement with a negative verb form.

> He **didn't study**. He **wasn't** ready for the test.

**non-action verb** A verb that does not describe an action. It can describe an emotion, a state, a sense, or a mental thought. We usually don't use non-action verbs in the progressive.

> I **like** that actor. He **is** very famous, and I **believe** he won an Oscar.

**non-count noun** A noun we usually do not count. We don't put *a*, *an*, or a number before a non-count noun.

> All you'll need is **rice, water, salt,** and **butter.**

**noun** A word that refers to a person, animal, place, thing, or idea.

> **Paula** has a **friend** at the **library**. She gave me a **book** about **birds**.

**noun modifier** A noun that describes another noun.

> Samantha is a **chemistry** professor. She loves **spy** movies.

**object** A noun or pronoun following an action verb. It receives the action of the verb.

> I sent **a letter**. He read **it**.

**object pronoun** A pronoun following a verb or a preposition.

> We asked **him** to show the photos to **them**.

**ordinal number** The form of a number that shows the order or sequence of something.

> The team scored 21 points in the **first** quarter and 33 in the **fourth**.

**period** A punctuation mark (.) used at the end of a statement.

> I'd like you to call on Saturday**.** We need to talk**.**

**plural** The form that means more than one.

> **We** sat in **our chairs** reading **our books**.

**possessive** An adjective, noun, or pronoun that shows possession.

> **Her** book is in **John's** car. **Mine** is at the office.

**preposition** A small word that goes before a noun or pronoun object. A preposition often shows time or place.

> Maria saw it **on** the table **at** two o'clock.

**present progressive** A verb form that shows an action happening now or planned for the future.

> I**'m working** hard now, but I**'m taking** a vacation soon.

**pronoun** A word that replaces a noun or a noun phrase. There are subject pronouns, object pronouns, possessive pronouns, and demonstrative pronouns.

> **He** is a friend—I know **him** well. **This** is his coat; **mine** is black.

**proper noun** The actual name of a person, place, or thing. A proper noun begins with a capital letter.

> **Tom** is living in **New York**. He is studying **Russian** at **Columbia University**.

**quantifier** A word or phrase that comes before a noun and expresses an amount of that noun.

> Jeannette used **a little** sugar, **some** flour, **four** eggs, and **a liter of** milk.

**question mark** A punctuation mark (?) used at the end of a question.

> Where are you going**?** When will you be back**?**

**regular verb** A verb that forms the simple past by adding *-d* or *-ed*.

> We **lived** in France. My mother **visited** us there.

**sentence** A group of words with a subject and a verb that expresses a complete thought.

> **We opened the window.**
> **Did they paint the house?**

**simple past** A verb form used to show a completed action or idea in the past.

> The plane **landed** at 9:00. We **caught** a bus to the hotel.

**simple present** A verb form used to show habitual actions or states, general facts, or conditions that are true now.

> Kemal **loves** to ski, and it **snows** a lot in his area, so he**'s** very happy.

**singular** The form that means only one.

> I put on my **hat** and **coat** and closed the **door**.

**small letter** The small form of a letter of the alphabet. We use small letters for most words except for proper nouns and the word that starts a sentence.

> **a**, **b**, **c**, etc.

**subject** The person, place, or thing that a sentence is about.

> **The children** ate at the mall.

**subject pronoun** A pronoun used to replace a subject noun.

> Irene works hard. **She** loves her work.

**syllable** A group of letters with one vowel sound. Words are made up of one or more syllables.

> One syllable—**win**
> Two syllables—**ta ble**
> Three syllables—**im por tant**

**third person singular** The verb form used with *he*, *she*, and *it*.

> Jessica **is** a reporter. She **works** for a TV station.

**verb** A word used to describe an action, a fact, or a state.

> He **drives** to work now. He **has** a new car, and he **is** a careful driver.

**vowel** The letters *a*, *e*, *i*, *o*, or *u*, and sometimes *y*.

**wh- question** A question that asks for information. It begins with *what*, *when*, *where*, *why*, *which*, *who*, *whose*, or *how*.

> **What**'s your name?
> **Where** are you from?
> **How** do you feel?

**yes/no question** A question that has a *yes* or a *no* answer.

> **Did you arrive on time?** Yes, I did.
> **Are you from Uruguay?** No, I'm not.
> **Can you swim well?** Yes, I can.

# Unit Review Answer Key

## UNIT 1

**A** 1. This is
2. These are
3. This is
4. This is
5. These are

**B** 1. She  3. It  5. We
2. He  4. They

**C** 1. ~~This~~ *These* are my parents.
2. ~~This~~ *Is this* your cat?
3. This is Pete. ~~Is~~ *He's* my brother.
4. ~~Is~~ *Are* these your photos?
5. ~~Im~~ *I'm* happy in this class.

## UNIT 2

**A** 1. spoons
2. classes
3. men
4. teachers
5. oranges

**B** 1. a pineapple
2. bananas
3. apples
4. an eraser
5. a notebook

**C** 1. This is ^*an* apple.
2. These are ~~fork~~ *forks*.
3. It's ~~a~~ *an* oven.
4. Three ~~person~~ *people* are in school.
5. These are ~~knife~~ *knives*.

## UNIT 3

**A** 1. It is
2. He is
3. She is
4. They are
5. We are

**B** 1. It's boring.
2. They're not **or** They aren't from Brazil.
3. I'm not a chef.
4. He's not **or** He isn't in Australia.
5. We're in class.

**C** A: Ali from Canada. ~~He~~ *is* a student. *He's* **or** *He is*
B: No. Ali ~~no is~~ *isn't* **or** *is not* a student. He's a chef.
A: Oh. ~~I~~ *I'm* **or** *I am* a student. I'm a teacher, too. I ~~be~~ *am* an

English language student. I'm a Portuguese

language teacher.

## UNIT 4

**A** 1. That
2. those
3. that
4. That
5. Those

**B** 1. He
2. Her
3. your
4. They're
5. It's

**C** A: Is ~~those~~ *that* your family in the photo?
B: Yes. That's ~~me~~ *my* brother, and that's my sister.
A: What are ~~they're~~ *their* names?
B: ~~He's~~ *His* name is Robert, and her name is Tammy.
A: ~~That~~ *Is that* your dog?
B: Yes. Its name is Spot.

## UNIT 5

**A** 1. d  3. e  5. b
2. c  4. a

**B** 1. Who
2. What
3. who
4. What
5. who

**C** 1. A: ~~What~~ *What is* **or** *What's* his job? Is he a dentist?

B: No, he's not. He's a doctor.

2. A: Is your sister single?
B: No, ~~she~~ *she's* not.

3. A: Is your mother a nurse?
B: No, she isn't. ~~She~~ *She's* a cashier.

4. A: ~~Is~~ *Are* you from Kenya?
B: Yes, ~~I'm~~ *I am*.

## UNIT 6

**A** 1. in
2. in
3. at
4. between
5. on the

**B** 1. at
2. in
3. on
4. across
5. next to

**C** 1. A: Is your apartment ~~in~~ *on* the second floor?
B: No, it's on the ~~three~~ *third* floor.

**2.** A: Where's the bank?

     B: It's First Avenue. It's between ~~from~~ 8th and
             *on*

       9th Street.

     A: Is it next the post office?
             *to*

     B: Yes, it is.

## UNIT 7

**A** **1.** Were      **4.** Was
   **2.** weren't      **5.** wasn't
   **3.** were      **6.** was

**B** **1. a.** he wasn't
      **b.** He was at the library.
   **2. a.** they weren't
      **b.** They were asleep.

**C** Sorry I ~~weren't~~ at the basketball game on Tuesday
           *wasn't*

afternoon. I ~~were~~ sick at home. It ~~be~~ really boring.
         *was*             *was*

~~Are~~ you at the gym yesterday? ~~Was~~ Amanda and
*Were*                    *Were*

Josh there?

## UNIT 8

**A** **1.** Where      **4.** How long
   **2.** How      **5.** When
   **3.** Who

**B** **1.** Where were you last night?
   **2.** I was at the movies.
   **3.** How was the movie?
   **4.** It was funny.
   **5.** Who was with you?
   **6.** Drew was with me.

**C** A: Hi. ~~What~~ was your vacation?
        *How*

   B: It was great.

   A: Where ~~was~~ you?
        *were*

   B: In the mountains.

   A: In the mountains? How the weather ~~was~~?
                  *was*

   B: It was rainy.

   A: How were you there?
       *long*

   B: A week.

## UNIT 9

**A** **1.** don't open      **4.** Don't worry
   **2.** Walk      **5.** Turn
   **3.** Don't eat

**B** New sentence:
Please don't start Unit 10.
**or** Don't start Unit 10, please.

**C** **1.** Please ~~to~~ stop at the corner.
   **2.** ~~You not~~ turn left.
      *Don't*
   **3.** ~~Turns~~ right, please.
      *Turn*
   **4.** ~~Don't please~~ park here.
      *Please don't*
   **5.** Don't ~~takes~~ the bus.
         *take*

## UNIT 10

**A** **1.** likes / doesn't like
   **2.** don't want / doesn't want / doesn't want

**B** **1.** live      **3.** has / have
   **2.** likes / like

**C** **1.** This is my brother Nelson. He ~~don't~~ look like me!
                         *doesn't*
   **2.** Nelson and his wife, Laura, ~~lives~~ in Brazil.
                     *live*
   **3.** Laura ~~is need~~ a new car.
          *needs*
   **4.** Nelson ~~work~~ as a mechanic.
         *works*
   **5.** They both ~~speaks~~ Portuguese.
         *speak*

## UNIT 11

**A** **1.** Do you go shopping
   **2.** Does your sister stay home
   **3.** Do your friends like
   **4.** Do you see
   **5.** Does Carlos speak

**B** **1.** A: Do…like     B: I don't
   **2.** A: Does…live     B: he doesn't **or** she doesn't
   **3.** A: Do…speak     B: we do
   **4.** A: Do…have     B: we don't
   **5.** A: Does…work     B: she doesn't

**C** A: Do you ~~works~~ out every day?
         *work*
   B: Yes, I ~~am~~.
      *do*

   A: Do you walk to the gym?
   B: No, I ~~not~~. I drive there.
      *don't*

   A: Does Amina ~~works~~ out with you?
             *work*
   B: No, she ~~don't~~.
        *doesn't*

## UNIT 12

**A** **1.** What time      **3.** Where
   **2.** Why      **4.** when

**B**  1. Where do your cousins live?
2. When do the fireworks start?
3. What does he do?
4. How does he like his job?
5. Why do you like Thanksgiving?
6. What time do you get up on New Year's Day?

**C**  A: How ~~Max celebrates~~ *does Max celebrate* his birthday?

B: He eats a huge meal.

A: What kind of food does he ~~eats~~ *eat*? And where *does* he ^

eat it?

B: He eats Italian food at his favorite restaurant,

Mangia.

A: How *do* ^ you spell "mangia"? And what ~~means it~~ *does it mean*?

B: M-A-N-G-I-A. It means "eat"!

## UNIT 13

**A**  1. c    2. d    3. a    4. b

**B**  1. A: How often do you skip lunch?
  B: I sometimes skip lunch.
2. A: What do you usually do on the weekends?
  B: I often go to the movies.
3. A: Do you ever eat fast food for breakfast?
  B: No, I never do.

**C**  A: ~~Never I~~ *I never* get up early. Do you get up early?
  *I usually get up early four days a week.* **or**
  *Usually I get up early four days a week.* **or**
  *I get up early four days a week, usually.*
  B: Yes. ~~I get up early usually four days a week.~~
A: Do you ~~see ever~~ *ever see* your friends after class?

B: Sometimes—but I usually see them on the
  *always*
  weekends. We ^ play board games ~~always~~. Do you

play board games?
  *sometimes* **or** *always* **or** *often* **or** *usually*
A: Yes, I ~~rarely~~ play them. They're a lot of fun.

## UNIT 14

**A**  1. short hair    4. thin
2. an    5. heavy
3. is

**B**  1. My roommate has a long face.
2. They are average height.
3. He is an unusual person.
4. It is a short book.
5. He has a nice smile.

**C**  A: What does your sister look like?
  *brown hair*    *green*
  B: She is thin, and she has ~~hair brown~~ and ~~a green~~

eyes.

A: Is she tall or short?
  *short*
  B: She is ~~a short~~.
  *short*
A: What about your parents? Are they ~~shorts~~?
  *tall*
  B: No, they're both ~~talls~~.

## UNIT 15

**A**  1. more fun    4. better
2. more exciting    5. worse
3. harder    6. tastier

**B**  1. Which is more entertaining, New York or
  Los Angeles?
2. Are amusement parks more interesting
  than museums?
3. Who is older, you or your sister?

**C**  I have two interesting pen pals—Jomo and

Abla. They are brother and sister, and they live in
  *older*
Tanzania. Jomo is ~~more older~~ than Abla, and he is
  *larger*    *taller*    *heavier*
also ~~more large~~. He's ~~more tall~~ and he's ~~heavyer~~. Abla
  *better*    *worse*
is a ~~gooder~~ student, but she's ~~more bad~~ than Jomo at

sports. They go to the same school. It's more crowded

than my school.

## UNIT 16

**A**  1. listening    4. 're watching
2. are playing    5. not looking
3. isn't raining

**B**  1. is playing    4. is sleeping
2. are visiting    5. is sitting, reading
3. are walking

  *He's not* **or** *He isn't*
**C**  1. ~~He not~~ standing. He's sitting.
  *waiting*
2. Bob and Maya are ~~wait~~ for us.
  *listening*
3. They're ~~listen~~ to a CD.
  *We're not* **or** *We aren't*
4. ~~We not~~ playing cards.

## UNIT 17

**A**  1. c    3. d    5. b
2. e    4. a

**B 1.** A: Is Ron getting a haircut?

    B: he is

  **2.** A: Are Dan and Janet celebrating their anniversary?

    B: they aren't

  **3.** A: Is it raining?

    B: it is

**C 1.** A: Is Annie ~~clean~~ *cleaning* her room?

    B: No, ~~she not~~ *she's not or she isn't or she is not*. She's writing a story.

  **2.** A: ~~Is~~ *Are* Ben and Jeremy doing homework?

    B: No, they ~~isn't~~ *aren't*. But it's OK. Tomorrow is a

    school holiday.

## UNIT 18

**A 1.** d    **3.** e    **5.** a

  **2.** b    **4.** c

**B 1.** What is Steve watching on TV?

  **2.** Why are you calling me now?

  **3.** What are you studying in the class?

  **4.** Who is taking you to work?

  **5.** Why are you taking the train?

**C 1.** A: Who *'s or is* teaching the class?

    B: ~~Mark's.~~ *Mark or Mark is*

  **2.** A: Why ~~you are~~ *are you* smiling?

    B: I'm ~~watch~~ *watching* a funny movie.

  **3.** A: What's your sister ~~wear~~ *wearing*?

    B: A blue shirt and jeans.

## UNIT 19

**A 1.** can't    **3.** Can

  **2.** can't    **4.** can

**B 1.** A: Can…understand    **2.** A: can't watch

    B: can't read      A: can't play

    A: can help      B: can do

**C** A: Pietro can't ~~dances~~ *dance*, but he can ~~to~~ play the piano.

  B: Can he ~~to~~ sing?

  A: Yes, he can. He can also teach music.

  B: Then he can ~~helping~~ *help* me. I want a music teacher for

  my son. Can he teach on weekends?

  A: No. He ~~no can~~ *can't* teach on weekends. He never works

  on weekends.

## UNIT 20

**A 1.** A: this    B: that's

  **2.** A: those    B: These

  **3.** A: That's

**B 1.** Mark's      **3.** Annie's

  **2.** children's    **4.** brother's

**C 1.** A: Is ~~these~~ *this* your new dress?

    B: No. It's not my dress. It's my ~~sister~~ *sister's* dress.

  **2.** A: Do you like ~~this~~ *these* glasses?

    B: Yes. I really like ~~that glasses~~ *those glasses or them*. You look smart

    in them.

  **3.** A: Why are you wearing your ~~dad~~ *dad's* jacket?

    B: ~~These~~ *This or It* isn't his jacket. It's my jacket.

## UNIT 21

**A 1.** coffee      **4.** water

  **2.** cereal      **5.** milk

  **3.** pizza

**B 1.** an    **3.** a      **5.** cup of

  **2.** any    **4.** Ø

**C** I always drink two ~~cup~~ *cups* of coffee for breakfast.

Usually I have ~~an cereal~~ *cereal or some cereal* and *a* slice of toast. Sometimes

I have fruit, like ~~a bananas~~ *a banana or bananas*. I also like ~~any~~ milk

and yogurt.

## UNIT 22

**A 1.** d    **2.** c    **3.** a    **4.** b

**B 1.** a    **3.** the    **5.** an

  **2.** ones    **4.** one    **6.** The

**C** Bozo's shoes are very strange. ~~Shoes~~ *The shoes or They* are orange

and yellow. ~~An~~ *The* orange shoe is big, and the yellow ~~ones~~ *one*

is small. He's wearing ~~the~~ *a* funny hat, too. He looks

like ~~the~~ *a* clown!

## UNIT 23

**A 1.** A: him      **2.** A: they

    B: He          B: them / we

**B** 1. her
2. him
3. them
4. her
5. them

**C** Thank you for inviting ~~we~~ [us] to the party on June 10. ~~Us~~ [We] can bring some cookies for dessert. ~~It~~ [They] are really good, and everyone likes ~~they~~ [them]. I don't have your address. Can you please email ~~them~~ [it] to us?

See you on Saturday!

## UNIT 24

**A** 1. moved
2. didn't graduate
3. didn't start
4. hired
5. expanded

**B** 1. attended
2. graduated
3. started
4. didn't work
5. didn't listen
6. failed

**C** 1. We started ~~last year~~ a business.
*Last year we started a business.* **or** *We started a business last year.*
2. He ~~no did~~ [didn't] graduate from high school.
3. Two weeks ago, I ~~move~~ [moved] to a new apartment.
4. She ~~was enjoy~~ [enjoyed] her vacation last summer.

## UNIT 25

**A** 1. got
2. made
3. ate
4. saw
5. wrote
6. went

**B** 1. Did you take
2. Did you get
3. Did Alicia take care of
4. Did Jack babysit

**C** 1. A: ~~You got~~ [Did you get] this book for your friend?
B: No, I ~~don't~~ [didn't]. She got it for me.
2. A: Did you go out last night?
B: No. Katharine ~~makes~~ [made] dinner for me at home. We ~~eated~~ [ate] a lot!
3. A: ~~Do~~ [Did] you pay for your parents' vacation last year?
B: Yes, I did. They went on a trip to Hawaii.

## UNIT 26

**A** 1. c
2. d
3. e
4. a
5. b

**B** 1. When did the accident happen?
2. How did the accident happen?
3. Why did he drive to the supermarket?
4. Who did he drive with?
5. Where did he take the car?

**C** A: What time ~~you~~ [did you] get to work this morning?
B: At 10:00 a.m. I was late because there was an accident on the bus.
A: Oh, no! What ~~happen~~ [happened]?
B: The bus hit a car. It was scary. People got hurt.
A: Oh, no. Who ~~they~~ got hurt?
B: The people in the car. An ambulance came to get them, but it took a long time.
A: How long ~~the ambulance took~~ [did the ambulance take]?
B: About twenty minutes.
A: Why ~~it did~~ [did it] take so long?
B: I don't know. But the people were OK.

## UNIT 27

**A** 1. How much
2. How many
3. How many
4. How much
5. How much

**B** 1. A lot
2. Not many
3. a little
4. A lot
5. Not much

**C** 1. A: How much time did you spend on a boat?
B: Not ~~many~~ [much] time. Only a couple of days.
2. A: How ~~much~~ [many] trips did you take last year?
B: Not many. Only two short ones.
3. A: How ~~much~~ [many] email messages do you send each day?
B: Each day? Only one or two. But I send ~~much~~ [a lot] of text messages—maybe twenty or thirty.
4. A: How much time do you spend online?
B: A lot ~~of~~. Maybe six hours a day!

## UNIT 28

**A** 1. Is there
2. there is
3. are there
4. there are
5. Are they

**B**  1. there  4. they
2. there  5. There
3. They

**C**  A: How was your trip to Hawaii?
B: Wonderful! There ~~was~~ *were* fantastic beaches, and *there* were

a lot of friendly people.

A: ~~Is~~ *Are* there interesting things to do in Hawaii?

B: Yes. You can swim in the ocean. ~~It's~~ *There are* a lot of
beautiful fish. And ~~they is~~ *there's or there is* a volcano. You need to

go to Hawaii.

## UNIT 29

**A**  1. I'm not going to play baseball
2. Argentina is going to win
3. It's not going to rain **or** It isn't going to rain
4. We're not going to have dinner **or** We aren't going
to have dinner
5. You're going to love

**B**  1. They are going to win.
2. We are going to be late.
3. The sun is not going to shine.
4. The game is going to start soon.
5. We are going to get there on time.

**C**  Jorge and I *are* going to go to a basketball game this

Saturday afternoon at 2:00 p.m. But there's one little

problem. Our friend's son ~~be~~ *is* going to graduate

from high school on Saturday, too. The graduation is

going *to* end at 2:00 p.m., so we *are or 're* going to be late for the

game. But we *are or 're* not going to miss more than half an

hour of the game.

## UNIT 30

**A**  1. b  3. e  5. c
2. d  4. a

**B**  1. is…going to be
2. is…going to start
3. are…going to get
4. are…going to go
5. are…going to talk

**C**  A: I got a new job. I'm going to be a producer.
B: ~~Is~~ *Are* you going to work full-time?
A: Yes, ~~I'm~~ *I am*.
B: When ~~you are~~ *are you* going to start?

A: Next month.

B: Are you going *to* take a vacation?

A: Yes, I'm going to go to Toronto for a week.
B: Who *are* you going to stay with?

A: My aunt.

# Key to Exercises with Guessed Answers

## UNIT 4

### AFTER YOU READ B

Space Needle

## UNIT 10

### EXERCISE 8

2. Rihanna comes from Barbados. / True.
3. A lot of people like Rihanna's music. / True.
4. People in Japan drive on the right. / False. People in Japan drive on the left.
5. People in Great Britain drive on the left. / True.
6. People live at the North Pole. / False. People don't live at the North Pole.
7. Penguins live in hot places. / False. Penguins don't live in hot places. **or** Penguins live in Antarctica. **or** Penguins live in cold places.
8. Most people have a lot of money. / False. Most people don't have a lot of money.
9. It rains a lot in the Sahara Desert. / False. It doesn't rain a lot in the Sahara Desert.
10. It snows a lot at the North Pole. / True.

## UNIT 12

### EXERCISE 8A

2. very interesting
3. freedom
4. 12:00 p.m.
5. 12:00 a.m.
6. a trip in a car
7. a family member
8. look at
9. enjoy a special day

## UNIT 25

### EXERCISE 7

2. False / The ~~English~~ *South African* police sent Nelson Mandela to prison.

3. False / Mahatma Gandhi was a famous leader in ~~China~~ *India*.

4. True

5. True

6. False / Harriet Tubman helped slaves in ~~Europe~~ *the United States*.

7. False / Martin Luther King Jr. wrote "Letter from ~~New York City~~ *Birmingham* Jail."

8. True

## UNIT 27

### EXERCISE 9

| | | |
|---|---|---|
| 1. b | 3. c | 5. a |
| 2. a | 4. a | 6. b |

## UNIT 28

### EXERCISE 8

**Suggested answers:**

2. Were there five national parks in the United States in 1871?
   No, there weren't. There weren't any national parks in the United States in 1871.
3. Is there a national park called Yellowstone National Park in Canada?
   No, there isn't. There's a national park called Yellowstone National Park in the United States.
4. Are there 10,000 national parks in the world?
   No, there aren't. There are 6,000 national parks in the world.
5. Are there many plants and animals in rain forests?
   Yes, there are.
6. Are there any farmers near the Amazon Rain Forest?
   Yes, there are. There are many farmers near the Amazon Rain Forest.
7. Are there any moose and deer in Yosemite National Park?
   Yes, there are.
8. Is there a big waterfall in Yosemite National Park?
   Yes, there is.
9. Is there a famous national park in Zimbabwe?
   Yes, there is. It's called Victoria Falls.
10. Were there a lot of tourists at Victoria Falls in the nineteenth century?
    No, there weren't. There are a lot of tourists at Victoria Falls now.
11. Was there a British king named Victor in the nineteenth century?
    No, there wasn't. There was a British queen named Victoria in the nineteenth century.
12. Is there a lot of noise at Victoria Falls?
    Yes, there is. The noise is from the waterfall and from airplanes.

# Information Gaps, Student B

UNIT 4

## EXERCISE 8  IS THAT A UNIVERSITY?

INFORMATION GAP  Work with a partner. Student A, follow the instructions on page 48.
Student B, follow the instructions below.

**STUDENT B**

- Look at the map. Student A has the same map with different information. Ask
  Student A questions about buildings 1, 3, 5, and 7. Complete the map.

  EXAMPLE:  **B:** Look at building 1. Is that a university?
  **A:** No, it isn't. It's . . .

- Answer Student A's questions about buildings 2, 4, 6, and 8 on your map.

  EXAMPLE:  **A:** Look at building 2. Is that a university?
  **B:** No, it isn't. It's . . .

- Compare your maps. Are they the same?

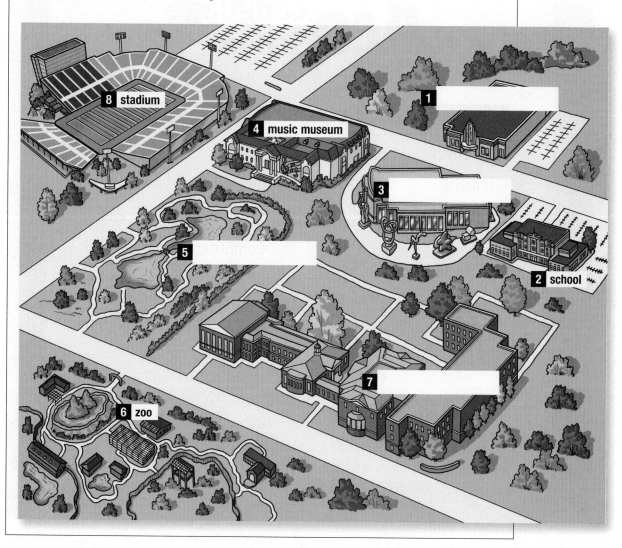

# EXERCISE 7  FIND THE CLASSROOM

INFORMATION GAP  Work with a partner. Student A follows the instructions on page 68.
Student B follows the instructions below.

**STUDENT B**

- The directory at Ace Language School is not complete. Ask your partner
  questions with *where* to complete your list.

  EXAMPLE:  **B:** Where's the main office?
  **A:** It's on the first floor in Room 101.

- Answer your partner's questions about his or her directory.

  EXAMPLE:  **A:** Where's English 1?
  **B:** It's on the first floor in Room 108.

## Ace Language School

| 1st FLOOR | ROOM | | 2nd FLOOR | ROOM |
|---|---|---|---|---|
| Main Office | *101* | | Spanish 1 | 202 |
| English 1 | 108 | | Spanish 2 | ___ |
| English 2 | ___ | | Spanish 3 | 210 |
| English 3 | ___ | | Computer Lab | 225 |

| 3rd FLOOR | ROOM |
|---|---|
| Chinese 1 | 303 |
| Chinese 2 | 309 |
| Chinese 3 | ___ |
| Library | ___ |

# EXERCISE 11 BOY SAVES MOM

**INFORMATION GAP** Work with a partner. Student A, follow the instructions on page 305. Student B, follow the instructions below.

**STUDENT B**

- You and your partner have the same story, "Boy Saves Mom." Some information is missing from your story. Ask your partner *wh-* questions in the past to find out the information.

EXAMPLE: **B:** Where did the accident happen?
**A:** In Ann's kitchen.

# Boy Saves Mom

On Wednesday, April 20, Ann Green had an accident. The accident happened in

_____ Ann's kitchen _____. She fell off a

chair and hit her head. Her son Max found her.

Max is four years old, but he's very smart. He

_____. A policeman

answered. He asked Max, "What happened?"

Max said, _____. The policeman sent an ambulance

to the Green's home. The ambulance took Ann to _____.

She is doing well there. Yesterday, she talked to a reporter. She said,

" _____."

- Your partner's story is also missing some information. The information is in your story. Answer your partner's questions.

EXAMPLE: **A:** When did Ann Green have an accident?
**B:** On Wednesday, April 20.

# Index